BLOOD CRIES AFAR

BLOOD CRIES AFAR

THE MAGNA CARTA WAR
AND THE
INVASION OF ENGLAND 1215–1217

SEAN McGLYNN

For Marie

First published in 2011

This edition published in 2015 by Spellmount,
an imprint of
The History Press
The Mill, Brimscombe Port
Stroud, Gloucestershire, GL5 2QG
www.thehistorypress.co.uk

© Sean McGlynn, 2011, 2013, 2015

British Library Cataloguing in Publication Data.
A catalogue record for this book is available from the British Library.

ISBN 978 0 7509 6391 6

Typesetting and origination by The History Press
Printed and bound in Great Britain by TJ International Ltd

Contents

Acknowledgements

This book has been a long time in the making. Whether it has been Bismarck's events being stronger than the plans of men or P.G. Wodehouse's Fate lurking around the corner with a piece of lead piping in its hand, circumstances have meant that I have left people waiting. I am painfully aware of this. My apologies to them all. That I did finish the book is in no small part due to a generous grant from the Society of Authors which came at a particularly crucial time; I am delighted to express my gratitude and appreciation to the Society.

In my first book I acknowledged my teachers over the years and medievalists who kindly invited me to speak at seminars and conferences. Here I should like to make mention again of Peter Coss for his understanding and learned insights and John Gillingham, whose work continues to be influential on my own. I would also like to thank Chris Harper-Bill: it was as an undergraduate in one of his lectures that I first learned of the little-known invasion of 1216 and became fascinated by it. I am very grateful to those scholars who, often a very long time ago now, have been gracious enough to provide me with unpublished papers of talks and advanced copies of articles relevant to this book. Tony Moore has been very kind in this respect. I have also benefited from Louise Wilkinson's research, and I am thankful to David Carpenter for directing her work my way. John Gillingham and Alexander Grant have also forwarded papers and useful comments. Special mention must go to Keith Stringer, whose work on the Scottish angle has been such a great help, and to the generosity of David Crouch and Stewart Gregory for an advanced look at their work on the wonderful new edition of *The History of William Marshal*; David Crouch's notes have proved invaluable. I have also benefited from a correspondence on national identity with the late Henry Loyn. My sincere apologies if I have unintentionally omitted others: as I say, it has been a long time. Looking ahead, I owe thanks to John France for directing me towards my next project.

In the work environment, I would like to pay tribute to past colleagues for their help and support: Joe Martin, Jo Sharrock, Dave Bates and Steve Ryan in

Bristol; Lara Price in Bath; and Jackie Duff at the Open University. And the same gratitude of course extends to my current colleagues who make my place of work so enjoyable: Andy Pickering, Stephen Page, Katherine Dray and Eddie Daughton. The students have been – and are – a delight to teach. At The History Press, Shaun Barrington has been an ideal editor to work with.

On the personal front, I still owe much to some wonderful friends acknowledged in my previous book: Robert Purves (always welcome on these shores); Steven Forrow (I have forgiven you – almost – for leaving London); Dr Anthony Cross (who, when not immured in the ivory towers of Oxford University, is encouraging me onwards in Bath); and the stalwart Stephen 'Gui' Rigby (with whom I put the world right and laugh at the folly of it all). New mentions this time around are: James, Meinir and (my goddaughter) Olwen Ottaway; Neil Trodden, whose detective work ensured we re-established contact; Michael Owen, who keeps me in touch with developments in the modern world; and my learned friend Glenn Renshaw, with whom over the years I have shared many hours of illuminating and productive debate on matters historical, social, cultural and political.

On the family front my thanks go to Liz, Dave, Josh, Jamie and Erin, not least for doing such a great job in looking after Mum. My mother remains a constant source of support, help and friendship and I will always be grateful to her. Sam, Maddy and Jenny have shown great humour, patience and understanding during my endeavours and at my being shut away in the study; you remain inspirational and the next one is for you. Finally, my love and thanks to Marie: even greater than her considerable assistance in helping with the translations of the Old French sources has been her practical help and support that have allowed me time and space to write. Her courage and resolve in overcoming serious adversity is remarkable and demonstrates that bravery is not merely present on the battlefield. This book is dedicated to her.

ABBREVIATIONS

AB   Anonymous of Béthune, *Histoire des Ducs de Normandie et des Rois d'Angle-terre*, ed. F. Michelet, Paris, 1840

AM   *Annales Monastici*, ed. H.R. Luard, Rolls Series, 1864–69

ANS   Brown, R.A. et al. (eds), *Anglo-Norman Studies* [formerly *Proceedings of the Battle Conference*], 1979–

ANW   Strickland, M. (ed), *Anglo-Norman Warfare: Studies in Late Anglo-Saxon and Anglo-Norman Military Organization and Warfare*, Woodbridge, 1992

BC   Barnwell Chronicler, *Memoriale Walteri de Coventria*, ed. W. Stubbs, 2 vols, RS, 1879–80

EHR   *English Historical Review*

HWM   *History of William Marshal*, ed. A. Holden, D. Crouch and S. Gregory, Anglo-Norman Text Society, 2002–2006

JMMH   *Journal of Medieval Military History*, eds B, Bachrach, C.J. Rogers and K. de Vries, Woodbridge, 2002–

MGH SS   Monumenta Germaniae Historica. Scriptores

MP   Mathew Paris, *Matthei Parisiensis, Monachi Sanctii Albani, Chronica Majora*, ed. H.R. Luard, RS, 1884–9

OEMW   Rogers, C.J. (ed), *Oxford Encyclopedia of Medieval Warfare and Military Technology*, Oxford, 2010

RC   Ralph of Coggeshall, *Radulphi de Coggeshall Chronicon Anglicanum*, ed. J. Stevenson, RS, 1875

Recueil   *Recueil des Historiens des Gaules et de la France*, Paris, 1734–1904

Rigord   Rigord, *Oeuvres de Rigord et de Guillaume le Breton*, ed. H.F. Delaborde, Paris, i, 1882

RS   Rolls Series

RW   Roger of Wendover, *Rogeri de Wendover Liber Qui Dicitur Flores Historiarum* [*The Flowers of History*], ed. H.G. Hewlett, RS, 1886–7

TCE   Coss, P. and Lloyd, S. (eds), *Thirteenth Century England*, Woodbridge, 1985

WB i   William the Breton, *Gesta Philippi Augusti* in *Oeuvres de Rigord et de Guillaume le Breton*, ed. H.F. Delaborde, Paris, 1882

WB ii   William the Breton, *Philippidos*, in *Oeuvres de Rigord et de Guillaume le Breton*, ed. H.F. Delaborde, Paris, 1882

Warfare and Medieval History

'War,' as defined by Clausewitz, 'is an act of violence intended to compel our opponent to fulfil our will.' This will is usually a political objective, hence Clausewitz's more famous, but also more controversial, dictum that 'War is nothing but the continuation of politics, with a mixture of other means.' He amplifies this verdict in the clarification: 'War is not merely a political act, but also a real political instrument, a continuation of political commerce, a carrying out of the same by other means.'[1] This is better known to us rendered as 'War is the continuation of politics by other means.' Although not all conflicts can – or should – be explained in such terms (some arising from emotional and irrational origins), this interpretation is basically sound and judicious; it is particularly apposite to the Middle Ages. Beyond the political objectives, we must also unearth the financial ones: these are rarely buried deeply but are frequently obscured by the noble ideals and moral justifications proclaimed by the warring protagonists. Politics means power means money. It is only rarely dangerous that too much cynicism is harmful to the process of historical interpretation; it is usually the case that the more cynical one is the closer one arrives at the historical truth. As I am forever telling my students, to really understand History you have to pick up the stone and see what is crawling underneath. As this book deals with warriors and not saints, it will adopt such an approach; but if these pages contain very few altruists, they do contain many brave men performing heroic acts in pursuit of their masters' objectives, however questionable their causes or motivations.

What Clausewitz applies to the modern world is equally germane to the medieval one. Medieval warfare was about land: its political and military control, the economic exploitation of its resources, the geographical implications it possessed for both security and offence, and the power and prestige it afforded its lord. Where these matters could not be satisfactorily resolved through marriages and inheritance, the resort to war was always a ready option. However, going to war was not always undertaken with the primary goal of subjugating an opponent to the belligerent's will: often – as before and since – its intent was to unite a people against a common enemy, to direct attention away from domestic problems and to reinforce a leader's authority among his own subjects. To confuse issues, these objectives could be combined with, and disguised by, genuine attempts at achieving grand designs at an enemy's expense. History is replete with examples of this, the medieval period offering no shortage of illustrations: King Henry V of England made spectacular military inroads against the French during the early fifteenth-century phase of the Hundred Years War, bringing political success both abroad and at home, thereby underpinning support for his shaky Lancastrian regime following Richard II's usurpation.[2] In John's reign, however, foreign wars abroad had the opposite effect, not least because they were so unsuccessful; where a leader's aim did not coincide with those of his more powerful subjects trouble at home was inevitable. The military intentions of medieval commanders were thus the same as generals from any historical period, but it would be wrong to deem them as the only ones that mattered: the aspirations of the medieval individual also demand consideration, even if, unlike today's electorates, they were unable to influence war-planning through the ballot-box.

Then, as now, military objectives were determined by the political environment; the purpose of this book is to demonstrate how military events determined, and were determined by, the political environment in England and France in the early thirteenth-century. Magna Carta, for example, a political and historical achievement of John's reign, was a low point for John and a manifestation of his military under-achievement. Special emphasis will be placed on how political failure for King John meant both political and military success for his Capetian enemies. The course of human history is sign-posted by military events. What would have been the history of Britain and Europe in the second half of the twentieth century had the British lost the Battle of Britain and the Russians lost on the Eastern Front? What of English history and the future British Empire had the Spanish Armada succeeded in 1588?[3] What if, in 1066, King Harold had not had to fight his great victory against the Norsemen at Stamford Bridge, just three weeks before his defeat in an extremely close-run battle at Hastings? And what if, during this battle, the formidable Anglo-Saxon shield wall had not chosen to break formation at a critical moment to pursue the Normans?[4] The French invasion of 1216 came extremely close to being a repeat of the conquest in 1066. Thus wars, and how they were fought, are crucial to our understanding of history.

This book explores and analyses the military activity during the French invasion of England in 1216 and the military events that led to this invasion (events for which a different outcome may easily have meant no invasion at all) and the profound consequences these had for the belligerents – and non-belligerents – involved. Such a study perforce concentrates on how engagements were fought, on explaining and detailing the methods of medieval warfare. The period under scrutiny here, and especially the invasion itself, provides an accurate and revealing portrayal of warfare between two Christian powers in western Europe during the Middle Ages; that is to say, a clearly political power struggle between enemies who shared religious, chivalric and social values.[5] The Angevin-Capetian conflict from 1202 to 1217 encapsulates nearly all the elements of medieval warfare in western Europe at this time, from the strategies and tactics of princes and commanders to the roles of individuals, whether soldiers or non-combatants, who fought and died both heroically and wretchedly. That these events have previously not received either a systematic military analysis or a monograph will hopefully afford this study some value.

Beyond the grand political and military schemes there are at least two other important reasons why wars took on such significance in the Middle Ages. One is the role of the monarch. Kingship was expected to be feudal and judicial, theocratic and religious, chivalric and martial: *rex* as *judex*, *sacerdos* and *miles* (the king as judge, priest and knight).[6] Medieval society was, after all, violent; the feudal agreement expected a lord to protect his people, which necessarily demanded ability in the military sphere and the employment of violence to bring about peaceful ends. A king poor in the profession of arms was prone to popular mockery, lack of respect and, crucially, loss of confidence by his subjects. In England the reigns of John, Henry III, Edward II and Henry VI are testimony to this. Such kings had to hope (in vain) for peace on the domestic and international scenes and, more realistically, for competent leaders of their armies. A mediocre king might get by on the latter; a poor one would not. We shall see how loss of military credibility could lead to loss of political credibility, initiating a vicious circle that could be broken only by a string of successes. When armies were evenly matched, political leadership could make all the difference.

The other main reason why war was so important to medieval history is too large to be addressed here in any detail: as Philippe Contamine explains, war in medieval history is 'an explanatory factor and is the product of a whole cultural, technical and economic environment'. In other words, medieval society was organised for war and can be understood only in the context of war. 'Medieval warfare,' therefore, 'is a massive and hence impossible subject.'[7] Its impact on the political environment will be considered, especially the effects of the Angevin-Capetian conflict on nascent nationalism in England and, to a lesser extent, France, arguing that, contrary to most modern opinion on this issue, a form of nationalism did exist at this time.[8] Some attention will be given to the military organisation of England and France in the early thirteenth century, but the focus will remain on military activity in the field: what happened, how and why. Even a narrative of such events should suffice to impress upon the reader the sheer enormity of time, energy and resources in blood and treasure that medieval monarchs poured into war. Contemporaries recognised this, as the chronicles of the age reveal, dominated as they are by war. It is from these chronicles that this book takes its lead.

Problems of Historiographical Interpretations

All sources, whether primary or secondary, require handling with care. Although this is especially true of contemporary authorities, historians of this period are blessed with some extremely well-informed chroniclers. In the vernacular we have the writings of the Anonymous of Béthune and *The History of William Marshal*; in Latin we have the monastic records of, among others, Guillaume le Breton (hereafter William the Breton), Ralph of Coggeshall and Roger of Wendover. The last of these has been disparaged by modern commentators; one contention of this study is that Wendover is generally an accurate and trustworthy source, and of particular value to the study of medieval warfare.[9] For the most part, the sources used in this book are strictly contemporary, the authors having lived through these events and in many cases witnessing them first-hand. An immediate problem with medieval sources, both Latin and vernacular, is the hyperbole of the writers when depicting incredible feats of arms against impossible odds: monastic chroniclers often imbued their numbers for armies (frequently an inflated 60,000) with biblical significance;[10] lay writers sometimes emulated the *chanson de geste* with exaggerated tales of derring-do. William the Breton's epic poem, the *Philippidos*, is especially culpable in these respects, yet it remains an invaluable literary work (his chronicle is far more sober in relating the events of his day). That said, the chief sources for this period are notable for their restraint and veracity (if not always their historical objectivity).

Although the sources are rightly approached with some caution, historians have sometimes been over-cautious in heeding contemporaries' accounts of suffering, dismissing tales of horror as the excited embellishments of clerics bemoaning attacks on church property and men of the cloth and the wickedness of soldiers sinning against God and his people. One extreme example of this form of writing comes from Symeon of Durham's description of Malcolm Canmore's Scottish invasion of northern England in 1070:

> Gazing upon the church of St Peter, blazing with the flames kindled by his men ... he ordered his troops no longer to spare any of the English nation ... It was pitiable to witness what they did to the English: some old men and women were beheaded by swords; others were run through with spears, like pigs meant for food; babies were snatched from their mother's breast and thrown high into the air and fell on the points of spears placed close together on the ground.[11]

That many such episodes could indeed be contrived and inaccurate does not obviate all such incidents; this study will argue that the descriptions of atrocities in the sources, especially in Wendover and William the Breton, deserve to be taken with the utmost seriousness. For all their vivid images of Hell, monastic writers seldom display the depraved imagination necessary to conjure up fabricated acts the equal of those the twentieth century has displayed in horrific abundance and reality. The power struggle following the break-up of Yugoslavia is, in many ways, reminiscent of medieval warfare with its sieges, massacres, burning of villages, the plight of the refugees and the appalling acts of cruelty perpetrated against soldier and civilian alike; but the crimes of Hitler, Stalin, Mao and Pol-Pot are on an altogether different scale. If a 'civilised' world can debase itself by such barbarity, why not the medieval one? Tragically, then as now, seemingly mindless brutality in warfare can serve a callous but calculating military rationale.

History is open to many interpretations; military history even more so. When thousands of men are engaged in conflict, it is impossible to gain a full and clear picture of the struggle. Wellington's choreographical allusion – that one may as well write the history of a ball as of a battle – is suitably apt and reinforces Clausewitz's fog of war, from which 'most reports are false'.[12] In the age of gunpowder the battlefield was obscured by smoke; in the Middle Ages natural elements were to the fore: in summer, dust clouds affected visibility and in winter, as ever, fog, rain and sleet caused problems.[13] Nevertheless, agreement among sources and participants allow for fairly detailed reconstructions and overviews of medieval military actions that are frequently enlivened further by striking individual episodes amidst the clash of armies. Many contemporary accounts capture much of the drama of medieval combat.

Historians of warfare in the Middle Ages have understandably displayed a preference for original sources written by men directly involved in the combat they describe: 'the vernacular brings us closer than Latin to the thoughts and actions of soldiers.'[14] Proper as this is, it has led to an unfortunate side-lining of clerical sources, which have been condemned as possessing 'little comprehension of military matters and even less interest in the complexities of strategy and tactics'.[15] This can be true up to a point, but such a judgement can be far from universally applied. From Bishop Odo at the Battle of Hastings in 1066, depicted wielding a club on the Bayeux Tapestry, down to the lowly 'bald' priest leading an assault on the Castle of Le Puiset in 1111, the clergy had always been active in warfare, so much so that special laws were formulated to cater for them when their status of immunity was compromised.[16] As will be seen later, Brother Guérin, Bishop Elect of Senlis, played a pivotal role in at the Battle of Bouvines in 1214.[17] An intellectual interest in warfare was also expressed by men of the cloth: Hugues de Noyes, Bishop of Auxerre (1183–1206), 'rejoiced in gathering a crowd of knights about him with whom he most gladly discussed military matters and also often re-read Vegetius [whose *De re militari* was the standard text on warfare in the Middle Ages] ... and he explained to the knights many of the lessons to be drawn from this author'.[18]

This interest extended to monastic writers who were no less affected by war and its outcomes. Monasteries were as likely to be in towns as in the remote countryside, and this meant that they frequently witnessed conflict at firsthand. Towns were politically and militarily important for several reasons: 'They produced a considerable revenue; they contained the largest clusters of population; they were often located at significant road junctions or river crossings ... They had mints, law courts and markets.'[19] They also had walls and castles. Not only were towns therefore obvious military targets, but often so were the monasteries within them: the great house at St Albans (with which Wendover was associated) was sorely troubled by both sides in the wars in England of 1215–17.

The social class from which most monks were drawn meant that there were strong ties between the *oratores*, those who prayed, and the *bellatores*, those who fought: monks had fathers, brothers, cousins, friends and patrons as knights. Monastic writers were only too pleased to honour these in their accounts of military actions that are described in monastic chronicles. Monastic communities could also be politically motivated: Wendover, in accord with most of his fraternity, was anti King John. Nor was conflict alien to the cloister: monks were engaged in their own spiritual battle against the forces of evil. Many monks, including Wendover, commonly describe a company of troops as *turma*, a term used at the monastery of St Maurice, for example, to denote the groups of monks in their shifts of round-the-clock worship in the choir of their church, which one commentator has called a 'powerful ritual weapon'.[20] H. E. J. Cowdrey, when discussing the *militia sancti Petri*, ponders whether *militia* should be translated as 'army' or 'knighthood' on one hand, or 'service' or 'obedience' on the other.[21] The practical need of the recourse to war was recognised by Abbot Marcward of Fulda: 'Not that it is proper that monks should inhabit anything but monasteries or fight battles other than spiritual ones; but the evil in the world cannot be defeated except by resistance.'[22] Monk and knight are most famously conflated in the Military Orders of the Hospitallers and Templars, the latter's formation being aided by St Bernard of Clairvaux.[23] Thus, among the various sources utilised in this study, the chief vernacular ones – *The History of William Marshal* and the Anonymous of Béthune – are fully complemented by the chief Latin ones – Roger of Wendover and William the Breton. All make an important contribution to our understanding of warfare in the Middle Ages.

Historians of medieval warfare have experienced many obstacles in pursuit of their subject. For a long time the unfashionable study of this subject has been dominated by retired generals and other ex-soldiers. However, the subject has spawned an academic history of its own, progressing from a limited understanding by generalists to exhaustive study by specialists. In the English-speaking world, Charles Oman's *The Art of War in the Middle Ages* held sway for much of the twentieth century;[24] fortunately, the truly appalling first edition of 1885 was rewritten for a greatly expanded and improved third edition in 1924 which, although now dated and misleading in places, remains in print as a serviceable and useful detailed study. From Oman stems the still readily accepted view that infantry declined as a battlefield force after Hastings until its revival in the early fourteenth century, when longbows, it is argued, ushered in the age of English victories epitomised by Crécy in 1346. Hans Delbrück, writing contemporaneously with Oman (and like him a non-medievalist), is more error-ridden. Although he was right to draw attention to the size of medieval armies, arguing that they were much smaller than was originally thought, he helped to perpetuate the myths of medieval warfare that became entrenched in the thinking of military historians: battles were all-important; they were fought almost exclusively by knights; battles usually occurred when one force inadvertently stumbled upon an opposing one; the ensuing *mêlée* was a confused series of individual combats fought by gung-ho knights seeking glory and renown; there were no tactical units; infantry was peripheral and became effective only with archery in the 1340s; knights felt that their honour would be sullied to fight on foot; they charged headlong into the enemy at first sight; leadership was poor; there was no discipline; tactics were rudimentary and strategy non-existent.[25] This caricature has been resoundingly disproven on all fronts by two decades of revisionism at the end of the twentieth century.

The publication of R. C. Smail's masterly study *Crusading Warfare 1097–1193* in 1956 should have instantly eradicated accepted thinking.[26] Unfortunately, perhaps due to its being specialist and scholarly in nature, its findings were picked up by only a few medievalists, and at a time when medieval warfare did not constitute a major area of academic research.[27] Its limited impact was also partly due to the failure to apply Smail's conclusions for the Middle East to Europe. He demonstrates how strategy, tactics, discipline, infantry and leadership all played major roles in the warfare of the period and that battle-avoidance was generally preferred to battle-seeking. In diminishing the role of battle he accentuated the role of the castle, placing logistics, ravaging and the taking and keeping of strong-points at the centre of medieval warfare. Many of Smails' views are echoed in J. F. Verbruggen's *The Art of Warfare in Western Europe During the Middle Ages* (originally published in Dutch in 1954; translated into English in 1997).[28] However, despite his recognition of the castle's importance, Verbruggen's focus remains on armies on the field of battle. His important work depicts clearly the professionalism of the medieval knight and dispels the myth of battle comprising large numbers of individual duels to show that knights fought in tactical units, a misuse of the sources having led to misunderstanding. He writes:

> In many instances we can show that historians … have simply not read certain passages in their source carefully. They have kept the name of the prominent nobleman who fought at the head of his unit, but in their account of the engagement they forget the words *cum suis, avec sa gent, cum sua acie*, with the result that the fighting of entire formations is represented as a duel …[29]

What knights learned from long years of training in small tactical units (*conrois*) they later employed in combat. Verbruggen also gives due attention to foot-soldiers, but again the emphasis is on the early fourteenth century.

With these antecedents, full-blown revisionism began in earnest in the 1980s, launched in 1984 by Philip Contamine's classic work, *War in the Middle Ages* (translated from the 1980 French edition) and by John Gillingham's seminal article, deliberately and provocatively titled 'Richard I and the Science of War in the Middle Ages'.[30] Contamine, in a passage already quoted, stressed the importance of warfare to medieval society and history as a whole. Gillingham gives prominence to the reality of warfare as experienced throughout the Middle Ages: ravaging, discipline, sieges, infantry, battle avoidance, etc. The flood of revisionist research that followed is incorporated into this work and referred to in the notes.[31] With the revisionist school of thought now prevailing (except in the area of military revolutions), inevitably there will be trends to counter-revisionism (a manifestation of the eternal cycle of historical debate). This has already been seen with the questioning of numbers, one highly respected historian taking Delbrück to task for the one thing on which he was probably right (relatively small army numbers);[32] another, more convincingly, believes that the necessary accommodation of new thinking on infantry should not leave the knight now on the periphery and also that discipline was, in fact, more of a problem than is sometimes considered.[33] By the twenty-first century, the study of medieval warfare has emerged into a major area of recognised research that has moved beyond the regular appearance of books on the subject: the annual *Journal of Medieval Military History* has produced eight volumes of leading-edge scholarship since its inception in 2002 and there is now a dedicated website from the *De Re Militari* group (www.deremilitari.org) that offers an abundance of invaluable information and resources to academic and layperson alike. In 2010, Oxford University Press published its massive three-volume *Oxford Encyclopedia of Medieval Warfare and Military Technology*, to present an authoritative account of our current understanding of warfare in the Middle Ages from scholars around the world (this author included). Medieval warfare remains, as Contamine noted, a 'massive subject'.

With all this in mind, the military events leading to the invasion of England in 1216, and the actual invasion itself, will be studied with the intention of revealing the true nature of warfare in western Europe in the early thirteenth century (and, by extension, the medieval period as a whole). Where similarities exist between the nature of warfare in this period and earlier and later medieval periods, these will be highlighted to press home the essential point that the Middle Ages saw relatively little real change in the art of war. Considerable attention will be devoted to styles of military leadership, especially in regards to the commanders-in-chief: King John, King Philip Augustus and Louis the Lion. Throughout this study, the main aim will be to show how war affected the history of this time and how it affected the people it caught in its terrible grasp. For just as war had its effect on society, so it took its toll on the individuals within that society. It is thus fitting to remember the words of the poet William Blake, who was moved to write the following lines on Albion by the historical events covered in this book:

The stars of heaven tremble: the roaring voice of war, the trumpet, calls to battle! Brother in brother's blood must bathe, rivers of death! O land, most hapless! O island, how forsaken! Weep from thy silver fountains; weep from thy gentle rivers! The angel of the island weeps! Thy widowed virgins weep beneath thy shades! Thy aged fathers gird themselves for war! The sucking infant lives to die in battle; the weeping mother feeds him to the slaughter! The husbandman doth leave his bending harvest! Blood cries afar!

William Blake, *Prologue to King John*[34]

ENEMIES: THE ANGEVIN-CAPETIAN STRUGGLE

Henry II

When, at the age of 21, the young Henry Plantagenet ascended the throne of England in December 1154, he established a new royal dynasty, the fame of which ensured its name would echo through the ages. His sons, the 'Devil's brood', included two of England's most legendary kings, resulting in a succession of three remarkable monarchs from 1154 to 1216. Henry ushered in an age of constitutional and legal changes against a turbulent background of political intrigue, diplomatic manoeuvring and, above all, war. But, first and foremost, he founded the Angevin Empire.

Son of the Empress Matilda, heiress of England, and Geoffrey, Count of Anjou, and grandson of King Henry I of England and Fulk of Anjou, King of Jerusalem, Henry was clearly born for great things; but even his natural ambitions must have been pleasantly exceeded by the relative ease with which he became King of England. One contemporary chronicler wrote: 'It is astonishing how such great good fortune came to him so fast and so suddenly.'[35] The struggle for the throne of England which had plunged the nation into the anarchy of King Stephen's reign was ended by the treaty of Winchester in 1153. By the terms of this treaty Stephen recognised Henry as his heir, *jure hereditario*. Stephen, worn out by the incessant strife of his reign and shattered by the sudden death of his eldest son Eustace, whom he had groomed to succeed him, relinquished any further serious dynastic ambitions for his own house and acquiesced to the demands of the Church, which sought peace for both sides, and to the barely tempered demands of his Angevin competitors. The treaty left Henry as the first undisputed heir and successor to the throne of England in over a century.[36] What Henry had only partially achieved by military force, fate had finished for him.

By the time of his Christmas coronation in 1154, Henry was already a hugely powerful figure on the European stage: Duke of Normandy, Count of Anjou and, through his inspired marriage to the divorced wife of King Louis VII of

France, Duke of Aquitaine and Count of Poitou. This match with Eleanor of Aquitaine had doubled his continental dominions and halved those of King Louis at a stroke. It was an irony of the French king's dissolved marriage that Eleanor had borne him only two daughters – a serious, if blameless, failing in any queen – but went on to provide her new husband with no less than four sons. However, despite this temporary blip for the French crown, the Capetian dynasty, founded in 987 and from which Louis was the eighth monarch, was notably fortunate in its long unbroken line of direct and relatively undisputed male successions; Louis later went on to produce a son with a new bride.[37] But Henry had married not only into power – he had also married into considerable trouble. For as much as Eleanor was bored by her unadventurous and unsatisfying life with Louis – she had complained that she had been married to a monk, not a king – it would seem that Henry was more than a match for this extraordinary woman; the result was a clash of two overbearing, ambitious and egotistical personalities. The marriage, even though a royal one, was not big enough to contain them. Henry, eleven years younger than Eleanor, took a series of mistresses, the most famous being Rosamund Clifford; Eleanor herself stood accused of infidelities during her marriage to Louis. Henry was a powerfully built, robust and energetic man who engaged upon an almost frenetically active involvement in the governance of his lands.[38] Eleanor, despite her allegedly amorous appetite, struck an elegant figure as queen and patroness of the arts.[39] In a manner reminiscent of the Empress Livia in Augustine Rome, she channelled her own ambitions through her male offspring; Henry, Richard, Geoffrey and John. These she turned against her husband, so much so that Henry compared himself to a picture in which an old eagle was being relentlessly harried and pecked by four eaglets.

For two decades Henry's reign was clearly a fruitful one. He re-established order and royal authority in England, leaving himself free to consolidate his continental interests; by 1173 he had accomplished this by becoming overlord of the neighbouring territories of the Vexin, Brittany and Toulouse, a tribute to his formidable diplomatic skills. All were of strategic importance and would prove to be so in the years of war that were to follow. He began the subjugation of Ireland and forged close links with Henry, Duke of Saxony, and also with Navarre and Lombardy.[40] The Constitution and Assizes of Clarendon in the mid 1160s added renown to his political authority and, notwithstanding the controversy over Archbishop Thomas Becket's death in 1170, 1173 saw Henry esteemed as perhaps the pre-eminent ruler in western Christendom. It was at this moment he faced the greatest challenges to his authority, all of which emanated from within his own family.[41] Motivated by King Louis of France, who never failed to meddle in and ferment Angevin familial discord, and by their mother Eleanor, Henry's sons allied themselves with disaffected barons and the King of Scotland in a military strike at the crown. However, a lack of synchronisation and coordination by the rebels doomed their revolt and permitted Henry to deal with and overcome one threat at a time. Henry was magnanimous in victory to his eaglets, but unforgiving of Eleanor: for the rest of Henry's reign, she remained in effective imprisonment.

In 1183 trouble brewed up again. In an acute manifestation of sibling rivalry the young Henry, who held Normandy, Maine and Anjou, allied with his brother Geoffrey, who held Brittany, against Richard, Duke of Aquitaine and their father. The two eldest sons were aided in their task by the new King of France, the eighteen-year-old Philip II. This dangerous instability threatened the Angevin power structure but was removed by the unexpected death from dysentery of the young Henry. Richard thereby became heir to the throne of England and inherited the elder brother's continental lands. Henry II wished to provide for John, his youngest and most favoured son, by giving him Richard's duchy of Aquitaine. Richard would have none of this: his many talents were already well established and he successfully countered all moves against him. In 1186 Henry was threatened by Geoffrey, again spurred on by King Philip of France; once again the premature death of a son – Geoffrey was killed in a tournament accident – saved Henry's position from greater danger. But the last years of Henry's reign witnessed no alleviation of his troubles. The scent of a new order was in the air and the old King found it increasingly difficult to shake off the hereditary hounds. His initially cordial relations with Philip of France broke down into open warfare. At first he was assisted by Richard against the French king, but then opposed by him. Inexplicably, Henry continued to favour John at the expense of Richard, his most gifted son. Prompted by fears for his inheritance and by Philip's sly encouragement, Richard joined forces with the French King in a well-organised military campaign against Henry over a battle-ground that was thus prepared for the conflicts of John's reign. Henry lost Le Mans and Touraine, and hence the struggle. In July 1189 he succumbed to the humiliating terms of Richard and Philip. Two days after signing his defeat, sick in heart and body, Henry died.

Richard I

True to the ever-changing nature of medieval alliances, when Richard became King of England the familiar pattern of Angevin-Capetian rivalry was renewed afresh, barely restrained even by their combined leadership of the Third Crusade (1190–2). Whatever King Philip had learned from the military genius of Richard in the Holy Land, he could not put it to effective use against him back in Europe, for Richard usually bettered the French King at war. Philip had returned home early from the crusade, making much of an illness that was afflicting him (*arnoldia*), but in reality his purpose was to lay claim to his inheritance of the county of Flanders, using the opportunity to make gains on Richard's continental territories in the English king's absence; he was not overly deferential to the protection afforded by the Papacy to crusader's lands. This was about the only time that

Philip made any real sustained headway against Richard; and what progress he did make was often in collusion with John, Richard's treacherous younger brother. On his return, Richard soon made good any losses he had incurred while in the Holy Land or while incarcerated by Henry VI of Germany.

Richard was adored by contemporaries for the chivalric hero he was; the judgement of historians has proved, until recently at least, to be more censorious, one damning him as 'A bad son, a bad husband, a selfish ruler, and a vicious man'.[42] The two main charges laid against him are his over-exploitation of England's resources to fund his 'foreign' wars and his wholesale neglect of his kingdom due to his absence fighting these wars on the continent, spending only a few months of his entire reign in England. The first of these charges will be discussed later in the context of Angevin military finance; the second has been comprehensively rejected by John Gillingham (though not universally accepted) who has shown the importance of Richard's continental lands to overall Angevin strategy.[43] Richard's assured judgement of character (except where his younger brother is concerned: he was extremely lenient with John's rebellions and alliances with King Philip of France) meant that England was always left in safe hands; indeed, as J.C. Holt has written of Hubert Walter, Archbishop of Canterbury and chief justiciar who governed England in Richard's absence, the King actually benefited from 'one of the greatest royal ministers of all time'.[44]

A further, neglected but extremely positive aspect is suggested here. Richard's victories abroad, brought about by his active involvement in warfare, denoted greater security for England, not less. One only has to examine John's pitiful record on the continent – which we will soon be doing – to witness the consequences of military defeat there, when unsuccessful campaigns were invariably followed by threats of invasion. In 1216 these threats were put into operation and became frighteningly real after heavy English losses in France. It has always been Britain's strategy to fight its wars on foreign soil, thereby preventing conflict on home territory. This strategy is widely understood in the more modern context of the Napoleonic wars of the early nineteenth century and the world wars of the twentieth century. Thus one historian of the Napoelonic wars has written for the early nineteenth century that 'in one sense Britain's defences began east of the Rhine with her Continental allies. Military dependence kept drawing Britain into European affairs.'[45] (In fact Richard carefully nurtured alliances with German princes.) Even in the twenty-first century, the British government has justified military action as far afield as Iraq and Afghanistan as a means to ensure safety at home. This is, as one historian of the Cold War put it, 'the age-old formula of security-through-expansion'.[46] The feudal nature of English medieval society does not preclude England, as many seem to think, from adhering to the wisdom of such a sensible 'age-old' policy in this earlier period. We can see this policy in action in the period of the Hundred Years War. Between 1377 and 1383, English strategy centred on taking and holding forts along the northern French coast to prevent further French and Castilian raids on the south coast which had culminated in an invasion of the Isle of Wight in 1377. This strategy was sold successfully to the commons, which granted the huge war funds for it, as a defensive measure. With the expiry of a truce in 1385, the French King Charles VI began preparations for an invasion of England the following year. He was in a position to do so because he had gained control of ports in Flanders from where he could assemble and launch his huge invasion fleet. This 'presented the most serious threat that England had faced in the whole course of the war, and provoked widespread panic in southern England'.[47] The fleet of 1386 gathered near Damme, in exactly the same place where the French King Philip Augustus had gathered his invasion fleet in 1213. Had John been as successful as Richard in his continental wars, then Philip would not have been in a position to pose this threat then or for his son to make the threat a reality three years later in 1216. This is the overlooked vindication for Richard's policy of fighting his wars abroad. This book will show how John's military failures combined with his political ones to leave England exposed to invasion.

Seen in this light, it is a measure of Richard's achievement that he did spend so much of his time fighting on the continent; likewise, it is an indication of John's shortcomings that in 1216 he fought his last war in England and against French invaders. It may safely be assumed that the French subjects of King Philip were happier during 1216–17 when their troops were inflicting the ravages of war on the English, than in the 1190s when Richard the Lionheart took the war to them. It is likely that contemporaries understood this; hence the English offered their grateful praise for Richard's military accomplishments, which were regarded in practical rather than merely jingoistic terms: the defence of the realm was a king's highest duty, and Richard performed it supremely well. It is therefore not surprising that fears of a French invasion abounded in England on Richard's death in April 1199, mortally wounded by a crossbow bolt shot from the battlements of a castle while suppressing a revolt in the Limoges. As William the Breton, no lover of the Angevin king, wrote of this event: 'God visited the kingdom of the French, for King Richard died.'[48]

The Angevin Empire

At the close of the twelfth century, the Angevin Empire stretched from the north of England to the Pyrenees, splitting modern France in half all the way down. It was a disparate collection of lands which included the peoples of Normandy, Brittany, Maine, Anjou, Limouisin, Angoulême, Agenais and Gascony at a time of pre-nascent French identity. Some of this territory, most notably Normandy, was held from the King of France as a suzerain; some of it formed part of personal patrimony. Holt has written: 'The Plantagenet lands were not designed as an "empire", as a great centralised administrative structure … On the contrary, these lands were simply cobbled together.'[49] Yet this construction worked: with little more to unite it than a common allegiance to its (usually absent) master, it managed to be a viable, indeed healthy, entity. Under Henry's and Richard's dynamic itinerant rule, the natural strengths of the empire came to the fore. As ever when examining territorial struggles, it is necessary first to establish the state of the regional economies. Gillingham has demonstrated these to be of great importance; thus they aroused the predatory interest of rulers, princes and magnates. 'Economically speaking the Angevin Empire may be described as a number of complementary regions bound together by a series of well-defined waterways,' he writes; the Angevins 'ruled over an immense trading zone'.[50] Chief among the commodities were grain, salt and wine, especially that coming from Anjou, Aquitaine, Bordeaux and Poitou. The busy traffic down along the Seine, Loire and Garonne testified to the economic viability of the empire which garnered great profits from this traffic in trade. Lucrative tolls, customs and licences added further to the Angevins' wealth. Economic strength translated into military strength; as the anonymous chronicler of Béthune notes, King Richard was 'extremely rich in land and resources, much more so than the King of France. He could raise a very large army from his vassals and mercenaries, for he was able to summon English, Normans, Bretons, Manceaux, Angevins and Poitevins. He also had numerous *routiers*, who inflicted much damage on the King of France.'[51] So here was another clear reason for Richard devoting so much of his time to the Empire: it was a source of funding for his wars and enabled him to continue his conflict on the Continent, outside his kingdom. England, too, was wealthy; but its relatively stable boundaries and greater centralisation of power, which owed much to the efforts of Henry II, meant that by and large it could confidently be left in the hands of competent administrators. The more volatile situation on the continent, with the Angevin frontier running contiguously with a hostile Capetian one (to which must be added the consideration of the more fragmented form of political life there) demanded greater attention. Although suzerains of France, the Capetians could lay claim only to personal royal lands centred on the Île-de-France, extending in a corridor from Artois in the north to Berry in the south.

Historians have drawn attention to the fact that contemporaries never addressed the Plantagenet dominions as an empire because they did not deem them as forming an institution.[52] However, in the Old French poem, *The Song of Dermot and the Earl*, written during the second quarter of the thirteenth century but following an earlier original, the Irish chieftain Dermot McCurrough speaks to Henry II of 'les baruns de tun empire'.[53]

Empire or not, the lands of the Angevin kings constituted the foremost political power of the time, and one well worth fighting for control of. Robert Bartlett believes that the danger to Capetian France from the Angevin Empire has been overestimated: 'For the Capetian Kings of France this accumulation of territories under the Angevins was not primarily a threat to their existing position but rather a large and potentially permanent obstacle to their ever doing anything about it. If the lower reaches of both the Seine and the Loire were held by Henry II and his sons, there could be no expansion downstream from the Île-de-France.'[54] This containment policy by the Angevins is an important factor; however, by 1214 John's fight to recover the Empire after its dismantlement sucked in the Holy Roman Empire as an ally and the existence of Capetian France was very much on the line. Ralph Turner believes that the Capetians held the military advantage, as Philip had a compact base in the Île de France, which made it easier for him to dispatch his forces 'to attack Angevin-held castles in the Seine or Loire valley'. By contrast, Richard and John had 'the disadvantage of defending a long frontier, extending from the Channel to the Pyrenees, stretching lines of communication and requiring dispersal of resources among widely scattered fortresses'.[55] This is a serious consideration; in the Russian civil war of the early twentieth century, a similar geo-strategic set up greatly assisted the Bolsheviks, compactly centred around Moscow, to defeat the dispersed forces of the Whites who, on the map, surrounded them. However, some of these disadvantages of the Angevins can easily be inverted into advantages: they could attack from anywhere on a long frontier, which in Normandy was close to Paris; the compact base around the French capital was threatened by a swift takeover; the wealth of areas within the empire meant that resources for war could be collected locally for regional fortresses; and the extent of the empire meant, as Bartlett hints, that it was harder for the Capetians to deliver a knock-out blow to their enemy. The events of 1204 and 1214 bear out these aspects of the strategic situation.

This informal empire was to be the arena for the climactic Angevin-Capetian clash. The years after Richard's death experienced an almighty contest between two of Christendom's greatest kings, the English and French monarchs, for the very existence of the Empire itself.[56]

John

Whereas Richard ensured his inheritance fell to him intact through his extraordinary efforts and abilities, John could boast no such merit when his turn for the crown came; he owed his position entirely to luck and to the services of the Grim Reaper, who had obligingly gathered to him John's three older brothers. Prince Henry, Geoffrey and Richard had all met premature ends; Richard, typically enough, struck down while in action. As the direct consequence, in 1199 John, fourth in line to the Angevin succession and 33 years of age that year, became King of England, Duke of Aquitaine, Count of Anjou and Lord of Ireland.

His position was not fully secure, and in some areas castles were victualled in preparation for and anticipation of any trouble that might have erupted. In

England his ascension to the throne was broadly undisputed, but in the French provinces there was a consensus that the young Arthur, Duke of Brittany and John's nephew through Geoffrey, had a better claim to the throne. Anjou, Maine and Touraine declared for Arthur, amid rumours that he also had the support of Archbishop Hubert Walter. The 12-year-old duke was taken under the aegis of Philip Augustus, who saw in him too good a chance to miss for trouble-making against the new King of England, just as his father had done. By a strange coincidence of history, John was with Arthur when Richard was killed. In one of his periodical bursts of energy, John made straight for Chinon to secure the Angevin treasury deposited there. Seizing the treasury was always the first action of any triumphant claimant to the throne: the financial resources thereby obtained signalled to his new subjects that they may hope for largesse in the form of gifts and patronage; but they were also made aware of the possible repercussions should they choose to resist someone who was now in a position to afford the employment of substantial mercenary forces in support of the new regime. John got off to a reasonably good start in England, gaining a measure of popular support by fixing low prices for Angevin and Poitevin wines. By the end of his reign he had created for himself one of the most controversial reputations, and possibly the worst one, of any monarch in English history.[57]

His legacy has led to some ambiguous judgements on his abilities, and there is still no consensus on his reign, though one has begun to emerge over the last decade. Stellar and Yeatman's humorous history of England, *1066 and All That*, published in 1930, conveyed a simplistic summary of John which held sway for a long time: he was 'a Bad Prince', 'an awful King', a 'wicked' monarch who 'demonstrated his utter incompetence' during 'his awful reign'.[58] Since then a great deal of scholarly revisionism of his reign has accentuated some positive aspects of John's monarchy, especially in the field of administrative processes. In 1902, Kate Norgate accused John of blunders in statecraft, errors in strategy, weakness, cowardice, sloth and superhuman wickedness.[59] Compare this to Alan Lloyd's assessment in 1973: 'He was himself an ingenious administrator and a shrewd strategist. When pugnacious barons dubbed him 'Softsword', they paid unwitting tribute to his preference for negotiation rather than violence. The inference that he was a feeble soldier is a false one.'[60]

In some ways these conflicting views reflect the times in which the historians wrote. The Victorian age, with exceptions such as Stubbs, admired the manly heroic figure cut by the chivalrous form of Richard (who, as we have seen, is himself the subject of conflicting views in the modern academic community) to the detriment of John who, it was believed, lacked the chivalry of big brother.[61] Many modern historians, more preoccupied with quantifiable information gleaned from official documentary evidence, and in reaction to unfashionable military history, praise John's undoubted administrative skills, sometimes effusively so.[62] But against this praise must be balanced Colin Richmond's telling observation that 'The records of government are all very well, but on issues that matter they do not tell the truth. In fact, they seek to obscure it.'[63] Favourable views based on bureaucracy accentuate chronocentric bias and preference, placing one skill at a premium over the other instead of valuing both as the two sides of the same coin. A good military commander in the Middle Ages had to be a good administrator: Richard the Lionheart excelled in both areas, hence his deserved reputation as a military genius; John excelled only in one, and even this was chiefly the result of his military failings which forced him to administer his kingdom ever more efficiently in an effort to find revenues to pay for the losses inflicted by war. Whatever today's sensibilities may be, medieval subjects expected their monarch to achieve success in war; as Ralph Turner neatly summarises it: 'modern scholars' admiration of kings such as John for attention to administration is anachronistic, applying standards of the twentieth century rather than the thirteenth.'[64] Growing recognition of this has seen John's reputation plummet. An important collection of papers from scholars published in 1999 to commemorate the 800th anniversary of John's accession to the throne is universally damning of the King, and the most recent research even challenges John's innovations in administration. David Crouch, writing in 2010, promotes wide, though not universal, current agreement in judging John's rule as 'ham-fisted' and the King as 'unpredictable and unreliable', whose 'irrational capacity for abrupt, extravagant, and uncontrolled resentment' put him 'outside the courtly world'.[65]

The balance must weigh heavily against John. Indeed, the greatest achievement of his reign, Magna Carta, was the result of his inability to rule effectively. With only some reservations, therefore, it is safe to concur with mitigated opinions of contemporary chroniclers, while bearing in mind John's record in administration. Gerald of Wales, virulently hostile to the Angevin house, declared that John 'feared not God, nor respected men'; Richard of Devizes depicted John as a raging madman, his face so contorted as to be unrecognisable; the more even-handed Barnwell writer says of John that 'he was less than successful' and 'a pillager of his own people'. Of course, such monastic voices had their own political and financial agenda, but John fares little better at the hands of secular sources. The anonymous biographer of William the Marshal portrays the King as a suspicious and resentful ruler, heedless to reason, blinded by pride and incapable of retaining baronial affection. The Anonymous of Béthune (whose master fought for John) labels John 'a very wicked man: he was cruel to all men … he ashamed many of the great men of the land, for which he was much hated.' The Anonymous goes on to relate how John set his barons against each other, 'happy to see animosity between them, and that he hated them through envy'; quite simply, 'he had too many bad qualities.'[66] This last assessment is one of the most telling; it confirms the inconsistency of the King and his woeful inability to manage people. Whereas Richard was an inspired leader of men, John was a Machiavellian manipulator, and not a particularly good one.

Was John mad? Contemporary depictions of his rages and rolling around on the floor gnawing frantically at straws would suggest this. But the question of whether John really was insane is debatable. Charles Petit-Dutaillis thought so, believing that John 'was subject to a mental disease known today and described by psychiatrists as the periodical psychosis ... Philip Augustus had a madman as his rival.'[67] Vivian Green, in his study *The Madness of Kings*, offers a more equitable judgement, questioning whether there is any real justification in labelling John as a madman; rather he was 'immature in behaviour and outlook ...His occasional bouts of energy, his rage and cruelty, his obsessive suspicions may well suggest that he was a victim of an acute personality disorder.'[68] Perhaps it would be more pertinent to say that those around him were the victims of his personality disorder.

The summation of faults displayed by John was dangerous in a king and disastrous in a medieval military commander. When John attempted to be assertive he often came across as shrill, cowardly and malevolent, as seen in his monstrous treatment of William de Braose's family (his wife and child were starved to death in a royal prison), his deadly intentions for the defeated garrison at Rochester and his duplicitous massacre and decapitations at Evreux in 1194. In W.L. Warren's memorable phrase, John 'could not resist the temptation to kick a man when he was down'.[69] He could not even keep his balance while doing so. In contrast, when Richard was assertive, the signal sent out was one of ruthless efficiency: his mass execution of nearly 3000 Muslims at Acre in the Holy Land, though reprehensible, at least had the merit of being an effective solution to a serious logistical problem, caused by an enemy failing to satisfy agreed demands.[70] The important point here is one of perception: whatever good John may have done, it was always overshadowed by his darker acts. Contempories considered him a loser, and so labelled him with the damning soubriquet of *mollegladium*, 'Softsword'.[71] Churchill believed that the British nation owes more to the vices of John than to the labours of the more virtuous monarchs (but then he also considered the loss of Normandy to be a good thing);[72] this was not the view of contemporaries, and their judgement was fairly sound.

Philip Augustus

Perhaps John's failings would have counted for less if he had been faced with a less formidable opponent: King Philip II of France. That Philip had made little headway against Richard in the 1190s is more of a reflection of Richard's qualities than Philip's shortcomings. Philip is the most important of all the seventeen Capetian kings of France: he did more than any other to create the foundations of modern France. Jean Flori, his most recent biographer, rightly claims that his reign constitutes 'a fundamental moment in the history of the French kingdom'

and he 'merits the title of the first King of France'.[73] He became monarch in 1180
when only fourteen. During his reign the very existence of the French nation
was constantly in peril, a danger that persisted until a climactic battle for survival in 1214, when John's allies were poised to deliver a crushing blow to Philip.
The Anglo–French conflict of the early thirteenth century is the story of a fight
for survival between the Angevin Empire and the Capetian monarchy. This contest was fought out within the boundaries of modern-day France, except during
the period 1215–17, when the war spilled over into England for its final round.
So bitter had the struggle become, by 1214 both sides seemed to veer towards
Catonic strategy: *delenda est Carthago*. Ultimately, France survived, and to this day
the French revere Philip for expanding and consolidating his kingdom and for
guaranteeing its long-term security.[74]

When John became king, Philip already had nearly 20 years of experience as
ruling monarch under his belt. He had been schooled in the art of kingship by
Henry II and Richard I, two of its great practitioners; his lessons were well learned
and consistently applied. However, in many respects Philip and John were evenly
matched. Philip was only two years younger than John. Both were possessed of
singularly unengaging personalities. Turner notes that Philip 'shared unattractive traits with John: lustful, authoritarian, cynical, suspicious, and treacherous';
Steven Runciman remarks on Philip's 'nervous disorder' and his predisposition
to indulge in 'underhand intrigue'; Elizabeth Hallam has written of 'cruelty,
treachery and authoritarian behaviour'. French historians have also noted his
unappealing features: Robert Fawtier accurately labels him 'a cautious, cynical
distrustful man'; Charles Petit-Dutaillis describes Philip's politics as 'flexible and
unscrupulous'; Flori, less critically, describes his character as 'complex and secretive' and also 'stern and severe' when compared to Richard the Lionheart.[75] Like
John, a picture of calculating slyness emerges; but unlike John, this unsavoury
quality was used to great effect, for Philip was a master Machiavellian, a schemer
whose machinations got results. For this reason, similarities in character are not
matched by similarities in reputation. Philip had developed talents at an early
age. In 1184 he was faced with a serious threat from Count Philip of Flanders,
'one of the shrewdest soldiers of the day' (under whom Richard the Lionheart
had served his military apprenticeship).[76] Henry II, who had afforded Philip a
considerable degree of protection during the latter's early years on the French
throne, brokered an armistice between the two sides for a year. The two parties
had to name their allies who were to be included in the agreement. King Philip
audaciously implicated his father-in-law, Count Baldwin of Hanault, by naming
him without prior consultation and without Baldwin ever having even taken the
King's side. Furthermore, Baldwin had no wish to antagonise his powerful and
dangerous neighbour, the Count of Flanders, who was at odds with the French
king. By this brazen move, the French King succeeded in achieving two aims:
he artificially represented his position as being stronger than it really was while

simultaneously manufacturing a useful split between Flanders and Hainault.[77] Philip was indeed 'a prudent and skilful diplomat',[78] no matter how dubious this diplomacy may have been. The French historian R.-H. Bautier has rightly praised Philip as 'a remarkable tactician of politics', who augmented his strength by his ability 'to judge allies and adversaries, and discover their weaknesses and profit from them'.[79] I would argue also that an even greater attribute was his capacity, which developed with his political maturity, to gauge and recognise his own debilities and limitations, especially in the military sphere.

Philip's phenomenal success offers one explanation for his great renown; another is provided by the panegyrical writings of the chroniclers Rigord and William the Breton, the official royal biographers: Rigord bestowed upon Philip the appellation of 'Augustus', complete with quasi-imperial overtones, and one altogether more flattering than 'Softsword' or 'Lackland', which English writers had stuck on John; William was sycophantically unstinting in his praise, regularly lapsing into eulogistical hyperbole. There was no battalion of hostile monks taking up their quills against him such as John faced in England. But Philip had some need of literary flourish in support of his martial endeavours: in another resemblance to John, Philip was not heroic material. A pale, sickly child who grew into a fat, prematurely balding young man, Philip was not the stuff of chivalric legend.[80] There is much truth in the accusation levelled by Gillingham that Philip was a 'timid soldier', but it is misleading to say, as A.L. Poole does, that he was 'not a great soldier' or, as Alan Lloyd concurs, he was 'not an outstanding warrior'.[81] Holders of this view might have cited the outburst of Philip's contemporary, the pathologically belligerent troubadour, Bertrand de Born, who charges Philip with being too soft ('trop mols') and chides him for 'hunting sparrows and tiny birdies' instead of pursuing the manly and noble past-time of war.[82] But Philip was to prove himself militarily as a commander-in-chief rather than as a fighting man.

The Treaty of Le Goulet

When John came to the throne of England in May, 1199, these two unlikely generals stood on the eve of unleashing upon each other the fury of their armies in a series of bitterly contested and viciously waged wars, which extended the established patterns of the Angevin-Capetian struggle. John and Philip were to be the chief instigators of the momentous events of the next eighteen years, but it would have been difficult for them to have forseen the desperate character that these wars were to take on, or the new levels of intensity that they were to reach. However, just before the storm was about to break, there came the lull. This appeared in the shape of the treaty of Le Goulet, signed on 22 May 1200. By the terms of this treaty, Philip Augustus recognised John as Richard's heir in all his French possessions, with Brittany held by Arthur as John's vassal. In return, John ceded the strategic Vexin and Evreux to the French king, reflecting, in part, Philip's recent military advances. Further terms were agreed as the two kings talked by themselves, surrounded by their retinues, at this border conference that a papal legate had done so much to bring about: John abandoned his alliances with Otto of Brunswick and some of Philip's vassals, which Richard had carefully cultivated;[83] he paid 20,000 marks to Philip as a succession duty, a feudal relief for taking up his continental inheritance; and the treaty was sealed by the marriage of John's niece, Blanche of Castille, to Philip's son, Prince Louis of France. Warm embraces between the monarchs were followed by John's summer visit to Paris, where he was lavishly entertained by his Capetian host.[84]

The salient features of the treaty formed telling portents of future events; alternatively, they may be viewed as actively shaping the future course of Anglo-French relations. Although the Norman Vexin was relinquished to France, Andelys and its defensive network, centred on Richard's magnificent 'bold castle' of Château Gaillard (also, but less accurately, called 'saucy' castle), remained in John's hands: this set the immediate scene for the epic struggle for Normandy in 1203–4. John's payment of the colossal sum of 20,000 marks for his continental territories defined his feudal relationship with his overlord, Philip of France: when this contract was ruptured in 1202 it allowed Philip, however tenuously, to justify his military moves against John in legalistic terms. And the marriage of Blanche of Castille to Louis was perhaps most significant of all: it gave the young Prince Louis his claim to the English throne in 1216.

It would be too much to assert that the treaty sowed the seeds of John's overwhelming troubles during his reign; equally, it is hard to see, as many historians do, that Le Goulet was something of a triumph for John in any but the most superficial of applications. 'Overall', writes one recent biographer, 'John had done well. He gained his goal by threatening force without seriously using it; and the settlement with Philip II bought him two years of peace, during which he would consolidate his power over his continental possessions. He seemed to be establishing control over his continental lands from the English Channel to the Pyrenees.'[85] This was certainly the impression John gave during his successful tour of his French fiefs from June to August 1200 – and the importance of impressions of power on the medieval mind should not be underestimated – but, as developments were to prove, ultimately John would have little to show for this consolidation. Instead, the treaty seemed to reveal John's habitual flaws in the area of Clausewitzian diplomacy: as John Baldwin succinctly summarises, 'Philip had extracted from John the major military objectives he had been unable to win from Richard.'[86] This brief statement captures the essence of Richard and John's competition with Philip Augustus. The payment of the huge relief stipulated in the treaty (itself a partial rebuttal to those who believe that Richard had all but bankrupted England) draws apposite comment from Warren: 'The significance of the relief demanded of John lies partly in the enormous sum asked, but even more in the demand itself and the agreement to pay. No one had ventured to ask it of Henry or Richard; they had simply taken possession and no one dared say them nay.[87] Previously the Angevin monarchs had, in effect, ruled half of France; but now the Capetians were asserting their feudal hegemony with John playing the part of compliant vassal. As Turner points out in his study of John, it was the King's signing of the treaty of Le Goulet, and not his subsequent military defeats, that earned him his label of 'Softsword'.[88] Gervase of Canterbury, who first recorded this judgement of contemporaries on John, believed that the King was right to settle for peace.[89] Historians have followed Gervase's lead, giving persuasive background reasons of war-weariness and economic concerns to explain why John was right to sign at Le Goulet.[90] One is tempted to add a more cynical explanation – that John's tendency to choose negotiations before a conflict rather than after it was perhaps a recognition that his own limited military skills could leave him in a worse bargaining position following any fighting. It may be that the collective wisdom of contemporary opinion reflected a clearer insight into the realities of the situation, perceiving as it does John's fatal flaw in kingship: his inability to play the role of warrior-king. Whatever the argument, ultimately John was to gain nothing lasting from the treaty. Sometimes it seems that whatever action John took, he was predestined to make a mess of it, and whatever path he followed it would leave him lost and bewildered.

Despite all his achievements, there was one area in which Richard had not left his brother a strong hand: relations with the Church in Angevin territory in France, especially beyond the Norman borders. Ralph Turner's study of Richard's administrative kingship in his French domains reveals the limitations of the King of England's influence. Being pious in the conventional sense, as Richard was, was not sufficient to smooth over matters of diplomacy, economics, peace and war, these being the chief practical and secular concerns of his episcopacy on the Continent.[91] Here Richard could not exert the leverage over episcopal elections that he could in England and thus he could not reap all the advantages that this entailed (which included those of vacancies and patronage).[92] Turner writes that the Angevins 'lacked the aura of sanctity that surrounded them in England as anointed kings. On the Continent, the French monarchs as heirs to the Carolingians asserted their role as protectors of the church even within the territories of their rivals, the Plantagenets. This tradition earned the Capetian rulers the devotion of French ecclesiastics who went so far as to support their French King against the pope.'[93] Certainly, Philip enticed the clergy with such sweeteners as free episcopal elections so as to lure their loyalties away from the Angevins; however, when his hand strengthened, Philip dispensed with the willingness to be so accommodating.[94] Where free elections did occur in the Angevin territory, the results could go against Richard's interests: in 1190 at Le Mans, the monastery of St Martin of Tours, which provided the Capetians with intelligence for the Loire

valley, elected one of its number to the bishop's chair.[95] Beyond Normandy, it
was only in Angers that Henry II and Richard succeeded 'in planting their own
clerks, bound to them by personal attachment and committed to the cause of an
Angevin empire'.[96]

There were serious problems even in Normandy, notwithstanding the close
political and ecclesiastical ties with England which constituted an Anglo-Norman
realm. Here, the strains and exigencies of continuous warfare were taking their
toll: pressures of financing military operations and, especially on the borders, raids
and depredation, focused the minds of the war-weary clergy evermore on peace.
Richard's demands had already led to an interdict on the duchy in the mid-
1190s, following a showdown with Walter of Coutances, Archbishop of Rouen
(whose toponym disguises his Cornish origins). At Andely, Richard had seized
the archiepiscopal manor there (together with its lucrative tolls imposed on traffic up and down the Seine) to build his mighty fortress of Château Gaillard.
After representations at Rome and an interdict, Richard settled with Walter by
compensating him with two other manors and the important seaport of Dieppe,
a mark of just how highly Richard valued the site.[97] Philip Augustus also recognised Andely's significance, as his father had before him (Louis VII had burned the
town in 1167).[98] During the peace made between Richard and Philip at Louviers
in January 1196, the French king, clearly appreciating its strategic importance, had,
in the words of one chronicler, 'demanded Andely for himself'.[99] But Richard
would not concede it: with the vital border fortress of Gisors and most of the
castles on the Epte having recently fallen into French hands, and with Vaudreuil
unable to control the road on the other side of the Seine, a weak point had
been opened in Rouen's satellite defences. Richard was therefore determined
that the Capetians should not obtain possession of Andely; instead, he planned to
build there a superb defensive complex (with offensive capability) to safeguard
the duchy's capital. He was, quite literally, laying the foundations for the key battle
of Normandy between John and Philip.

In the tense military stand-off at the turn of the century, England needed
Richard, not John, to counter Philip of France. As the Archbishop of Rouen pres-
ciently lamented on hearing of Richard's death: 'What hope remains to us now?
There is none, for, after him, I can see nobody able to defend the kingdom. The
French will overrun us, and there will be no one to resist them.'[100]

2

THE CONQUEST OF NORMANDY, 1200–1204

The treaty of Le Goulet should have ushered in a period of relative stability between the kingdoms of England and France. For Philip it granted space to sort out his problems with the Papacy over his bigamous marriage to Agnès of Méran; for John it meant time to consolidate his inheritance of the English crown. Both countries were in a position to benefit from the increase in trade that peace would surely bring to them; this was particularly important to John who would have wished to recoup much of the huge sum of 20,000 marks that he had agreed to pay his overlord, Philip, by terms of the treaty, in return for formal recognition of his continental fiefs. John visited these fiefs on a comprehensive tour between June and August of 1200. From Dieppe in Normandy to St Sever in Gascony, he was accompanied by his army in a formidable display of power, designed to impress upon the many rebellious factions within his empire that he possessed the means and determination to force his will upon his widespread dominions. As a further incentive to cooperation, John took hostages as guarantees of good behaviour.

Whatever success this 'triumphal progress'[101] might have achieved in its tacit aims of intimidation, it was utterly nullified by one of John's greatest political blunders: his crass insensitivity to Hugh le Brun and the Lusignans. This episode reveals how John's acute political awareness was, as was so often the case, squandered by his hopeless inability to manage people or inspire them to place their confidence in him as their lord. Discarding his first wife, Isabella of Gloucester, with an ease that must have been the envy of Philip of France, John determined to marry another Isabella, the twelve-year-old daughter and heiress of Count Ademar of Angoulême, claimant to the country of La Marche. He wed her in late August and whisked her back to England. This swiftness of events was in a large part prompted by the uncomfortable fact that Isabella had been betrothed to John's vassal, Hugh le Brun, Count of La Marche and head of the most influential baronial family in lower Poitou. John's action was one of a series of offences he committed against the Lusignans (he would argue these were in response to slights against him), but the elopement with Isabella proved the most instrumental in the decisive struggle that was to follow. His motives for marrying Isabella had little to do with lust – although this cannot be entirely discountenanced, as nudging contemporaries pruriently suggested – and even less to do with romance, as some chroniclers and historians have also suggested; instead they were generated by a keen grasp of geo-politics. John wished to prevent Hugh's marriage to Isabella as the concomitant territorial control would not only have created a physical barrier to his communications between Poitiers and Bordeaux along the network of Roman roads, it would have also dangerously empowered the already refractory Angoulême lords. There was also the major consideration that the existing power structures in Aquitaine might be overthrown: John was fearful that if Hugh combined possession of the counties of Angoulême and La Marche with the lordship of Lusignan, then any shift in his allegiance away from the English crown to Philip of France would cut Aquitaine in half and make it virtually impossible to hold.[102] The affair might have ended favourably for John had he suitably recompensed Hugh for his loss of face; instead he fixed on a vindictive course which added insult to injury: in place of making amends he offered trial by single combat (by champions of course); worse, in the spring of 1201, he invaded the county of La Marche, seized it in his new wife's name and attacked the Norman county of Eu, which belonged to Hugh's brother, Ralph. Daniel Power has written of the importance of this affair: 'John's military inadequacies alone do not explain' his unfolding position; 'equally significant were his deteriorating relations with the Lusignan family since 1200.'[103]

John had feared a strengthened Lusignan family agitating under the aegis of the Capetians; now, by his own actions, he had forced a weakened but embittered family decisively into the French camp. Hugh and Ralph appealed to King Philip against John's shabby treatment of them. Philip, as overlord to the Duke of Aquitaine, heard this appeal with some discomfort. His relations with the Papacy over his matrimonial problems were still at a sensitive stage, despite the lifting of a papal interdict on France, and John's display of power on inheriting his continental lands in 1200 may well have served its purpose in earning Philip's cautious respect. Furthermore, John had added to his war chest in 1201 when he summoned his troops to Portsmouth. There the expeditionary force was equipped for a campaign that John had arguably never intended to embark upon. Instead, his purpose in gathering this army was to appropriate the soldier's campaign funds, being the money that they had brought with them to cover their expenses while serving the host: as one chronicler succinctly puts it, 'He took from some of them the money they would have spent in his service and let them return home.'[104] The money thereby collected was used to employ 200 mercenaries in Normandy: one half under the command of William Marshal, the other under Roger de Lacy – two generals who were to play such a large part in the coming wars. But Philip's own position was improved by a settlement of differences with Rome and by the death of Count Theobald of Champagne. This latter event meant a sudden wind-fall for the French crown: the Count's heir was a minor, which allowed Philip, as overlord, temporarily to add the substantial resources of this great fief to those of the royal demesne.[105]

The two kings entered into a period of seemingly successful negotiations, culminating in John's stay in Paris at the end of June, where he was lavishly entertained by Philip. The treaty of Le Goulet was confirmed and John promised Philip to have the Lusignan matter settled in his court as Duke of Aquitaine. John's troops, however, continued to harass Lusignan forts and to lay waste French territory in the Touraine. The Lusignans pressed Philip to act on their behalf, and by 1202 he was prepared to do so. John's foot-dragging over fulfilling his prom-ise of the previous June had incited Philip to demand, somewhat ambitiously, the surrender of the most important castles in Normandy – Falaise, Arques and Château Gaillard – as security for his word. John continued to 'make his excuses', as Gervase of Canterbury correctly identified them, [106] and by April, Philip, as feudal overlord, could not be seen to be waiting any longer. Nor did he wish to do so. When, despite having pledged as security the two small satellite castles of Château Gaillard (Tillières and Boutavant), John failed to heed a summons to the French royal court to respond to the charges of injustice raised against him, he was judged, *in absentia*, as a contumacious vassal and condemned to forfeit his lands held of Philip: his fiefs of Aquitaine, Poitou and Anjou were to revert to the French crown.

Mirebeau and Anjou

The fragile agreement of Le Goulet had already been violated by both Kings: John had renewed his support for his nephew Otto of Brunswick's claim to the imperial throne; Philip had engaged his daughter Marie to Arthur of Brittany, thereby re-establishing ties with John's enemy. But Philip's dramatic judgement meant all-out war. Hostilities were immediately opened by French attacks on Boutavant and Tillières, both of which were taken and razed to the ground.[107] John set up his campaign headquarters at Pont l'Arche in the Seine Valley where he must have rued his change of fortune. He had lost valuable allies to the Fourth Crusade, upon which the Counts of Flanders, Blois and Perche had embarked; and the Counts of Toulouse and Boulogne were transferring their allegiances to Philip.

The French King swept through the north-eastern frontier, meeting with little resistance until he reached Gournay.[108] Philip's strategy had been to isolate Gournay by first taking the castles in the Forest of Lions. With this achieved Gournay had only its formidable defences to rely upon. The castle was situated in marshland and was protected by three curtain walls, wide and deep moats and the river Epte. It lay under the control of a loyal Angevin officer by the name of

Brandin and both he and the garrison were offered considerable rewards by John if they maintained a successful defence. Philip, however, whose military achievements lay primarily in his skill as a castle-breaker, rose to the challenge with great ingenuity. Seeing that the castle was all but impregnable to anything but a lengthy siege, he turned, as he so often did, to his engineers. He instructed them to break the dam wall of a large weir that lay farther up the river. The result was an inundation the sheer power and volume of which so compromised Gournay's defences the garrison was compelled to surrender. William the Breton claimed the whole area looked like a sea. Philip rebuilt the defences and by mid-July had moved to Arques, which lies on the Varenne river and which protected the vital port of Dieppe (that Richard I had given to Walter, Archbishop of Rouen, in exchange for Andely and the construction there of Château Gaillard). John hoped to raise the siege here by cutting off French supplies: he intended to do this himself by land while his ships from the Cinque Ports did likewise at sea.[109]

In the southern theatre of war Arthur led his Bretons and Poitevin allies up the Loire valley into the strategic nerve centre of the Angevin Empire. As a rival claimant to the throne of England, the teenaged Arthur (he was born in 1187), who had been brought up in the French court with Philip's son, Prince Louis, was an obvious weapon in Philip's armoury. The French King had knighted him and accepted his homage for Brittany, Anjou, Poitou, Maine and Touraine – on the provision that Arthur could seize them. Philip intended to keep Normandy for himself. Philip had furnished him with money and 200 elite knights and sent him to Poitou where his forces were augmented by the Lusignans, Savary de Mauléon and other barons, including feudal contingents from Berry and Bourges. In all, Arthur may have been at the head of 1000 men when he marched on the Castle of Mirebeau at the end of July. This castle, lying between Angers and Poitiers, was at that moment offering hospitality to his grandmother, and John's mother, the redoubtable Eleanor of Aquitaine, now approaching her eighties but still a major player on the political scene. Despite Philip's characteristic advice to proceed cautiously, the proud and headstrong Arthur was not inclined to miss this opportunity of bagging such a great prize. Eleanor managed to despatch an urgent letter to her son, begging him for his immediate assistance. John, already moving south, met her courier near Le Mans on 30 July. Prompted by William des Roches, the castellan of Chinon whom John had made Seneschal of Anjou following his alienation from Philip, he marched with truly remarkable speed to Mirebeau, which his troops reached within 48 hours, having covered a distance of some 80 miles.

The sources do not agree on the events at Mirebeau, but a detailed composite picture can be drawn up. The anonymous narrator of Béthune, the most complete and reliable of the sources, relates that the town of Mirebeau surrendered but the castle, to which the garrison had withdrawn, remained defiant. Arthur requested Eleanor to leave the castle; she expressed her indignant surprise at the affrontery of his actions. Arthur's force billeted in the town and settled down for a siege, unaware of John's rapid approach. Early in the morning of 1 August, the English king's army under the lead of William des Roches, burst upon the besiegers. The startled look-outs sent up the cry of 'To arms! To arms!' Ralph of Coggleshall claims that all the town's gates except one had been secured; the Anonymous confirms that the Poitevins had been unable to close this gate. It was presumably through this poorly defended entrance that William and his troops stormed into the town. Once in, they fought to open the other gates. The element of surprise was total and had been used to the fullest advantage by the royalist forces. Geoffrey de Lusignan, we are told, did not stir himself from his breakfast dish of pigeons; if this were true, he must have mistakenly considered his defences secure enough to deter a precipitous assault. Others were not so confident. Hugh le Brun and his brother Ralph mounted their horses and rushed to the gates where they were met by the sight of William des Roches' men breaking through. Royalist troops cascaded along the streets of Mirebeau, converging on the town centre. In the ensuing combat, des Roches is recorded as having three horses killed beneath him. We are led to believe, somewhat improbably, that even John entered the thick of the mêlée that erupted throughout the town. The Poitevins were completely routed. No one of any consequence escaped. William the Breton, forever making excuses for the defeats suffered by the French and their allies, claims that John's soldiers had made a cowardly and, by implication, unchivalrous night attack that offered Arthur's forces no chance of a spirited resistance. Relying on the effects of the day's labours and drink to put the besiegers into a deep sleep, William depicts the royalist troops creeping furtively into the town and overcoming their opponents who were still in their beds (as if this somehow places the French troops in a better light). Roger of Wendover's account differs slightly again and should not be entirely dismissed: his *Flores Historiarum* becomes contemporaneous around this time. In his version, the besiegers left the town 'in pompous array' to meet the oncoming Angevin troops. Both sides drew up in battle order and engaged with each other. The royalists gained the upper hand and Arthur's force withdrew hastily to the town; but they were pursued so closely by the royalist cavalry they were unable to close the gates behind them (other references remark on an unsecured gate) and both sets of belligerents entered the town together. Although none of these sources mention it, it is possible that at the crucial stage of the battle some of Eleanor's garrison in the castle sallied forth to aid the relief army, thereby catching the besiegers in the middle of two hostile onslaughts. Whatever the exact details, John's decisive response to the situation at Mirebeau had earned him a great victory.[110]

John's swift reaction to the threat faced by his mother reveals his ability to act rapidly in a crisis. His forced march to raise the siege offers a good example of the need for a military commander to act quickly and decisively. However, this in itself was not enough: the efficacy and use of such rapid movement was equally important. John might easily have rushed headlong into an ambush; we might suppose that William des Roches provided him with good intelligence of the enemy's disposition. Philip Augustus had once been caught by acting over-zealously in a military situation and inadvertently hurled himself into a dangerous ambush – although William the Breton unconvincingly claims that this was both understandable and excusable given Philip's unrestrained martial vigour and eagerness for the fray.[111] John would also have recalled how Richard failed to lift the siege of Aumâle in 1196: his attempt to surprise the French camp after a forced march floundered because of the well-entrenched and thoroughly pre-pared defences of the besiegers.

Although the Omanian school of thought on medieval warfare has been dis-counted, we can see how its thinking may have developed when we encounter such instances of spontaneous reactions by medieval generals. The idea that sol-diers, and knights in particular, had only to get a whiff of the enemy to charge headlong into battle is exaggerated; indeed, medieval commanders placed great emphasis on battle avoidance. Chroniclers, especially those favourable to the subject of their attentions, liked to stress the resoluteness of the commander who responded immediately and boldly to any danger. The real skill lay in know-ing when to act quickly and when not to act at all: some military actions were undertaken with the express purpose of provoking the enemy into taking steps that were to their ultimate disadvantage (a major strategy of the 1215–17 war in England). John's response to Mirebeau was appropriate and vindicated by the hugely successful outcome. He was well aware of the benefits that speed could bestow upon a commander. His father, Henry II, said while campaign-ing in France: 'Many castles, farms and cities lie exposed to us which we can easily overrun by a forced march.' His brother Richard, the epitome of ener-getic generalship, characteristically commented: 'To those who are well prepared, delay has always been and always will be dangerous.' John would have also remembered the great effectiveness of Philip's speed in raising the siege of the important Castle of Vaudreuil in 1194. William the Breton was astonished by this remarkable forced march:

> I am amazed
> That he [Philip] could, like a giant, complete an eight day march in three;
> And who could not be astounded that this king, with his troops,
> Fully armed, travelling as if with wings rather than feet,
> Could make so many days' march in so short a time?
> What runner or pilgrim with winged feet,
> Having fulfilled a vow and wishing to return home,
> Can boast of having ever similarly covered
> One hundred and fifty miles in three days?

It is interesting to compare the rate of this march (150 miles in three days) with John's (80 miles in two days); unsurprisingly, both impressed contemporary observers.[112]

John had done well. He appreciated the urgency to raise the siege before it succeeded through storming, mining, bombardment or the arrival of reinforcements; Mirebeau would be hard to win back if the castle fell into enemy hands. As John was to find to his cost later, the loss of an important stronghold could prompt a rapid realignment of alliances and defections to the side deemed to be gaining the upper hand in the contest. John was justly elated by his victory – he did not have too many – and expressed his joy in a letter sent to England telling of his 'happy success' in seizing over 200 prisoners. Among the captives were Arthur himself (seized by William de Braose), Geoffrey de Lusignan, Hugh le Brun, Andrew de Chauvigny, Raymond de Thouars and Savary de Mauléon. No wonder he crowed that 'he had got the lot'; Warren assesses that 'not until Crécy were English arms to gain so resounding a success.'[113] If John had deliberately provoked the Lusignans into revolt through his marriage to Isabella, it had seemingly worked out brilliantly. The shock-waves hit King Philip at Arques, where his siege machines had been pounding the town's defences for over a fortnight. He immediately raised camp, abandoned the investiture, and force-marched his troops to Tours, but arrived too late to salvage anything from this heavy defeat. With nothing to be done but to assimilate the new political and military situation into a new strategy, he returned to Paris. William Marshal pursued the French army, hoping to inflict telling damage during its retreat; but the French kept their discipline and withdrew in good order and did not expose any weaknesses that could be exploited by the harassment of the Angevin soldiers. This pursuit was limited, being curtailed by effective and well-executed counter-measures put into operation by Philip. As he withdrew, he left the Norman borders in flames, sparing neither churches nor monasteries. It was one of only two major victories over Philip.[114]

At one blow John had become master of events. Arthur of Brittany and Geoffrey de Lusignan were incarcerated in the mighty fortress of Falaise; Hugh le Brun was thrown into the *donjon* of Caen Castle. Many of the other prisoners were shipped to Corfe Castle in England, where a dramatic postscript to events occurred. Amongst these prisoners was the romantic adventurer Savary de Mauléon, who led an attempted prison break-out. Having apparently made four guards drunk, he took possession of the keep, which then had to be invested by English troops. Tellingly, 22 of the prisoners starved to death rather than surrender, an indication of the harshness of the conditions of their captivity. Savary, through the mediation of the Archbishop of Canterbury, Hubert Walter (who was sympathetic to Arthur's cause), came to terms with John: his wife and mother were amongst the hostages he had to pledge for his future loyal service.[115] The one remaining possible focus of revolt, Viscount Guy de Limoges, also fell into John's hands by September. Not only had the opposition leadership been removed; with their capture came the enormous military assets of many of their castles. But John failed miserably to capitalise on his extraordinary good fortune. With no lessons learned, once again his egregious mishandling and poisonous mistrust of his most powerful subjects had disastrous consequences. If indeed John could not resist kicking a man when he was down, nor could he retain his balance when putting the boot in; the result was usually John ending up on the floor.

It was, ultimately, John's treatment of his most illustrious captive, Arthur of Brittany, that caused him to squander the aces in his hand. William des Roches, whose invaluable assistance at Mirebeau was given on the understanding that he would have a say in Arthur's fate, went unheeded when he pleaded for Arthur's release. John had, instead, moved Arthur from Falaise to Rouen, capital of Normandy. Dark rumours soon spread concerning Arthur's fate and his suspected murder; speculation abounded in much the same way as would in the similar case of Richard III and the princes in the tower, when another English monarch stood accused of slaying his nephews, but again without conclusive evidence. A story of Ralph of Coggeshall relates how John had attempted to blind and castrate Arthur (to prevent any heirs laying claim to the throne), only to be prevented by the king's chamberlain, Hubert de Burgh. It has been suggested that Arthur actually died from shock after being castrated. By Easter of 1203 it was widely believed that John had done away with Arthur. Two contemporary writers offer circumstantial evidence for Arthur's murder. The Annals of Margam claim that John, drunk one night after dinner, killed his nephew with his own hands and threw his body, attached to a heavy stone, into the Seine. Though dramatic, this is a serious account: Margam Abbey had for its patron William de Braose, who was with John and party to events at this time, which may have been a reason for de Braose's downfall. William the Breton paints an even blacker picture of John, who coldly murders Arthur after taking him out alone in a boat at night, plunging his sword into his stomach, and then rowing three miles in darkness on the Seine before dumping the corpse overboard. However, it is highly unlikely that John was possessed of enough courage to risk being alone with Arthur, or even capable of rowing three miles. But the agreement on the use of the Seine for the purpose of disposing Arthur's body does lend some verisimilitude to this aspect of the accounts. Later assertions that Arthur had died of self-pity or in trying to escape by swimming across the Seine have done little to alleviate suspicions. Whatever the real story, it is highly probable that John did have Arthur slain; certainly, this is what the Bretons believed.[116]

It was John's treatment of young Arthur that prompted William des Roches' defection to Philip Augustus; he took Viscount Aimery de Thouars with him to the French side. The Bretons responded to the rumours of Arthur's murder by going on the warpath; they took Angers while William and his rebel allies took control over most of the Loire's counties, blocking the movements of John's

agents between Le Mans and Chinon. The citadel at Tours managed to hold out
for John until 1204: abandoned by des Roches' man, Hamelin de Roorta, Tours
was placed under the command of Brandin, one of John's mercenary captains; it
was subsequently lost and partially regained. Loches and Chinon, under the mercenary captain Gerard d'Athée and Hubert de Burgh respectively, resisted until
1205. Vital as these strongholds were, they were isolated pockets of resistance in
expanding enemy territory. John had even to send a mercenary force under Peter
des Préaux to rescue his queen from Chinon. Chinon was a great administrative centre (David Carpenter has suggested that the loss of its records was very
significant) and an Angevin treasury; its fall was a deep psychological blow for
John. This grim situation was entirely of his own doing. William des Roches was
the most vacillating of vassals but, as Powicke observes, his actions were those of
intelligent ambition. Had John kept him loyal he would have retained this vital
region, which would have been 'the most important guarantee against the loss
of Normandy'.[117]

His desertion marked a trend. The great majority of the Poitevin nobility had
relations or friends taken prisoner by John at Mirebeau, and his cruel treatment
of his captives lost him any residual goodwill. John's talent for alienating those he
needed had come to the fore. Fearful of being bogged down in Anjou, John sent
out peace feelers to Philip; unsurprisingly, Philip rejected these. English sources
blamed the disaster that was to follow on the mass desertions of the continental
baronage, but with more skilled and energetic military leadership, John may have
minimised even this great wave of treachery that was now unleashed; instead, he
succumbed to fatalistic lethargy, allowing des Roches and his allies further successes in Anjou. The defections gathered momentum. Hugh de Gournay went
over to Philip and delivered up John's castle of Montfort, having let in French
troops at night.[118] Count Robert of Alençon triggered further tergiversations
with his change of allegiance to Philip; by 1203, John was bereft of important allies
north of the Loire. But it was the military blows that struck the hardest. John's
castle at Vaudreuil had been stocked up with provisions and strengthened against
the French King's obvious designs on Normandy. Philip prepared for a lengthy
siege of this strategic fort but, to everyone's amazement, its English commanders, Robert Fitzwalter and Saer de Quincy, capitulated without a fight. Vaudreuil
served two major purposes: an offensive one as a launching pad for expeditions
into the Vexin; and a defensive one as an important satellite protection to Château
Gaillard, itself the chief bulwark for Rouen and hence Normandy. With Vaudreuil
and now also Conches in his hands, and the counties of the Loire increasingly
under allied control, Philip was able to focus on the great but formidable prize
of Normandy.

The marches of Normandy were the most heavily fortified areas of France.
John was relying on their defences to absorb anything that Philip could throw
at them. Normandy was of vital importance to both England and France. The

French crown wished for access to the northern seaboard and for control of the mouth of the Seine, not least because Paris, the seat of the French government, lay up river and was vulnerable to attack. Normandy offered a different prospect to Philip than the regions of the Loire. Although there had been substantial 'continental drift' between England and Normandy, much Norman sentiment remained pro-English: many barons, including William Marshal, held territory both there and in England; the kingdom and the duchy were also bound by strong trading and commercial interests. The network of castle defences; the resources in men and money; the ease with which reinforcements could be sent unhindered across the Channel – all pointed to the belief that an energetic resistance would ensure Normandy's safety.[119] But Philip had probed deep into the eastern regions of the duchy, and John was left placing his hopes on the garrison at Château Gaillard. Normandy's fate hung on its defence.

The Siege of Château Gaillard

The siege of Château Gaillard was the great set-piece of the struggle for Normandy. The castle itself was justly renowned by contemporaries as a marvellous feat of engineering. Sited on a dramatic crag overlooking the confluence of the rivers Gambon and, crucially, the Seine, this castle was the prized personal project of Richard the Lionheart. He had endured an interdiction on Normandy to build his 'beautiful castle on the rock', his 'saucy castle' as it is often called ('bold' or even 'hardy' castle may be more accurate translations). It was constructed in one startling phase between 1196 and 1198, a remarkably short time. Richard spent more than £11,500 on it, more than on all his castles in England during his entire reign, an amount that came to more than twice Normandy's total annual revenues. The castle was the heart of its own complex defence system that included the island fort of Île d'Andely, the new walled town of Petit-Andely, the fortifications of the original town of Andely, a stockade and outlying forts. It represented the apogee of castle-building and techniques, and it was with good reason that the writers of the age considered it impregnable. It was here that one of the most dramatic sieges – arguably *the* most dramatic siege – of the entire Middle Ages was carried out between the end of September, 1203 and March 1204.[120]

The place of Château Gaillard in history has been immortalised by William the Breton's hugely detailed, and therefore invaluable, accounts. He was an eyewitness to most of the events that occurred there and this is reflected in the space he devotes to it; other chroniclers, in comparison, barely mention the siege in more than passing.[121] Despite the epic qualities of the siege and its enormous consequence for the course of English history, its details have been largely overlooked by writers outside France, the last major published accounts of any note in English being those by Kate Norgate in 1887 and 1902, with my contributions on one aspect of the siege from the last few years.[122] What follows is based closely, but by no means exclusively, on William the Breton's description of events, especially as laid down in his *Philippidos* (a source which requires some careful handling and which, due to its abstruse nature, has not been used by historians as much as William's more straightforward chronicle).

Having descended down the Loire by boat, taking Saumur and Loudon along the way, King Philip of France returned to Normandy to invest Château Gaillard. He began by isolating it. With Vaudreuil already in his hands, in August he besieged another satellite fort of Radpont. This resisted for three weeks before surrendering in late September; a substantial garrison of 20 knights, 100 sergeants and 30 crossbowmen was taken prisoner. Philip then rested and reinforced his men before fully investing the defence complex at Château Gaillard. The flow of events was going his way. His soldiers had raised John's siege of Alençon and regarrisoned Tours; William des Roches and Philip's mercenary captain Cadoc had taken possession of Angers; by April 1203 Le Mans was in Philip's hands; his allies were making advances throughout Anjou. Pushed out of Anjou and Touraine, John resorted to ravaging Brittany, possibly to draw enemy forces away from the pincer formation they had developed. But he achieved nothing. His army and resources were needed on two fronts, in the south-west and the north-east; it was in the north-east that Philip's grip was hurting most.

The French army marched up to Petit-Andely and pitched camp on the bend of the river opposite the town. Philip, ever cautious and realistic, knew his objective was both daring and ambitious, and prepared for a lengthy siege. The castle was in the charge of Roger de Lacy, the Constable of Chester. Roger of Wendover describes this seasoned and ruthless soldier as 'noble and warlike' (both Richard and John rated him highly as a commander) and this was not just the view of the English chroniclers; the heroic defence that he and his garrison were to make become widely recognised. Roger was an Englishman with no landed interests in, or attachments to, Normandy; he stood to benefit only from the English king's fortunes and was therefore completely loyal to John. Indeed, in 1199 de Lacy had hesitated in his support of John's accession to the throne and had consequently fallen under the king's suspicion; here was his chance to prove himself in his lord's eyes. His first defensive measure was to destroy the bridge joining the left bank to the island, thereby denying the French both crossing and easy communication to the facing banks. Philip therefore had need to construct his own bridge, but this process was hampered by the defensive stockade across the Seine, which obstructed the transport of materials necessary for the bridge's construction. Philip's initial objective was to remove this obstacle.

For this task, he relied on what proved to be the first of a series of extraordinarily brave acts performed during the siege. While Philip's siege machines and artillery gave covering fire to keep down the heads of the defenders (and hopefully at the same time inflict some useful damage on the defences), a group of

young Frenchmen, possibly led by Galbert de Mantes, swam under a hail of fire
to the stockade and hewed at it with axes. Given the river's strong currents, the
weight of the axes and the exertions of swimming and axe-wielding, it is likely
that the fatalities suffered by this group were not only due to the barrage of
missiles raining down on them from the castle, but were also due to drowning.
Eventually they hacked a gap wide enough to allow large boats through. The
passage thus created, though distinctly uncomfortable for those who had to pass
through it under the eyes of the castle, was essential not only for the construction
of the new bridge but also for the supply of the camp, including livestock and
provisions, needed to sustain a long siege. It was Philip's intention to starve the
garrison out.

Philip immediately set about organising the building of the bridge. For this
he assembled a number of broad, flat-bottomed barges and ferries that worked
the Seine transporting commercial goods and livestock along and across it. These
he had bound together to form a pontoon bridge. Strengthened by stakes, the
bridge was able to support the erection of two tall, strong towers on four particularly large boats. These towers served the dual purpose of defending the
bridge and directing arrows on the enemy walls. The bridge was a substantial
piece in itself, and an early indication of the scale of engineering works necessarily brought to bear on the Angevin defences. With the bridge now complete,
Philip led the greater part of his forces over the water and tightened the siege of
the town. William the Breton, in a suitably overblown reference, likens Philip to
Xerxes, the Persian King who famously crossed the Hellespont by similar means
in the fifth century. The French pitched another camp and attacked the island
fortress from both sides. Having fully bottled up the besieged, and having captured Château Gaillard's satellite forts, the French were free to roam the Vexin
at will, foraging and plundering the region's fields and dwelling places to the
extent that feeding his huge army provided no overwhelming logistical problems for Philip. The French King had clearly understood the need to neutralise
not only the direct military threat posed by the satellite garrisons but also their
capacity to hamper the essential task of foraging and provisioning to meet the
insatiable demands of such a numerous besieging force. Philip, ever the master of
poliorcetics, paid as much attention to the no-less important but prosaic details
as to the grander, more militaristic ones. No doubt the booty from these operations kept the troops happy too and helped maintain morale: well fed and with
opportunities to line their pockets, the French soldiers would have enjoyed
higher spirits than their hemmed-in English counterparts; but they were lulled
into a false sense of security.

John, never far from Rouen, was roused from his ineffectual meanderings into
one of his periodical bursts of intelligent and focused activity. In the early phases
of the Normandy campaign, he treated the flood of ill-tidings about the military
situation with seeming equanimity. Roger of Wendover reports that John's

reaction to being told that the King of France had entered his territory, taken many of his castles and dragged off their commanders to prison ignominiously bound to the tails of horses, was to reply nonchalantly: 'Let him be; whatever he takes from me now I will one day recover.'[123] Now, however, at the very end of August while staying in Rouen, he proposed a daring plan to raise the siege at Château Gaillard. No doubt hoping to emulate his spectacular success at Mirebeau, John devised a scheme involving a night attack on the French lines. In this plan hatched by the King and William Marshal, two English divisions were to make their way by land and river to Andelys. In the combined operation the land force would fall upon the camp while over 70 transport vessels, laden with provisions pillaged from the Channel Islands and protected by a flotilla of small war ships, would re-supply the garrison on the Isle and break the pontoon bridge. Secondary sources have too readily accepted the numbers William the Breton provides for this relief force. He puts the figures of the Angevin land troops at 300 knights, 3000 mounted sergeants and 4000 infantry, plus a mercenary force under the infamous *routier* captain Lupescar; the naval element is said to have consisted of pirates under their commander, Alan, and 3000 Fleming soldiers. A total of perhaps 11,000 men is highly improbable: one modern estimate calculates that the French King had only around 2300–2600 paid troops on the Norman marches in 1203–4, and of these only 250 were knights, the rest being made up of infantry and crossbowmen.[124] William inflated the figures to create a sense of great odds pitted against the French. Nevertheless, it is clear that this was a major operation and one designed at least to match the French in military capacity. On receiving John's orders, William Marshal immediately put the plan into motion.

Whether through over-confidence and poor guard detailing by the French or through the skill of William Marshal, the English land force approached undetected to the main camp on the left bank peninsula shortly before dawn. But the plan went wrong from the start: the fleet was late for its part in the operation. John's strategy had been a sound one, and clearly caught the French off guard, but perhaps it had been conceived too hastily. He and his advisers had overlooked the crucial factor of when the Seine could be best navigated upstream that night; consequently, the flotilla was delayed in its journey against the tide. The Marshal, probably unaware of the flotilla's problems, would not in any case have wished to hold back his attack: if he waited he would lose the advantage of the cover of the night and in the meantime increase the risk of being discovered by the French, a certainty as daylight approached. The better and greater part of the French army had crossed to the other bank; Philip had left only a smaller contingent at the camp. Attached to the siege camp were the non-combatants: 'merchants, *ribaldi* and scroungers, and all those who march to follow the army camps in order to sell all sorts of things', writes William. These lay drunk and in a deep sleep in the fields outside the camp (which was almost certainly fortified). At the appointed hour, the Marshal launched his onslaught. His men rushed on the camp. The element of surprise was total. The camp erupted in terrified panic as the alarm went up. All who could, fled to the pontoon bridge in a frenzied effort to escape to safety on the other side and away from the slashing and hewing of English swords and axes. Over 200 were cut down. Such was the weight of numbers on the bridge it partially collapsed: it could not sustain the panicked rush of so many. Already one English objective had nearly been achieved.

William des Barres, the great French general whom William the Breton labels 'the flower of chivalry', and who was everything William wished his King to be, halted this precipitous flight. He admonished the fleeing troops and organised his own company of soldiers for a counter-attack. He had torches lit to deny the English the cover of darkness and ordered rapid makeshift repairs to the bridge. When temporary repairs had been put into effect, des Barres' banners led the French back across the bridge and headlong into a bloody engagement with the English. The English force could not hold the bank or camp against this onslaught and were soon routed; they suffered many casualties, dead and wounded, and a large number were taken prisoner. William Marshal made good his own escape. It is unsurprising that the Marshal's biographer, who offers copious details of the great warrior's military career, omits this serious defeat in his writings.

Just as the French were recovering from the exhausting encounter and celebrating their victory, they were faced with the second wave of the English attack: the flotilla had arrived. But it was late. The misreading of tides ensured that the counter-attack had lost its synchronicity. As dawn broke, the English ships could be seen making their way up-river to the isle. Once more the cry of 'To arms!' went up. French troops lined both banks and the pontoon bridge; crossbowmen were ordered to take up positions on the bridge's towers. The bridge was afforded the greatest protection; it was the priority of attackers and defenders alike; on it stood des Barres, Simon de Montfort (of Albigensian Crusade fame) and the elite of the French troops. Alan and his sailors displayed extraordinary courage and determination in pressing on into the midst of the enemy that were arrayed on three sides, especially as the Marshal's forces were in retreat. His flotilla had been discovered sooner than he had counted on and the Marshal's assault had obviously alerted the French to the presence of danger. As his ships drew near the bridge they were met with a shower of arrows, javelins, stones and other missiles. Their position in the middle of the river afforded some protection and they doggedly held their course. They reached the bridge with a crash of timbers and a downpour of arrows, crossbow bolts, sling-shots, stones, logs, pieces of iron, boiling pitch and tar let loose by the French lining the bridge and manning the towers. Persevering bravely against this barrage, the English began to attack the fabric of the bridge and to strike at the cables, stakes and boats which held together the beams of the bridge. A deadly hand-to-hand mêlée ensued. William the Breton relates the violence of the combat almost gratuitously, but he captures the horror of medieval combat. Blows by the sword inflict terrible injuries with deadly efficiency: eyes, hands, feet and ears are lost by many victims. Throats are cut. Stones crush skulls. Axes shatter knee caps and clubs spatter brains. One man is engulfed in boiling tar and another sees his intestines hanging from his stomach. It is only when a huge beam of oak is toppled on two boats, crashing into them and holing them that the deadly encounter took a decisive turn. The boats manoeuvred about and employing their oars, retreated down the river, still incurring heavy losses. They were pursued by some young French sailors under the command of Jean le Noir and Galbert de Mantes, the latter proving himself to be one of the heroes of the siege. These caught up with two English vessels and captured them with the complements of crew, soldiers and booty. The rest of the attack flotilla fled to Rouen. John had failed to lift the siege of Château Gaillard.

The hearts of the garrison trapped in the island fortress must have sunk as they watched the disaster unfold before their eyes and as the flotilla withdrew into the distance. The English offensive had concentrated French minds and shaken them from their complacency; reminded of their own vulnerability, they intensified their action against the island. The besieged had placed some hope in a wooden palisade before the fort as an extra line of defence. It was here the French now turned their attention. Once again Galbert was instrumental in events. Some incendiary devices were prepared and secured in water-tight containers. These were attached by ropes to the waists of a group of men under Galbert's lead.[125] This group swam unobserved (it is not clear whether what follows occurred in the day or at night) to the far, eastern side of the island, which was not so closely guarded: the defenders believed that the castle above them extended security to this part of the wall and had accordingly intensified their manpower on those points most under direct pressure. When in range, the French swimmers hurled their incendiaries at the palisade, which immediately caught fire. The breeze whipped up the flames and carried them into the fort itself. Soon all was engulfed in the conflagration and the whole fort went up in smoke. The shouts of triumph from the French looking on from the river banks were matched by the cries of horror from the isle. As the garrison attempted to seek safety from the blaze, its already critical plight was worsened by the barrage of stones and arrows that continued to assail them from the siege towers of the French. A few managed to escape in boats, but many were overcome by fumes as they cowered in the fort's vaults. The palisade had proved to be not their saviour, but their nemesis. The French took to their boats and crossed with ease to the island, seized the survivors and made themselves master of the place. King Philip's men had won him two spectacular early victories: the repulsion of the English relief force and the taking of the Île d'Andely, a vital step to taking the castle itself. For John in Rouen, the news was grim indeed.

As William the Breton, who had such a keen military eye, said: 'The island fortress having been taken, it was easy to take the town.' This was something the townspeople of Petit-Andely had anticipated: witnessing the fall of the fort, they fled headlong *en masse* into the opened gates of Château Gaillard, placing their trust in the castle's walls now that their town's main defence and garrison had been lost. For many it was to be a fatal mistake; for many more the short path to the castle led them to unimaginable and unforeseen horrors. To prevent the empty town and fort from being retaken and in order to press the siege of the castle more closely, Philip filled them with his own people. These comprised not only the garrison needed to guard the place and to assist in the siege, but also new inhabitants – settlers – who, through the spoils of war, now took possession of the fugitive's homes (Edward III did the same thing at Calais in 1347 after winning an eleven-month siege there, and crusaders cast out the defeated townspeople of Carcassonne in 1213). The two forces to whom this task fell were both mercenary elites: one company under a certain Walter; the other under the famous captain Cadoc, Philip's counterpart to Mercadier, Richard the Lionheart's mercenary captain, and now John's. Philip placed great trust in Cadoc; so much so that his company received the lucrative sum of 1000 French pounds daily. With the town and fort occupied, Philip's next task was familiar to a commander who had taken a strongpoint by force and intended to keep it rather than destroy it: the repair of the damage done (especially to the bridge) and a general refortification and reprovisioning.

It was at this point, with the castle securely invested, that Philip left to personally conduct the siege of Radpont, which fell in less than three weeks. John, still smarting from his recent defeat, did nothing for this important satellite castle, but instead withdrew to Falaise and Mortain, possibly with the intention of recruiting fresh troops. Radpont's garrison had made a few spirited sorties, probably prompted by dwindling supplies, but to no avail. Philip wanted to lead his army onto Rouen, but this was not practicable in military terms while the castle of Château Gaillard continued to cast its formidable shadow over French ambitions, tying down vast resources of the French kingdom. With its soldiers occupying the banks, the island fort and the town, the castle's garrison was easily contained; but an investiture of Rouen, with its reputation of impregnability, would be a lengthy, and hence hazardous process. Château Gaillard had to be taken first.

Patiently and realistically settling down for a long siege, Philip appreciated that bombardment and storming were unlikely to produce results on their own. And so he resolved to starve the besieged out. He set in motion a series of monumental engineering works. Huge trenches of circumvallation and contravallation were excavated the length of the siege force's perimeters. These were designed to prevent sorties from the castle and to defend the French siege camp from any further outside relief attempts. One leading historian of the fall of Normandy has cast doubt on these trenches being excavated, but overlooks clear contemporary evidence for this.[126] Seven wooden forts (*brestaches*) protected both trench lines and were placed equidistant from each other; each had its own moat and drawbridge and was of considerable strength. All were filled with soldiers. Within the greatly fortified camp the French army, soldiers and camp followers alike, prepared for winter by building wooden and thatched huts to replace their tents. They had created their own small town. Here they were to live – and some die – until the spring. The harsh winter that followed bore witness to perhaps the most tragic episode in all the decades of Angevin–Capetian conflict.

The Useless Mouths

At some unspecified time early on during the siege, the castle's commander, Roger de Lacy, the Constable of Chester, regretted having opened his gates to the inhabitants of the captured town, Petit–Andely, whose number had been swollen by an influx from the surrounding region, all of whom had sought refuge in the castle from the French forces.[127] He realised that with so many mouths to feed his garrison, which had little hope of fresh supplies, would be unable to sustain the siege for long. By itself, however, the garrison had sufficient stores to sustain it for a year. On one occasion, William the Breton informs us that many thousands of non-combatants had taken shelter within the castle's precincts, but this is clearly an inflated number; the exact figure is hard to ascertain: an upper estimate of 2200 and a lower one of 1400 can be calculated. In order to preserve the stores that would be quickly exhausted by these 'useless mouths'[128] de Lacy evicted some 500 of the oldest and weakest amongst them. The French took pity on the feeble group that emerged from the castle gates and allowed them to pass safely through their lines. A few days later a similar number were turned out from the castle and, being equally incapable of aggression, they were also permitted to cross the besieger's lines.

King Philip was absent from the siege at this stage, away campaigning and organising help for his Breton allies who were being troubled by John in an attempt to draw the French away from Château Gaillard. When he heard of this lenient treatment of the refugees, he immediately sent orders forbidding the safe passage of any further non-combatants expelled from the castle, regardless of their age or wealth; and he also ordered that any further groups were to be driven back to the fortress. He was keen to ensure that as many people as possible whittled down the garrison's supplies. De Lacy resolved to send out the remaining townspeople, judging his victuals as sufficient for twelve months if only the garrison and most able men remained in the fortress; all the rest were cast out. The number of this last group of men, woman and children was possibly as high as 1200, but was probably nearer 400; it comprised the weakest and most vulnerable of the refugees. William wrote that de Lacy knew he was sending them to certain death.

What followed was a full-scale tragedy to match any of the worst horrors of the Middle Ages. When this ragged and disorderly band spilled from the castle they believed that they were going to rejoin their families and fellow townsfolk in safety; but instead they were to be subjected to warfare in its most vicious form. They were not met by the opening lines of the besieging forces, but by a hail of arrows and javelins. The French had followed their new orders. The refugees flew back to the castle only to find the gates locked and bolted against them. The guard responded to their pitiful entreaties to allow them back into safety with the words: 'I do not know you; go and search for shelter elsewhere: it is forbidden to open the gates to you.' With this the soldiers on the battlements hurled down stones and fired arrows onto the terrified masses huddled below. Racked with fear and panicking from the incomprehensible violence of their erstwhile protectors, the wretched crowd withdrew from the foot of the castle walls, and moved out of reach of the missiles and into no man's land between the besiegers and the besieged. There on the rocky slopes beneath the castle, they were to remain for three winter months.

Finding what precious little cover they could on the steep, barren and rocky gradients around the fortress, the people tried to protect themselves from both the elements and the artillery barrages by harbouring in the shallow fissures and clefts in the rock face. These offered little shelter from the wet and cold of winter. William was astonished by the harshness of those within the fortress: it was not surprising that the enemy should prevent the group passing through their own lines; but that they should be condemned to 'a wretched and miserable existence' by the inhumanity of their own friends and relations was truly shocking to him. These poor people had sought refuge for themselves and their goods in the strongest castle in Christendom, only to be ejected and abandoned by their own side. All they had with which to sustain themselves were wild herbs, rarely to be found in winter, and the waters of the nearby river.

William catalogues the horrors that these people were driven to by deprivation and starvation. A chicken that had come out of the castle was fought over by the strongest of them and consumed with its feathers, bones, eggs and excrement. A baby that had just been delivered was snatched from its mother by ravenous men who ripped up the infant and devoured the parts. The starving wretches feasted on the dogs that de Lacy had kicked out of the castle. He did not want these animals to consume even the scraps of the garrison's food, and he was probably moved by a belated compassion for the plight of the people whom he had defended at the start of the siege. According to William these dogs were skinned with bare hands, although use was undoubtedly made of any arrows that had fallen into no man's land. When these dogs had been eaten, so too were their skins. William wrote that all feelings of shame were suppressed in the fight for survival. For three long, bitter cold months the desperate souls were tormented by hunger, existing in a nether-world where many 'neither lived nor died; being unable to hold onto life, they could not quite lose it'. In fact, at least half perished from starvation and hunger. But for the waters of the Seine, all would have died.

King Philip returned to the siege in February 1204 and witnessed the horrible results of his earlier orders. When the emaciated survivors saw the resplendent sight of the French monarch, given to corpulence and regally attired, crossing the bridge to the island fort, they called out for mercy and for a release from their slow death. William, always ready to praise Philip, rejoices in the king's clemency when he commands that the wretches be released and fed. William witnessed amongst the ragged band a man still resolutely clutching onto a dog tail. When told to throw the tail away the man refused: 'I shall only part with this tail that has kept me alive for so long when I am full on bread.' There was, however, further tragedy in the ending to this episode, which adds veracity to William's eye-witness account: deprived for so long of proper food and nourishment, most of the survivors gorged themselves on their first real meal with fatal consequences. Some historians have sensed hyperbole in all this. However, even in medieval times, it was known by some people, the writer Wofram von Eschenbach incuded, that it was dangerous for starved people 'to gorge on empty stomachs'. At Belrepeire, his hero Parzival, having raised the siege there, fed its famished inhabitants while being aware of this danger, 'so he gave them enough food and no more'. Numerous attested accounts from history reveal an authenticity to William's writing at Château Gaillard.[129] With this pitiful chapter of the siege concluded, the more familiar business of war was resumed.

Historians have had relatively little to say on these events, yet they lay bare the commonplace reality of warfare rather than the glamorous but rare spectacle of battle: the non-combatant was as much at risk as the knight, and frequently perhaps even more so. William's graphic account may give the impression of being artificial and sensationalist, but it actually bears close similarities with other chroniclers' harrowing descriptions of different sieges. The situation at Château Gaillard was repeated twice during the Hundred Years War. At the siege of Calais in 1346–7 Edward III allowed the 1700 poor sent out by the garrison to pass through his lines, even giving them food and money. But then he sealed the investment and left 500 to die from appalling hardships in no-man's-land. Those that were left behind suffered agonies from hunger. A message for help from the besieged was intercepted by the English: it read that dogs, rats and cats were being eaten, and nothing remained but to eat each other. Henry V's siege of Rouen during 1418–19 was almost an exact repetition of Château Gaillard, similarly lasting six months over Christmas. The besieged were soon short of food. The eyewitness chronicler John Page informs us:

They ate up dogs, they ate up cats,
They ate up mice, horses and rats.

Here a rat cost 30 pence, a mouse sixpence; those in the town were fortunate enough to add vegetable peelings and dock roots to their meagre fare. Those expelled from the town and denied access through the besieging lines of the English endured the winter starving in the ditch surrounding the walls. Some 5000 were said to have died of hunger or from exposure in the winter downpours. Starving children, their parents dead, begged for food; an infant was seen trying to suckle from its dead mother; there were ten or twelve dead to everyone alive; and there were rumours of cannibalism.[130] The heart-rending scenes depicted by William the Breton at Château Gaillard were repeated throughout the Middle Ages on various scales.

The motivation for Philip's response to the outcasts at the siege was clear enough: he was using hunger as a weapon. All the sources attest to the presumed impregnability of the fortress, and Philip believed that it could only be taken by blockade and starvation. As William, a seasoned observer of war wrote, 'it is cruel hunger alone that conquers the invincible.' The chronicler and French royal biographer Rigord declared that Philip's intention was to take the castle by 'hunger and want…in order to spare the blood of men'. But this is either naïve or disingenuous, attempting it as it does to portray a compassionate king: the unmitigated suffering of the non-combatants involved little actual blood-letting. Such a policy of starvation took its toll at Château Gaillard. The English chroniclers believed it to be the principal reason for the fall of the castle: Ralph of Coggeshall wrote of the garrison's shortage of victuals; Roger of Wendover thought that Roger de Lacy made a gallant but doomed sortie so that he might die by arms rather than of hunger.[131] The role of hunger as a significant military weapon will be seen again later when we investigate the siege of Rochester in 1215; here we shall limit ourselves to focusing on why it was that the non-combatants were made to suffer so terribly.

From Philip's point of view, the situation was straightforward. First, by forbidding the outcasts to make the short walk to safety he hoped to oblige the garrison to take them back into the castle and so exhaust the garrison's stores many times faster than would otherwise have been the case. This was especially desirable as we may assume that these people brought foodstuffs with them into the fortress, thereby unwittingly providing more victuals for the soldiers there and increasing their ability to hold out even longer. Starving the garrison out by the burden of extra numbers would facilitate an early surrender at relatively little cost in blood and treasure for the French. Secondly, showing mercy meant revealing a potentially fatal weakness. If King Philip let 'the useless mouths' through his lines then other towns and castles would also expel their non-combatants whenever Philip might besiege them; in this way their stores would last longer and the siege would be protracted, probably without success for the besieging forces. Philip Augustus did not earn his reputation as a castle-breaker by displaying any such weakness. Finally, the fate of those outside the walls reminded those within the castle of what awaited them should the blockade run its full course: the victims offered the besiegers an opportunity to apply some psychological pressure.

Roger de Lacy's motivations on the English side are more complex and, as this episode has been largely neglected by historians, never fully examined. Why should such a renowned and respected warrior (one chronicler describes him as 'vir magnificus et bellicosus') resort to such cruel tactics against his own people? For a medieval commander to be successful required a degree of ruthlessness that affronts modern sensibilities. Obviously, de Lacy wanted to preserve his food supplies long enough to maintain a lengthy resistance; and such was the strength of the castle under his command he could hope to hold out as long as his stores did. Those that were not of use to the castle's defence were therefore thrown out. To have accepted them back in would have been as much a sign of weakness as any leniency that Philip might have displayed; it would also have utterly defeated the military objective of defending the fortress – and according to the anonymous writer of Béthune, de Lacy had vowed that he would only come out of the castle dragged by his heels.[132] De Lacy has been blamed for his 'terrible blunder' in allowing the townsfolk to enter the castle in the first place, only to force them out later. But this overlooks the basic feudal obligation of a lord to protect his vassals. A more practical concern was that if a lord failed in his duty, his people might actively seek another lord they deemed more capable of protecting them: the thirteenth-century *Schwabenspiegel* asserts 'We should serve our lords for they protect us; if not, justice does not oblige us to serve them.'[133] Furthermore, at the time when he accepted the refugees into the castle, it was more than probable that a fortress as important as Château Gaillard would be quickly relieved. We have already seen how King John had sent out an expeditionary force to raise the siege, and it was only after its failure that de Lacy sent out the non-combatants.

Historians have made little of a letter sent by King John to de Lacy, and have not made any possible connection between it and de Lacy's expulsion of the non-combatants. This might be of something of an oversight as the letter clearly implies that no more help would be forthcoming, and that de Lacy must look to his own devices:

> We thank you for your good and faithful service, and desire that, as much as in you lies, you will persevere in the fidelity and homage which you owe to us; that you may receive a worthy reward of praise from God and from ourself, and from all who know your faithfulness. If however – which God forbid! – you should find yourself in such straits that you can hold out no longer, then do whatsoever our trusty and well-beloved Peter des Préaux, William of Mortimer, and Hugh of Wells our clerk, shall bid you in our name.

The letter, though undated, seems to have been written in early November in nearby Rouen, capital of Normandy.[134] It is possible that de Lacy received this letter before removing the townsfolk from the fortress, and perhaps only took this extreme measure when he knew the garrison had been left to fend for itself.

He did have the option of surrender at this point, and the letter appears to accept such a possibility. But the letter is ambiguous on this score: John does, after all, express his wish for de Lacy to 'persevere'. The charge of holding a lord's castle was a heavy one, especially when the castle was as important as Château Gaillard and the lord was King John. Medieval chronicles bear witness to the fate of the commanders who were too ready to capitulate. The Duke of Norfolk wrote in 1453: 'it has been seen in many realms and many lordships that for the loss of towns or castle without siege, the captains that have lost them have been dead and beheaded, and their goods lost.'[135]

William the Breton and some modern French historians have condemned de Lacy for his 'cruel and pitiless decision' in expelling the refugees, but to do so ignores the exigencies of war and the situation in which the castellan found himself. If such large numbers were kept within the castle precincts – unfed, but at least with the benefit of shelter from the winter – they may have risen up against the garrison who denied them food and overwhelmed them by sheer weight of numbers.[136] They may also have been driven away from the foot of the castle walls to minimise the chances of the outcasts effectively doing the work of the enemy through covering a surprise night attack by scaling the walls. Lowly *ribaldi*, the non-professional element in armies, had achieved something similar when they scaled the walls of Tours in 1189. It is interesting to note that only after their three months of deprivation did Philip judge this group as 'unable to harm anyone'; but William the Breton had drawn the same conclusion when they were first ejected, describing them as 'inutile bello'. At least by sending the people out de Lacy could hope that there was a chance the French would allow them to pass through as they had done with the first two groups.

Some French historians have equally been too quick to follow William the Breton in praising Philip's show of mercy when, on his return to the siege, he was so moved by the plight of the outcasts he relented on his earlier instructions and ordered that they be freed and fed. William makes the most of this humanitarian gesture of the French king, who was 'always responsive to supplicants, because he was born to have compassion for unfortunates and to always spare them'; he was 'moved by the lamentations ... of those who had already suffered too much'. Philip Augustus was moved probably as much by military considerations as by charitable ones: he feared 'the not improbable outbreak of a pestilence which might easily spread to his own entrenchments'.[137] This was an ever present fear at siege camps, where numbers could be decimated by the spread of disease. In the siege camp at Avignon in 1226, 'There arose from the corpses of the men and horses which were dying in all directions, a number of large, black flies, which made their way inside the tents, pavilions and awnings, and affected the provisions and drink, and being unable to drive them away from their cups and plates, caused sudden death amongst them.'[138] It was during this siege that Roger of Wendover suggests that Philip's own son, Louis VIII, died from the dysentery that had spread through the besieging camp. More important to the French King than the alleviation of the suffering of the non-combatants was the need to keep his forces at full strength to press home the siege.

The End of the Siege

Philip may have simply wanted the refugees out of the way for an assault on the castle. Throughout the winter the castle had been bombarded and assaulted, but with few tangible results. Spring was imminent and with it could be expected a renewed military campaign by John. John had slunk back to England in early December, having dismantled a number of castles which he feared Philip might make use of on his advance to Rouen. These were not the actions of an inspiring military leader. Shortly after Christmas the King of England was at Oxford where he organised the granting of war subsidies from both the laity and the clergy. This was the beginning of a concerted effort to raise war finances: tallages were levied on towns; privileges and concessions went on the market; goods in ports were taxed at a fifteenth. Scutage was also collected: a number of barons were fearful of losing their lands in Normandy and were therefore prepared to pay 'shield-money' in lieu of providing an actual military presence on campaign.[139] Philip had probably heard of these preparations. Further delay incurred mounting dangers and left unfinished business in other territories, especially in Poitou; Philip could not afford to have the best part of his army indefinitely tied down at one siege, no matter how important. John's inactivity over the last three months was not going to last. By the end of February 1204, Philip was making ready to storm the castle.

Another phase of major engineering works now took place. Philip concentrated his forces around the narrow stretch of land that reached out to the castle rock. This was the only accessible approach to the castle, a fact reflected in the intricate construction of the castle itself; its design was focused to counter any attack from this direction. By massive military landscaping, the whole area before the castle was flattened and widened, an enormous task which involved the breaking-up and removal of rocks. The purpose was two-fold: to provide a quicker and safer approach to the castle's outer defences; and, most importantly, to facilitate the movement of siege machines – ballistae, mangonels, trebuchets – closer to the castle walls. Protected runs allowed soldiers to fill the ditch before the salient tower with various materials, thereby creating firm ground for the belfries to threaten the walls; but it remained highly dangerous work. It was clear to the defenders what the French had in mind, and they directed their fire on these manoeuvres, inflicting heavy casualties. Nevertheless, the task of filling the moat was continued, its importance and dangers understood by those taking it. At the siege of Acre, directed by Richard the Lionheart and King Philip during the Third Crusade just over a decade earlier, a story circulated of a mortally wounded woman asking for her body to be thrown into the town's moat to fill it and to help with the attack.[140] The crusading spirit was not so prevalent at Château Gaillard; but the exercise and its purpose remained the same, ensuring the loss of many lives in its accomplishment. The defenders were equipped with their own mangonels and ballistae, which they used with varying effect. The protected path to the ditch had enabled at least one very large belfry to be drawn up to the walls. From this huge wooden tower, crossbowmen and archers aimed their bolts and arrows down on the garrison with deadly results, easing the plight of the French working to fill the moat.

Events suddenly speeded up. Before the moat was half-full, the French descended ladders into the moat and then set them up on the other side. The ladders, however, were too short to be of much use and the soldiers had to resort to using their daggers and swords to assist them in clambering up the rock to the base of the walls. These men were terribly exposed to the missiles falling down on them from above; covering fire from the belfry together with the shields strapped to their backs and held above their heads afforded them some protection. In the siege tower the crossbowmen and archers of Périgas Blondel demonstrated why they were so highly regarded, and so well rewarded, by King Philip. The air whistled with sounds of bolts, arrows and slingshots from both sides. Philip, exhorting his men onwards from the front ranks by the edge of the ditch, exposed himself to the dangers of the fierce combat and was struck several times (if we are to believe William the Breton), but his shield and armour protected him from serious injury. However, it is unlikely that Philip had forgotten Richard I's fate five years earlier and probably orchestrated the assault from a reasonable distance.

At the foot of the salient tower which formed the apex of the two angled forward walls, the French used picks to dig out a hole at the wall's base large enough to provide them with shelter from the stones and arrows cascading down on them. From here Philip's miners went to work. The contemporary chronicler Robert of Auxerre identifies the importance of miners to the French king: they operated like moles and followed Philip everywhere.[141] These miners are a prime consideration in Philip's reputation as a castle-breaker; they had gained much experience from services to their employer, especially at successful sieges such as Le Mans in 1189 and Boves in 1185. As these sappers mined under the foundations of the tower they supported the roof over their heads by means of sturdy timber pieces, cut from tree trunks. They excavated the mine in relative safety; the defenders had not yet organised an effective counter-mine to break in on the French tunnel and halt their progress. The miners piled up some tinder, lit it and hastily withdrew from the mine as the timbers burned. They got out just before the props went and the roof caved in. With its foundations eaten away and all the underpinning gone, half of the tower came crashing down into the moat, filling the air with dust. Not only did this leave a breach through which the French could storm; the masonry rubble from the tower also helped to fill the moat further and made a passage across it easier. Faced with the immediate prospect of storming, Roger de Lacy ordered his men to torch the buildings of this outer ward of the castle, not wishing to leave the enemy any useful materials or cover and also probably with the intention of buying some time for a retreat. This hastily done, the garrison manning this untenable sector withdrew quickly across the drawbridge to the castle's middle bailey. Before the flames had died down or the smoke had cleared, the French, led by Cadoc, poured through the breach to take the outer ward. On the ruined remains of the tower he raised his banner.

The middle bailey was guarded by a ditch 30 foot wide and a strong wall; it was no less formidable than the first defences. The French were keen to keep up the momentum that they had just created and did not allow themselves to be daunted by this broad moat and staunch rampart. They immediately launched themselves on a follow-up attack. A group of sergeants scouted around the edge of the ditch in the standard practice of searching for a relative weak point in the defences. They found one. Almost inevitably, given his misfortunes in war, it had been created by King John. A year earlier he had a building added to the middle ward. William the Breton describes the building's upper storey as consisting of a chapel and the lower one a latrine, 'against religion', he complains, appealing to spiritual outrage. At a shallower part of the ditch Peter Bogis and some comrades scrambled unseen down and across the moat until they were directly beneath the chapel window. Bogis, standing on the shoulders of a companion named Ralph, with considerable agility was able to reach the window and pull himself up. Remarkably the window had been left unbarred and Bogis climbed into the chapel. An alternative version puts forward the idea that Bogis, presumably of slight build, actually clambered up the latrine chute and opened up the window from the inside. Either account should not be dismissed: during the First World War, one of the most powerful fortresses in the world was taken in a very similar manner.[142]

From the window Bogis lowered a rope to his men and pulled them up. Once inside, the band of Frenchmen began to break down the door to the interior of the ward. The noise of their efforts alerted the defenders who feared they were about to be subjected to a mass break-in by the enemy. As before, in their panic they decided to abandon this ward also, and so they fired it (although it is possible that they may have intended only to burn the building the French were in). Then they hurried back to the strongest part of the castle – the inner bailey which housed the keep. As the French troops outside the castle watched this drama, they feared that Bogis and his group had been engulfed by flames. They had in fact taken shelter in a vault used as an armoury and survived the blaze. To the undoubted cheers of their onlookers, Bogis and his men emerged from the smoke to cut the ropes of the drawbridge and lowered it to their fellow soldiers. The French troops rushed across.

The inner bailey was enclosed by a 500ft wall eight feet thick. It was less a wall than a series of seventeen D-shaped towers, or convex buttresses, providing tremendous strength and the capability for withering flanking fire. The keep itself, surrounded by its own ditch 50 feet across, was the same thickness as the wall. De Lacy was left with less than 180 men to defend it, a sufficient number under his experienced leadership, although fatigue would have been a further factor with which to contend. However, like the middle bailey, this part also suffered from a major design flaw. The gate-house, though well positioned at an awkward point for attackers, had no drawbridge; instead the ditch was spanned by a bridge hewn out of the rock itself. Thus the weakest part of the inner ward – its entrance – could not be protected by the wide ditch. That noted, any approach across this bridge might expect to encounter the deadliest barrage to repel it. The most intense action of the whole siege now led to its climax.

Philip sent forward a siege machine known as a cat. The cat, *catus*, also known as a sow, *scrofa*, was a reinforced roof on walls – in effect, a huge, mobile shield – under which soldiers and engineers could approach a stronghold's walls to damage its fabric or to undermine it. The French mining operation met with effective resistance. Roger de Lacy now ordered a counter-mine to be excavated; this opened up on the French mine where the French miners were attacked and forced to retreat, their work only partially completed. By early March an enormous petraria, called 'Chadaluba', was brought to bear on the walls, discharging its artillery of large stone blocks against the ramparts. The wall, weakened both by the effects of Philip's miners and, ironically, by de Lacy's counter-mine, collapsed when struck by the petraria for the third time. The besiegers, seeing the creation of this breach, hurled themselves forward. They scrambled up and over the tumbled masonry and stormed the breach in force.

Despite the hopelessness of the situation, de Lacy and his men fought on. Even now they disdained what would have been the most honourable of surrenders. However, overwhelmed by sheer weight of numbers, they were soon under physical restraint and led away in chains. They were lucky not to have been slaughtered on the spot: the laws of war placed the fate of victims of a successful storming in the hands of the victor. According to the anonymous chronicler of Béthune, de Lacy met with a relatively lenient, if ignominious treatment. Each day throughout the long siege, when called upon to yield up the castle, de Lacy defiantly replied that he would never surrender the fortress, even if he were dragged out by his feet. His heroic defence did indeed end in this dishonourable manner.[143] He and his garrison were shackled in irons. King Philip had finally taken Château Gaillard.

Both the Anonymous of Béthune and Roger of Wendover provide alternative endings to the siege. Both agree that the English were, at the last, starved out (Philip's early strategy). The Anonymous states that the garrison capitulated after exhausting their food supply, which included their horses. Wendover claims that de Lacy and his men, 'preferring to die in battle to being starved', mounted their warhorses, rode bravely out of the castle in a daring sortie, and killed many of the enemy before they were eventually overcome, and then only with great difficulty.

These two accounts offer plausible scenarios; but it must be considered that they cover the siege in only a few lines, and the details concern themselves with only the siege's finale.[144] William the Breton, despite his faults, was an eyewitness to these dramatic events.

In the warm afterglow of victory following the brief outburst of triumphalism meted out to de Lacy, Philip afforded a genuinely magnanimous treatment to the enemy commander who was detained prisoner on parole in France. De Lacy was one of the few men King John placed consistent faith in: he contributed £1000 toward paying his ransom to secure his release from France; on his release he made him sheriff of Yorkshire and Cumberland, entrusting him to help defend the volatile north from Scottish incursions.[145] John had recognised the great, if ultimately futile, service de Lacy had rendered the English crown by his lengthy defence of Château Gaillard; it was the king's own fault not to have profited from de Lacy's defence. By the time of the siege's conclusion at the end of the first week in March, de Lacy had been left with some auxiliaries, 120 men-at-arms and 36 knights. Only four defending knights were killed during the siege.

For six months, Philip's army, estimated at between 2300 and 2500 strong on the Normandy frontier at this time, was preoccupied with this siege; but John had failed to secure any advantages from this situation. Powicke ponders whether the garrison would have performed even better in a less 'complicated' castle; he questions whether the castle's defences were too restrictive; if its 'elaborate arrangements' were 'mutually injurious'; or, indeed, if it was too scientifically advanced for its defences to be fully understood and exploited by its garrison.[146] These are valid questions; however, de Lacy was an experienced commander and, over the course of the siege, would have studied, analysed and exhausted all of the castle's defensive potential. What is curious is that such a justly renowned castle, rightly considered as the apogee of castle-building, should have, in John's chapel and the bridge of rock, such serious design flaws in its innermost defences. Whatever the possibilities might have been, the English and French forces had played their part in perhaps the most epic siege of the entire Middle Ages. Its consequences were soon apparent to all.

The Collapse of Normandy

John heard the news of Château Gaillard's fall on the day he was making his hunting arrangements for his return to the duchy. But John was never to return to Normandy as its duke. Philip immediately established his grip on the region by repairing the castle's ruined defences so that they were, in the words of William the Breton, 'more solid than they had ever been'. Given Philip's eye for detail and his mastery of siege warfare, this is wholly credible. This was the castle that symbolised control of Normandy. The implications of its loss were grasped straightaway by the duchy's inhabitants; within three months it was totally subjected to French rule. Philip, ever the cool customer, did not let success go to his head. His gaze was set on Rouen, the capital of Normandy, and which lay farther down the Seine.[147]

Rouen prepared for the siege: resources and supplies poured in while the defences were made ready. The city's strong walls and triple ditch made it a formidably strong objective (as Henry V discovered during his six-month-long investiture of it between 1418–19). Its Angevin loyalties were reinforced by those who had fled to the city before the Capetian advances. All the time negotiations prompted by the Papacy continued apace, but these were little more than diplomatic formalities and they achieved nothing. It was during these talks that William Marshal, in an act of *realpolitik,* paid homage to Philip for his Norman lands while still serving his English lord.

Contrary to what might have been expected, Philip did not make straight for the city but instead directed his army to the west: a strategy which was to reap great reward at minimal cost. John's preparations for war, initiated at Oxford just after Christmas, were now tardily coming to fruition. If Rouen held out against a besieging French force then Philip could expect to face another relief expedition from England, this time larger than the one he had confronted at Château Gaillard and while deeper in hostile territory. Rather, he determined on the piecemeal territorial conquest of Normandy, leaving its capital isolated and increasingly surrounded, and hence reducing its strategical value. On 7 May he took Argentan and the satellite castles of his next objective, Caen. Intelligence gathered from Norman deserters revealed Falaise to be deeply demoralised, a condition not unsurprising giving Château Gaillard's recent loss. The stronghold of Falaise withstood the French forces for only a week, despite the extensive defence excavations John had recently carried out there; Lupescar, its commander, bowed to the tide of events and went over to Philip, taking his mercenaries with him. It is possible that Lupescar's actions were in part prompted by financial incentives offered by the townspeople of Falaise who did not wish him to resist the French king: they feared the material and personal damages that a siege would inflict on them, a telling effect of Philip's ruthlessness at Château Gaillard. With Falaise gone, Caen soon followed without a fight; with it went Bayeux, Lisieux, Coutances, Barfleur, Cherbourg and lesser places. In the first week of May, Breton forces under Guy de Thouars, burning with revenge for Arthur's murder, had broken through Normandy's southwestern defences and destroyed Mont Saint-Michel, a task which had to be completed quickly as the tides that transformed the rock into an island gave them only limited opportunities to do so. They then moved on to sack Avranches, linked up with French forces and joined Philip at Caen. Here Philip divided his army into two. Guy de Thouars, the Count of Boulogne (erstwhile ally of John), William des Barres, a large body of French knights and the mercenaries who had changed sides at Falaise completed the subjugation of south-western Normandy where castle after castle fell in rapid succession, a sure sign of military and political momentum. Philip, meanwhile, now turned to Rouen.

Philip must be given full credit for his strategy. The successful sweep south west and link-up with the Bretons left, as Philip intended, the ducal capital exposed and friendless. The political and psychological effects of this were as important as the explicitly military ones. Prince Louis attempted a similar approach during his invasion of England in 1216–17 when he was confronted by Dover Castle: he temporarily abandoned the difficult siege of this castle to first subdue lesser ones around it. John, too, tried this for London in 1216. In eastern Normandy all that was left of John's defences were Arques, Verneuil and Rouen itself; these decided to act in unison during the crisis. They saw clearly that the writing was on the wall in one form or another. The duchy's records of government had already been shipped to England before the end of May; and the indecent haste with which Falaise and Caen had capitulated had done nothing to stiffen the resolve of the remaining Angevin pockets. They felt the acute vulnerability that Philip had designed for them.

At Rouen we witness another example of why Philip Augustus had such a reputation for the subjugation of strongholds. Force and logistical expertise were not the only ingredients of his poliorcetic success. Before the gates of Rouen, he played on the defendant's fears, self-interest and common sense to come to an agreeable conclusion. Faced with the might of Philip's conquering army, the leading figures of the capital's community considered, as Falaise did, not only the mortal dangers they faced but also the financial threats that a siege would entail. Rouen's civic and trading riches rested in large measure on its privileges and rights; if John could no longer guarantee these then Philip might instead; but he would only be predisposed to do so if the city submitted quietly without forcing him to expend French blood and treasure. Philip, ever cautious and calculating, had been alert to such sensibilities throughout the Normandy campaign and had confirmed the liberties of the places now under his control. This had happened at Falaise, the fate of which was so influential on decision making in Rouen. If resistance failed, the capital's jealously guarded and coveted privileges could be revoked and instead granted to rivals.

Rouen's military commander, John's 'trusty and well-beloved' Peter des Préux, assessed the long-term hopelessness of the situation. He knew that only direct intervention from England could save the situation and harboured doubts that King John would provide the *deus ex machina*. Peter, who had enjoyed a close friendship with Richard the Lionheart, knew John's character and had less faith in him than his predecessor; John, conversely, had relied heavily on Peter and his brothers over the years in keeping Normandy secure. Rouen could look to its own formidable defences for a while if it so wished, but the balance of gains and losses made this option an unattractive one. Des Préux and the castellans of Arques and Verneuil made a truce with Philip on 1 June, in which all three agreed to surrender if help was not forthcoming within 30 days. They wrote to John in supplication and could not have been overly surprised by the tone of John Softsword's reply: they were not to expect any help from him and they were to act as they saw fit. This was not an exhortation to arms that would steel his subjects' nerves to counter Philip's threats, for the French King had added psychological intimidation to the incentives for surrender. Philip had explained to the citizens, governors and castellans of the towns and castles in his path that they should accept him as their lord now that John had abandoned them (not least by fleeing to England at Christmas). Wendover writes: 'he begged them as a friend to receive him as their lord since they had no other; but he declared with an oath that if they did not do so willingly, and dared to vie against him, he would subdue them as enemies and hang them all on the gibbet or flay them alive.'[148] After Château Gaillard, few doubted this threat. Hostages had been offered to Philip and their safety, along with that of the city, was put before faith in John. On receiving John's reply, de Préaux did not even wait for the truce to expire; on 24 June the strong fortresses of Arques, Verneuil and the capital of Normandy, considered invincible by many, surrendered to the French king. John had already lost Maine and Anjou. Now, too, Normandy was lost.

This was a momentous occasion in English history. Nicholas Vincent has recently summed up its significance: 'it fatally tarnished the military and political reputation of King John and set the Plantagenet kings on the road to harsher taxation, failed attempts to recover the duchy and, in the aftermath of this failure, the breakdown in relations between kings and barons that resulted in Magna Carta. King John's road from Normandy to Runnymede was a straight one.' David Carpenter has judged that 'The Capetian Conquest of Normandy was a turning point in European history. It made the Capetian kings dominant in western Europe, and ended the cross-Channel state.'[149] The French were in command of the northern seaboard. Paris, at times within just a day's ride of English forces in the twelfth century, was now safe. And England lay under threat of invasion.

3

War, Politics and the First Invasion Attempt, 1205–1213

The Impact of the Loss of Normandy

John's loss of Normandy was as disastrous to England as Philip's conquest of the duchy was beneficial to France.[150] The long-standing Capetian goal to obtain control of the northern seaboard and expel the English from Normandy had been spectacularly achieved. The tables had been decisively turned: now it was England that was under threat from invasion, and it immediately went on invasion alert. Of course, the new geo-political reality did not preclude further English campaigns into French territory – these were still mounted on a large scale – but a real psychological and material blow had been delivered to the English. For over a century, the duchy had been viewed primarily as a strong forward post on the continent for invasion into France; in strategic terms, it was an offensive asset. Now, however, the English believed that they had lost a defensive asset, a large buffer zone that had kept the French from operating on the shores just across the channel. The gains also further secured their access to the Flemish coast, not least because now they could more safely assemble and move ships along the coast. Implicit in Richard's continental campaigning was an understanding of this. But the disaster had implications far beyond geo-politics; the consequences for domestic politics, royal finances and, above all, military considerations, are the subject of this chapter.

Relations Between the Powers in the Early Thirteenth Century

In the brief survey of the relationships between European powers that follows, the dealings between England and France with the Empire and the Papacy were dominated by two overriding concerns: for England, all efforts were concentrated on regaining the lost territories in France; for France, the wish was to consolidate and expand gains on her home territory, an objective that could be aided by taking the offensive to England itself. Invasions of England remained an active option of French policy exercised into the eighteenth century, and threatened (as we have seen in chapter one) into the nineteenth. English dreams of recovery in France began fading after the Hundred Years War, despite the long drawn out and optimistic claims of royal titles over the centuries; invasions by Edward IV and Henry VIII did little to keep these dreams alive. In reality, such campaigns and assertions of sovereignty were used more to apply political and diplomatic pressure in pursuance of much more modest objectives. The loss of Calais in 1558 during Queen Mary's reign finally put paid to the hereditary hopes of the English crown (but not the claims).

Long before then all hopes of re-establishing the Angevin Empire had been abandoned: the empire technically came to an end in May, 1259, by the Treaty of Paris.[151] This treaty, concluded by John's son and successor, Henry III, and Philip Augustus' grandson, Louis IX, saw the English renounce all claims to Normandy, Poitou, Touraine, Maine and Anjou. In a poor return for this, the English King was acknowledged as Duke of Aquitaine, for which he paid homage to the King of France. Although the treaty did mark the formal demise of the Angevin Empire, it did little to alleviate Angevin-Capetian or Anglo-French rivalry, the antagonism persisting for centuries to come.[152] As argued in chapter one, Richard the Lionheart's continental campaigns were undertaken as much for the good of England's security as for his own Angevin patrimony, and the security concerns for both sides remained to the fore long after 1259. War and politics may be tribal, religious, dynastic, national, civil or inter-communal, but they remain war and politics, they remain power struggles. In 1204, the struggle that led ultimately to the Treaty of Paris might have led instead to Anglo-Imperial dominance of France or to another Norman conquest of England. These years of diplomacy, alliances and sporadic campaigning led to the pivotal, epochal engagement at Bouvines in 1214 and the French invasion of England in 1216.

Anglo-Imperial Relations

England's close relations with Germany went back a century to 1114 when Henry I married off his daughter Matilda to the Emperor Henry V, an 'early warning to France'.[153] Commercial ties with continental Europe grew even stronger as a result of this. One such tie was the burgeoning Flemish cloth industry's demand for English wool, something that inevitably intertwined political and economic interests between the two regions throughout the medieval period. This trade connection was instrumental in attracting the Counts of Flanders away from Capetian influence. There was also a great deal of trade with other areas of the empire, especially Cologne and the Rhineland. Under Henry II, relationships with the empire had become so close there was even a resentful backlash in

England, John of Salisbury railing: 'Who has appointed the Germans to be judges of the nations?' and calling Germans 'brutal' and 'headstrong'.[154] Such outbursts of national indignity should be remembered when we discuss the effects on English identity caused by the French invasion.

The Angevins forged a significant alliance with the powerful German Welf dynasty when Henry the Lion, Duke of Saxony, married Henry II's second daughter, Matilda. The Welfs were second only to the imperial Hohenstaufen dynasty in Germany, with whom Henry also remained on good terms, even when hosting the Duke of Saxony during his political exile in England in the 1180s. This bound the Angevin-Welf families ever closer together: the King became guardian to the Duke's children, and the Duke may even have been present at the King's death. A new balance of power had developed during Henry's reign. The purpose was to squeeze France in the middle. Now, 'France was always the actual or potential enemy, Germany, as in the time of Henry I, the natural ally of England.'[155]

Under Henry II's sons, the alliance continued to strengthen, with Richard being typically, even extravagantly, generous in funding the Welfs and Henry the Lion's son, his nephew Otto of Brunswick, in particular. He also offered money fiefs to other princes from Germany and the Low Countries. One historian has accurately judged these alliances as being 'of fundamental importance in that phase of English foreign policy which ended disastrously at the Battle of Bouvines in 1214'.[156] Directed against the Capetians, these alliances also served the related ambition of securing the imperial throne for Otto, the election of whom as King of the Romans in 1198 (and hence future Emperor) was regarded by at least one contemporary as Richard's greatest achievement.[157] A more immediate success was the transfer of allegiances of the Counts of Flanders and Boulogne away from Philip and to Richard, another objective of the alliance; Renaud de Dammartin, Count of Boulogne, was to be a large and powerful thorn in Philip II's ample flesh until 1214. Both these Counts had made treaties with Philip Augustus the previous year. For Flanders, Baldwin of Hainaut was motivated by the commercial interests of his country (as discussed above), while Renaud held genuine grievances against the King of France, but was also a ruthless opportunist. These Counts protected Normandy from a French attack in the north, while simultaneously making incursions against the French in Artois. The alliance was cemented with the sending to Flanders of 280 English troops.[158] The Hohenstaufen reacted to the election of a Welf by electing in turn their own man, Philip of Swabia, brother to Emperor Henry VI who had died in 1197.[159] This set the scene for two decades of civil war in Germany. Politics, diplomacy and warfare in western Europe were all subsumed by the resulting clash between the Angevins and Welfs on one hand, and the Capetians and Hohenstaufens on the other.

By the terms of the Treaty of Le Goulet in 1200, John was to end his financial support to Otto, but when war broke out between England and France in 1202, he quickly resumed a formal alliance with his nephew. For his part, Otto IV

justified payments from England with plans to invade France at Rheims and
Cambrai, forcing Philip to fight on two fronts – the established strategy of the
allies. In 1207 he was enthusiastically received in London and ceremoniously
feted by John. His fortunes received a great fillip in 1208 when his rival, Philip of
Swabia, was assassinated. The next year, Pope Innocent III crowned Otto IV Holy
Roman Emperor in Rome, only to excommunicate him just a month later over
his territorial ambitions in Italy.[160] This confrontation served to nudge the pope
into the Capetian-Hohenstaufen orbit and Otto even more decisively into John's,
the other papal bad boy. John now had a nephew on the imperial throne. The
Angevins and Welfs began in earnest to forge a broad anti-Capetian coalition with
real teeth that was to dominate European politics for the next six years. To this
end, John sent his half-brother, Earl William of Salisbury, to Germany with a letter
addressed to four archbishops, two bishops, two abbots, four margraves and five
dukes.[161] In England, there were a number of Germans, mainly mercenaries, who
held favour at John's court; some were military commanders of strategic castles
such as Berkhamsted, while others held lucrative offices.[162] Although John had initially somewhat neglected the alliances formed by his brother, he soon took them
up again with energy. Much of the recent negotiations were directed by the Count
of Boulogne, who had been in regular contact with John since 1209 via the mercenary pirate, Eustace the Monk. The Count declared his public support for John
when he and several other princes, including Count Ferrand of Flanders, signed
the Treaty of Lambeth in May 1212, by which the signatories promised to make a
separate peace with France. John declared that he wished 'these things to be done
publicly so that our friends may rejoice and our enemies may be openly con-
founded'.[163] John continued to pour money to Otto – as much as 10,000 marks on
one occasion alone – until an uprising in Wales forced a tightening of the purse
strings and put a hold on his military plans to recover his lands in France.

France

France's relations with Germany, as with so many nations of the time, can be
understood on the basis of 'my enemy's enemy is my friend.' All sides manoeuvred to thwart their opponents, real and potential. With a number of powers in
the mix – Angevins and Welfs, Capetians and Hohenstaufens, the Papacy, Flemish
princes and even Iberian kings – the possibilities for a changing rota of friends
and foes remained high. The pope fell in and out with everyone, but John and
Philip remained pretty much constant with their alliances (with some occasional
bumps on the road). Philip Augustus had a particular antipathy towards Otto, not
least for the latter's active assistance to Richard I in his campaigns against France.

French animosity towards the empire stretched back over the years (just as
it was to go forward, too). The victory of Philip's grandfather, Louis VI, over a

German invasion in 1124 was a celebrated highpoint in Capetian tradition, helped by Abbot Suger's account in *Life of Louis the Fat*.[164] Philip's gravitation towards the Hohenstaufens was a natural response to the Angevin–Welf alliance. Early in the 1190s Philip and Emperor Henry VI made a secret alliance against Richard I; some contemporaries believed that Henry's incarceration of Richard, shipwrecked on his way back from the Crusades, was at Philip's behest (and probably John's, too). Certainly, the Capetian did his best to keep Richard in prison by offering all manner of financial incentives to Henry. Capitalising on his opponent's imprisonment, Philip conspired with John to put the latter on the English throne. John did homage to Philip for Normandy and, with the opportunistic Count Renaud of Boulogne temporarily amenable to Philip, 'a Capetian King of France was for the first time in history in a position to threaten England from the sea.'[165] Philip lost no time in arranging an invasion fleet at Wissant in Boulogne.[166] An invasion of England was in Philip's mind in summer 1193, long before his son undertook the 1216 enterprise. That he could think about such an undertaking was due to the synchronicity of vital developments: the temporary rapprochement with Renaud Dammartin and the extraordinary luck of Richard's captivity. In 1193, Philip married Ingeborg of Denmark, primarily for the help this would afford him in his struggle with England: marriage meant (dubious) Danish claims to the English throne and also a strong fleet and army, offering the prospect of a two-pronged attack on England.[167] This combination did for Harold in 1066.

Richard was not greatly perturbed by his brother's revolt, later dismissively, but perceptively, saying that 'my brother John is not the man to conquer a country if there is anyone to offer the feeblest resistance.'[168] England remained loyal to the captive King (there was deep suspicion and mistrust of John already); Roger of Howden reports that Richard's officials repaid the trust he had placed in them: 'The justiciaries of England and the faithful subjects of our lord the King manfully resisted [John] and inflicted upon him great loss.' The seaports were strongly garrisoned and the Channel and potential landing places watched over vigilantly, so that the French could be prevented from disembarking their troops and those of their Flemish allies. Members of an advanced scouting party did get ashore but were taking prisoner and thrown in chains. The bulk of the force 'did not dare land'.[169] A bizarre, personal twist added to Philip's problems. The day following his wedding night, he inexplicably repudiated his bride, bringing down on himself the wrath of the papacy and burdening him with years of conflict with the Church.

To compound matters, Philip now also faced the imminent prospect of Richard's release: negotiations for his ransom were in progress between the English government and the Emperor. Philip's bids to purchase Richard from Henry were exploited by the Emperor who saw in them an opportunity to exact an even higher bid from England and to apply pressure for a prompt payment. Henry had no intention of auctioning Richard to Philip: his grandiose plans for universal supremacy, of the type that so exercised John of Salisbury, led him at this early stage to work towards a weak and vulnerable France. Richard's release in 1194 created panic among his enemies. Howden reports that Philip warned John of the news: 'Look to yourself; the devil is loose.'[170] And look to himself John promptly did: he fled to the French court. The threat from John and Philip was over.

The unexpected death of Henry VI in 1197 from a typhus-like fever changed everything.[171] Henry's son, the future Frederick II, *stupor mundi* (the wonder of the world), was only three years old when his father died, leaving it easier for the Welf Otto of Saxony to be elected King of the Romans the following year. This piled on the bad news for Philip. Richard's nephew, whom the King had already favoured with the title of Count of Poitou, brought great prestige and potential backing to the Angevins. The tide turned more in France's favour when in 1199 another sudden death shifted the balance more to his liking: Richard the Lionheart was killed at the siege of Châlus Chabrol. With John now King of England the French monarch faced a far less dangerous opponent.

Henry's death should have been a relief to Philip as the Emperor had disregarded the Capetian-Hohenstaufen alliance and had even made Richard, as one of the terms of ransom, an imperial vassal, urging him to wage war on France. Henry wanted Richard to undermine France's power for him. But Otto being catapulted towards the imperial throne was far worse for Philip; he feared him far more than he feared John. Fortunately for him, the internal strife in Germany that followed Philip of Swabia's election ensured that Otto was preoccupied with securing his own position domestically before venturing into foreign affairs. In 1198, the French King had sent Bishop Nivelon of Soissons to Worms to sign an alliance treaty with Philip of Swabia, undeterred by the Duke's excommunicant status. The French king's concerns for security on his eastern and north-eastern borders took precedence over religious formalities. As King John started to fall out of favour with the pope in 1206 and was himself excommunicated, and as Otto suffered a string of defections, Philip of Swabia's position strengthened and Capetian policy towards the empire fleetingly appeared to be vindicated by triumphant results – until Philip's murder in 1208.[172] The Duke of Swabia's death was considered by many to be God's judgement, and support for Otto of Brunswick became widespread. Philip attempted vainly to promote his preferred candidate, Henry of Brabant, with 3000 marks and implored the pope not to crown Otto. Otto easily won the day and in 1209 the diplomatic mission from the Earl of Salisbury resulted in the formal Angevin-Imperial coalition against France.

Dire as this was for Philip, he at least had the satisfaction of seeing Otto excommunicated almost immediately after. This was scant consolation and did little to effect the political situation for the time being. The ever-vacillating Count of Boulogne judged Philip now weak enough to declare publicly against him with the Lambeth Treaty, by which he paid homage to John, and thereby posed a real threat from north-eastern France. Philip, who never trusted Renaud, had seized some of his fiefs and occupied part of Boulogne. France was on alert for enemy advances from the north, east and west; in the south it was heavily engaged with the Albigensian Crusade against the Count of Toulouse and the Cathar heretics.[173] Neither Philip nor John neglected the Iberian peninsula: the French monarch allied with Castile in 1202, bolstering that kingdom's claim for English Gascony; to counter this, John allied with Castile's enemy, Navarre. But the ever-turning wheel of fortune presented new opportunities, and even now Philip was preparing another expedition to invade England. That this was the case had much to do with the state of papal politics.

Papal Relations

Inextricably intertwined in the international politics of kings and emperors was, as ever, the Papacy. Its overarching concern was to prevent imperial designs on Italy and its lands there; it is easy to forget that it was a state in its own right. It was never a biddable task to dissuade the King of the Romans and the Holy Roman Emperor to desist from such plans, and both Otto IV and Frederick II suffered excommunication over this issue. The Papacy was just as eager as other protagonists to play 'my enemy's enemy', at various times supporting and then opposing the English and French kings depending on the situation with the empire. Thus Innocent III ignored Philip's pleas not to crown Otto of Brunswick as Emperor but, following his bull of excommunication, channelled his support to the youthful Frederick Hohenstaufen. Innocent was pope between 1198 and 1216. Considered as one of the greatest popes of any era, he was brilliant, wildly ambitious, calculating, cynical, skilful, ruthless and obstinate, displaying all the characteristics of a successful temporal prince; his term in office, not coincidentally, saw a period of tremendous changes within the Church.[174]

For France and England, relations with the Papacy were determined as much by the domestic scene as by the international one, and it is the former that now requires some attention here. Philip Augustus' troubles were of a personal nature. Most rulers of Christendom had run-ins with Rome but, as the eldest daughter of the Church, France and her kings had fewer than most (though these were often serious). The Ingeborg affair caused a severe rupture. In 1193, when nearly 28 years of age, Philip married the eighteen-year-old daughter of the previous King of Denmark and sister to the current one, Cnut VI. Her dowry included 10,000 marks and, as mentioned above, the prospects of a large navy and a claim to the English throne. If Philip's motives for marrying Ingeborg were political, his motives for rejecting her after their wedding night can only be supposed. Temporary impotence has been given as one reason. His attachment to his mistress, Agnes of Méran, and the Danish King's alliance with Otto IV certainly prevented any reconciliation. Philip asked his bride to return to Denmark; she refused. The Gallican church granted Philip his divorce, but Rome reversed the decision and clerical opinion within France was split. Intimate details emerged from the royal couple: Ingeborg claimed that the marriage had been consummated; Philip that it had not. In 1196 he married his mistress (her father had close Hohenstaufen connections), further distancing himself from Rome. Philip refused to succumb to papal pressure with the result that Innocent placed France under interdict from January to September 1200. Philip's treatment of Ingeborg was cruel and vindictive: he kept her imprisoned until 1213 with few comforts and denied her material and spiritual solace. Even Philip's encomiastic biographers, Rigord and William the Breton, sided with the rejected queen (and with Rome). Only with the death of Agnes in 1201 was there room for more substantial conciliatory measures. Philip finally released Ingeborg and accepted her back in court in 1213. The date is significant: it was the year of a planned invasion of England and Philip wanted Denmark and the Papacy on his side.

Philip was largely successful in resisting papal interference in domestic matters of state: in 1203, when attacking Normandy, he refused point blank to obey the pope's orders to make peace with John (had he done so history may have been very different). Forceful as he was, Innocent was not heavy handed in his dealings with Philip. His decretal of April/May 1204, *Novit ille*, sent to the episcopacy in France, laid out his powers to intervene not as a temporal overlord (*ratione feodi*) but as a moral leader (*ratione peccati*). In effect, this marked papal acknowledgement of Philip's increasing power. The letter was written when Normandy was on the point of total collapse and after Philip's understandable refusal to acquiesce to the papal nuncio's instruction to settle a truce with England.[175]

The same year, the Papacy repeated its request for French help against the Cathar heresy in the south of France. A French-led crusade began in 1209; in 1215, Crown Prince Louis joined the expedition. In 1210, Innocent was also seeking Philip's help against Otto IV. By 1213, a number of factors had improved Philip's hand. Most of Toulouse, the centre of the heresy, had been subjugated; Philip had smoothed over relations with the Papacy over the Ingeborg affair; a new understanding began with Denmark; his ally Frederick Hohenstaufen was elected as King of the Romans in December 1212; and King John was embroiled in his own serious difficulties with Innocent: all contributed to make 1213 a propitious year for an invasion of England.

Just as Philip's problems with the Papacy can be traced to a specific moment in time – his repudiation of Ingeborg – so, too, can John's: the death of Hubert Walter, Archbishop of Canterbury, in July 1205. As one historian has noted: 'the election of an Archbishop of Canterbury generally occasioned a conflict.'[176] This is an understatement for the crisis that was precipitated by the election of Walter's successor.[177] For all his failings, John handled the ensuing crisis with tremendous skill, displaying, as he did periodically throughout his reign, a keen, if spasmodic, intelligence and understanding of affairs. The death of Walter deprived John of one of one of medieval England's great officers of state. Gillingham judges him as 'a resounding success. No king had a better servant'; Holt as 'the ablest and most effective of all chief justiciars and one of the greatest royal ministers of all time'.[178] John was not so generous: he celebrated Walter's death as a liberation that finally afforded him complete authority as king. Walter's efficacy as a minister had certainly encroached upon John's absolute freedom of political movement, and his demise granted John an opportunity to replace him with someone more flexible. Sidney Painter believes that in John's dealings with Innocent III, 'the fiercely intransigent attitude of the King in this dispute can only be understood in the light of his relations with Hubert Walter'; John 'was determined that the next primate should be a man in whom he had complete confidence and who owed him his position to his favour'.[179]

Unfortunately for John, Innocent supported a candidate that did not have royal approval. This was not unusual in itself, but the pope brought to his office new ideas of papal power and he wished to implement many of them in the secular world. The pope had eventually settled on Stephen Langton for the vacant see of Canterbury; John's man was the royal *familiaris* Bishop John de Gray of Norwich. The involved election process saw many twists and turns, the two parties taking their position to the papal court. In December 1206 Innocent insisted that John agreed to Langton as archbishop. John refused and cleverly spun out negotiations until Innocent lost patience and declared an Interdict on England in 1208. John was right to reject Langton on a number of levels. Submitting to the pope on this issue would set a precedent for further papal interference and restrict the king's vital tool of royal patronage. Roger of Wendover has left us with a favourable impression of the cleric: 'a genuine Englishman', 'skilled', discreet' and 'accomplished'.[180] But given Langton's later anti-royalist, pro-baronial bias, these plaudits are unsurprising. Innocent was sufficiently impressed by Langton's intellectual work to have made him a cardinal. (Langton's revised arrangement of the books in the Bible and his rendering of these into chapters remains with us today.) Modern historians are not unanimous in their opinion of Langton; Turner considers him to have been 'a man of little originality, a casuist in his thoughts'; in his acceptance of the archbishopric 'he showed little practical sense … he was either very arrogant or very obtuse'.[181] The most important relevant reason for John's refusal to accept Langton was political: the cleric's connections with France. He had lived in Paris for years where 'he belonged to a circle of Parisian masters with pro-French views, who contrasted the Capetians' just rule with Angevin tyranny'.[182]

Events proved John's suspicions of the papal candidate correct, the Archbishop being a foremost figure in measured anti-royalism. His ties were not just political but intimate: his brother Simon was from the hardliner section of the baronial movement, 'a more ardent, less balanced man than the Archbishop, inclined to headstrong speech and violent partisanship', who, as a rare fragment from French records show, had been receiving subsidies from Prince Louis from as early as 1213.[183] Stephen Langton returned from exile in 1216 in the same ship that

carried Louis to England for the Prince's great campaign. When Innocent consecrated the 50-year-old Langton as archbishop in 1207, John refused him entry
into England. And so began the Interdict.

The imposition of the Interdict caused some confusion among the clergy over
its implementation.[184] Broadly speaking, it meant the cessation of church services
and restrictions of the sacraments; bodies were laid to rest in the woods, ditches
and by the roadside without the services of a priest. However, much religious
life continued relatively unaffected, as 'clergy and laity learned to accommodate'
the Interdict.[185] It is a slightly puzzling period for historians, as sources tell us
very little indeed about the Interdict's impact. Politically, more telling was John's
excommunication in 1209 for obduracy in the face of papal pressure. This was
designed to put the King outside of Christian protection and thus remove
subjects' obligations to him. But as a spiritual measure, its currency had been
devalued in Innocent's hands by his repeated resort to it for political purposes. In
Innocent's Europe, it was almost a rite of passage for independent secular princes
and it may even have encouraged some bad-boy male bonding between John
and his excommunicated allies, Otto of Brunswick and Raymond of Toulouse. In
theory, excommunication conveyed the threat of justified opposition to an anath-
ematised ruler; although serious, it nevertheless depended upon the domestic
political situation for efficacy. In reality, its effect in England was limited, successfully countered in many ways by John's effective propaganda campaign across the
country. One contemporary monastic annalist's exaggerated opinion was that 'all
the laity, most of the clergy and many monks were on the king's side'; as Turner
drily and perceptively puts it, people 'felt little excitement about the issue of free
episcopal elections'.[186] Another historian writes, 'the only people really disturbed
by the sentence on John ... were some of the English clergy.'[187] Some felt compelled to move overseas, including all but two bishops, John de Gray and the
growing, soon to be towering, figure of Peter des Roches at Winchester.

John picked up the papal gauntlet unperturbed and sensing opportunity. He
does not seemed to have lain awake at night fretting over the eternal perdition of
his soul; indeed, he probably slept contentedly having busied himself profitably
exploiting the English church's now weakened position. This was the real bonus
in John's tangled dealings with the Papacy during this period: he employed his
dexterity to pocket a proportion of the Church's wealth, tapping ecclesiastical
resources to fill his depleted war chest. He did this chiefly through confiscation of clerical property and fines. In a creative display of humour, causing both
financial and moral embarrassment, he held the mistresses of the clergy for
ransom. The overall effect of the Interdict was a windfall that solved his financial
concerns for years, raking in over £65,000 profit during this period of exclusion
from Rome.[188]

By 1212, however, the deteriorating political situation and the fear of papal
deposition heightened the danger of a French invasion. Philip Augustus was

capitalising on support from Innocent and casting his eyes towards England; with John excommunicated, an invasion would be cloaked under the moral aegis of a crusade, just as in 1066. John was now ready to submit to the Papacy, and when he did, it was in a spectacular fashion: in May 1213 he accepted Langton as archbishop and rendered England and Ireland as papal fiefs. By putting his lands under Rome's suzerainty and holding them as fiefs of the pope, John was placing himself under the protection of Innocent as his over-lord. Any offensive action now taken by the French would be deemed an attack on Rome. Roger of Wendover is right to claim that the motivation for John's capitulation was Philip's preparation for invasion. As the Barnwell annalist wrote:

> The King provided wisely for himself and his people by this deed, although to many it seemed ignominious and a monstrous yoke of servitude. For matters were in such extremity … there was perhaps no other way of evading the impending danger. For from the moment he put himself under apostolic protection and made his kingdom part of St Peter's Patrimony, there was no prince in the Roman world who would dare attack him or invade his lands.[189]

John had taken a hugely significant step but, nonetheless, it should not be over-dramatised. William the Conqueror rejected the same arrangement from Pope Gregory VII in 1080, but contemporary princes generally took a pragmatic view: Poland, Denmark, Portugal, Sweden, Sicily and Aragon were all papal fiefs. Even Richard I had temporarily paid homage for his kingdom to the Emperor as a condition of his release and captivity. Innocent was delighted by this augmentation of Rome's power, prestige, political influence and finances. For John the results were soon to manifest themselves. In October 1213, Innocent was writing to England expressing his 'special care and concern for our well-beloved son in the Lord, John', that all should 'remain steadfast in loyalty to the said king', and warning against any instigation 'to move a step against the king'.[190] Only a few months earlier Innocent had been likening John to a ruthless, cornered foe, treacherously feigning peace.[191] The King had freed himself from excommunication and now worked towards freeing England from the Interdict; this release came the following year after suitable financial recompense had been made to the injured Church in England. John had pulled the rug from under baronial opposition and Philip's seeking of a papal blessing for his enterprise in England. His submission has been hailed as a political masterstroke.[192] Certainly, John had contrived to make a virtue out of failure. But, as will be seen in the next chapter, his triumph was a short-lived one, ended by military defeat on the continent. For the time being, however, it left John in the ascendancy. In 1213, even the tide of war was to turn his way.

Armies

The subject of military service and obligation in medieval England has generated
much literature. The focus of this study is on actual warfare, and so organisation
for war – an enormous area that encompasses the most salient preoccupations of
medieval government and economy – will be addressed here only summarily.[193]
From the outset, though, I should state that I do wonder how great the influence
of these matters was in directly military terms. Statistics are notoriously unreliable, and their application to medieval warfare even more so, where records are
fragmentary and incomplete. Figures and sums on papers do not always guarantee
a clearer picture of the front line and are there for guidance.[194] Soldiers fall sick,
records are falsified and money designated for military spending in one sphere is
siphoned off elsewhere. So often, and especially for this period, official records tell
only part of the story.

Money and manpower were – and remain – paramount concerns of military
commanders. Lack of both could certainly affect expeditions: Henry III had to
abandon his French campaign in 1229 due to logistical failings, while manpower
recruitment difficulties in the Holy Land imposed a major constraint on crusading policy. All princes were forever looking to increase their revenues for war
spending; we have just seen how John exploited the Interdict to this end. But as
R.C. Smail so succinctly put it: 'No Christian ruler of the twelfth century had
an army at his disposal which met his needs in full.'[195] This is a crucial point to
appreciate: generals always lacked the resources they wished for, but this did not
prevent endemic warfare in the Middle Ages. Leaders kept a close eye on recruitment and the purse strings for they knew how decisive these things could be;
but ultimately they kept fighting with what resources they could muster, often
starting out in the hope that the fortunes of war would favour them and thus
allow planned campaigns to be seen through. It is important to examine war in
the Middle Ages the right way around: warfare and politics affected money and
recruitment more than money and recruitment affected warfare and politics. War
was the primary initiator. The role of politics and military effectiveness, whether
through skill or luck or both, determined events far more decidedly than just
the size of an army or the state of the coffers. In June 1399, Henry Bolingbroke
sailed to England with fewer than 50 men; one contemporary chronicler claims
that he had no more than fifteen soldiers. By August he had effectively usurped
King Richard II and taken his place. In 1485, Henry Tudor became Henry VII
even though his expeditionary force was very small initially, and remained outnumbered at the opening of the Battle of Bosworth.[196] Political momentum
and unfolding events had proven of first consequence as it had in Normandy in
1204. The collapse of the Angevin Empire was fairly sudden and dramatic, and
came after decades of Anglo-French warfare that had only tweaked pre-existing
border frontiers, indicating that in military terms the two sides were fairly evenly

matched. The momentary imbalance that sowed disaster for England was the political and military inadequacy of John's reign.

Scholarship has long since countered the amplified role of feudalism in military organisation, in which a knight received a land-fief from his lord for 40 days' military service. Money was ever at the heart of military contracts. In 1066, on the eve of William the Bastard's invasion of England, one contemporary informs us of the Duke's troops requiring pay for their military services.[197] Even the 40 days military service was not definite as the feudal system was flexible enough to adapt to needs. Robert of Torigny tells of Henry II's invasion of Wales in 1157, when 'every two knights equipped a third', thereby producing a smaller force than the King could call upon but one that would serve for longer in the field.[198] Even when the allotted period expired in normal service, it was possible that 'the troops were simply taken into royal pay at the end of the obligatory forty days.'[199] This reduction in quotas seen in Henry's reign became an increasing feature of recruitment into royal service. It was notably employed by Richard I in 1194 and again by King John in 1205 when, under threat of invasion, he ordered that nine knights should fully equip and send a tenth.[200] By 1218, Hervey Bagehot, Lord of Stafford, was summoned to provide five knights; the survey of knights' fees in 1166 had stipulated 60.[201] Personal service and garrison duty was increasingly commuted by scutage and payment, the money substitute directed to the employment of mercenaries (although restrictions were placed on these by Magna Carta). Levels of equipment were stipulated for all ranks, as Henry II's military reforms of 1181, recorded in the Assize of Arms, demonstrates: all freemen were to supply themselves with weapons and military equipment according to their wealth. Philip Augustus was sufficiently impressed by these to implement similar reform in his own kingdom. Tellingly, the Assize did not distinguish between feudal and non-feudal obligation.[202]

Armies consisted of a range of fighting men with varying degrees of military skills, from the poorly trained recruits of a general summons or forced conscriptions, as with France's *arrière-ban*, to the fine-tuned professionals of knights and engineers. The universal levy was the full-scale mobilisation of the whole kingdom. In the confusion of civil war from 1215–17, it was not an easily implemented contingency. John had recourse to it in 1205 and 1213, both occasions that threatened invasion from France.[203] At the other extreme was the military household, a permanent force of knights and their retinues available for immediate action on the king's orders and the backbone of his army. Stephen Church's thorough and important study of John's household calculates that the King could muster a force of nearly 100 knights.[204] But he also shows how these numbers could not always be relied upon, as the political situation of 1216–17 affected many loyalties. The military household was very close to being a standing army, ever present as a military body or rapid reaction force to enforce the king's will. This had clear advantages, but disadvantages also. As Robert Bartlett summarises it: 'They were always there; but then again, they were always there.'[205] Like mercenaries, the household did not come cheap.

Forces fluctuated in size according to need. The numbers employed in the expensive business of castle garrisoning can be used as a political barometer: large garrisons in times of uncertainty and perceived danger; skeleton garrisons (if any at all) in times of peace.[206] As will be seen later, the role of garrisons was a central feature of the war of 1216–17, during which at least 209 castles were involved. This is a huge number, but not a surprising one as medieval warfare was predominantly castle warfare; the invasion exemplifies both. For this reason, engineers, miners and siege experts were highly valued as effective members of an army, as we have seen at Château Gaillard. Also valued were the highly developed skills of crossbowmen and archers, the former particularly valued in sieges; these combined to inflict more recorded fatalities in medieval warfare than any other combatants. As indicated above, it can be a hopeless task to pursue definitive numbers from bureaucratic or any other records. Armies generally comprised hundreds rather than thousands, except for the largest campaigns and battles, as at Bouvines. Powicke emphasises the 'distinction between the permanent nucleus of knight and men-at-arms, and a changing kaleidoscopic force by which they were accompanied'.[207]

Military organisation in France was not radically different from in England; we have already mentioned Philip Augustus affected in France his own version of Henry II's Assize of Arms. We know a good deal about Philip's military establishment from the survival of important documentation from his reign: the royal government registers and the *prisia servientum*, a war levy.[208] Philip oversaw a radical transformation of French administration and, just as historians have credited John's success in bureaucratic government, many more have acknowledged the efficacy of Philip's reforms. Jim Bradbury believes these lay at the heart of the French king's success: 'It was *because* Philip had set about reforming and streamlining royal administration, and therefore royal wealth and resources, that all his successes had come about.'[209] Certainly, Philip's ability to translate his resources into military hardware and manpower was a significant element in his conquests, but it was more political momentum, not least when generated by military triumphs, that played a crucial role in determining the outcome of conflicts. These could – and often were – affected by the military organisation, but the actual unfolding of events was far more important.

Given the documentation, it is no surprise that Philip's war machine has been extensively studied, providing a clearer sense of French military organisation.[210] The nerve centre of Philip's army, like John's, was the household of the king, from which he took the counsel of such men as Batholomew de Roye, William des Barres and the Clément family (who, in Henry, provided the marshal of France). The army, in its various forms, took its orders from the Constable and the marshal. Knights were expected to be fully kitted, while the equipment of sergeants or footsoldiers was specified in less detail. Many of the latter came from communes within Philip's domain: for example, Tournai, Laon and Sens were obliged to provide 300 men; Beauvais, 500. Other towns, as with Corbeil, provided a cash equivalent. Monasteries were also expected to do their bit, supplying packhorses and weapons, logistical organisation being no less vital.[211] Whereas English – or, more exactly, Welsh – archers were already developing a formidable reputation, so were Philip's crossbowmen, as we have seen at Château Gaillard. Contemporary illustrations of the Battle of Bouvines depict crossbowmen discharging their weapons on horseback. Absolutely crucial to Philip's success was his contingent of engineers and miners, whom sources say accompanied him everywhere. Once more it is worth reiterating that medieval warfare was more about sieges than battles, and so Philip's siege achievements are owed in considerable measure to his engineers. Of course, mercenaries were ubiquitous, and Philip relied heavily on his greatest mercenary, Cadoc. One historian has estimated that Philip could call on in total some 3000 knights, 9000 sergeants, 6000 men from urban militias and as many thousands of footsoldiers as he was ready to hire.[212] These are approximate, total figures; no single French army was ever comprised of these numbers as far too many variables came into play. Troops were needed to face various threats, potential and real, from England, the Empire, Flanders and internally; there were also the Albigensian crusade and castle-garrisoning duties to be considered. John, in addition and in conjunction with civil unrest, faced military threats from Wales, Scotland and France. Both kings, however, had their permanent military forces in their households.

Philip's military structures were physically reinforced by his fortress policy in France. His reign saw Paris fortified with walls and the Louvre Castle. Across his lands, a sustained and massive fortification programme led to town walls and castles being constructed or bolstered throughout his reign from 1190 onwards. He is credited with introducing to France a new, stronger style of architectural defence in the shape of cylindrical towers, demonstrated by the *donjon* of the Louvre.[213] More than this, Philip used his fortress network intelligently, permitting a good deal of autonomy to castellans, unlike John's approach in England and Normandy which 'was ruthlessly *dirigiste* and opportunistic from first to last'.[214]

This period saw important developments in the navies of England and France.[215] For the latter, acquiring the northern seaboard after winning Normandy necessitated considerable expansion of its fleet to project greater maritime power. For a long time John has received credit for establishing the royal navy. Ships were recruited into royal service in a similar way to men. The Cinque ports of the south coast (Hastings, Rye, Sandwich, Hythe and Romney) were traditionally required to provide 57 vessels for fifteen days of service; more merchant ships could be hired or commandeered to augment this for a form of merchant navy. Warren argues that the loss of Normandy compelled John to adopt a coherent maritime policy.[216]

Clearly, adverse circumstances forced him to devise a new front-line defence on
the Channel and he accordingly increased the number of ships available under
his command: between 1209 and 1212 he had built 20 new galleys and 34 other
ships.[217] Turner describes the new situation: 'The English Channel was no longer
an internal waterway for an Anglo-Norman realm but a boundary with the hostile
French; a navy was needed to protect the kingdom's coasts.'[218] John Gillingham
has challenged the claim that John was founder of the navy, persuasively pointing
out instead that it was Richard who deserves credit for this. Richard saw to the
construction of Portsmouth as a naval base and he maintained a very active maritime policy, whether in raids against pirates at St Valéry in 1194 or in protecting sea
routes to La Rochelle.[219] As argued earlier, his absenteeism in no way reduced his
concerns for England's safety. And Richard was, after all, responsible for the huge
logistical enterprise of the Third Crusade. A fleet, like castles, was needed as much
for offensive purposes as defensive ones.

It will be seen in this narrative how the English were considered to have a
distinct advantage over the French in naval matters. Already early in Richard's
reign there were indications of this. During the Third Crusade, Philip had to
borrow naval transport from Richard in order to continue his expedition. A pro-
Ricardian author delights in recounting how Philip entered Messina harbour in
just one ship to be met by a jeering crowd, immediately followed by Richard's
impressive fleet making a spectacular entrance to an ecstatic reception.[220] Naval
considerations were paramount in Philip's marriage to Ingeborg of Denmark at
a time when his maritime assets were limited. But as he increased his territory
and power and won huge stretches of seaboard (extensively in the north with
Normandy, less so in the west with Pointhieu), so his mind turned to invading
England and thus ship-building. Although Bradbury believes the 'formation of
fleets in 1213 and 1217 was the origin of a French royal navy', Mollat du Joudin
claims that 'it is impossible to see in the improvised fleets of 1213 and 1217 the
origins of the navy ... The fleets of Philip Augustus were occasional and ill-
assorted.'[221] Philip was never to match John in this crucial sphere of warfare.

Finances

All these men, castles and ships had to be paid for. Medieval government was
nothing if not geared to war, and war finance forever drove government bureaucracy. Government records of the time have permitted close scrutiny of the
countries' finances. Here the difficulties with numbers are even more vexing
than army sizes. It is extraordinarily difficult to track and categorise all national
income for a medieval state, but for our period there is the extra complica-
tion of inflationary pressures. There is little consensus among historians as to
how marked these pressures were, and the differing degrees to which England

and France were affected by them, but much important work has been carried out in this area.[222] Some historians place inflation at the heart of John's
political difficulties, one arguing that 'the rise in prices was probably a purely
English phenomenon' and another, consequently, that 'no king of England was
ever so unlucky as John.'[223] Others, however, see inflation in both England and
France; Georges Duby writing of revolutionary changes in France, while David
Fischer makes the case that before the 1220s prices rise were barely percep-
tible.[224] The most recent study, by James Masschaele in 2010, summarises the
economics and inflation debate and argues that the early thirteenth century was
a period of very substantial growth. He cautions judiciously that conclusions
are not easily drawn, concluding wisely that Magna Carta is 'first and foremost
a political document'.[225] Most medievalists would agree, however, that the eleventh and twelfth centuries underwent momentous transformations in society,
government and economy, 'the most profound and most permanent change that
overtook Western Europe between the invention of agriculture and the indus-
trial revolution.'[226] These changes, and the monetisation that went with them,
enabled kings to undertake ever-more protracted wars.

Much scholarly economic debate has also been focused on the comparative
wealth of John and Philip.[227] Despite the glaring discrepancy in geographical
area ruled by the two kings before 1204, to the Angevins' obvious advantage,
many historians argue that such factors as Philip's higher wages for his troops
provide clear evidence for the greater resources of the Capetian king. Thus
John faced the dilemma that 'a wealthier master was outbidding him.'[228] John
Gillingham, however, in his sensible analysis of these matters, argues convincingly that 'it must be certain that at the start of his reign John was significantly
richer than Philip'; he further emphasises that it is 'how financial resources
were employed rather than the sheer volume of money that is more crucial'.[229]
Nicholas Barratt's detailed surveys of the financial situation gives Philip an
advantage in dispensable cash, but notes that this was negated by the greater
costs of hiring his soldiers.[230]

So many statistical variables come into play I remind readers of my caution in
discerning hard-and-fast financial reasons for cause and effect in military affairs
and in the outcome of the wars discussed here. The fiscal exactions of John were
clearly instrumental in the production of Magna Carta, but, in the subsequent
conflict, John's ability to wage war and hire mercenaries was never seriously curtailed. Indeed, unplanned-for exigencies such as the Interdict actually helped to
fill his war coffers. Figures actually show that John's revenues could increase considerably at times of crisis, at just the moment when he needed them most. It
strikes me that John employed the threat of French invasion to this end, to extract
further revenue increases from his subjects. Political and military factors were far
more decisive in determining the outcome of the Angevin-Capetian struggle,
and to these we now return.

Campaigns, 1205–06

The winter of 1204–05 was a harsh one in England; for John, it must have been especially bitter as he reflected on the calamitous past year. He did not see the loss of Normandy as permanent; but then, no King of England and Duke of Normandy could allow themselves that thought, or be known to be thinking along such lines. The Barnwell chronicler, more favourably disposed towards John than other commentators, might have considered Normandy's loss inevitable, but that did not make it anything less of a disaster and humiliation for King and country.[231] John's determination to recover his patrimonial lands in France should not be doubted, but his attempts – and inability – to achieve this compounded his problems, leading to the ultimate disaster at the end of his reign with the French occupying London and one-third of his kingdom. As James Holt has observed, 'John's most decisive action was not that he lost Normandy, the Touraine, and the old Angevin influence in the Midi, but that for ten furious years he devoted all his attention to regaining what he had lost.'[232] Relationships with the church, the barons and the exchequer all contributed to John's ignominious end, but it was ultimately war that was his undoing.

Anjou was gone; Maine was gone; Normandy was gone. Now, in the summer of 1204, Philip Augustus turned his attentions to Poitou and Aquitaine.[233] In August, Philip set out with a large army to subdue the region, defended for John by the Seneschal Robert of Turnham. Philip was aided by the Lusignans, still smarting from John's treatment in 1202, and by William des Roches. The chronicles have little to say on these events, but it is clear from Rigord that this was a major expedition.[234] Philip's greatest asset was the political momentum won from Normandy, as potential resistance bowed to the incoming tide, and within a few weeks most of Poitou was gone too. A few Angevin outposts held out: Niort; Thouars; the crucial port of La Rochelle, now a frontier town; and the powerful castles of Loches and Chinon, the latter a major centre of administration and a treasury. Philip had Loches and Chinon blockaded over winter before returning to them in spring the following year. Defended respectively – and, it would seem, heroically – by Gerard d'Athée and Hubert de Burgh, these held out until Easter and mid-summer, Chinon witnessing a last-gasp sortie that failed to break the siege. These lengthy sieges appear to have the epic qualities of Château Gaillard, but with no writer such as William the Breton to chronicle them, we cannot say how the sieges were fought. De Burgh and d'Athée joined Turnham and hundreds of others in captivity, but were ransomed by John at great expense; he needed such loyal fighters as these.

Meanwhile, John had held a series of major councils from January, including one with all his tenants-in-chief, to exact a heavy scutage for the defence of the realm, for he feared England was under imminent threat of invasion. How real this perceived threat was is debatable, and it may have been the case that, as suggested earlier, John was using this as an excuse, even if partly genuine, to lay claim to war finances in general. Ralph of Coggeshall reports that soon after John sent 28,000 marks for an army of 30,000 men to defend Gascony.[235] There was a threat of invasion but it was as much a political threat as a military one. The wily Philip had been successfully coaxing Renaud Count of Boulogne and Henry Duke of Brabant to pursue their wives' claims to lands in England. John had to calculate whether, should he lead a major expedition abroad, these powerful soldiers might take advantage of his absence to agitate in England and persuade the barons, of whom John was even more distrustful now that he blamed them for the loss of Normandy, to abandon him. England was therefore placed under invasion alert. All males over twelve years of age were made to swear that they would protect the country from foreigners and the country was organised for war with a muster for defence in April. The south and east coasts were under the watchful eyes of royal officers. These bailiffs had orders to regulate the passage of ships into and out of the harbours, and even passing by; only those with a royal licence were allowed freedom of movement. This was not just a security measure against possible incoming forces and to disrupt possible communications with enemies across the Channel; it was also a way of garnering naval resources for John's fleet and the imminent expedition to the Continent.

The preparations, completed by June, would suggest that John was planning an attack on two fronts, from a landing north in Normandy and from the south in Poitou. Ralph of Coggeshall conveys the enormous scale of the expeditionary forces, calculated to have cost one-quarter (£5000) of the king's annual revenue and in which some '14,000' sailors and '1500' ships were said to have been involved.[236] Even the prisons were emptied. John claimed that this act of clemency was 'for the good of his mother's soul'; in fact, he was ensuring a ready supply of fighting men. It is notable that this amnesty did not extend to those convicted of treason, for treason was ever at the forefront of John's troubled mind. At this time he was spitting blood on William Marshal's recent return from France where he had paid homage to King Philip for his lands there; this was a unique arrangement by an English baron and did little to settle John's already frayed nerves.

This expeditionary force was possibly the largest gathering of military forces yet witnessed in England. But it never embarked upon its campaign. Archbishop Hubert Walter and William Marshal (fresh back from France, remember) persuaded him that it was not worth taking the risk. All manner of reasons were proffered by the two as they clutched at the King's knees, begging him not to go: it left England open to invasion; Philip was too strong; the Poitevins were not to be trusted; too much was at stake. Weeping and crying, John acquiesced – only to change his mind the following morning and spend the next few days sailing up and down the Channel before finally disembarking having achieved nothing. This almost comical – and hugely expensive – episode has never been fully understood. Perhaps by the final act John was hoping to shame his barons into following him; perhaps he was attempting to save face by giving the impression that he was up for it while his meeker barons were not; perhaps he was stewing in a tremendous sulk. But the cancellation of such a massive campaign was a major incident. Turner says that the cause was 'in part from a baronial resistance to overseas service in principle and probably in larger measure from their exasperation with John's money-raising methods'. Warren offers further credence to this when writing what Hubert and William feared, 'and the King assumed, was that if he attempted to put to sea he would be faced with something like a sit-down strike'.[237] William Marshal was clearly influential in proceedings, no doubt his new self-interest adding eloquence to his persuasiveness. Also of possible consideration but overlooked is the fact that the invasion threat, by which the country had been mobilised, was in fact no longer so pressing by this time as Philip's focus and efforts were evidently directed to the south in Poitou, and so a pre-emptive strike was no longer deemed necessary by many of the barons.

In the end, two much smaller forces were dispatched to the continent under John's illegitimate son Geoffrey and his illegitimate half-brother, William Longsword, the Earl of Salisbury. La Rochelle was reinforced, but it was a case of too little, too late for the castles of Loches and Chinon, both of which were in ruins from their sustained bombardments. John had done even less for these than he had for Château Gaillard. The message sent out to the baronage in western France was not reassuring for John's allies, current or potential.

The harnessing of such a massive force was thus a significant waste of effort and resources; however, John made some financial capital out of it: before the troops were dispersed, he exacted a payment – an immense sum according to one chronicler – from them in commutation of military service. The money collected went towards the campaign of 1206. Although not as grandiose as the 1205 force, the fleet and the host it carried that arrived at La Rochelle on 7 June were still very impressive. It is not known why so many barons were present on this expedition, but it has been suggested that John had browbeaten individuals into submission by personal visitations and no doubt, by promises and threats.

John first marched to Niort to give heart to the garrison exposed in what was now Capetian territory. He then moved deep into the south-east of Gascony to besiege some new enemies at Montauban. Alfonso III of Castile had laid claim to the Duchy through his wife Eleanor (John's sister) and was backing it up with force to the extent that he had besieged, and had failed to take, Bordeaux. It was essential that John countered this threat to avoid being squeezed from north and south. Montauban was an impressive fortress, but John was not daunted. His siege artillery battered its walls and defenders until, just after a fortnight of this, his soldiers, 'greatly renowned in this type of warfare', as Roger of Wendover says, 'scaled the walls and exchanged mortal blows with their enemies'.[238] The castle fell on 1 August and with it came great booty and prestigious prisoners. John earns much credit for this action by which he ended the peril to his territories here. However, important as it was, a glance at the map will show just how far the action was from Poitou and Normandy; success at Montauban had merely prevented his predicament from deteriorating.

From now until October, John directed his operations back in Poitou, Touraine and Anjou. Many barons still preferred John over Philip Augustus, the proximity of the latter in Paris many found to be overbearing and intrusive. Aimery de Thouars was one such: although rewarded as Seneschal of Poitou by Philip for coming over to his side previously, the habit-forming turncoat viscount now returned to John's fold. Our view of feudalism and homage to lords can sometimes blind us to just how superficial allegiances can be. Princes knew this and bidded at baronial auctions to gain support for their various campaigns. The same year Philip Augustus had attempted to win over Raoul d'Exoudun, Count of Eu, by offering him the whole of Poitou for five years and a bundle of money and soldiers besides, because 'you are one of the most powerful barons of Poitou and there is no one more suitable to conduct his [Philip's] business in south-west France.'[239] It is easy to be cynical about the cupidity of barons (and correct, too), but families could not choose where their masters fought out their wars, and they had to adapt accordingly when war came. John's campaign had chosen Poitou as the centre of his campaign for four major reasons: it possessed the highly fortified safe port of La Rochelle; it was closer to the developing events in south-east Gascony; it was also central to thrusts northwards into his lost territory; and because John felt that despite their infamous capriciousness, the barons here were more likely to prove loyal than anywhere else (which says something about his expectations). The allegiances of barons were to prove equally crucial to the protagonists during the invasion of England in 1216–17.

Three weeks after his success at Montauban, John was back at Niort, near La Rochelle, with Savary de Mauléon. It was at this juncture that Aimery de Thouars, no doubt taking note of Montauban and John's seemingly committed military efforts, decided that the Angevin monarch now offered more favourable prospects than the Capetian one and so aligned himself once more with John. In so doing, he delivered northern Poitou back into John's hands. Boosted by his improving fortunes an emboldened John raided into Anjou; when he could not procure boats for a crossing of the Loire, in a demonstration of determination, he forded it, much to the amazement of one chronicler. He ravaged his way back to his ancestral home of Angers, which he took on 8 September. He set up court here for a week, then moved even farther north to La Lude and back over the next five days. His intention was probably to send a minatory message to contumacious and rebellious vassals; but the message immediately following Angers was more equivocal: he destroyed at least parts of the city – Rigord says 'totally' – and quitted it hastily.[240] It was a clear statement of force, but also one that said he was not staying. As John moved back south to Thouars, Aimery attacked Brittany.

Philip's response to John's operations was measured but decisive. In spring he had already moved into Brittany, reaching Rennes and taking Nantes. With him was William des Roches and the royal heir, Prince Louis, gaining valuable experiences of warfare while still just a teenager. The French King's march on Angers in September was enough for John to head for safer ground south. Philip pursued him to Thouars and besieged him there. The campaigns of 1205–6 have received little attention from the chroniclers, and the siege of Thouars even less. However, a troubadour, apparently writing at the time of the siege, has left us a song in which he calls on Savary de Mauléon, 'a good knight at the quintaine', and his comrades-in-arms to defend 'your fortress'.[241] Philip's forces ravaged Aimery's lands in front of his eyes while his siege machines kept up the pressure on the town.

The campaign had ground to a halt and so, on 26 October, a two-year truce was arranged. The terms reflected the new state of affairs brought about by John's expedition. The truce recognised that for Poitou, the land north of the Loire, just retaken by the French, fell under Philip's control, while that to the south, just won by John, fell to English rule. Many historians consider this a very positive result for John: Poitou was substantially back in Angevin hands and he had 'succeeded in securing his position from Poitou to the Pyrenees'.[242] Nor should it be forgotten, as it often is, that John had also regained the Channel Islands.[243] But in reality these was only very modest recoveries, as if a football team losing 6-0 at half-time comes back to score a goal and goes on to lose the mach 6-2 at full-time. John made no demands on Normandy, Brittany, Maine, Anjou and the Touraine. In fact, John did not even sign the truce personally. The evening before the truce was confirmed, he had slipped back to La Rochelle. It may seem surprising that Philip went along with the truce – after all, he was at Thouars with a large army – but he was keen, as always, to consolidate and secure. As Warren nicely puts it: 'He was still digesting Normandy and wanted time to complete his meal.'[244] John, meanwhile, had to ruminate on his next steps. He had plenty of time to do so. He left La Rochelle in December and returned to England. It would be another seven years before his army was back in France for a fully fledged campaign to recover his lands.

1207–12

As with so many truces, Thouars did not last. Philip broke it and by the summer of 1207 was ravaging Aimery's lands across the Loire; by 1208 the Viscount and John's stalwart Savary de Mauléon were his prisoners.[245] However, the political map of Poitou changed little. This period saw a distinct lull in the Angevin-Capetian conflict, as both kings preoccupied themselves with other matters. The launch of the Albigensian Crusade against the Cathar heretics in 1209 (preparations had begun a year earlier) meant a sizeable portion of French soldiers went south to fight in the Languedoc.[246] Philip himself was still digesting Normandy, seeing to the realignment of his great fiefs in his kingdom as a result of this; while Brittany, Champagne and Auvergne were at the forefront of those aligning themselves with Philip, Flanders and Boulogne led those who looked across the Channel to John as a way of maintaining greater independence.[247] Both John and Philip were deeply immersed in ecclesiastical and diplomatic matters as we have seen, attempting to forge or repair important political relationships as their circumstances dictated with the pope, Emperor and subjects, and all with a mind to the future Anglo-French conflict. Philip took the opportunity to initiate an extensive fortification programme, which included Paris, and went on occasional campaigns to slap the wrists of recalcitrant barons.[248] John, on the other hand, was involved with military expeditions on a grander scale (not including a muster in 1208 which was probably prompted by an invasion threat). These should not detain us long, but they are worthy of brief discussion as they reveal the threat posed by his enemies on the Celtic borders of the British Isles and they provide context for their roles during the French invasion. They also reveal that John had greater martial accomplishments here than abroad, and that he did not lack anything in the form of military experience.

Warfare with Scotland, Wales and Ireland was nothing new for English kings. Rulers in these countries were ever ready to take advantage of their neighbour's monarch when his attentions were engaged elsewhere. The Auld Alliance between France and Scotland, cemented to increase the discomfiture of England at times of war, was very 'auld' indeed, and will be seen to be operating effectively at this time. When John's battle with the Papacy left him with but one representative of the episcopate in England (Peter des Roches; John de Gray was made justiciar of Ireland in 1210), Scotland offered a ready refuge for the bishops that exiled themselves from his kingdom. Fall-out with some of his barons in 1208–9 had resulted in a bitter conflict between the monarch and the powerful William de Braose, who fled to Ireland where he joined up with William Marshal, still out of favour since refusing to go on the 1206 Poitevin expedition. William the Lion, King of Scotland, perceived an opportunity to cause trouble here, as did Philip Augustus.[249] In August John went north with an imposing army and William, knowing that John was 'prone to all kinds of cruelty' submitted and was forced to come to humiliating and costly terms.[250] This left John free to deal with Ireland, where the de Lacys led the anti-John faction. (By now, William Marshal was once more back with John.) Again, a show of overwhelming force by John was enough to quell trouble: he took with him some 800 knights and 1000 infantry – a clear sign that invasion fears had abated in England now that Scotland had been forced to come to terms. This show of strength limited actual resistance; even at Carrickfergus the garrison of the well prepared and strongly fortified castle 'behaved like cowards', writes one contemporary, and opened their gates to John.[251] This campaign is often hailed as an outstanding success for John, but

Sean Duffy argues persuasively that the view 'that the 1210 expedition was an out-and-out triumph needs to be considerably modified'.[252] However, the Irish barons were to remain at least predominantly loyal during 1215–17. John's crassness almost inevitably revealed itself in Ireland, when he laughed at a native king who rode bareback, thus causing offence to the Irish. Such inappropriate behaviour had more serious implications when directed against his own barons.

With John in Ireland, the Welsh got up to some serious mischief, Llewelyn the Great (as he was to be later known) instigating, says one Welsh chronicler, 'cruel attacks on the English' as he attempted to make inroads in south Wales.[253] John acted in the summer of 1211 with another large English army precipitating another full-scale retreat by the enemy: Llewelyn made a strategic withdrawal to Snowdonia. However, John's campaign did not go smoothly and had to be abandoned when his army ran out of supplies and famine sapped the host's strength. A second, more thorough expedition set forth in July: more men, more supplies and more engineers to build castles. Llewelyn agreed to harsh terms.

It was at this moment that John has been deemed master of the British Isles. The Barnwell annalist observed, in a well-known passage: 'In Ireland, Scotland and Wales there was no one who did not bow to the nod of the King of England, which, as is well known, was the case of none of his predecessors.' But the annalist also goes on to say: 'And he would have appeared happy indeed, and successful to the height of his desires had he not been despoiled of his territories across the sea, and under the ban of the Church.'[254] His achievements were in fact decidedly mixed. Ireland was a partial success, Scotland was rendered quiescent for a few years, and Wales took up arms again in 1212. Serious as these threats had been, they were not comparable to the one posed by Philip Augustus' France; victories against princes, subjects and a comparatively weak and impoverished Scottish monarch offered no indications of a similar outcome against the ever-growing power of his Capetian opponent. But that was what he had planned for 1212.

Dominating the British Isles, John was feeling increasingly confident. His nephew was now Emperor Otto IV; Renuad de Dammartin, Count of Boulogne, had sailed to England in May to pledge his service to John; following him came the Counts of Flanders, Limbourg, Bar and Louvain to voice their opposition to Philip. What was more, his war coffers were full – although he still had to pay the political price for this. The desertions weakened Philip, but should not, however, be seen as a sign of weakness: a paradox of increasing, centralised power was that the stronger the monarch became the more he provoked resistance from those who saw their own powers being encroached upon, causing those feeling threatened to seek help from foreign powers. This was also to be a feature of English politics in 1216 and up to the end of the Tudor regime.

John was now in his strongest position for nearly a decade. But it was a fleeting moment. Activity at Portsmouth in the spring and summer of 1212 was at its most intense for six years, as John's officials and commanders made ready for the long-awaited expedition to Poitou. All across the country, John's efficient government machine was put into operation to ensure full recruitment and provisioning for the full-scale expedition: extra money was raked in by means of the forest laws; writs were sent out across the country to summon knights; government men roamed the land to ascertain exactly the military service owed to the King. But John's forces did not go to France; instead, they went to Wales.

Llewelyn had managed to forge an alliance with erstwhile enemies and competing princes to rise up against John.[255] Roger of Wendover relates how 'the Welsh burst fiercely from their hiding-places, and took some of the English king's castles, beheading all they found in them, knights and soldiers alike'; they torched several towns and amassed 'great quantities of plunder'.[256] Decapitation was an almost ritualised aspect of warfare in Wales and Ireland.

Llewelyn had been spending time at John's court and may have grown to distrust him even more; he and the Welsh princes were gravely concerned by the King's castle-building programme and the obvious implications of this for control in Wales. Fearing this expansion of muscular English power, Llewelyn had secured a treaty with Philip Augustus around May or June. As Ifor Rowlands points out, John may well have had intelligence about this, which would explain the scale of the Welsh campaign; John feared a political alliance like the Franco-Scottish one that had loomed in 1209.[257] Initially, John had sent only a small force to aid the Marcher lords, but awareness of an accord with France may have made him reconsider with a much larger force. The treaty served Philip especially well as it delayed, and ultimately prevented, English troops attacking his lands.

The army that mustered at Chester in late August was a massive one. John and his royal household had quickly but effectively ordered to the host over 6000 labourers and 2230 skilled carpenters and ditchers: he was planning not only to recapture lost forts but also a massive extension of his castle-building programme. Historians have speculated that he was on the eve of achieving in Wales what his grandson Edward I would later in the century. John was in a ruthless mood. On arriving at a second muster point of Nottingham, the first thing he did was to execute 28 Welsh hostages. Two died following castration, but most were hanged on a gibbet; the youngest was only seven. John then sat down to dinner. His dining was ruined: not by the deaths of the youths he had just ordered, but by the arrival of chilling news. In a foretaste of what was to come, Llewelyn had also been conspiring with the barons. John was informed of a plot either to kill him, or to abandon him, possibly ending in the same fate, to the Welsh. Poised to invade Wales, the whole enormous enterprise unravelled in an instant. John immediately marched north to intimidate the centres of baronial unrest there. Eustace de Vescy and Robert Fitzwalter, the chief conspirators who led the revolt against John over the next few years, fled to Scotland and France and John returned to London. This was the third major expedition John abandoned. Cancelled campaigns were not uncommon in medieval warfare, but three on this scale was telling and a waste of money painfully extracted from his subjects for no tangible ends.

The year 1212 did not get any better for John. The news from Europe was grim, too. Philip Augustus seized English ships in French ports; John reciprocated in England. His allies there were faring badly: Count Raymond of Toulouse was succumbing to the French-led Alibigensian crusade; Emperor Otto was on the defensive and Pope Innocent III had offered a counter-imperial crown to Frederick Hohensatufen, with whom Philip had now made an alliance. Whether known to John or not at this stage, the baronial discontents at home were agreeing terms of homage to Prince Louis, Philips' heir, for when he was crowned as the next King of England. According to the widely spread prophecies of Peter of Wakefield, a mystic wondering about in the north of England, this was going to be sooner rather than later. Unfortunately for Peter, and distinctly lacking foresight, he prophesised neither the gaol sentence in Corfe Castle that John arranged for him nor his being tied to the tail of a horse, dragged to Wareham and hanged. No wonder Wendover observed that in 1212 John 'had almost as many enemies as barons'.[258]

1213

Relationships with the Papacy proved crucial this year. Over Christmas, Stephen Langton and the Bishops of London and Ely had gone to Rome to press for action against their King; Innocent, currently in ascendancy in Europe, was feeling receptive to their calls for intercession and was keen to turn the screws on John, issuing him with an ultimatum for June. Wendover writes that in January the pope wrote to Philip, commissioning him to undertake a crusade against a John deposed by the Papacy and to claim the throne of England for the Capetians. This may have been an exaggeration of the contents of secret letters from Innocent; more recently, academic opinion has moved to discount the deposition because French chroniclers do not discuss it, as they surely would have done had it been the case. However, William the Breton, in his neglected *Philippidos*, does talk at this stage of Philip taking vows to act 'against the schismatics' (*contra schismaticos*) in England.[259] Given the alliances forged the previous year, it is likely that there was at least an understanding of what Philip had planned (and chroniclers were soon certainly to give this impression). And what Philip had planned, with or without the blessing of a fully fledged crusade, was a French invasion of England in 1213.[260]

Philip had been assiduously preparing for this for some time. He was now taking advantage of developments in Artois and Flanders, along the north-east seaboard of France, where he had seized land from Renaud, Count of Boulogne and towns from Ferrand, Count of Flanders, pushing the former into John's camp and leaving the latter wavering. The nature of these disputes is complex but John was quick to offer assistance to disaffected French subjects just as Philip was to English ones. Renaud of Dammartin was a key player in the years 1213–14. He was always ready to change sides and the French King was rightly suspicious of his shockingly poor record of loyalty. Philip, whose patience he had tried, determined that this was going to be the last time. Historians have differed in their judgement of Renaud: 'This remarkable, cultivated, ambitious, and versatile man' says one; 'unstable' another.[261] It is safe to say that he was an opportunist who, like many French nobles, feared Philip's growing regional power. The territory gained by the Capetian gave him more and better opportunities for invasion staging posts, and assembly points were established at Gravelines, Boulogne and Damme. At Soissons on 8 April, Philip held a major council in readiness for the enterprise of England, attended by the great barons of his kingdom. Louis was to take and hold England as an apanage; even if crowned king, he was still to defer matters of land redistribution and homage to his father.

John was now facing his gravest threat since the loss of Normandy and he made careful and thorough preparations for war, as he had the previous year. In a letter to all the sheriffs in England, he called for mercenaries to join him and demanded that all who were obliged to take up arms muster at Dover 'to defend our person and themselves, and the land of England'.[262] This patriotic exhortation was backed up with menace: John made it clear that he wanted to know who came and who did not; those who failed to make an appearance were to be branded as cowards and condemned to slavery. A huge army ('sixty thousand', of course) gathered on the coast. John also ensured that the navy was at full strength and readiness; stronger than the French in this area, he planned to intercept the French in the Channel and 'and drown them in the sea before they could even set foot on land'.[263] His navy sharpened its fighting skills with raids on Dieppe, Fécamp and on the Seine. John's confidence in the navy was in sharp contrast to his confidence in his barons: another reason why John placed so much emphasis on maritime defence was that there was less likelihood of being deserted on the field of battle, a real fear of his.

It was at this critical juncture that John played what most historians agree was his masterstroke: he submitted to the pope. On the 13 May he met the papal legate Pandulf, accepted Langton as Archbishop of Canterbury, agreed compensation payments to Rome, and agreed to render England as a papal fief. England was now under the special protection of the pope. The Barnwell annalist captured both the logic and the shame of this action: 'The King provided wisely for himself and his people by this measure, although to many it seemed ignominious and a monstrous yoke of servitude.' He goes on to say that there was no swifter or more effective way of avoiding the looming threat, for now, as we have seen above, 'there was no prince in the Roman world who would dare attack him or invade his lands.'[264]

But Philip Augustus was just such a Prince. He was not so easily deterred from a major campaign as John, even after Pandulf warned him in the third week of May that to persist with the invasion would incur an excommunication. Philip was livid with the legate at this turn of events, railing at the injustice of it all after he had spent 'sixty thousand pounds' on fitting out the expedition in the name of the pope. To rub salt in his wounds, John had dramatically upstaged Philip's own reconciliation with the Papacy. In an overlooked episode, at Soissons in April Philip was reconciled with Ingeborg, thereby healing a significant, long-standing rift with the Church and garnering even greater blessings for his enterprise. Surely this would have played a major factor in influencing John to make his own, even greater, reconciliation with Rome the following month? The diplomacy of this period was intense indeed.

Philip persisted with his great undertaking nevertheless. Warren has reflected on why Philip should press on with the invasion at all. One factor may have been that his awareness of baronial feeling against John augured well, as it had before the fall of Normandy; and another that it was a way of preventing John landing his army in Poitou. But Warren believes that the whole operation was 'hazardous', extremely 'optimistic', and that these wasted resources would have been better deployed in annexing Aquitaine. He sums up with: 'One can only conclude that Philip's sense of mission against the house of Anjou had reached the proportion of megalomania, and that he would not be satisfied with anything less than its complete destruction.'[265] Philip was far too prudent and meticulous a King for this assessment. Aquitaine, with its loyalties and economic connections to England and distance from Paris was a challenge of a different order, as Philip knew and history was to prove. We have not long seen how he took his time to consolidate his conquest of Normandy, and settled for a truce at Thouars in 1206. Ambitious? Undoubtedly. Megalomaniac? Unlikely. Preventing John's expedition to Poitou points to the real reasons. The opportunity to take the war to England was probably paramount in his thinking, for the same reasons we have discussed for Richard fighting his wars in France. Philip would be sparing his own subjects while giving the message in the starkest of terms to John's that the English King was failing in his primary obligation to protect them. Also important were the unknown consequences of kicking down John's front door. If his whole house started shaking then the barons could bolt outside and run towards Philip. This proved to be the case for Louis in 1216.[266]

All that Philip needed to proceed with the invasion was the active support of Ferrand of Flanders, not least to secure the French positions along and behind the Flemish coast. Philip, however, was not prepared to return the Count's towns and so Ferrand, son of King Sancho I of Portugal, declared on 24 May at Ypres that he was not prepared to join with the Capetians. The implications of this were clear: Ferrand would gravitate fully into the Angevin orbit and Philip would have to count him as a foe. Philip turned his war machine on Flanders.

What followed was an intense outburst of brutal and sharp warfare. The French King wanted Bruges and Ypres, preferably – always preferably – by negotiation if possible. Ghent required a siege. He advanced his invasion force into Flanders, 'destroying everywhere in his path by fire, and putting the inhabitants to the sword'.[267] He led the bulk of his forces – up to 240 knights and 10,000 infantry – to Ghent leaving behind a contingent to protect his fleet that had followed up from Gravelines to Damme. The fleet was too large (William the Breton gives a figure of 1700 ships) to all beach or dock here, so the rest anchored at the mouth of the River Swin. Ferrand quickly entered into a formal alliance with John who did not delay in sending help and in great force – perhaps as many as 700 knights augmented by mercenaries – under the command of Renaud de Dammartin, Hugh de Boves and William Longsword, the Earl of Salisbury. In a remarkably short time, on Thursday 28 May these arrived not far from Damme at Muiden. The main French force was still at the siege of Ghent. Those left with the fleet, including the mercenary captain Cadoc, were too preoccupied with the ransacking of Damme and the ravaging of the surrounding area to notice the threat; in so doing, they had left the fleet largely without defence. The allies arrived at Swin on Saturday 30 May to the astonishing spectacle of this huge but vulnerable target. Salisbury seized the moment and immediately launched a surprise attack on the fleet. It was a violent and spectacular success. John's men cut the cables of 300 ships laden with corn, wine, meat, flour, wine and arms and other stores; they stripped another 100 of their supplies before burning them. The biographer of William Marshal paints a vivid picture of 'ships at sea burning and belching forth smoke, as if the very sea were on fire'. The booty was immense; the effect on Philip's invasion was terminal.

On the Sunday, Ferrand joined up with the allies who then hoped to capitalise further on their victory by turning on Damme itself. Philip, who knew the power of forced marches, responded to the news with accustomed celerity. The *Philippidos* has the French King declaring; 'There is no point in stopping to hold counsel ... The only thing to do now is the work of our arms.' For the sake of speed, he dispatched Duke Peter of Brittany at the head of squadrons of light cavalry to relieve Damme, with other troops under the King following as quickly as possible. The first troops arrived on Monday. This time it was the allies' turn to be surprised. The Duke, Prince Louis and William des Barres went for them at speed. The latter took to flight and to their ships. The tide was out, leaving a large number of ships still settled on the banks, so hundreds of John's men could not escape by sea. Some clambered into small boats but many drowned in their haste. There was much slaughter; William the Breton puts allied fatalities at 2000, an inflated figure probably, but still an indication of the scale of the carnage. The French took numerous prisoners, Count Renaud narrowly escaping being one of them. The counter-attack was small consolation for Philip. Seeing the extensive losses incurred by his fleet – Wendover talks of 'irreparable damage' – he knew the invasion was over. He torched what remained; not 'out of his mind with rage' and frustration as William Marshall's biographer claims, but to prevent their being taken by the enemy. The presence of a strong English fleet offshore would have kept the rest of the French trapped at Damme anyway.

Philip once again sent out his incendiaries into Flanders and took Ghent. He eventually withdrew having achieved few conclusive results other than the unintended one of strengthening support for Ferrand against him. Even Damme was lost as the war continued intermittently into the spring of 1214. In England, John was overjoyed at this remarkable victory. Not only had the Damme operation brought spoils and glory, it had destroyed any invasion attempt for a considerable time; Philip's naval forces had still not recovered by the following summer. John wished to profit from the momentum he was gaining and to deploy his buoyant forces, morale high, in a major Poitevin campaign in July. This involved yet another muster. The response was overwhelming indifference. Knights grouped together to approach the King to tell him that their constant readiness since spring, as decreed by John, meant that their financial means had been exhausted; they were prepared to go with John if he met their expenses, but John would have none of this. Barons from the north, that centre of anti-John sentiment, refused point blank to accompany the king, making the case that their feudal obligations did not extend to service overseas. As Ralph of Coggeshall also points out, they claimed 'that they were already too worn out and impoverished by expeditions in England'.[268] John's temporary mastery of the British Isles had come at a high price. There had been at least five military musters over the previous year – four in 1213 alone – and the barons had had enough. In addition to these considerations, it is worth remembering that a campaign of national defence against a foreign invader who brought war into one's own territory and threatened to appropriate land was always likely to elicit a more positive response than one for conquest abroad. In successfully denying the King for the first time they had laid down a significant marker.[269] Once again John flew into one of his incandescent rages, and once again he took to the sea, this time to Jersey, in the forlorn hope that he would be followed. He was not.

John still headed a considerable force of mercenaries and continental troops. With these he went North again to repeat his earlier exercise of intimidation and to bring the Northerners to heel. Now another great victory – his diplomatic adeptness with the Papacy in May – exacted a small but telling toll: at the end of September Archbishop Stephen Langton chased after the King and at Northampton warned him that his actions contravened oaths and agreements made at the time of his submission to Rome. Langton threatened John's army with excommunication and the King gave way. On 3 October at St Paul's in London, John formally rendered, through the papal representatives Pandulf and Cardinal Nicholas of Tusculum, his kingdom of England to the Papacy. For the rest of the year the terms for the final settlement were agreed. These were not as onerous as they may seem. As Christopher Harper-Bill has concluded, John 'lost remarkably little of the additional revenues he had accrued to the royal coffers during the Interdict, nor ... of his effective ecclesiastical patronage. The political advantage, moreover, which stemmed from his submission to the Papacy was considerable, both before and after his unexpected death.'[270]

John continued to feed his finances into war preparations, pay-rolling his mercenaries and his continental allies, chiefly Emperor Otto of Brunswick, Count Renaud of Boulogne and Count Ferrand of Flanders. In the south, the picture was not positive. His ally King Pedro of Aragon had been killed at the Battle of Muret in September 1213, and a defeated Count Raymond of Toulouse came to England at the end of the year to receive a substantial payment. But it was affairs on the border of north-east France that really mattered. Here John's abundant war subsidies kept the French engaged in costly, wearing warfare and helped to bring over the leading princes of the region, such as the Count of Holland and the Dukes of Brabant and Limburg, to England and her allies. As one historian has noted, 'Immense sums were poured out by the English treasury in support of these princes, and large numbers of Flemish knights were retained in the king's service by annual pensions charged on the exchequer.'[271] John's finances had help to buy and finance an impressive coalition. Whatever the relative wealth of Angevins and Capetians, as discussed earlier in the chapter, neither side had their military ability seriously curtailed by financial constraints.

John set a date at the beginning of February for the next planned expedition to Poitou. In further readiness, he made a truce with the Welsh and enlisted the reformed church hierarchy to smooth out issues of contention in his realm. Ferrand paid homage to John in Canterbury in January 1214 where, no doubt, war plans were made. Geoffrey Fitzpeter's fifteen years as justiciar ended with his death in October; John replaced him with Peter des Roches, the sole loyal representative of the episcopacy in England in 1210, in January. It would seem that in the middle of November John had held a war meeting in Oxford. His distrust of his barons, always strong and worsened by their defiance in the summer, was such that he ordered them to come unarmed. The domestic political situation had clearly not improved; nonetheless, despite Ralph of Coggeshall's observation that 'few earls, but an infinite multitude of knights of lesser fortune' sailed with John, Turner has noted that 'a good number of his nobility actually accompanied the King to Poitou.'[272] However, this was not a sign of commitment and loyalty, Turner adding that these included 'some who would join in the rebellion against him by the next spring'.[273] John left Portsmouth on 1 February accompanied by his wife and treasure. Most of his faith was placed not in his barons, whose presence with him was as much political as military, preventing them from conspiring at home (as many of those remaining did), but in his mercenaries, the Poitevins, and his powerful allies. This was the moment John had been waiting for since 1206. Everything was now poised for a monumental and decisive clash. The gathering war clouds were about to unleash an almighty storm that broke over Bouvines, one of the single most critical battles of the entire Middle Ages.

4

The Battle of Bouvines, 1214

John landed at La Rochelle on 16 February 1214. There had already been two failed attempts at a full-scale Poitevin expedition, but this time it had at last come to fruition. Now was John's opportunity to make good the crushing losses of 1204 and to re-establish the Angevin Empire. Behind him and in his absence he had left the kingdom in the capable hands of Peter des Roches, whom he had appointed justiciar on the eve of his departure, leaving his barons grumbling at having a foreigner set over them; before him lay the alliance he had so carefully nurtured, designed to win back his lands by delivering a crushing blow to King Philip of France and the whole Capetian dynasty. The strategy was simple and sound. John's army would apply pressure in the Poitou region, creating a diversion for the French forces in the west. Meanwhile, the main body of the coalition's forces would move in to France from the north-east. Philip would therefore be threatened by great danger on two fronts. The scene was set for one of the most decisive battles of not only the entire Middle Ages, but of Western European history as a whole.[274]

La Roche-au-Moine

John's campaign had an auspicious beginning. Using La Rochelle as his one secure base (kept loyal to England by its trading interests), John sought to strengthen his position by control of the surrounding regions before attempting to engage with Philip. He met with immediate success. By 8 March, 26 castles and strongholds were restored to him. One siege gives a measure of his rapid advance: the Castle of Milécu, just a few miles south-east of La Rochelle, had been fortified against the Angevin King by Porteclin de Mausé; John besieged it on Sunday 2 March and had taken it by Tuesday. At Limoges, Viscount Gui, like so many of the barons of Aquitaine, offered homage to John: 'I could not resist him or await your help,' he later wrote to Philip Augustus; 'for the future you may not rely on me.'[275] John

marched deep into Gascony and then swung north. His progress was unhindered
by the Lusignans with whom he had now come to an accommodation (some
fifteen years too late, it could be argued). However, one of the Lusignan brothers,
Geoffrey, remained alienated, and John, maintaining his momentum, launched
a short, sharp military strike against him, lasting five days in mid-May. John was
buoyed by his victories and, keen to convey his potency abroad to domestic mal-
contents in England, he was quick to write home with his good news, which
Wendover records:

> We ... crossed with our army to Mervant, a castle belonging to Geoffrey de
> Lusignan; and although we might not believe that it could be taken by assault,
> we, on the day after, which was the eve of Whitsun [17 May], took it by force
> after one attack, which lasted from early in the morning until one o'clock.
> On Whitsunday, we laid siege to another of Geoffrey's castles, called Vouvant,
> in which was Geoffrey himself and his two sons; and when our petraries had
> assailed it continuously for three days so that a chance for taking it was immi-
> nent, the Count of La Marche came to us and caused Geoffrey to throw himself
> at our mercy with his two sons, his castle and all that was in it.

There was still more success for John. At the same time as this operation, the
unfortunate Geoffrey had another of his castles besieged by Prince Louis of France
at Moncontour further to the east. John led his forces there and Louis withdrew.
John consolidated his agreement with La Marche and trumpeted his victories in
his letter home: 'Now, by the grace of God, we have been given an opportunity to
carry our attack against our chief enemy, the King of France, beyond the Poitou.
And we inform you of this so that you may rejoice in our success.'[276]

With his position south of the Loire now firmly reinforced, John turned his
attention northwards. He made a feint towards the French army in the east and
then headed northwest towards Angers, the capital of his ancestors. Just as he
appeared set to encircle it after yet more gains, he made a forced march west
and took Nantes in mid-June. An important seaport, Nantes could prove most
useful to John in his future plans to retake Normandy from the south. Its value
was emphasised by its garrison under the command of Robert of Dreux, cousin
of King Philip and brother of Peter, Count of Brittany. In what both William the
Breton and the Anonymous of Béthune consider a reckless move, Robert led
his soldiers and some armed citizens to a bridge that lay just outside and which
John's army needed to cross. From here, he began taunting the enemy. He was
soon to regret his rashness as in the ensuing combat he and between fourteen and
twenty knights were taken prisoner.[277] The effects of this Angevin success were
soon felt downriver at Angers, the city capitulating swiftly to John on 17 June.
No doubt John's victorious progress – and that vital force of momentum – had
influenced the city's prompt surrender, but William des Roches, King Philip's

Seneschal of Anjou, had already made the decision not to defend the city. The ruined walls of Angers had not been repaired following John's previous campaign. Instead, des Roches focused his efforts on the city's satellite castles, which had been reinforced. This was to prove a wise move. Taking Angers had been a great symbolic and propaganda victory for John, but, like before, a hollow one: it was in his hands for just a few weeks, it could not be held by him in hindsight, as William des Roches had known with foresight.

One of Angers' satellite castles was La Roche-au-Moine (also written as La Roche-aux-Moines). This had been constructed and recently munitioned by des Roches to guard the Nantes-Angers road from attack by the Angevin garrison of nearby Rochefort. John now directed his whole force against the new castle, a further indication of his plans to use Nantes as a naval base for the reconquest of Normandy. He also needed La Roche-au-Moine for his advance on Le Mans and then, perhaps, Paris. And if things went badly for him, the castle would cover his retreat back to the coast. A concentrated barrage began on 19 June as John's artillery attempted to batter down the castle's tower and walls.

The garrison's vigorous defence was to prove fateful. The siege has received scant attention, even from French historians, despite its consequences. The silence of English historians is perhaps explained by the paucity of contemporary sources: Roger of Wendover provides the only English perspective. The Capetian version is once again related by the quill of William the Breton, never slow in seizing upon and trumpeting a Capetian victory.[278] For all our knowledge of political and diplomatic history, La Roche-au-Moine shows us the importance of military outcomes in explaining so much of history; for if La Roche-au-Moine had fallen to John as quickly as had the other strongholds in the campaign thus far, subsequent events may well have turned out drastically different: the whole allied expedition of 1214 may have turned on this minor siege.

John's substantial army was augmented by the Rochefort garrison, under the command of Paies de Rochefort, a brigand knight in the best tradition of the robber baron. The French defenders of La Roche-au-Moine were soon under attack, but fought valiantly against John's onslaught. As was common with those hard-pressed by investiture, the defenders cannibalised their surroundings, dismantling whatever they could find, including beams and wooden supports from houses, to hurl on their attackers. William the Breton then offers another of his revealing, intimate observations of warfare. A crossbowman by the name of Enguerrand, a huge brute of a man well-deserving of his appellation 'Monastery-breaker' (perhaps suggesting he was one of Rochefort's men), advanced up to the castle ditch under the protection of a large mantlet shield carried by a youngster. Each day from behind this shield Enguerrand shot bolts at the garrison with impunity, causing great consternation. A French crossbowmen by the name of Pons came up with an idea to meet this threat. He attached one end of a long, thin piece of rope to a bolt and the other to a fixed point next to him. He shot the crossbow bolt directly into the mantlet where it embedded itself. He pulled the rope towards him and dragged both it and the boy into the moat. Enguerrand, left defenceless and exposed, was immediately struck down by a fatal hail of arrows as he attempted to withdraw. John was enraged by this setback and by Pons' demonstration of delight at the success of his ruse. According to William the Breton, Pons called out: 'Get away from here, King, and leave us in peace, for fear that you will meet a similar death.'[279] Apparently John did withdraw a little to direct the assault from a safer distance; he (and no doubt Pons, too) would have remembered the manner of his brother's death from a crossbow bolt at Châlus Chabrol in 1199. John then erected gallows (a typical siege practice of his) to intimidate the garrison: if they did not yield immediately he would grant them no quarter. But the garrison fought on. However, after a fortnight's intense combat had taken its toll, with the garrison exhausted and deprived of sleep, the defenders were brought to the point of surrender. But help was on its way.

At the end of April, Philip Augustus and his host had been at Châteroux on the borders of Berry and Poitou. Faced by enemy advances on two fronts – John from the south-west, the coalition allies under Otto from the north-east – he split his forces: he led his army to meet the allies, while his son, Prince Louis, went to Chinon to meet the threat of John. With Louis went the experienced general Henri Clément, the marshal of France. Philip knew this division of forces was risky but he had little choice other than to react exactly as the coalition wanted him to. If he concentrated entirely on the danger emanating from the Low Countries, John would have a relatively free rein in regaining his lost southern territories; but if Philip focused on John, he left the way open from Flanders to Normandy and Paris.

The French king, intending to reinforce his army by feudal and municipal levies on his way northwards, left Louis with a substantial force: William the Breton's figures put this at 800 knights, 2000 men-at-arms and 7000 infantry, to which were later added the 4000 men under William des Roches and Aimery de Craon, the veteran warrior and respected commander. This may be an inflated figure, but essentially Philip was mobilising his kingdom in a war of dynastic – even national – survival.

Louis was at Chinon when he heard of the dangerous predicament of the garrison at La Roche-au-Moine. Hesitant to act precipitously as he was outnumbered and acutely aware of the combined peril to the Capetian monarchy, he sent to his father for instructions. The French crown was extremely fortunate that the garrison at La Roche-au-Moine held out long enough for a reply to reach Louis. When it came it was decisive: raise the siege. (The Anonymous of Béthune attributes the decision to Louis heeding the advice of Clément.) The order was informed by political and military awareness. If the English advance was not checked increasing numbers of barons from the Loire would defect to the Angevin cause in a reverse of the tide that flowed to the Capetians during the conquest of Normandy; Philip was acutely aware of the power of momentum. And for once during the campaign John was pinned down. Since landing at La Rochelle his movements had been intentionally erratic to keep Philip guessing while simultaneously assessing the extent of Capetian strength since his return to Poitou. After Philip's move towards the north-east, John had continued to confuse Louis with his movements by never staying at one place for any length of time. Now that had changed. John had set himself squarely before La Roche-au-Moine, so much so that from here he summoned not only fresh horses, but also his wife, children and treasure. Louis had a firm target and clear instructions for his military objective. He prepared his troops and advanced on John.

At this time Louis was 26; he had acquitted himself well in the Flanders campaign of the previous year but was now facing the greatest threat that he and his father had ever known. He was aware of the importance of avoiding any rash mistakes at this crucial juncture. Louis was quite unlike his father in most respects. Small and pale, in contrast to his father's burly countenance, he was nevertheless imbued with the chivalric spirit of a true knight that was so lacking in his father. Coupled with his energy in time of war he earned for himself the soubriquet of 'The Lion' from his later biographer, Nicholas de Bray. He was a true warrior who loved fighting and who risked his life in its pursuit. But he was not recklessly impulsive; rather, he was a highly effective and competent commander who took time for the necessary logistical preparations before starting military operations. Between 1211 and 1226 he spent over four complete years in the field; by his death he had participated in seven major campaigns, including crusades in southern France.

All this was befitting an alleged descendant of Charlemagne, as eagerly presented by Capetian propagandists. To the fore of these was Gilles de Paris, who wrote his epic poem *Karolinus* for Louis to assist him in emulating his great ancestor. Such a gift would not have been lost on the learned and cultured Prince who had also received Rigord's *Deeds of Philip Augustus* and William the Breton's own epic poem, the *Philippidos*. Louis is an altogether more attractive, vibrant figure than his clever, scheming, calculating father, gaining an almost saintly reputation for himself by fathering a saint, the great monarch St Louis IX (born just two months before these events at La Roche-au-Moine). Louis' religious influence on his more famous son should not be underestimated. Louis has sadly been much neglected by historians despite his significant impact on the medieval world. This is largely due to the brevity of his own reign (1223–6) and, to a greater degree, his being overshadowed by his remarkable family: his father, Philip; his son, St Louis; and his formidable wife, Blanche of Castile.[280]

Louis' army was poised to descend upon John's siege camp on 2 July. Through his scouts John learned of Louis' approach and of the French inferiority of numbers. John did no seem to need much bidding by his spies: he arranged his army in battle order ready to meet the oncoming French. At the vanguard of the

French forces was the marshal, Henri Clément, a man 'small in stature but great in heart'.[281] With the French were William des Roches and Aimery de Craon, the only two major barons present (there were eleven with Philip). A large French force under the heir to the throne was about to engage with a larger English force under the King of England. The scene was set for an epic and potentially decisive encounter between the Angevin and Capetian dynasties.

But it never happened. John's Poitevin's barons, under Aimery de Thouars and including the Counts of la Marche and Eu, refused to fight. They declared themselves unprepared for pitched battle. This refusal may have been on military grounds – battle avoidance was a common stratagem in medieval warfare – but given the superiority of English numbers (a fact agreed by both English and French sources) this is unlikely. More probably the real reason – or excuse – was, as William the Breton suggests, the Poitevins' reluctance to fight against the immediate forces of their suzerain. Such action was not without precedent: the Poitevins had also baulked at fighting Philip in 1206; and in 1159, John's father, Henry II, declined to come to blows with Philip's father, Louis VII, at Toulouse for the same reason. Wendover's accusation of treachery may be too judgemental, although Aimery de Thouars had a reputation as an habitual turncoat and certainly had a chequered career: this Seneschal of Anjou and custodian of Chinon had fought with John before 1202; with Arthur of Brittany after 1202; Philip Augustus made him Seneschal of Poitou after taking it in August 1204; in 1205 the Thouars family returned to John's side and in 1208 his son was captured by Philip. In 1214, concerns for the best interests of his family and castle are likely to have dominated his reasoning; the doubt over events in the north-eastern sector may also have played a part.

The barons withdrew leaving John exposed to uncertainty in his ranks; where some led, others could follow. He was never an assured and confident commander who could rely wholeheartedly on his soldiers' loyalty, and he suffered for it. His string of military victories came to an end at La Roche-au-Moine. Before the advancing French, he fled back to La Rochelle where his campaign had started with such promise four months earlier. This retreat was nothing if not determined and swift, covering 115 km in two anxious days. It is possible that John thought Philip's whole army had returned to the region. La Roche-au-Moine was a rout without a battle, its pathetic anti-climax summing up John's sudden and complete reversal of fortune. Wendover claims that when Louis heard of John raising camp he actually feared that John 'would attack him, and fled in the opposite direction from King John's; and thus each army ignominiously taking to flight, turned their backs on one another'.[282] If this did happen, the French withdrawal was only momentary as their scouts would have passed on news of John's own retreat. Before long the valiant garrison of La Roche-au-Moine were pillaging the deserted English siege camp, for in its haste the Angevin army had left all behind it: siege engines, tents, clothes, money and valuables. As the

French came onwards many of the English who had not been so quick to flee were harried, many drowning as they attempted to cross the Loire in overladen barges; stragglers were cut down by the French vanguard. The skirmish was a bloody one. Among those slain in the pursuit were John's chaplain (William the Breton's opposite number) and Paies de Rochefort, mortally wounded in two places. Henri Clément died a few days later, probably from wounds sustained in the encounter, possibly exacerbated by fever. The pendulum had swung in Louis' direction and he quickly capitalised on his victory by undoing much of John's work during his Poitevin campaign. He rapidly retook many of the castles recently lost to John, razing to the ground those of Montcontour and Beaufort; garrisons were placed in all the strategic strongpoints; he ravaged the lands of Aimery de Thouars and many of the region's towns; and, significantly and sym-bolically, he regained control of Angers, throwing down the defensive wall hastily erected there by John. Any person found from John's side was clapped in irons. Anjou was back under Capetian dominance once again. The only clouds over the spectacular success were the marshal's death and the uncertainty over his father's fate in Flanders where the German-Flemish coalition forces were advancing.

Philip Augustus' cause had been greatly served by his son's achievement. The bold but necessary decision the King had taken at Châteroux to split his army into two had been vindicated by events in Anjou. The defence of La Roche-au-Moine had brought the French the time needed to launch a direct attack against a previously mobile English army and its Poitevin allies. The result was, at one blow, the end of John's advances in Poitou and the firm securing of one of the two fronts against France. However, back at La Rochelle, John had not given up Poitou yet. His army had been put to flight, with him leading the way, but it had not been destroyed. He still intended to co-ordinate his strategy with his allies in the north-east, where they held the initiative, and in the second week of July he wrote back to England calling for reinforcements to pursue his military opera-tions. His dissembling letter unwittingly reveals the anxiety that had crept into his thoughts: 'Everything is, by God's grace, happy and prosperous with us ... We earnestly entreat those who have not crossed with us to come to us immediately ... Know that if any of you have incurred our displeasure, the best way to make amends is by answering this summons.'[283]

Any defeat was serious and potentially disastrous for a military commander, but only subsequent events could determine whether this would be the case. Poole calls the encounter at La Roche-au-Moine a 'disaster' for John, as indeed it proved to be; Sivèry rightly believes that John's defeat here was a major factor leading to the French invasion two years later.[284] Yet had the outcome at Bouvines been reversed by a coalition victory, John's defeat would have been of relatively little consequence; for the French this scenario would have been their equivalent of Harold's great victory at Stamford Bridge in 1066 and the swift negation and irrelevance of this a few weeks later at Hastings.

What would an Angevin victory at La Roche have meant, if anything? The pressure on Philip Augustus in north-east France would have intensified even more, and his defensive inversion of a Schlieffen-like plan would have been widely perceived as a failure. But it is doubtful that John would have pressed for Paris, still some distance off with the inevitable dangers of over-extended supply routes and exposed vulnerability deep in enemy territory, and with the bulk of Louis' army still in the field. Only an overwhelming Agincourt-style victory would have made this a feasible option. Ralph Turner goes further, opining convincingly that John did not even have plans for an assault on Normandy, seeking instead 'a decisive victory elsewhere in France that would convince the Norman nobility of Capetian weakness, and persuade them to return to Angevin allegiance'.[285] This accords with my emphasis on the importance of political momentum in medieval warfare. However, Daniel Power's analysis of John's strained relations with the Norman aristocracy would seem to make this hope optimistic;[286] but John was probably hopeful that pragmatic self-interest and the new political reality would win them over.

And what of John's fickle Poitevin allies? Their policy of a weak Capetian neighbour and a distant Angevin overlord could now be improved upon: a serious blow by the coalition against Philip would offer the enticing prospect of an impotent Capetian overlord on the one hand, and a weakened John on the other. Aware of the coalition's intentions, did the Poitevins see practical political autonomy beckon?

Why, then, did John choose to fight (assuming he did)? Battle avoidance was common operational practice in the Middle Ages. It is likely that John did not wish to lose the momentum he had built up with all its impressive results. A victory would have added tremendous impetus to the powerful – and potentially almost irresistible – momentum he already had in progress. His earlier victories and superior numbers would have boosted his confidence, and John had a tendency to oscillate sharply between over-confidence and pessimism about the situation. And with the powerful Poitevins momentarily gathered on his side, it is understandable that he should wish to make use of them. We have seen how his early military victories affected the political environment, persuading leading figures such as the Count of Nevers to line up with him. This tide of allegiance could prove even more effective than military victory in the field and could certainly be shaped by it. John would surely have learned this the hard way from the loss of Normandy, especially after the fall of Château Gaillard (and he would be reminded of it again in 1216). Perhaps he hoped that taking La Roche would have a similar effect, albeit on a smaller scale. For the same reason, Philip wanted Louis to take decisive action at La Roche: as important as raising the siege was the opportunity to break John's momentum of success. Philip simply could not afford to allow John's continued progress across the region to become a victorious promenade; the political consequences may have been too damaging, not

least in how it could affect his efforts to raise armed support to counter the imperial threat in the north-east.

Such factors would have determined strategy. The French victory did not
release a great deal of men from this sector to the north-eastern one. Louis' army
of 800 knights and thousands of footsoldiers was not strong enough to finish
off John, and did little more than ravage the lands of the Viscount of Thouars,
having crucially retaken lost castles; John had to be contained in La Rochelle and
Capetian garrisons were placed in all the newly taken strongholds of the territory
regained. But Louis had secured this front and neutralised the King of England.
The Angevin momentum had been broken. This was the important significance
of La Roche. But for Bouvines, the overlooked encounter at La Roche-au-
Moine would be recognised as a major French victory. Some chroniclers certainly
deemed it such, with Matthew Paris going so far as to claim, rather dubiously, that
La Roche was celebrated as the major Capetian success of 1214.[287] A sober verdict
on Louis' victory at La Roche is provided by the Anonymous of Béthune, who
wrote: 'Know that it was a good thing of which his father was very well aware.'[288]

Despite his letters home and over-optimistic plans, John's active role in the
coalition had been reduced to a relatively passive one of tying down much of
Louis' army in this region of France when it was sorely needed elsewhere. The
fate of John's designs in France and that of the Capetian monarchy was about to
be decided in the north-east and without his direct involvement.

The Battle of Bouvines

From Châteroux, Philip had hurried north to meet the even greater threat
facing Normandy and Paris. The long years of careful coalition building by John
(structured on the relations formed by his brother Richard) now culminated in
an impressively powerful league united against France.[289] This league had manifested itself as a formidable host in the Lowlands, poised to press down into
France. John's brother, William Longsword, Earl of Salisbury, was, tenuously, the
commander-in-chief of this grand army, but his command was neither readily
accepted nor undisputed among the other elite generals. Otto IV, Holy Roman
Emperor, was the prominent figure, but his force was a relatively small one and
Salisbury's prominence reflected the input of the coalition's chief paymaster:
John. Joining them were the contingents of Count Ferrand of Flanders, Count
Renaud de Dammartin of Boulogne, Count William of Holland and the Flemish
troops under Hugh de Boves, the last having been recalled from John's service in
England for this great campaign. The allies also added to their ranks the Dukes
of Limburg and Brabant, Count Conrad of Dortmund and many other important barons and the troops they brought with them. They awaited the late arrival
of John's nephew, Otto of Brunswick, who was eager to crush Philip, not least

because the Capetian supported Frederick Hohenstaufen, Otto's rival claimant to the imperial throne. The delay of Otto and his German princes left the coalition host ravaging and pillaging Ponthieu, and organising attacks on the far north-eastern border. Philip, meanwhile, was granted precious time to muster the feudal host against the impending danger: barons, knights, men-at-arms and communal troops were quickly gathered and reinforced by some of Louis' knights now spared from Anjou. This great mobilisation was reminiscent of the call to arms in 1124 sent out by Philip's grandfather, King Louis VI the Fat, when the French kingdom was imperilled by another threatened invasion from the empire, at that time under Henry V. The lack of uncoordinated troop movements amongst the present coalition meant Philip could organise his defensive force, albeit hastily.

By 23 July both sides had mustered their hosts: the coalition at Valenciennes, the French at Péronne. Philip led his army, totalling perhaps 1400 knights and 6000 infantry, through Cambrai and Douai to Flanders. Pillaging supplies for his army and burning what he could not use from his enemies' lands, his intention was also to cut the allies' lines of communication to the coast and also to prevent Otto's force from joining with Salisbury's. This move may have offered the possibility of the French launching a surprise attack on Otto's rear, from the side he least expected, enabling the French to deal first with a much smaller force before engaging the main body of enemy troops: with John contained in Anjou and Otto's army repulsed, Philip could hope either for victory against Salisbury or, more probably, Salisbury abandoning his campaign altogether, having already lost two of its three main elements. Imperial scouts were active, however, and informed Otto of French movements when he was at Valenciennes (from where he was pondering his advance on Paris), with Philip now behind him at Tournai by 26 July. Tournai was one of the two normal operational headquarters for French campaigns in Flanders (the other being Lille). It had been taken by the Flemish a year earlier, but was now recaptured by a French force working in advance of the main column. Otto countered by a move to a strong position at Mortagne, just seven miles to the south of the French position, which left Philip feeling that he had overreached himself as was now exposed to both Salisbury's and Otto's armies, the exact situation he had hoped to avoid. Despite both sides having good local geographical knowledge, many of the protagonists having estates in the region and local urban militias predominating in the armies, the two forces managed to pass each other unknowingly.

It is likely, as John France has suggested, that Philip was playing for time in the hope that the disagreements among the coalition leadership would lead to its collapse. Philip would also have anticipated the negative impact on the coalition from the defeat of John's forces. William the Breton, characteristically but unconvincingly, depicts Philip as impatient to attack his enemy, only to be restrained by his military advisers (whom Philip almost invariably heeded).[290] Instead the French made a rapid retreat along the Roman road to Lille early on 27 July. This suggests that it was never Philip's plan to directly engage the enemy, but only to prevent them from joining forces; once he had failed in this, he withdrew his army. Many historians believe that Philip was actively seeking a decisive battle with the allies, but the Anonymous of Béthune, the author of the *History of William the Marshal*, and the Marchiennes accounts concur in that Philip was endeavouring to avoid contact with the enemy; Roger of Wendover's narrative clearly indicates that the French had taken up a defensive rather than an aggressive position on the battlefield. Even more than most military commanders, the unheroic Philip appreciated the tactic of battle avoidance. However, despite William the Breton's constant lapses into unobjective panegyrism, his account remains the best and fullest description of the battle, as he was eyewitness to the events that were to take place that fateful day.[291]

Sunday 27 July was a scorching summer's day. Philip had sensibly stopped at the bridge of Bouvines, on the Tournai-Lille road. Here he had shade and, more importantly, his men and horses had a plentiful supply of water from the Marque flowing beneath the bridge. The refreshment was all the more welcome after the dusty rigours of almost constant marching in the summer heat. Philip carefully arranged a fortified camp. Meanwhile the coalition forces were also on the move to keep within striking distance of the French while still determining what course of action they should take and when. Philip's scouts had informed him that the allied forces had struck camp, but he believed they were making for Tournai and not for him. The leadership of both sides was anxious about the gravity of what was at stake on such a momentous occasion. The tension was possibly less strained on the allies' side. They were confident as they held their council of war, dividing up the regions of France between them as their spoils of imminent victory. Otto – who had by now joined up with the main force ahead of most of his troops – and Count Renaud of Boulogne were reluctant to initiate battle on a Sunday, especially as all their troops were not yet drawn up. A plan was discussed to allow the French to retreat in the hope that their morale would be sapped and the army would be further weakened by desertions, but this was rejected despite its merits. They were persuaded against hesitation by John's leading mercenary, Hugh de Boves, who disparaged them for wavering and cast aspersions on their courage if they failed to attack Philip immediately. In a phrase employed by the energetic royal generals Henry II and Richard the Lionheart, Hugh warned them, 'Delays are always dangerous when things are ready'; and added, for good measure, a sting in the tail with, 'It is easier to talk than act.'[292] They prepared for battle.

Hugh probably had three motivations for so forcefully exhorting the allies to adopt his strategy. First, in one sense, things *were* ready: Hugh wished to catch the French army, stretched out along three miles of the road, divided as it crossed the bridge (the potential efficacy of such a move can be evaluated by the crushing defeat suffered by the English against the Scots at Stirling Bridge in 1297). Secondly, and as he reminded his allies, they were beholden to King John for his generous payments in subsidising the campaign and therefore were honour-bound to deliver battle for John's sake. The English King's reverses in Anjou made a victory in the north even more imperative; if the cat-and-mouse movements of shadowing enemy troops continued there was a danger that the coalition might dissolve before it had played its full part. Finally, Hugh de Boves was a mercenary captain who had prospered under his paymaster John; of all the allies he had the least to lose and the most to gain. Wendover calls him 'a brave soldier but a cruel man … he spared neither women nor young children'.[293] The thought of fighting on a Sunday did not weigh heavily on his shoulders. The chroniclers make much of the blasphemy of fighting on the Lord's day, especially William the Breton who never missed an opportunity to blacken the foe's evil reputation, but too much of this has been made by both contemporaries and modern historians. Fighting on Sundays or holy days was far from uncommon: in 1264, Simon de Montfort spent Easter, the holiest event of the Christian calendar, storming the defences of Rochester and attacking its tower, and incurred very little censure for doing so.[294] The decision to attack was perhaps swung by the perception that the French were in full retreat and thus were vulnerable.

While Philip was taking shelter from the sun under an ash tree, the allies arrived at Cysoing, a mile south-east of Bouvines, and, catching up with the French rearguard, lanched into them. In charge of the rearguard were Viscount Adam of Melun, Duke Eudes of Burgundy and Brother Guérin, Bishop-elect of Senlis. Guérin was a veteran Knight Hospitaller who now, at 58 years of age, was ready to take his place amongst the French episcopate. His experience of warfare made him an invaluable adviser to Philip, and he was instrumental in the battle that was about to take place. From his hill-top vantage point he saw the allies fast approaching. He instructed the Viscount to hold the enemy off with his light cavalry and crossbowmen. The Anonymous of Béthune offers a slightly different, and possibly more accurate, account. According to him the rearguard took up position in a small wood and delayed the enemy's advance with crossbow fire. The rearguard struggled to catch up with the main army but had to stop and turn to face the enemy five times. It was soon hard-pressed; the allies were not intending to harass the retreating French column, but to destroy it. Guérin, assessing the seriousness of the situation, had ridden up the three-mile column to warn the king. Philip took counsel with his commanders, most of whom thought the march should continue, believing that Ferrand, who was leading the enemy attack, was not about to give battle; a minor deviation of Otto's course (to find fording points across a stream) was misconstrued as an intention to avoid an engagement. Then Gérard la Truie came up the column to warn the King of the escalating combat. The French were in imminent risk of succumbing to the coalition's intention of being caught stretched out, but now at the worst possible juncture with the army on either side of the River Marque. By this stage, most of Philip's army had crossed, leaving a relatively small number of footsoldiers and the greater part of

his cavalry dangerously exposed on the east side. It was made clear to the king, by
Guérin above all, that battle avoidance was no longer an option: the French had
to stand and fight.

Philip entered a nearby chapel to pray for victory. When he emerged the cry
of 'To arms!' went up; armour was donned, bridles were tightened and echelons
put into order. The majority of soldiers that had already crossed the bridge were
recalled and the bridge itself, having just been reinforced to take the strain of the
baggage train and the large numbers of men crossing, was now destroyed to harden
the resolve of the French and to stem any thoughts of flight from the battlefield.

Roger of Wendover's narrative diverges markedly from the other sources. He
places Philip's army within the fortified camp, behind the French wagons and
carts. Although at odds with the other contemporary sources which tell of battle
orders confronting each other on classical lines, Wendover's slant does not lack
plausibility. Such fortified camps were not new and were a common response
to dangers faced by an army on the move, attaining their fullest development in
the Hussite wars of the fifteenth century. In 1124, when also faced by an imperial invasion, Louis VI drew up wagons in circles, 'like small castles' according to
the chronicler Suger, to allow tired and wounded soldiers to retire from battle to
seek attention and to be refreshed by water. It may be that Wendover was confusing similar arrangements at Bouvines with the actual battlefield. At the Battle of
Alençon in 1118, in which Henry I of England suffered a major defeat, Count
Fulk of Anjou positioned his army within a fortified enclosure from which
he made sorties against the enemy (a point to recall when considering Count
Renaud's tactics at Bouvines). And in 1197 when Philip was campaigning in
Flanders, his opponents under William Marshal and Count Baldwin of Flanders
explored the possibility of organising carts in a defensive barrier against him, from
behind which battle could be offered. It is also worth reiterating Philip's cautious
and defensive nature and his hopes for battle avoidance. Intriguing though this
possibility is for one of the most epic and best documented battles of the Middle
Ages, the general conformity of the other major sources demands that they be
taken as forming the basis for any consideration of Bouvines, with William the
Breton's eye-witness account providing the core (but not all) of what follows.[295]
It is prudent to assume, therefore, that the baggage camp took up its customary
place behind the army and guarded it from surprise attack (aided at Bouvines
by a clear view of the surrounding area and with greater protection afforded by
adjoining marshes).

With the cavalry back across the river, Philip dispatched 700 of them towards
Cysoing to counter the allies' vanguard. This was effective: it forced the allies to
halt and to organise an equal and opposing cavalry force under Count Ferrand. A
classic cavalry engagement was to ensue, allowing the French to quickly move their
troops to face the enemy where they arranged themselves smoothly into battle
order less than a mile north-east of Bouvines. Philip took up his position at the

centre of his arrayed forces, with the French national war banner, the Oriflamme of
St Denis, set by him. There was consternation amongst the allies now they had lost
the initiative. Otto's men, engaged with the French rearguard and hoping to catch
their foe unprepared at Bouvines bridge, were not themselves ready for pitched
battle at this stage. Their own column, about four miles long, would take hours to
be fully arranged into battle order as Count Renaud had earlier warned. Indeed,
the Flemish sergeants from Bruges and Ghent were too far to the rear to play any
part in the engagement, and the allies' ability to fully utilise their tactical units was
hampered by this incapacity to deploy all their forces. Nevertheless, Otto had the
bulk of his forces with him and, having led them northwards, he likewise arranged
his battalions which, like the French, were heavily dominated by infantry.

The two armies spread out and faced each other on a broad plain. In the best
tradition of medieval bias, each side proclaimed itself to be heavily outnumbered
by the enemy: this allowed victory to be magnified and defeat to be mitigated.
Estimates give the allies superiority in numbers, further evidence for Philip's
attempt to avoid an engagement. The coalition comprised some 1300–1500
knights and 7500 infantry, opposing 1300 cavalry and 4000–6000 infantry for the
French.[296] However, a rough balance was probably created by the delay in bringing all the allied troops up to the battle. On this brilliant summer's day the French
had the advantage of facing south-east with the sun at their backs; the allies, facing
north-west, had the sun shining directly into their eyes. Among the many banners
and flags by which the various army units identified themselves, three stood out
before all the others. On the allies' side, looking positively demoniacal to William
the Breton, was the imperial banner, a golden dragon and an eagle mounted on
a *caroccio*, a war chariot. The French King displayed his two sacred banners: the
golden fleur-de-lis on an azure background and the *oriflamme*, carried into battle
by French monarchs, especially at times of national peril.

The banners were placed in the middle of each line with the commander-in-
chief. These lines were arranged in the standard battle formation of three divisions
which collectively stretched to perhaps 2000 paces across. With Otto at the centre
of the imperial line was his personal bodyguard and imperial troops, positioned
behind a phalanx of infantry. To his left was Ferrand of Flanders, whose battalion was dominated by light cavalry.[297] It is hard to be certain about the precise
course of action in the most confused, initial stages of the combat, but I believe
that the Ferrand-Guérin cavalry encounter would have taken place in phases,
from early contact through to the full onset of battle. Their initial contact, as
mentioned above, allowed time for the armies to be drawn up on the battlefield,
but I do not see this encounter as being constantly contested; the first lull, as the
forces measured up to each other, and any subsequent ones, would likely have
allowed the cavalry forces to draw up very roughly in the lines of battle. After
cavalry waves attacked they would withdraw to reform, reorganise and rest, their
mobility permitting them to shuffle into an overall position in the line of battle

described here, even if not in perfect order. On the Emperor's right wing were the knights and mercenaries of the Earl of Salisbury, Hugh de Boves and Renaud de Dammartin; their infantry was also to the fore. Directly opposite Otto was Philip, surrounded by his household troops with his loyal and veteran friend, William des Barres; when the communal infantry arrived on the scene they positioned themselves in front of Philip. To Philip's left, facing de Boves, Salisbury and Boulogne, were Bishop Philip of Beauvais with his brother Count Robert de Dreux and their men, Thomas de St Valéry with his knights and infantry, and the forces of Ponthieu under their Count, William. On the right wing, under the command of Guérin and facing Ferrand, were Duke Eudes of Burgundy, Count Gaucher of St Pol, Viscount Adam de Melun, their troops and those of Champagne. Each of these warriors led their own cohorts of troops which facilitated coherency in command and combat.

In the clarity afforded by a bright sun, the soldiers could distinctly make out the opposing lines: the men, the horses, the gleaming weapons and armour and the rich colours of numerous banners. Philip of France, in a pre-battle oration that combined nationalism and religion, exhorted his troops to fight together and at the same time. Behind him could be faintly heard the chant of his chaplain, William the Breton, leading another household clerk in prayers for France's triumph: 'Blessed be my Lord who leads my hand into battle' (Psalm 143) and 'Lord, the king will rejoice in your strength' (Psalm 20). Late in the afternoon, the full battle commenced.[298]

It was Guérin who had opened hostilities on his flank. His early correct assessment of the enemy's intentions had been crucial in granting the French the time they needed to draw up their forces. Now his judgement was once again critical. He realised that the more time passed the more allied soldiers would be drawn up on the battlefield, thereby outnumbering the French. He needed to take advantage of the allies' lack of organisation as they attempted to deploy troops arriving on the battlefield from their column of march. He had already efficiently arranged the French in battle order, ensuring that their line had spread out wide enough to avoid being outflanked and so that all the troops could fight simultaneously. Taking advice from St Pol, Guérin launched a cavalry charge of 150 mounted sergeants from Soissons. The purpose of this light cavalry change was to disrupt the opposing Flemish formation, softening and loosening it up for a charge by heavy cavalry. The Flemish absorbed the attack comfortably, inflicting severe damage on the French: the brunt of the casualties was felt amongst the unarmoured horses; only two sergeants were killed in the charge. The Flemish knights waited for their moment to counter-attack: William the Breton claims that they considered it beneath their dignity to engage with mounted men-at-arms; it was probably also equally true that they were disciplined enough to refrain from breaking ranks too early, something that Guérin had hoped for. With so many horses lost the men of Soissons had to fight on foot or retreat. Two Flemish knights, Walter of

Ghistelle and Baldwin Buridan, then led a charge against the Champanois heavy cavalry, escalating the conflict. After the clash of the first shock had broken the lances of the knights, swords were drawn and wielded. Amongst the division from Champagne, Pierre de Rémy and his men distinguished themselves by capturing the two Flems who had led the charge. Another Flem, Eustace of Machalen, cried out, 'Death to the French!', foolishly drawing attention to himself: some French soldiers grabbed hold of him, ripped off his helmet and struck him dead with a knife thrust beneath the ventrail.

The next divisions to commit themselves to the battle were those of Gaucher de St Pol and Count Ferrand of Flanders. Ferrand's move into the fray forced back the knights of Pierre de Rémy in its diagonal drive to King Philip's position, but a charge by St Pol, a follow-up to the Soissons' first attempt, cut deep into the enemy's ranks. In fact the sheer impetus of this charge by St Pol's elite knights took them straight through Ferrand's ranks and they could then, having brought their mounts about, attack from the rear. Much of Ferrand's force became surrounded when confronted by a further onslaught from the Viscount of Melun and his men. These charges inflicted heavy losses among the Flemish infantry, many of whom were hemmed in by warhorses and their riders, with blows raining down on them. The knights on both sides were not so easily dispatched: their armour afforded great protection even when unhorsed from their high, mounted battle platforms (horses were a primary target) they were not easily killed. The French then launched a third wave of cavalry, led by Count Jean de Beaumont, Mathieu de Montmorency, Duke Eudes of Burgandy, Viscount Adam de Melun and the Count of Sancerre. The Duke, a corpulent 50-year-old (like Philip) fell to the ground when his horse was killed beneath him. This was a moment of danger for the French: if the Duke were taken prisoner there might be a collapse in morale at a critical stage. In the Anonymous of Béthune's slightly different version, Arnulf of Oudernaarde came to blows with the Duke and attempted to kill him by forcing his dagger through the helmet's eye-hole. Immediately the Duke was surrounded by his men, probably his household bodyguard; these protected him while another horse was brought up for him to remount. When back in the saddle, he was urged to leave the fray for some rest, but he refused: he plunged back into the fight to avenge himself for the dishonour of being unhorsed.

The Duke was not the only knight on the French side to find himself in trouble. Michael de Harnes was pierced by a lance between his hauberk and his thigh which pinned him to his saddle and his horse as both lay on the ground; he was rescued by his comrades who placed him on another horse. Michael's commander, Hugh de Malevine, also had his horse slain (by Walter of Ghistelle before his capture), and like many other knights that day he had to fight on foot, but 'with no less skill'. Meanwhile the Count of St Pol and some of his men had withdrawn from the press: exhaustion in battle, especially when covered in armour in blazing heat, sapped the strength and endurance of even the fittest warriors. While regaining his breath, he caught sight of one of his knights surrounded by Flemish troops. He replaced his helmet and rode to the beleaguered knight's assistance. Charging with his head bent low over his horse's neck he broke into the throng of enemy troops (and, given the nature of a full-blown mêlée, no doubt forced aside some of his own infantry in the process). He then stood up in his stirrups and struck down with his sword from the mobile platform of his *destrier*, carving a way out for his companion. St Pol was repeatedly struck by the lances and pikes of the Flems, but neither he nor his horse was brought down. He returned to his knights, regrouped them and led them back into the thick of the action. St Pol's bellicosity proved too much for the Duke of Brabant: never fully committed to the imperial cause, he fled the field.

The encounter between the French right wing and the allied left wing raged to and fro for up to three hours before the balance tilted fully against the Flemish. Count Ferrand had lost his horse and was fighting on foot, but he was slowed down by serious wounds and exhaustion: he had been in the action continuously and was by now 'half-dead'. Hugh and Jean de Mareuil fought their way to the Count, but Ferrand was forced to surrender to save his life as he was no longer able to physically defend himself. His capture was a turning point: with their leader taken prisoner and their ranks severely depleted, the Flemish surrendered, fled or were killed.

The confusion and reality of the battle are not easy to convey, but William the Breton gives an excellent contemporary eyewitness and informed depiction of its true nature in this scene from Bouvines:

… From both sides the combatants engage with each other over the whole plain in a mêlée so thick that those who are striking and those who are being struck are so close together that they can hardly find the space or opportunity to stretch out their arms in order to deliver more vigorous blows. The vestments of silk attached over the armour so that every knight can be recognised by his signs have been slashed and ripped into a thousand shreds by the maces, swords and lances that beat upon his armour to break it, so that hardly anyone could distinguish his friend from his enemy. Someone is lying on his back on the ground, his legs in the air; another falls suddenly on his side; a third is thrown head first, his eyes and mouth filling with sand. Here a cavalryman, there a footsoldier voluntarily surrender themselves to irons, fearing to be struck dead more than to live vanquished. You could see horses lying here and there across the field, breathing their last, others with entrails bursting from their stomachs; others felled from having been hamstrung; and still others wandered here and there without their masters, freely offering themselves to whomsoever wished to ride them. There was hardly anywhere that one did not find a body stretched out or a horse dying.

With perhaps as many as 169 knights killed (some ten per cent), Bouvines was indeed a bloody battle by the standards of the day.[299]

The central divisions had by this time experienced the same vicious realities of battle. The infantry of the French communes – from Beauvais, Compiègne, Corbie and Arras – arrived on the battlefield only just before Otto's battalions advanced on Philip. These French footsoldiers had not been able to answer the recall at Bouvines with the same swiftness of the cavalry, and they had been in the van of the column on its march to Lille. When they saw Philip's fleur-de-lis standard, carried by Galon de Montigny, they drew themselves up in front of the King's household knights. Hardly had they done so when Otto's troops were upon them. These communal levies were unable to withstand the allies' charge and the Emperor's knights crashed through the King's battalion. Seeing the imminent danger to the King, William des Barres led the household knights in a counter-thrust as Gui Mauvoisin, Stephen Longchamp, Henry Count of Bar and others rushed to protect the king. Unbeknown to the French at this time, the allied commanders had sworn an oath to target Philip in the battle. While the knights of either side were engaged, German footsoldiers penetrated further through the lines of the communal infantry and household knights to reach King Philip himself. Armed with their pikes and billhooks they reached out for Philip on his horse. One hook from a pole-arm secured itself in Philip's chainmail between his head and chest, and the King of France was brought head first to the ground.

If any episode from the pages of medieval history should dispel the myth of the insignificance of infantry in warfare, this is it: common footsoldiers had unhorsed a French king and were now poised to kill him. The killing of the enemy's commander, especially when he was the greatest power in the land, usually presaged the end of the battle: Harold's death at Hastings in 1066, Richard III's at Bosworth in 1485 and Pedro II of Aragon's at Muret in 1213 (still fresh in the minds of the combatants at Bouvines) were all decisive moments in those battles. Now the Capetian monarch was faced with the same fate. Philip managed to drag himself to his feet with the billhook, wrenched from its owner's grasp, still hanging from his neck. But the German soldiers continued to set about him. French trumpets sounded the alarm warning of the King's peril; Galon de Montigny frantically waved the national banner as an urgent message of the danger facing the monarch, and hence the whole French army. In one of the battle's many acts of bravery, the distress signal was immediately acted upon by the household knight Pierre Tristan who dismounted and put himself between his King and his assailants, holding them off while Philip mounted Pierre's horse 'with surprising agility' and escaped to relative safety while Pierre was killed by the infantry. The Capetian King had been saved by the sacrifice of a gallant knight who had reached him in time and by the efficacy of medieval (and particularly royal) armour.[300]

The battle now raged more fiercely than ever. Stephen Longchamp, another household knight, was killed immediately in front of the King, the victim of a new type of weapon: a slim dagger with three sharp edges which could slide through weak points in a suit of armour. This is how Longchamp died, pierced through his eye to the brain by a thrust through his helmet's eye-hole – the most common method of dispatching a well-protected knight.[301] With Philip remounted, and all his German attackers slain, the French centre-division began a concerted counter-attack against the imperial battalions, gradually pushing them back. The intensity of the fighting took on an almost poetic character to spectators. This was a battle of epic proportions, the contest of a generation, which saw both armies unleash all their mighty force in the ultimate drama of violence. As William the Breton wrote of this stage of the battle: 'Thus began the marvellous fray, the slaying and slaughtering of men and horses by both sides, as all were fighting with wonderous virtue.' Broadswords, clubs, lances, maces, spears, bows, crossbows, daggers, pikes, axes, falchions, billhooks, slings and bare hands were all utilised in the combat, each taking its toll.

The pendulum had swung the other way and the fight was now taken to Otto. The Emperor in turn found himself threatened with mortal danger. French knights began cutting their way through to him; by this stage many knights would not regroup for any further charges and had dispensed with their lances in favour of swords and close-quarter weapons. Roger of Wendover depicts the Emperor bravely wielding his single-edged sword (probably a falchion) like a billhook and in this manner he kept the French at bay. But Pierre Mauvoison, 'more powerful in arms than he was wise in the ways of the world', managed to grab Otto's bridle in an attempt to lead his horse out of the mêlée and the Emperor into captivity – a prize that would have earned him great renown and fortune. But Otto's bodyguard had formed a tight formation around their lord and Pierre was thwarted. Gérard La Truie also managed to reach the Emperor; he unsheathed his knife and stabbed him full in the chest, but the weapon was unable to pierce the chainmail. Gerard swung his knife again and missed, instead plunging his weapon deep into the eye of Otto's warhorse which had reared its head just at the critical moment. The horse convulsed with death-throes but managed to lurch away, carrying its rider out of immediate danger before falling down dead, throwing Otto into the dust and leaving him vulnerable and exposed, the moment of maximum danger for a knight. Bernard von Ostemale rode up to his master, promptly dismounted, and bravely offered him his own horse, knowing that in doing so he faced almost certain capture or death. Otto, equally promptly, jumped on Bernard's horse. But he was not out of harm's way yet. Guillame des Barres, the Barrois, renowned Seneschal of France, was doggedly pursuing the Emperor as he attempted to make his escape to a safer position during the battle's most heated phase. Des Barres managed to grab Otto by the neck, but could neither pull him from the saddle nor wrench off his helmet to cut his throat before the imperial bodyguard fell on him. Count William of Frise, Gerard von Randeradt, Otto von Tecklenburg and some Saxons had broken away from Otto's now retreating contingent to deal with des Barres and save the Emperor. They killed his horse, bringing des Barres down and compelling him to fight on foot. He was not to be taken easily.[302] He fought 'like a raging lion', his dagger in one hand and his sword in the other, his shield presumably lost. He had to stand fighting alone for some time as he had pushed far ahead of his companions. Some, such as Gautier de Nemours ('The Young'), Guillame de Garlande and Barthélemy de Roye, had stressed the need to guard the King some distance back, lest he be exposed to the enemy once more. (In the *Philippidos*, William the Breton contradicts his prose account: in verse he unconvincingly portrays Philip as leading the surge to reach Otto.) Des Barres was at the point of succumbing when Thomas de St Valéry led a successful charge of cavalry and infantry through to him, forcing off the German knights and providing him with a horse and rescue.

By now the Germans were fighting a rearguard action, buying time for the Emperor's escape with their freedom and their lives. Many of those taken by the French were the elite of the Teutonic chivalry chosen for the imperial body guard for their bravery, loyalty and prowess. As Otto was escorted to safety off the field, Counts Conrad von Dortmund, Otto von Tecklenburg, Bernard von Ostemale (who had obviously found a horse to replace the one he had offered up to the Emperor) and Gerard von Randeradt, were amongst the many who courageously hindered the French advance, thereby sacrificing their own chance to evade capture. Only when further resistance was futile did they surrender. The imperial *caroccio* was destroyed in the combat and the battered standard was seized by the French. The golden eagle had lost its wings and the dragon was broken. This shattered symbol of imperial authority was brought to Philip.

But the battle was not over; indeed, it was about to enter a particularly bloody phase. On the French left flank the struggle continued as furiously as ever, with no sign of either side gaining the upper hand as they fought over the dead and dying bodies of their fallen comrades and enemies. Renaud de Dammartin, Count of Boulogne, was proving himself the most effective allied commander on the field of battle, and his mercenaries the toughest soldiers. Easily picked out by his large helmet and distinctive physique, the Count supported a weighty lance made of ash that few but he had the strength and skill to carry. Renaud had formed his *routier* infantry into a large circle or horse-shoe shape of two ranks of closely-knit pikemen. From within this defensive position the Count led his heavy cavalry in charges against the French, possibly in the form of tactical thrusts when and where they were needed. When his cavalry needed rest or regrouping it withdrew into the relative safety of this bristling enclosure. From here the Count and his men made several sallies.

Historians of the battle have made much of the Count's tactics, usually to praise them as an innovative and effective deployment of infantry. Misguided modern authorities express pleasant surprise that foot soldiers could play an important role at all. The attention these tactics have attracted may in large part be due to William the Breton's assertion that they represented 'a new form of warfare'. William is extremely well-informed on military matters and remains one of the best but least utilised sources for medieval warfare, but it is unlikely that Renaud's manoeuvres were, as William believes, entirely novel. For all William's first hand experiences, he actually witnessed very little in the way of pitched battles, rather he was present at a number of skirmishes and encounters, some of them substantial in themselves, but nothing on the scale of Bouvines. We have already mentioned Alençon in 1118 and Louis VI's tactics in 1124, both occasions offering examples of ad hoc defensive enclosures on the battlefield. On the latter occasion Suger, who gives the fullest account of events, spoke of a circle defended like a 'castle'; William the Breton gives almost exactly the same term in the *Philippidos* to describe Renaud's formation, which he likens to a 'castle under siege'. Variations of such tactics were employed in the crusades, including the Third Crusade of 1191–2, in which Philip had participated; they were used with great effect by Richard the Lionheart at the Battle of Jaffa, which occurred just a few days after Philip embarked on his return journey home to France, which may explain their novelty to William.[303]

With the Count of Boulogne was Earl William of Salisbury, known as 'Longsword' on account of his martial ability, and his force of mercenaries. These two formidable warriors were engaged in a bitter mêlée with the French left wing, where they faced Count Robert de Dreux, Thomas de St Valéry, Bishop Philip de Beauvais and the Count of Ponthieu, all with their formations. According only to the *Philippidos*, the Bishop of Beauvais saw the battalion of his brother, the Count of Dreux, under extreme pressure from Salisbury's contingent, and so the Bishop rode up the Earl and bludgeoned him on the head with his mace (*clava*). As an ecclesiastic he was not permitted to shed blood and so did not wield a cutting weapon such as a sword or an axe (the Bayeux Tapestry famously depicts Bishop Odo of Bayeux in the thick of the fighting at the Battle of Hastings swinging a dangerous looking club). Such was the blow delivered by the Bishop it shattered the Earl's helmet and knocked Salisbury to the ground on which he landed with so much force that the imprint of his body was left upon it. Remembering his modesty as a cleric, the Bishop then judiciously permitted a knight called Jean to take Salisbury as an immensely prestigious prisoner and to receive the reward for him. Given William's propensity in his poem to inflate his heroes, it would not be too difficult to argue that it was in fact Jean who had taken the Earl prisoner in the first instance and had captured him after a struggle, perhaps having been instructed to do so by the Bishop in an endeavour to lift the acute pressure that his brother was under.

The loss of Longsword came amidst a flurry of losses that sapped the allies' power. Hugh de Boves, the keenest advocate of delivering battle to the French, is nowhere mentioned in the fighting and we only hear of him (from Wendover and William the Breton) when he flees from the battlefield. De Boves' hasty departure was precipitated when he became aware of Count Ferrand's capture and recognised that the collapse of the Emperor's central division was imminent. Ironically, and in contrast, it was the Count of Boulogne, who had vehemently opposed the engagement, that fought on the longest and hardest. But by now he had little support: Longsword and Ferrand had been captured; de Boves and the Emperor had fled the field. The contingent from Bruges, witnessing de Boves' withdrawal, at once sounded a general retreat, further depleting both the centre and the left wing. The Flemish infantry that had at this stage only just arrived on the scene and who might have made a significant difference to the day's outcome had the battle been delayed, realised that there was little point in committing themselves to the fray at this late stage. With the centre and left gone, and with the series of battlefield desertions and captures, Boulogne was left to fight alone.

Count Renaud's tenacious resistance and the stand of his mercenaries marks the conclusion of this epic battle in a suitably dramatic fashion. He fought so valiantly that even William the Breton had to admit admiringly that 'his unbridled valour did not permit anyone to vanquish him', and his great accomplishment with weapons and in fighting 'loudly proclaimed that he was the true issue of French parents'. Praise indeed from William. Temporarily safe within his enclosure of pikemen the Count was nevertheless exposed to the dangers of arrows and missiles and from combat during his sorties, the more so now that he had only five or six knights left in his command. Hopelessly outnumbered, he perhaps continued the struggle in the hope that the allied army could regroup and return to the field. He was taking a huge risk but had much to gain from Philip's defeat: in 1211 the King of France had deprived him of his lands, and Renaud was making a determined effort to capture or kill the King. During one of his sallies the Count confronted a sergeant called Pierre de la Tournelle, who was fighting on foot as his horse had been slain. Pierre quickly approached the Count in best infantry tradition, attempting to bring down the rider by disabling his horse. Renaud's horse may well have been stationary, hemmed in by the press of battle. Pierre was able with his left hand to lift up the horse's armour, which was held in place by broad straps, and expose its belly. He drew his sword and plunged it deep into the *destrier's* groin and into its guts, right up to the sword's guard. One of Renaud's knights, seeing his lord's mount fatally struck, grabbed the bridle of the dying horse and, against the Count's will, began leading it out of the fray. But this knight was set upon by the brothers Quesnes and Jean de Coudon and knocked to the ground. Renaud soon followed him, landing on his back with his horse collapsed on top of his right leg, pinning him to the earth.

There followed an unsavoury scramble to take the Count prisoner and thereby claim an invaluable prize. A swarm of knights closed in on Renaud with this aim in mind. The Coudon brothers were about to bind him while Jean de Rouvrai and Hugh and Gautier de Fontaine appeared on the scene where they proceeded to argue over who should take the Count of Boulogne captive. Jean de Nestle then bustled among them to stake his claim, even though, says William mockingly, 'he had fought no one in the course of the whole day.' While this unseemly squabble ensued to determine a lucrative outcome to the day's events (thus portraying clearly the profiteering nature of chivalry), Count Renaud's life remained in peril as fighting continued around him. Comotus, a young commoner (*garcio*), who by dint of his lowly birth could lay no claim to such a noble prize, was doing his best to slay the Count. This servant of Guérin tried raising the side of Renaud's hauberk to stab him in the stomach (or to emasculate him), but the knife was denied entrance by the quality of armour, the chausses being securely attached to the mail shirt. He then managed to rip off the Count's helmet and inflicted a nasty head wound. Comotus was preparing to slit the Count's throat while Renaud desperately tried to fend him off with his hands as he lay trapped underneath his horse. Just as Comotus was about to deliver his *coup de grâce,* his master Guérin arrived on the scene to stay his arm. Renaud willingly surrendered himself to the bishop-elect, securing his safety by becoming the prisoner of the most powerful figure present. Hardly able to stand and covered in his own blood, Renaud was dragged to his feet. While this was occurring, the Count of Boulogne's loyal knight, Arnulf of Oudenaarde, led a desperate rescue attempt. The Count was forced by a series of blows to clamber onto the back of a packhorse and, under the guard of Jean de Nesle and his men, he was led off to King Philip. Arnulf and his comrades were all captured.

There was still one last drama to be played out on the field of battle. Some 400–700 of Renaud's Brabançons remained in their tight-knit formation, bristling with their pikes. The French cavalry, who had for the most part discarded their lances earlier in the battle, were extremely wary of these mercenaries: 'They, with their pikes longer than knives and swords, and moreover lined up in an invincible formation of triple ranks of walls, were so cleverly disposed there was no way that they could be breached.' The healthy respect that knights had for footsoldiers is highlighted by this episode. Philip was taking no chances with his valuable cavalry: he would not have forgotten the defeat inflicted on his knights by Henry II's infantry at Gisors in 1188. But for this last display of defiance the French commanded the battlefield; they were thus free to re-equip the cavalry with lances to take on the mercenaries. Philip ordered overwhelming force to be used in crushing the mercenaries. Up to 2000 infantry and 50 cavalry under the leadership of Thomas de St Valéry were sent against them. The cavalry shock charge that followed succeeded in its task of breaking up the defensive wall of pikes; such was the clamour of battle it was impossible to hear the blare of trumpets. Although not mentioned anywhere by William the Breton, archery probably played its part in loosening up the mercenary ranks. We know from the Anonymous of Béthune – and we would expect anyway – that bowmen were present. Despite their lowly status, it is nevertheless surprising not to hear of their actions in the battle; as William the Breton attests on other occasions, they were an effective component of medieval armies. As we shall see later, field armies, especially those made up quickly as the French one was in 1214, included a large element of garrison troops – predominantly archers and crossbowmen. When St Valéry's cavalry had achieved their initial task against the mercenaries, it combined with the infantry to move in for the kill. The pikes and fearsome double-headed axes of the mercenaries could not counter the sheer weight of numbers pressing against them. They were slaughtered. According to William the Breton, St Valéry's force suffered only one minor casualty, a remarkable result given his earlier alarming description of the mercenaries. But it is likely that here William is only referring to the cavalry: infantry losses, invariably much higher due to lighter armour and the limits of chivalry, were not a noteworthy statistic for most chroniclers. With the mercenaries' last stand ending in their massacre, the killing had finished. The battle was over.

Aftermath

Most battles, especially major ones, do not end cleanly on the field of conflict: there is usually a substantial mopping-up operation afterwards which involves further casualties. At La Roche-au-Moine the Marshal of France probably received a mortal wound when pursuing the fleeing enemy. After the Battle of Hastings in 1066 it is thought that some victorious Norman cavalry fell into trouble in a steep ravine when, in the 'Malfosse incident', in pursuit of the defeated forces, they encountered a last stand of Anglo-Saxons. Nor is this solely a feature of medieval warfare: at Waterloo in 1815 the French put up a number of rearguard actions to hinder pursuit. This may have been the role of Renaud's mercenaries at Bouvines. Bouvines, however, did end on the battlefield. Philip, ever cautious, knew that he had won a seminal victory, and wished immediately to consolidate his huge gains rather than seek further, indefinite ones. He did not want his army dispersed in running down the enemy; as William the Breton explains, 'The King did not want our people to hunt further than a mile for the men in flight because of the danger of little known paths and the oncoming night and, also, so that the captured princes and wealthy men would not escape.' This last point is what Philip feared most: an enemy that regrouped and counter-attacked when his own army was scattered. Although a concerted regrouping of the allied army was improbable given the scale of the defeat, the loyalty and ties of self-interest many had for their captured lord may have prompted an attempt to snatch certain prisoners from the French. It was this haul of captives that Philip had netted for himself which made Bouvines such an eminently satisfying victory for him. Of over 130 knights that had fallen into his hands, 25 were knights banneret and five were counts; held at his will were his great enemies Count Ferrand of Flanders, Count Renaud of Boulogne and King John's brother, Earl William of Salisbury. The Anonymous of Béthune wrote: 'It was a marvel that the number of barons, knights and sergeants taken was so great.'[304] While many of his great confederates were locked in chains, Emperor Otto made good his escape, heading for Valenciennes and spending the night at the Abbey of St Sage. The allied coalition that a few hours earlier had threatened the very existence of Capetian France had been smashed.

The ordinary French soldier also had his gains. When the trumpets sounded the return from the pursuit, the troops could revisit the battlefield to scour for booty. The enemy had been scattered, the prisoners had been secured and the wounded were being attended to – now the profits of war had could be harvested by the survivors.[305] William the Breton's eye for detail is revealed in the following scene depicting the aftermath of the battle, when soldiers scavenged amongst the corpses of men and horses:

> Here someone takes a *destrier*, there a sturdy rouncey offers its head to a stranger and is tied with a rope. Others take abandoned weapons from the field; one grabs a shield, another a sword or a helmet. Someone else leaves happy with some leggings while yet another is pleased with a breastplate and a third gathers clothes and armour. Happier still and in a better position to withstand the caprices of fortune is the one who can seize the horses laden with baggage or swords hidden under their bulging covers ...

This business-like picture captures the reality of a battle's anti-climactic conclusion. The spoils of war would certainly be impressive as seen here: golden vessels, precious implements, silken vestments and various other forms of booty meant that some wagons were so laden they required sixteen horses to pull them. Nor should it be overlooked that the wagons were often of considerable value themselves. One wagon, however, was not taken as war booty: Emperor Otto's *caroccio*. This was axed 'into a thousand pieces' and burned so that no trace of it remained. The wings of the eagle were repaired and Philip sent this imperial symbol to King Frederick of Sicily, Otto's rival claimant to the title of Holy Roman Emperor, a tacit semiotic message to Frederick as to whom he owed his new-found security and his gratitude.

Just as Philip had prayed for victory before battle, so now he would have given thanks to God for his stunning success. With the company commanders having been recalled from the hunt (they no doubt had hoped to come upon Otto) and rested in their tents, the question of prisoners was dealt with. Philip had the captured allied leaders summoned to him. Those from his own kingdom were his own liege men and, as they had conspired against the King, were guilty of high treason; the custom of the land permitted beheading for these. However, in the event, all the prisoners were spared their lives; prison or ransom was to be their fate. In chains and ropes the captives were bundled onto carts and transported to scattered prisons. In total, over 300 prisoners were taken: a catalogue of prisoners drawn up in August records that 110 knights were taken to Paris, sixteen were placed in the safekeeping of great lords and the most important three came under the charge of officials of the royal household: Count Ferrand of Flanders was assigned to Barthélemy de Roye; Count Renaud of Boulogne to Jean de Nesle; and Earl William of Salisbury to Count Robert de Dreux.[306] The prisoners carted to Paris were incarcerated in two *châtelets* that guarded the bridges linking the Île-de-la-Cité with the banks of the Seine. Others were imprisoned in the Grand Châtelet, from where three later escaped. Ferrand remained in the donjon of the recently completed Louvre until he was set free in 1226. Salisbury was soon released by negotiations; it had always been Count Robert's intention to exchange him for his son who was held by King John, a transaction that John did not initially accede to (Philip of France had rewarded Count Robert with his important prisoner with this transaction in mind). The harshest treatment was handed out to Renaud de Dammartin, Count of Boulogne. He was no longer to be a constant source of trouble for the French King: he was taken to the castle at Péronne and shackled in chains. Thirteen years later, still in chains, he died.

The day after Bouvines Philip headed back to Paris. Public rejoicing had already begun throughout France. The common people lined the route of the king's return to the capital, cheering their monarch and heaping insults on the Count Ferrand and the other prisoners. Official celebrations were organised everywhere in the kingdom, but especially in the capital, where unrestrained revelries lasted day and night for a week. Unsurprisingly, the mood in the Angevin royal camp in Poitou was one of shock. When John heard of the news 'he was thrown into despair', records Wendover. 'Since I have become reconciled to God, and submitted myself and my kingdom to St Peter and the Roman Church', bewailed John, 'nothing has gone right for me, and every misfortune has befallen me.'[307]

John, however, remained prepared to continue the fight from his position south of the Loire. John had ordered his justiciar in England, Peter des Roches, to arrange 300 Welsh reinforcements to be sent to him by the end of August. He was right to feel the need for them. Philip, with characteristic alacrity, marched his army of up to 2000 knights and accompanying infantry south into Poitou in a major show of confidence and strength, halting at the Castle of Loudon with John only fifteen miles away. Although the size of the French victory at Bouvines is hard to overestimate politically, John's position in Poitou was not entirely hopeless. The barons of the region were wary of the possible consequences of an overly strong Capetian monarchy; as Baldwin points out, Philip's arrival south to join his son Louis did not intimidate John's Poitevin allies as much as he may have hoped.[308] Certainly, Philip did not carry through the threat implicit in his action, despite the assertions of some French historians that Philip was poised to conquer Poitou.[309] The French King was not prepared to put his spectacular gains at risk in another battle: in addition to the very real advantages won at Bouvines was the enormously enhanced prestige of Philip's reputation as soldier, victor and King, which had practical power applications of its own. An unnecessary encounter and possible minor defeat would have blemished his aura of conquering hero. Worse, the wheel of fortune could turn dramatically against him: on 1066 Harold of England marched from decisive victory at Stamford Bridge to utter defeat three weeks later at Hastings, the great earlier triumph becoming a footnote in history. Prompted by Pope Innocent III, eager for peace in Christendom so that he could launch another crusade, the two sides came to terms at Chinon on 18 September in a truce that was to last five years from the following Easter. This truce merely extended the one of Thouars in 1206. Baldwin believes that it reveals an actual weakening of King Philip's position south of the Loire. With the exception of the loyal Angevins Aimery de Craon and Juhel de Mayenne, Philip's document was not underwritten by any notable baron of the Loire region. Unlike in 1206, John's co-signatories now included the leading Poitevins, with the Counts of La Marche and Eu and the families of Thouars, Lusignan and Larchevêque: 'Faithful to their reputation, the Poitevins preferred to stand with a distant and weaker suzerain.'[310]

Against this must be set the submission of Viscount Aimery of Thouars and other Poitevin barons to Philip and, argues Gillingham, 'Philip's relative lack of interest in this part of the world.'[311] Put into context, Poitou simply was not as important as the north: 'Philip was always more interested in invading England than in completing his takeover of the continental lands of the Angevins. This was because the threat to Normandy came from England not from southwest France.'[312] This threat, it may be added, could be turned on its head regarding England: as we have seen, Philip's conquest of Normandy gave him a vital stretch of northern seaboard from which he could menace John's kingdom. Thus the stalemate in Poitou was deliberately anti-climatic and not worth Philip's whole-hearted attention. Both he and John had experienced enough antagonistic relationships with the Papacy and neither had much to gain from reviving such troubles at this immediate juncture by rekindling the conflict. Philip, with an eye to events in England and his hoped for enterprise, was, according to Ralph of Coggeshall, more interested in the 60,000 marks offered to him by John, an indication of how weak contemporaries judged John's position in Poitou.[313] The truce allowed John to hold the line south of the Loire for the time being.

Much has been written about the consequences of Bouvines, one of the most significant battles in European history, but it was how it was fought – and won – that altered the course of subsequent events. If the French forces had not been so well ordered and so well led; if the coalition army had not been so precipitate; and, above all, if Philip of France had been killed or captured, as was so nearly the case: the whole future of Europe might have been radically different. As Painter noted, 'If Bouvines had been won, John would have been the dominant power in western Europe.'[314] John's continental policies and alliances, so expensively fostered, would have come to fruition; Otto IV would have remained Emperor; the barons in England would have recovered their lands in France; Philip Augustus would not have been the instigator of France as the leading power in Europe; Magna Carta may never have happened; and there would have been no invasion of England. Thus 'Bouvines deservedly ranks among the world's decisive battles.'[315]

As it was, John's position had in reality collapsed and his great financial outlays had been for nought. It was the King of France who was now Western Europe's pre-eminent monarch. Capetian France was secure in itself and more threatening than ever to England. England prepared for the worst. In late August John sent his word to his formidable justiciar and serving regent, Peter des Roches, to munition Dover Castle and make ready for his return. Des Roches had already organised defence measures for the Marches, where a sudden spate of Welsh incursions indicate that the news of John's crushing defeat had reached home, and the Welsh were the first hostile element to capitalise on it. With John far away with his army in Poitou, there was real alarm that Philip might undertake a rapid invasion. By early September des Roches was prudently engaging men to keep a discreet vigil on the coasts; he also seized foreign merchant vessels that may have been carrying French men and horses.[316] Des Roches and the country waited tensely for John's return.

France, in contrast, settled down to enjoy the new political dawn. Flanders was now effectively under French control[317] and Aquitaine could be safely dealt with later; John's own troublesome subjects in England held promise for help in a favourable outcome here. Just as John's problems were mounting precariously, so Philip's were subsiding; as the Anonymous of Béthune wrote: 'After this, no one dared to wage war against him, and he and the whole of his land lived in great peace for a long time.'[318] Bouvines was Philip's last – and greatest – direct combat involvement, a fitting end to his successful military career. He had no need to continue his role as general in the field: his son Louis, a more martially inclined man than his father, had proven his worth and now took the lead in active military matters.[319] Bouvines granted Philip the luxury of becoming an administrative king; he could safely retire from the rigours of campaigning.

The year 1214 therefore witnessed a remarkable change in European politics, and deserves to be regarded as one of the watersheds in history. Bouvines had changed everything. Contemporaries, such as the Anonymous of Béthune, realised this. But in 1214 the now largely forgotten engagement at La Roche-au-Moine was considered by many, such as the Minstrel of Reims, to be nearly as significant as Bouvines. We must remember that without Bouvines, La Roche would be hailed as a major Capetian victory, as it was at the time. A century after these dramatic events, which saw John's plans totally crushed on his two fronts, one French chronicler wrote of these two great Capetian victories as having occurred simultaneously, as if divinely synchronised. He says that Philip and Louis sent out messengers at the same time to pass on news of their success. These messengers, one from the south and the other from the north, met at Senlis. Having shared their joyous news, 'they raised their hands to Heaven, giving thanks to the Lord whom by wondrous coincidence, had granted the father and son to triumph over their enemies at the very same moment.'[320]

John, however, was on the eve of the most intensive warfaring period of his life. He and his allies had failed decisively on the continent. His two great armies, one in the north-east and the other in the south-west, had been seen off one at a time by the French: better coordination of troop concentrations, more prudence at Bouvines and better luck on that historic battlefield (Philip, remember, was fortunate to have survived) might have changed everything. But it had all gone so completely wrong; the fortunes of war had turned comprehensively against him. John left La Rochelle in early October, never to return to France. On his journey back to England he must have been filled with foreboding. He had left his kingdom in a state of political unrest; his shattered foreign policy would only add fuel to the fire. On his return in mid October he prepared for civil war.

5

Magna Carta, Civil War and the Countdown to Invasion, 1215

John and the Anger of the Barons

The state of John's mind as he sailed back from La Rochelle in mid-October 1214 can be easily imagined. Even if he had come to terms with the massive defeat at Bouvines – and the defeat did not stop him conducting government business and making plans for the future – he knew that he was returning to a kingdom that was approaching boiling point in terms of political discontent; the heat had been rising before he had left England and the Bouvines disaster could only fan the flames of opposition. Following his allies' defeat, John had sent secret instructions back to England to put his castles in a state of readiness in expectation of the trouble to come. In his absence, the justiciar Peter des Roches – soldier, bishop and chief administrator – had done nothing to cool things down. Incessant demands on the baronage for service and money were made all the more grating to them by the elevation of this foreigner over them. His lack of popularity can be gauged by a contemporary rhyme that was not designed to be flattering: 'The warrior at Winchester, up at the exchequer / Sharp at accounting, slack at the scripture'.[321] John had increasingly reacted to his own distrust of his countrymen by importing men from France, especially Poitou, and placing them in high office at the expense of English candidates. This abuse of patronage, as the disaffected regarded it, was compounded by the physical reinforcement of foreign mercenaries in the realm, adding to the perceived threat of arbitrary government. The political events in England leading to Magna Carta and civil war have been much studied and need not detain us for long here in what is a military study of events. That said, the political context needs addressing briefly, as do the reasons for the personal animosity of the leading rebels against their king, so that we have an understanding of the motivations that compelled men to take up arms in a civil war.[322]

John had earned for himself the label of a loser; 'Softsword' had rarely seemed so appropriate as a sobriquet. The successes that John had achieved in the military sphere, and which some historians view favourably for his record, were all temporary and could never balance out the disasters of 1204 and 1214. David Carpenter has succinctly summarised the impact of the latter, following the massive defeat at Bouvines:'In Germany it undermined Otto and set up Frederick II. In Normandy it ended the chance of an Angevin recovery. In Europe it made King Philip supreme. In England it shattered John's authority and paved the way for Magna Carta.'[323] The contrast with the enhancement of Philip Augustus' reputation could not have been clearer. Philip's panegyrist, William the Breton, pretty much concludes both his books on the King with the Bouvines climax, even though Philip was to reign for another decade. This purposeful neglect can be explained largely by how unexciting the rest of the reign was in comparison prior to Bouvines: overwhelming military success had brought France relative peace and security, as the theatre of war moved to England itself. Richard I's policy of fighting his wars abroad was, as suggested in the first chapter, a highly effective and successful one; criticising him for his military absence is a misunderstanding of fundamental defensive strategy. Now Philip benefited from the same luxury: he had all but finished the war on his home territory, and he could now take it to England.

John's inability to show anything concrete for his vast outlay of national treasure inevitably led to the sensible conclusion that his squeezing the country for money to fight more wars was tantamount to throwing good money after bad. Finances lay at the root of John's problems, just at it lay at the heart of politics; above all, money was needed for war. Baronial reluctance to fund John's overseas campaigns arose from resentment at expectations of scutage and military service, which itself was of course extremely costly, as John was told in no uncertain terms in 1212 and especially 1213. The refusal of the northern barons to heed the summons in 1213 resulted in John attempting a military display of power in the north before Archbishop Langton stopped him. This resentment went back to the 1205 scutage: Robert Fitzwalter and Roger Bigod were resolutely against the King from this point. John's habit of imposing a scutage and then abandoning the expedition funded by it did nothing to foster mutual trust. 1214 saw the scutage rate hit a record high; Peter des Roches failed miserably to reach his tax targets since May and on his return in October John demanded three marks per fee from those who had not, in his mind, fulfilled their obligations to him in Poitou. This increased anger especially in East Anglia and the north. Henry II had levied eight scutages in 34 years; John levied eleven in just sixteen. The tactless, indeed, aggressive manner of John's financial exactions antagonised his subjects further. The sale, exploitation and manipulation of justice but failing to deliver it fairly in the courts; pressurising the Jews who in turn pressurised their baronial debtors; the instatement of over-eager royal officials seeking income for the crown such as the ruthless Brian de Lisle in the north and the promotion of insensitive foreigners such as Engelard de Cigogné as sheriffs; the use of hostages as coercion;

the seizure of land by will; and always tax, tax, tax, like the onerous aid of 1207: the pressure on the barons was severe and unrelenting.[324] And John never had anything to show for it.

It was the increasingly arbitrary nature of exactions and rule that caused the most unsettlement. A particularly personal and unpleasant tactic of John was the use of amercements. These were ostensibly a system of penalties for those convicted for offences against the King's peace; in reality they were a means by which barons bought the King's goodwill. Robert de Ros, Sheriff of Cumberland, failed to keep some prisoners in custody and was fined 300 marks. Thomas de St Valéry sought the King's goodwill in 1209 probably for no other reason than he was the brother-in-law to William de Braose who had fallen from favour with John. In 1210, Robert de Vaux, another northerner, offered John 750 marks and five top quality horses so that, according to the official pipe roll, the King 'would keep quiet about the wife of Henry Pinel'.[325] Amercements could be extortionate: William of Cornborough died in gaol because he was unable to pay his. As Ralph Turner says of John, he 'became master at enmeshing those who had lost their favour in administrative difficulties that could result in financial ruin. John made the most of his ability to entangle his subjects in debt.'[326] A substantial element of John's financial policy might therefore be described as part extortion and part blackmail for political ends. He might have found sympathy and help a better way to ensure loyalty; no wonder men such as Robert de Ros joined with the rebels in 1215. Debtors like Gilbert de Gant and Henry d'Oilly were also well represented among the rebel ranks; James Holt has identified the upheaval of 1215 as, in part, 'a rebellion of the King's debtors'.[327]

We can perceive in all this the distinctly unpleasant nature of John's vindictive character. This is best exemplified by his notorious treatment of Willaim de Braose and his family, 'one of the defining events of the reign'.[328] John's actions were part of his suspicion of powerful nobles and his desire to cut them down to size; Ranulf of Chester was on the receiving end of this trait in 1203–4, as were William Marshal and de Braose in 1205–7. It was the latter who suffered the full brunt of John's animosity. De Braose, a close advisor of the king's, had done well out of John; many barons had benefited from the king's patronage and largesse, thus delaying a united front against him for far longer than might otherwise have been expected. De Braose was Lord of Bamber and Barnstaple and a Marcher Lord in South Wales with land around the Gower. In 1201 he had been offered the honour of Limerick in Ireland by John, for which the baron promised to pay £666 annually for five years. Six years later he had managed only £468. This lack of payment, coupled with de Braose's affiliation with William Marshal and, more seriously, possible involvement with the Welsh, served to heighten John's anger and mistrust. He ordered his justiciar in Ireland to raid the baron's land and seized his lands in Wales. De Braose attempted military action to regain three of his castles in Wales but failed; he burned some of Leominster and killed some of John's

crossbowmen and sergeants before taking refuge in Ireland. As seen above, John
even marched to Scotland in 1209 to ensure no help was received in Ireland from
that quarter before making for Ireland in 1210. De Braose attempted to make his
peace with the King, but John seemed hell-bent on destroying him, proclaiming
him a traitor, and demanded an impossible 40,000 marks payment from him. De
Braose's wife, Matilda, and son were taken hostage and imprisoned in Windsor
Castle. The baron could not find the money for their release and, ignobly or prag-
matically, fled to France. In 1210, John had Matilda and her son starved to death
in a dungeon. This shocking news spread like wildfire across the country, made
all the more horrible by lurid details of the position in which their bodies were
supposedly found: she slumped between her son's legs with her head lying on his
chest, having gnawed at his cheeks for food.

John sent out a carefully detailed public letter explaining the financial and
political reasons for his actions, revealing an awareness that his actions were causing grave disquiet. It has been reasonably argued that John had to pursue his
course ruthlessly: once one baron was indulged with non-payment of debt, all
would try for the same treatment. But another convincing argument could be
made that in fact William was not his target after all – Matilda was. Perhaps money
was only the excuse John put forward for such extreme action and another reason
is needed to explain why John was so implacable and vicious. This other reason
may be the de Braoses' knowledge of John's involvement in the death of Count
Arthur of Brittany. De Braose had in fact captured Arthur at Mirebeau and was
around John at the suspected time of Arthur's death. Interestingly, de Braose was
the patron of Margam Abbey the annals of which offer a unique insight into
the young Count's murder, laying the blame squarely on John during a drunken
rage.[329] It is worth asking whether de Braose felt that his position of influence
combined with his knowledge of John's dark secret led him to believe that he
could be relaxed about the payment of his debt to the King. If so, he was playing a
dangerous game that backfired tragically. A key moment in the affair came when,
as was John's custom, he demanded the de Braoses' sons as hostages. Wendover has
Matilda paling at the prospect, explosively declaring in front of John's officers: 'I
will not hand over my boys to your master King John, who wickedly murdered
his nephew Arthur, whose custody had been honourably granted.' Just as revealing is William's measured response; upbraiding his wife for her foolish (that is,
dangerous) words, he said: 'If I have offended him [John] in anyway, I am and shall
be ready to give my lord satisfaction, without hostages, according to the decision
of his court and of my fellow barons.'[330] The 'without hostages' provision might
easily be taken as damning, for hostages were habitually surrendered to John by
barons, even by those deeply antagonistic towards him. John was 'enraged' and
from this point on did not relent until Matilda's death.

It may be wrong to look at this whole, terrible affair from just one angle, either
financial or personal; both would have been important and both had serious

political implications. Why this case is so significant, and why it has been afforded so much space here, is because it shows the alienating combination of John's greed, inept management of people and his arbitrary viciousness that did so much damage to him. All of England quickly came to know about these events; the barons now felt more vulnerable and edgy than ever: if John could treat one of his leading nobles in this capricious and disgraceful way, who among them could be sure of their own safety and that of their families? Historians have rightly and consistently made much of the consequences of John's fatally flawed and paranoid character. In 1961 Warren wrote that 'the king's ability to cripple his vassals was all the more disturbing in John because he was capable of using it for no very good reason – a caprice of his twisted suspicions, his dislike of men simply because they were great and powerful'. He adds, 'Even if the barons accepted John's explanation, they could only have been more alarmed, and felt more dreadfully insecure, at this terrible illustration of the king's interpretations of his rights. Even the mightiest among them could be crumpled if they lost the king's "goodwill", and the goodwill of a king, moreover, who was so suspicious and mistrustful.'[331] In 2010, David Crouch, in the most recent assessment of the Braose case, says that it reveals the king's 'irrational capacity for abrupt, extravagant, and uncontrolled resentment that put John outside the courtly world. He was unpredictable and unreliable.' Sidney Painter has called the Braose affair 'the greatest mistake John made during his reign'.[332]

John delighted in adding insult to injury, and rumours abounded of his licentious behaviour at court. Such stories may have been added after rebellion had broken out as a form of justification for taking action against the monarch. Certainly, William the Breton did not hesitate to lay into the Angevin enemy by claiming that John took advantage of his half brother Earl William of Salisbury's captivity in France after Bouvines to seduce his wife. Two of the rebel leaders both accused John of adultery, not with commoners and servants, but with women in their families: Eustace de Vescy claimed John attempted sex with his wife, while Robert Fitzwalter accused John of having forced himself upon his daughter. Clearly there was great rallying, anti-John propaganda to be made here, and again the effective warning was sent out that if the wives and daughters of great nobles were vulnerable to John's advances, then no one's family was safe, no matter how elevated they were. These stories are likely to have been more than merely malicious gossip. It could not have been easy for such proud nobles as Fitzwalter and Vescy to admit to such stories. The Anonymous of Béthune – not a monastic chronicler, remember – condemns John because 'he lusted after beautiful women and because of this he shamed the high men of the land, for which reason he was greatly hated.'[333] Even government records make a knowing nod towards this, probably with dark humour: the chancery rolls record that 'the wife of Hugh de Neville gives the lord King 200 chickens that she might lie one night with her lord, Hugh de Neville.'[334] Other kings had been serial adulterers, not least John's father, Henry II, whose 'adultery was conducted on a truly regal scale'; he was able 'to make free with the women even of his greater barons'. That John's 'crimes against women' were not tolerated in the same way says something not only about their nature, but also about his personal stature, authority and the character of his misrule.[335]

So there were plenty of reasons to take up arms against the King: political, patronage, personal (often deeply personal) and financial. John was overwhelmingly responsible for this state of affairs: his crass incompetence in dealing with his magnates, his erratic behaviour and his spiteful, almost sadistic violence, this displayed in destabilising, arbitrary and unchivalrous kingship marred by persistent military failure, all fused into a programme of opposition to John and a *casus belli* in the autumn of 1214. This amalgamation of grievances did not help in settling upon a single, rallying cry of rebellion. This makes it harder to identify the rebels as a homogenous group, a task made all the harder, as we have seen in France, by the fluctuating allegiances of knights and barons. Individual bones of contention might more easily be settled by mutual self-interest than a raft of demands; some would show allegiance to the side that most threatened their own land. With the crisis of 1212, John had shown that he could be flexible and pragmatic when the occasion – and pressure – warranted, the Barnwell chronicler noting that suddenly the King 'began to conduct himself more civilly to his people and the country subsided'.[336] It was then that, crucially, John healed his differences with William Marshal to get him back on side. However, John seemed inherently incapable of sustaining such judicious and measured behaviour for any length of time and the baronial party formed into a recognisable movement.

For David Crouch, in his recent important article on paranoia and the barons in King John's reign, a real measure of the how critical matters were can be seen by the number of 'corporate baronial letters suddenly flying everywhere', arguing that 'statements of joint baronial positions and beliefs are the most evocative symbols of crisis. Things have to be really bad to get the barons to work that closely together.'[337] Already by late summer 1213, according to Ralph of Coggeshall with some exaggeration, 'nearly all the barons of England formed an association to fight for the liberty of the Church and the realm.'[338] The appeal to Church and rights of liberty was a strong one. James Holt takes a more jaundiced view of the rebels' cause. 'It was a rebellion of the aggrieved, of the failures' (the two should be taken separately and include those wronged and those who lost out on patronage and advancement); it was 'a protest against the quasi-monopoly of privilege by the King and his friends'. At its most significant it was 'a call, not to break bonds, but to impose them ... on the monarchy'.[339]

A highly vocal defence of the Church and liberties of the realm gave the opposition honourable and attractive ideals; while these provide convincing cover for more practical concerns, these concerns, no matter if self-serving in practice, had genuine connections with the liberties being fought for. Crouch says of the aristocracy that 'Even under John's ham-fisted rule it was by no means predisposed to rebel, and it took a lot to bring it to the point of resistance.'[340] Rebelling against the king, even one as undeserving as King John, was not to be undertaken lightly, and many baulked at the idea. An exact rendering of who was in the rebel ranks is no easy task, not least because of the fleeting allegiances mentioned above. By May 1215, of some 197 baronies in England, only 39 had declared for the rebels; however only a similar number openly expressed their support for the king. The majority stood to one side, wishing either to avoid becoming embroiled in the conflict or waiting to see which side gained the advantage. Thus, with the arrival of the French a year later, the number of rebel barons grew in the summer to 97 but may have dramatically dropped after John's death. The numbers in themselves do not tell the whole picture: variables are introduced by the relative wealth and strength of barons, the size of their knightly retinues and whether these retinues were largely loyal or not. This last factor is a matter of debate amongst historians. John was aware that knights might have multiple fealties (William Marshal brought the point sharply home in 1204), and sought to take advantage of this in 1212 and 1213 by summoning knights to discuss matters of the realm at a national assembly, but this has 'never earned John any credit as one of the fathers of the English Parliament'.[341]

Historians have emphasised the three major regional groupings of the barons. In the north, its chief leaders were William de Forz, the Count of Aumale, John de Lacy and William de Mowbray, and Eustace de Vescy, one of John's most implacable enemies; including Lincolnshire, this group also counted Gilbert de Gant and William d'Albini (Roger of Wendover's patron) among their number. Contemporaries labelled the rebel barons collectively as 'the Northerners', probably because the seeds of rebellion had been sown there most fruitfully with resistance to service and scutage in 1213–14, but also because animosity towards John was generally at its most bitter there. From East Anglia and Essex came the most important group: Robert Fitzwalter, Lord of Dunmow in Essex; Roger Bigod, Earl of Norfolk; Richard de Clare, Earl of Hertford; Geoffrey de Mandeville, Earl of Essex; and Robert de Vere, Earl of Oxford (whose lands were overwhelmingly held in Essex and Cambridgeshire). Given the number of earls, it is not surprising that this group provided the main leadership of the rebels; the soon to be established baronial council comprised no fewer than twelve men from this group. Less emphasis has been given to the western rebels, chief of whom were Henry de Bohun, Earl of Hereford; Giles de Braose (unsurprisingly), Bishop of Hereford; and William Marshal's oldest son, also William (who had spent time as one of John's hostages). Important recent research has redressed the neglect of this region and argued for its more significant role in the rebellion.[342] From elsewhere, the chief men of note were Saer de Quincy, the Earl of Winchester with land in Northamptonshire and Cambridge, and the baron William de Beauchamp with lands in Bedfordshire.

The leadership of the rebels has not been viewed favourably by historians: Poole says that 'the leaders do not inspire confidence'; Warren condemns
Fitzwalter, the elected leader of the rebels, as 'altogether disreputable and mis-
chievous, rescued from ignominy only by his great fiefs, and owing his leadership
to his dominating aggressiveness'. He and Eustace de Vescy were little more 'than
baronial roughnecks'.[343] The Anonymous of Béthune tells the colourful story of
how Fitzwalter's son-in-law, fellow rebel Geoffrey de Mandeville, once killed a
servant during an unseemly row taking place near to where the King was staying.
When John threatened Geoffrey with hanging, Fitzwalter challenged the King
with 'You will not hang my son-in-law! By God's body you will not!' before
threatening intervention with 200 of his knights. At Geoffrey's trial, his father-in-
law turned up with an estimated – but completely implausible – 500 knights.[344]
Fitzwalter and Saer received opprobrium for giving up Vaudreuil so easily to King
Philip in 1203, but there is uncertainty over this episode. Fitzwalter clashed with
John in 1210 over the rights to a priory which he ravaged, prompting the King
to send troops against him and he was declared an outlaw in 1212 for his part
in the assassination plot; his estates were seized and two of his castles, including Baynard's Castle in London, were destroyed. Influential as these groupings
were, regional associations were just one of the ties that bound them together.
As seen above, kinship and marriage were important, as was friendship; Robert
de Ros and Eustace de Vescy were brothers-in-law to the new King of Scotland,
Alexander II.

But most significant 'was their shared hatred of King John on account of personal wrongs done to them'.[345] These wrongs included being denied privileges
and rights; having castles, lands and offices withheld without justification; cor-
rupted justice and extortionate fines; excessive, punitive royal debt collection;
the favouritism towards foreigners; personal affronts to families and honour;
exorbitant demands for failed military campaigns; and the sheer arbitrariness of
a vindictive royal will. Underneath it all lay a deep and bitter resentment against
the monarch. The rebellion that began in England in 1215 had been a long time
in gestation, and John was its feckless father.

Magna Carta and Civil War

The peace that John and Philip had made was formulated to last until Easter 1220.
While it signified military disaster on the Continent, it freed the Angevin King
to focus on the dangerous unrest in his own country which, in turn, had itself
been stoked further by John's military failure. However, although clearly by far
and away still the dominant military force in England with his network of royal
castles and influx of mercenaries, his position was much weaker than ever before;
the domestic opposition had increasingly fused into a substantial entity with a

focus on personal opposition to the King.[346] John tried to make amends where he could with conciliatory gestures. In November he attempted to win over the Church and Langton in particular through a charter which granted freedom and swiftness in ecclesiastical and abbatial elections; the reservations he attached to it rendered the offer less generous than it seemed and Langton remained more inclined to the rebel cause than the royal one. Overtures to the Welsh princes Llewelyn and Maelgwn failed to secure them to his side. Robert de Ros and John de Lacy were sweet-talked and substantial efforts were made to retain the loyalty of barons who were at risk of wavering.

In parallel with these emollient moves were sensible, practical ones. Knights from Savary de Mauléon were due in February and from Hubert de Burgh, Seneschal of Poitou, in March. John's continental mercenaries, principally Poitevin in origin, were distributed to royal castles under the command of Falkes de Bréauté. Strengthening of garrisons meant not only that castles were well prepared for defence, but could also readily launch a force in the field in the locality. Increased garrison sizes were a clear indication of heightening tensions on the political barometer. When discussions between the opposing factions broke down in January, this garrisoning was stepped up further, as exemplified by Nottingham and Scarborough. In October, Nottingham Castle received 20 men, more were sent in late January and six knights were dispatched there in February. At Scarsborough at the end of March, the garrison comprised no fewer than 10 crossbowmen and 60 soldiers; within three weeks it had climbed to 13 crossbowmen, 72 soldiers and a minimum of 10 knights. Throughout autumn and winter the castles themselves underwent repairs and had their fabric reinforced: Northampton, Mountsorrel, Corfe, Winchester, Oxford, Hertford, Wallingford, Berkhamstead and the Tower of London all appear in the records as undergoing such work; that many of these were soon to see action reveals the necessity of such operations.[347]

The contumacious barons had also been busy. They, too, were forging and reinforcing links, aiming first at John's principal princely enemies in Wales, France and Scotland. It was not just the Northerners who had ties with the Scottish; connections went deep and wide across the barons and the royal court as Keith Stringer has shown.[348] The sixteen-year-old Alexander II came to the throne of Scotland only on 5 December 1214; he was very possibly in consideration by the barons for the title of the next king of England, four centuries before James Stuart achieved this. But the availability of Prince Louis of France, backed by the might of the newly victorious Capetian monarchy and the prospect of lands being regained in Normandy without war, proved easily the better prospect. It was this line of communication that was pursued most enthusiastically.

The baronial party is believed to have met at Bury St Edmunds in the autumn of 1214 under the guise of a pilgrimage. Here they attempted to bolster their platform of reform by appealing to Henry I's famous coronation charter, which

promised the King's commitment to adherence to rights of custom and regula-
tion of the correct intercourse between the baronage and the monarch. For some
historians such developments point to a real attempt at reform by the community
of the realm for the betterment of the crown's subjects; for others, they merely
represent a fig-leaf to cover the naked self-interest of over-mighty nobles. The
cynical interpretation is probably closer to the truth, but that should not blind us
to the programme of genuine reform that manifested itself with Magna Carta, no
matter how self-serving the motivation behind it. The precise events leading up
to Magna Carta are not known in great detail but what is has been told elsewhere.
The very nature of conspiracy and surreptitious meetings inevitably mean that
even the best-informed commentators of events can take us only so far. Even
with the 24-hour-media coverage and information overload of the twenty-first
century we still perceive only glimpses of the reality behind decisions made by
governments going to war.

In the second week of January 1215 the disaffected barons met with John in
London. They turned up in what seems to be a display of force and demanded
that John keep true to his absolution oath taken at the time of his reconciliation
with the church and uphold the ancient laws and liberties of the realm as indicated by Henry I's coronation charter. (It is not clear whether they wished to see
this reissued, or a new one drawn up.) John tallied and procrastinated, promising
to give such grave matters lengthy consideration. If true to form, he would have
initiated a series of one-to-one meetings with individual barons to cajole them
and encourage their loyalty, thereby weakening the baronial party by desertions.
Safe conduct was granted the rebels and it was agreed that their grievances would
be addressed by 26 April.

The time was used by both sides to bolster their positions with appeals to
Rome, where John, as a prized feudal supplicant, was more readily heard. John
cynically and cleverly increased his leverage here by swearing the vows of a crusader on 4 March; by taking up the cross, he could expect, by church law, even
greater papal protection. On a less spiritual propaganda level, he brought in more
mercenaries from the Continent (Savary de Mauléon had now landed in Ireland)
while the baronial party appealed to King Philip in France. Following the January
meeting, John ordered throughout the country that the oath of allegiance to him
to be pledged anew as liege homage, so that men swore to 'stand by him against
all men', which was taken by his opponents to be 'contrary to the charter'.[349]
Safe conduct letters were issued in February and April to allow for negotiations
between the King's party and the baronial one. The actions taken by John in this
period are not easily interpreted. On 13 March John sent some of his Poitevin
allies home, thanking them for their readiness to serve but telling them that they
were no longer needed. Did this mean he was feeling confident of a favourable
outcome? Or was he meeting some demands of the rebels to play for time? A
week later, letters from the pope to the Archbishop of Canterbury were on their

way to England, his support a vindication of John's papal policy. These letters set forth the 'three-fold peace terms' (*triplex forma pacis*) wholly in support of the King. The pope took to task the clergy and episcopate (including Langton) for not mediating to the King's advantage, condemned all conspiracy against the King on pain of excommunication, and praised John for submitting England to the Papacy. By the time this epistolary reinforcement had arrived in England in late April or early May, the situation had deteriorated dangerously.

Delay did not suit the barons. The circumstances approaching the pre-arranged meeting of 26 April to settle issues were increasingly discouraging. They knew in early March that they had lost any hope of papal support or even papal ambiguity and they did not wish to see the impact of this support for John grow to their disadvantage. They wished to provoke John into action that would be characteristically unmeasured and so unite baronial opposition against him. They were well aware of John's deliberate policy of procrastination and vacillation, the latter designed to throw out mixed signals and stir up uncertainty among the barons not yet fully committed against him. On 13 April another meeting was held with some of the barons at Oxford, possibly to set the agenda for the forthcoming conference. In further readiness, the barons mustered at Stamford in arms and in great force. Wendover puts their number at 'two thousand knights, other cavalry, sergeants and infantry, armed with various equipment'.[350] Wendover, displaying a rare anti-baronial moment, calls this gathering a 'pestilence', possibly affected by the hindsight of the bloodshed that was to follow. Among the five earls and 40 barons present he lists Robert Fitzwalter, Eustace de Vescy, Robert de Ros, Saer Earl of Winchester and Geoffrey de Mandeville. This show of strength was designed both as an insurance policy and to intimidate the King at the imminent meeting (although for some historians the barons' intent by this time was solely military). But this long heralded conference, arranged in January, never took place.

John permitted smaller scale talks to continue, but buoyed by his papal backing, he was confident that he, rather than the barons, could set the agenda. He sent Langton to clarify the baronial demands at Brackley, near Northampton, a day after the scheduled but cancelled meeting. The barons were guided by Langton's coherent political reform programme that held broad appeal, but as Painter has observed and as we have discussed above, there was more to it than this: 'The leaders of the baronial party were the king's personal enemies. Their chief object … was to avenge old injuries real or fancied and to secure their private rights – lands, castles, and privileges that they felt John or his predecessors had deprived them of.'[351] They set out in detail the laws and ancient customs of the kingdom that they expected to see verified and, says Wendover, 'declared that, unless the King immediately granted them and confirmed them with his own seal they would, by seizing his castles, lands and possessions, force him to give sufficient satisfaction'. On hearing these demands, John's sarcastic comment was: 'Why do these barons just not ask for my kingdom?' Sarcasm turned quickly to rage and he swore that he would not enslave himself by granting the barons their demands. He refused to be pacified by Langton or William Marshal and had his uncompromising reply sent back to the rebel camp. Their immediate response was to openly defy the King by 5 May, by breaking their homage to him (*diffidatio*), and to reaffirm Fitzwalter as their leader, but now in a clearly military capacity, as 'Marshal of the army of God and the Holy Church'. The storm had finally broken and the war had begun.

War

With occasional truces, the war was to last over two years. Its first military operation was launched by the barons against Northampton Castle directly following their act of defiance. John, in typically uncommitted fashion, had tried to step back from the brink with an appeal for arbitration on 9 May which revealed admission of wrongs that needed righting; this was immediately rejected and followed up with a royal writ two days later commanding his sheriffs to seize the lands and chattels of the rebels. While this served to strengthen the opposition against him, he countered this to some extent by granting their possessions to his own supporters, thereby encouraging royalist loyalty. The rebels meanwhile had begun their two-week siege of the major royal castle of Northampton. The castle held out under its mercenary captain Geoffrey de Martini because the barons, though arrayed splendidly for war, had no siege machinery at this early stage; they had hoped that Henry de Braybrooke, Sheriff of Northampton and predisposed to the rebel side, might have been able to persuade the garrison to surrender. But John's defensive measures had been intensified during April: Bristol, Salisbury, Norwich, Oxford and London had their defences strengthened; William Marshal had supervised the garrisoning and readiness of royal castles throughout the country; and men had been brought in from Poitou and Flanders. From the latter came Robert of Béthune, patron of the anonymous chronicler who furnishes us with such valuable information about the war. We know little of the action that took place at Northampton, but among the dead was Robert Fitzwalter's standard bearer, shot through the head with a crossbow bolt. With the resistance clearly set to hold, the rebel force moved on to the lesser fortress of Bedford Castle, held by William de Beauchamp, which did open its gates to them.

It was not a promising start, but at least the rebels were nonetheless gaining important momentum; once they had led the crossing of the Rubicon, others followed, not least many from the younger generation of sons and nephews of the great baronies, 'hoping', judges the Barnwell chronicler, 'to make a name for themselves in war'.[352] With Winchester firmly under the control of his lieutenant Savary de Mauléon, John dispatched Flemish mercenaries under his brother-in-law William Longsword, ransomed back from the French, to secure London. John was looking dominant – but that all changed in a moment: the barons beat them to the capital. When messengers reached them at Bedford with news that the citizens of London were ready to support them, they rushed down to the city where, in the evening of Sunday 17 May, they found, as they had been told, the capital gates open to them in a welcoming gesture of embrace. (The Anonymous of Béthune says that the gates were shut but unguarded; the Barnwell annalist claims that the barons made use of ladders left unattended from the refortification works.) They swiftly entered the city, set up guards at all the gates, and proceeded to the next order of business without delay: they plundered the supporters of the King and the Jews, even tearing down the houses of the latter to utilise their stones in strengthening the defences. Although the Tower held out for the time being, Baynard's Castle, the city's second major fortress, though damaged, had for its master Robert Fitzwalter; it was his faction within the city that had helped the rebels land this most critical of prizes.

The occupation of the capital was obviously an immense and prestigious fillip for the rebels. Not only had they control of London's wealth, large population and surrounding regions, especially Essex; it also provided a tremendous recruitment boost, especially among waverers. As Fitzwalter was to write later that year to his rebel cousin William d'Albini (also written as d'Albini, d'Aubigny and d'Aubigné): 'You know well what a great benefit it is to you and all of us to keep the city of London, which is our refuge; and what a shame and danger it would be to us if by our own fault we lost it.'[353] Its strategic value was as important as its economic and political ones, as it allowed the barons to ship in reinforcements safely from France. It remained in baronial hands throughout the entire conflict and was a major thorn in the loyalists' side all this time. It proved a major bargaining counter in the Magna Carta negotiations that developed soon afterwards; indeed, it could be argued that its loss forced John to agreement at Runnymede.

Immured securely in London, the rebel leadership sent out letters across the land to earls, barons and knights 'who appeared to still remain faithful to the king, though only pretending to be so'. These letters were more threatening than exhortative, as Wendover indicates: the London party 'encouraged them with threats, as they considered the safety of their property and possessions, to abandon a King who was perjured and who waged war against his barons, to unite with them to stand firm in a fight for liberties and peace; and if they declined to do so they would be treated as public enemies, with war raged against them, their castles knocked down, their homes and building burned down, their parks, warrens and orchards destroyed'.[354] This is an eternal dilemma of war: being forced to take sides. Wendover claims that the stratagem was effective, with the greater part of the undecided barons now joining them. Among this number were John de Lacy and Robert de Ros. John had wooed these to no effect; what really mattered was the military – and hence political reality – on the ground. Although Wendover is exaggerating the tide away from John, it was nonetheless real, as Coggeshall corroborates: London caused 'many daily to go over to the army of God'. John was so shaken by the loss he 'was besieged with terror and never left Windsor'.[355] Wendover claims that the King was so abandoned, the pleas of the exchequer and the sheriff's courts, central to royal administration, came to a halt throughout England, 'because there was no one to make a valuation for the King or to obey him in anything'. Comments such as this serve to demonstrate how military events and momentum rapidly have an impact on politics.

The news grew worse for John elsewhere as this momentum grew for the barons. Philip Augustus was in contact with the barons, and sent over, probably without official public sanction, the naval mercenary Eustace the Monk transporting siege equipment for the rebels, much needed if they were to break John's network of over 100 royal castles.[356] Over the next month Northampton was lost (the townsfolk rose up against the royalist garrison, killing some of them) as were Lincoln, Chester and Carlisle, these last two also defecting. In Wales and Scotland, Lleywelyn and Alexander were mobilising to capitalise on the situation. Rebellion had broken out in the south-west by the second week of May under William de Montague, William Malet and Robert Fitzpain. John sent the Earl of Salisbury at the head of a Flemish force to lift the siege of Exeter there; however, his intelligence was faulty and the city had already been taken. At Sherborne Castle, Earl William heard that the rebels were prepared to meet him in ambush with knights, sergeants and Welsh archers on the road through woods that he had to take to reach Exeter; he was told that his forces would all be captured and so he returned to the King at Winchester. Here his half-brother the monarch scorned him for his lack of resolve: 'You are not good at taking fortresses.' The Flemish were ashamed by these words. John ordered that they make a further attempt. The Anonymous of Béthune, from whom this account comes, tells us that his master Robert was stung into oratory to encourage his men for another expedition on 24 May, declaring that he would rather take a chance 'either to die or conquer, rather than retreat shamefully.'[357] Even when informed that enemy numbers had increased so that that they were now outnumbered by an improbable ten-to-one, they were not deterred. The rebel force was actually not confident in meeting the loyalist forces: on hearing of their approach they abandoned Exeter to them and fled. We shall see in the next two chapters how troops being deployed to a siege was often enough to end the siege without engagement; for this reason it was a central strategy employed throughout the conflict.

Regaining Exeter was a small victory which did little to change the seismic upheavals of May and early June. John continued to play for time, granting safe conducts for negotiations, writing to the pope for help and all the while planning to build up his military resources to crush the rebels when the time was right. With the situation so fluid, it has been argued that John also wanted time to determine which of his barons were still loyal and who had deserted him. But again we see the central flaw of John's military leadership: indecision and procrastination. His optimistic plans for recovery were always for the future rather than for the present. He responded to the loss of Normandy with an apathetic claim that it could all be recovered quickly; his continental campaigns succeeded only in retaining Gascony from the Iberian threat, not in regaining Angevin territory and hence preventing Capetian consolidation; and now he was once again failing to act decisively. Had John moved resolutely against the rebellion in its first stages, he may have prevented it gaining successes and all-important momentum. Painter suggests that he held back from easy victory 'in order to satisfy the pope and the rest of the baronage of the correctness of his conduct.'[358] However, John's failure to meet with the baronial party on 26 April only served to confirm his unreliability to the rebels; by this stage, anyway, they had long ceased to trust him. But the appeals to the pope, as with his letter mentioned above, highlight the point made about John deferring decisive action not only to a later date, but also to external agencies rather than his own. It could easily be assumed that John's sanguine front was a mask for a justifiable lack of confidence in his own ability to solve crises. Painter goes on to make the valid argument that a concentration of royal garrisons and mercenaries might easily have overwhelmed the rebels while in the open field, but London, Fitzwalter's 'refuge', changed all that. 'Clearly John had waited too long.'[359] Instead, he concentrated on reinforcing his castles and ravaging the lands of his enemies. We have already stressed the importance of London. We shall see later how John's failure to deal with it again reveals his lack of resolve and how this led to his military failure. It was John's wish to gain time that led him to Runnymede and one of the most famous events in English history: the sealing of Magna Carta.

The Magna Carta Interlude

In mid-June, John finally met the barons again face-to-face by the Thames halfway between the rebel camp at Staines and his castle at Windsor. Here they presented to him the 'Articles of the Barons', their programme of reforms, which became, with little emendation, the Great Charter. The baronial party had worked on this for months, with the help of Stephen Langton. A cerebral pragmatist, Langton was excoriated by Innocent for his involvement with the rebels and was suspended from his position as Archbishop of Canterbury by the papal legate Pandulf and summoned to Rome; he remained out of England until 1218. Three meetings between 10 and 19 June saw Magna Carta agreed upon. Central as this document is to English constitutional history (and it is still evoked in court cases today, much to the dismay of judges), it is important to keep it in its medieval context. It is not a charter of liberty in the American constitutional sense as declaimed in the Declaration of Independence, but rather a charter of liberties. The charter is dominated by financial matters relating to feudal incidents, such as reliefs, which were no longer vaguely designated to be 'reasonable' (the

interpretation of which was very different between crown and subject), but fixed
at £100 for a barony and 100 shillings for a knight's fee. The rights of widows and
minors under wardship were protected to permit volition against highest bid-
ders. Finances are also addressed in clauses dealing with debts, tariffs and consent
for scutage. The arbitrary and corrupt nature of the justice system was another
primary concern for the barons, who, as we have discussed, had long suffered
under exploitative fines used as much for political purposes as judicial ones. Two
consecutive clauses state: 'To no one will we sell, to no one will we refuse or delay
right or justice'; and, more famously, 'No freeman shall be arrested or imprisoned
or disseised or outlawed or exiled or in any way destroyed, neither will we set
forth against him, except by the lawful judgement of his peers and by the law
of the land.' Security issues are dealt with in clauses dealing with the return of
hostages and lands and castles and another calling for the removal 'from the kingdom of all foreign knights, crossbowmen, sergeants and mercenaries, who have
come with horses and arms to the detriment of the kingdom'. Both concerns
over security and patronage through the presence of foreigners holding office
and hence power is seen in the preceding clause which demands the removal
of named alien servants of the state such as Gerard Athée, Guy de Cigogné and
Geoffrey de Martigni. The conditions of the charter were designed to maximise
a broad appeal; they reveal explicitly the heart of baronial protest against John's
autocratic and capricious government.[360]

The most radical and uncompromising clause of all is the last, 61. It is also by
far the longest and aims to insure the preceding provisions. By this clause, the
barons wish to present themselves as acting for 'the community of the realm'
by establishing a council of 25 barons who will oversee the King's adherence to
the charter. That this council would be inherently anti-John was ensured by the
rebels' insistence that the members should be drawn from their own number. If
they deemed a complaint against the King justifiable and if he did not address it
satisfactorily within 40 days, this ultimate security clause gave them the power
to organise the whole land to seize his lands, castles and possessions. The lack of
any faith in John's word and promises as monarch had been enshrined in a legally
binding document. For some commentators, one King had been replaced by 25
kings. David Carpenter judges that 'the restrictions placed by Magna Carta on
the workings of kingship were unprecedented and profound'; Warren says that
John 'was virtually reduced to the role of executive officer of the law under the
supervision of a baronial committee'; while Galbraith calls the last clause 'the
most fantastic surrender of any English king to his subjects.'[361]

When negotiating with the barons, John was all urbanity and reason; but
Mathew Paris writes that when he withdrew from the talks he gave full expression to his humiliated outrage: 'he gnashed his teeth, rolled his eyes, grabbed sticks
and straws and gnawed them like a madman, or tore them into shreds with his
fingers.'[362] John did not actually sign the charter or perhaps even seal it himself,

but he did agree to it. That he did so reflects partly his relative weakness at the time after the losses listed above, especially London; however, this was a relative weakness to his earlier position, as John was still the leading military force in the land. More typically, he was again putting off a decisive reckoning, confidently and correctly expecting the pope to declare the document null and void, agreed to under duress and altogether illegal. Almost ironically, a King whose reign was characterised by arbitrary law was appealing to legal justification of his own position. Again, John's duplicity is revealed. As Holt says, 'Throughout, even when he sealed Magna Carta, John had not the slightest intention of giving in or permanently abandoning the powers which the Angevin kings had come to enjoy.'[363] John reluctantly acquiesced to the charter because he never intended to heed it. But in his acquiescence he paid the high personal price in abasing himself before his barons.

Not that the barons ever believed that John was going to turn over a new leaf and become the model of a constitutional monarch. They did not trust him before and they did not trust him now. Most protagonists on both sides realised that what had occurred at Runnymede was little more than a prolonged truce. Some of the barons themselves paid little attention to the charter and began plundering royal lands; others took recourse to this action because the King was dragging his feet in implementing the restitution of land, castles and property to them as the charter stipulated he should. Many southern barons planned gathering at a tournament in Stamford on 6 July to 'celebrate the peace'; such meetings were well known to be mustering points for armies. They changed the venue and date to a week later back in Staines as they feared venturing too far from the capital. (Here, the Tower of London was placed under the supervision of Archbishop Langton.) For the barons involved, it allowed them practice in war games and strategies as well as giving them the excuse to bear arms. Neither side relaxed their guard after Magna Carta; rather, they prepared for the next round of the conflict. Elsewhere, royal officials were given a hard time in performance of their duties and barons fortified their castles (including those recently received back from the King), and even built new ones.

John's faith in his papal ally and overlord was rewarded in the technical sense, but not a practical one. In August, Innocent III annulled Magna Carta in the strongest terms, excommunicated 30 leading rebels and had Langton suspended. But the reality of the situation was dictated by raw power on the ground and not by spiritual vindication; the latter was useful but it was never going to be decisive. For all that John's putative 'masterstroke' in submitting to the Papacy has been lauded for its Machiavellian and cynical creativeness, it did very little indeed in bringing him any worthwhile success in the ensuing conflict. John placed too much emphasis on papal support, but that did not mean he failed to make more practical preparations from overseas. While his castles were readied for immediate action, abroad troops were being raised in Aquitaine and Flanders, where the leading mercenary captain Hugh de Boves was active. He even tried to win Philip Augustus over by making extravagant promises, but as the Barnwell annalist so succinctly put it, 'others had been to him beforehand'.[364]

The temperature rose precipitately in mid-August. The barons were refusing the charter condition for the return of London to the King by the 15th, and the King refused to meet the barons at a pre-arranged meeting in Oxford on the 16th, claiming that he had been badly treated and was in personal danger from them. Episcopal interventions for the Papacy failed to bring the sides any closer together, and the pope's annulment of 24 August and the excommunications that followed shortly for their leaders and the whole of London served only to remind the barons that they had to rely on their own devices. There was no longer any middle ground: the choice was between war and submission. They chose war. Their talks with Prince Louis of France intensified.

The Return to War

All sides could smell war in the air, coming with the change of season in September. John placed his family in the secure royal stronghold of Corfe Castle. He meanwhile sailed at the end of the month to the impressive fortress that is Dover Castle where he awaited Hugh de Boves and his army from the continent: Poitevins, Flemings, Brabantines and Gascons were all expected. From here he could also check any potential threat from France and restrict access to London from the east. Rochester Castle was to play an important role in this strategy. Sporadic military operations broke out, a stuttering start to renewed hostilities. Rebel forces besieged Oxford while some of the London garrison headed eastwards to Ospring in Kent to block any potential advance on the capital by John. The king, hearing of their advance while at Canterbury, retreated hastily to Dover; the barons, no less fearful, made for Rochester. The Anonymous of Béthune sarcastically comments that thus both sides were vanquished without a blow being struck. John suffered a major setback on 26 September when Hugh de Boves' large contingent of reinforcements were drowned in a channel storm; countless bodies, including that of the leader, were swept up onto the beaches of the south coast. Much treasure and coinage, so necessary for the payment of the royal mercenaries, went down with the ships. The survivors struggled into Dover.

On 2 October, John instructed his brother, Earl William of Salisbury, to visit ten royal castles and form a field army from their garrisons, while his leading mercenary captain, Falkes de Bréauté, was sent on 4 October to take command of the midlands and the west. Along with William Marshal, John relied heavily on these two commanders to lead military operations. William, illegitimate son of Henry II and the Earl of Salisbury, was an intelligent and capable soldier with long experience in serving John: commander of the royal fleet, he had led the naval victory at Damme and fought bravely at Bouvines where he had been captured and ransomed. Warren says that he 'was the only one of the greater barons with whom John was on terms of back-slapping intimacy'.[365] John would often send him casks of wine and help him out with his gambling losses (he was a card partner of the King). John felt comfortable with his half-brother, a blood relation whose illegitimacy rendered him, in theory at least, less of a threat. Falkes de Bréauté played a central military role throughout the conflict. A veteran mercenary leader, capable of raising large, professional forces for service in his master's armies, Falkes raised himself to a position of significant political power and influence. The bastard son of a Norman knight, he was perhaps John's most loyal commander; it was a relationship not built on respect but on the surer foundations of money and reward. He accumulated important castles in the southern midlands from Oxford to the borders of East Anglia and a favourable marriage to a rich widow. He also accumulated a reputation for brutality when Sheriff of Glamorgan (one of several shrievalties) a characteristic which seems to have marked his youth; his first name is reputed to derive from a scythe with which he had slain a knight. His contemporary reputation and popularity was low: a bastard foreigner who had worked his way up to be a favourite of the King, his ruthless plundering of abbeys served only to ensure that the monastic writers gave him a terrible obituary for posterity. He will be a regular companion in our story of the war.[366]

The focus of the struggle was, for the time being at least, in the south-east corner of England. With the rebel leadership moving tentatively eastwards from London, and John in Dover with his surviving reinforcements from the continent. With both sides poised to engage each other bloodily and dramatically at Rochester, it is perhaps an opportune moment to assess the state of play. The King held the better hand with a number of 'powerful advantages'.[367] Turner points out how the loyal barons, such as William Marshal and Ranulf of Chester, were the only ones who could put major feudal forces into the field. This was not always entirely reassuring for John, though, who held deep suspicions of both men. At the same time the Marcher lords had to consider the irruptions of the Welsh under Llewelyn and other princes, and therefore had to look west as well as east. Royalists had to look north, too: like, the Welsh, the Scots also entered into alliance with the rebels, providing important military assets to them that cannot be overlooked. Royalist earls such as those of Warenne (Surrey) and Arundel (Sussex) owned important castles not just in the south and East Anglia, but also in the north. John's royal coffers never seemed to empty to the point where he would fail to employ mercenaries in strength; the machinery of royal government, though creaking under the pressures of war, together with control of the countryside ensured that the influx of funds to the royal cause continued to a considerable degree. The military organisation of the realm also meant that the King could afford the engineers and costly equipment and machinery necessary for siege warfare.

The role of castles and town was crucial in medieval warfare, but in this one especially.[368] Of 209 castles identified as being directly involved in the struggles, 72 were royal and, significantly, fourteen were episcopal; Rochester was the one remaining episcopal castle not under John's control. Diplomatically, the Church and Papacy were on the King's side, even if John considered Archbishop Langton a bare-faced traitor. The only leading ecclesiastic on the rebel side was Giles de Braose, Bishop of Hereford. The military strength this support afforded the royal cause came not just in castles but also in knightly quotas. By September 1215, all the royal castles except Hertford, Bedford, Carlisle and Colchester, and possibly York and Rockingham, were firmly in John's command, with garrisons captained by steadfast loyalists. Of the 123 baronial castles involved, 51 were owned by loyal barons; 7 held by neutral barons were in John's hands; and 12 rebel castles were under the supervision of royal constables. This left the rebel barons with only 53 castles: they were outnumbered three-to-one on this most telling of military assessments. The royal castles were also more impressive: perhaps fewer than half the rebel castles were constructed in stone, with only some 20 being tellingly redoubtable, compared to about 50 of the royal castles.

The loyal barons also held not just more but better castles.[369] That the stronger barons tended to remain loyal also meant greater manpower resources. They could impose scutage on their own vassals and employ professional soldiers to match those in the service of the Marcher lords. These combined with John's mercenaries to form a fighting force of considerable experience. By comparison, relatively few baronial knights could be termed veterans; of the leadership, only Saer de Quincy, William d'Albini, Roger de Crecy, Robert de Ros, William de Mowbray and Robert Fitzwalter were tried and tested campaigners. At this stage it was, as one historian has called it, 'a war of professionals against amateurs'.[370] No wonder the rebels looked abroad for powerful allies.

In Prince Louis, they found one. Channels of communication had long been open in one capacity or the other with the Capetian court. Philip Augustus might have sent surreptitious help, but, given the situation with the Church and, to a lesser extent, his post-Bouvines truce with John, he could not be seen to do so overtly. His son, however, offered an alternative strategy. The King could make a show of disapproval of the Prince's involvement in the war, while tacitly encouraging it. It is even possible that he directed the rebel leadership to his son. Given the seriousness of the situation described above, the rebels called directly on Louis to assist them in September; having broken allegiance with their own king, they sought a new one. Louis, restless, ambitious and war-like, responded positively. A fig leaf of justification was required to warrant Louis' newly discovered claim for the English throne. He proffered two. The first was a hereditary one through his wife, Blanche of Castile, granddaughter of Henry II; as far as successionary claims went, this was a blatant case of queue-jumping. The other was due to a putative, but unverified, condemnation of

John in the French court following the murder of Arthur of Brittany; this was entirely disingenuous: as we have seen in Philip's pseudo-feudal justification for expropriating Normandy from John, the Capetians, unlike the Papacy, had no overlordship of England. Both claims were hopeful and unrealistic and given purely for form's sake. The barons had their *jus ad bellum*, and now Louis could pretend that he had his.

In making this appeal to a foreign Prince to rule over England, the rebels lost much of their moral cause and damaged their broadly-based programme of reform; the appeal, believes one leading historian, 'proved that the rebel barons were a faction, no longer representative of the community of the realm, a propaganda plus for King John'.[371] While this statement is undoubtedly true, it was clearly the right course of action for the rebels to take; it did much to transform their position. A point not often made is that a period of political uncertainty beckoned in the future even without the current civil strife. John's heir to the throne was the seven-year-old Henry. This meant a minority, and a minority meant aggressive vying for position and influence as regent and royal advisers. For some who feared losing out in this scramble, the prospect of a foreign Prince, in all likelihood ruling from a distance in Paris, was a preferable option. And there was the added bonus of an early departure from the scene by John. Without Louis, the rebels' military position was relatively weak. It might be argued that they had previously held the moral high ground and that they had derived propaganda value from this. Little good did it do them. While such things were important and seen to be such by contemporaries, they were only of real practical value if they produced tangible gains with men on the ground and increases in military materiel. These were to come with Louis, and what a difference they made to the course of the war. While a final agreement between the two parties was being negotiated, Louis made his preparations.

War across the Land

The hesitant atmosphere of conflict erupted into full warfare with the epic siege of Rochester in mid October. Rochester lay on the road between London and Dover. Its strategic importance came from its ability to hinder – or aid – communications with the continent, guard the mouth of the channel, and threaten London.[372] On 11 October, Reginald of Cornhill, who was holding the castle for Stephen Langton, allowed in a band of rebel knights under William d'Albini. D'Albini, an experienced war leader and one of the baronial 25, was Wendover's patron at Belvoir, so it is not surprising that the midlands chronicler furnishes us with the most detailed account of the siege. Robert de Béthune had also just come over to John at Dover, and so the Anonymous also provides us with a directly contemporary account involved in the heart of the action.

D'Albini had heeded the calls from the rebels in London to come south from his stronghold in Leicestershire and give assistance. Having provisioned his Castle Belvoir there with arms, victuals and loyal men he made for the capital and was received warmly. They told him of their plan to block the Dover to London road by securing Rochester Castle. Their priority was, as Fitzwalter had made clear, keeping London safe. To Rochester they dispatched a force of selected men under d'Albini's command. When Cornhill let him in, he found the castle so woefully lacking in all things necessary to withstand an investiture that, under pressure from his men, he was forced to consider whether to abandon the castle altogether. However, he rallied his men, who comprised 95 knights and 45 sergeants, to avoid the shame of deserting their duty; they went through the town and took what they could into the castle. The precariousness of their frontline position and the proximity of royalist forces meant that they dared not venture outside the town to collect supplies from the surrounding area. Doing so might have left them exposed to ambush from an advance royalist force; John himself was at the town two days later.

Robert of Béthune warned John that he underestimated the enemy 'if you go to fight them with such a small force'. John was unconcerned, replying 'I know them too well; they are nothing to be made much of or feared.' It is unlikely that John was undermanned, given the numbers of men who had just crossed the channel; John had been waiting for these before taking any major actions, and he could react to the new developments in Rochester in force. The reinforcements included large numbers of crossbowmen, essential for the successful prosecution of siege warfare. Wendover is more realistic in saying that the King brought a multitude with him, even though he would, naturally, wish to emphasise the scale of opposition faced by his patron.

The Barnwell annalist and Ralph of Coggeshall tell us of John's first objective: the destruction of the bridge over the Medway. This was a priority as it would greatly hinder reinforcements from London coming to relieve the siege. The threat of a relief force falling upon a besieger's camp was always to the forefront of a besieging commander's mind; the events at Mirebeau in 1202 were repeated throughout the Middle Ages and we will be seeing them again at Lincoln in 1217. John sent a group of men in boats to row under the bridge and set fire to it from below, which they achieved despite being fiercely assaulted by Robert Fitzwalter's group of 60 knights, sergeants and crossbowmen guarding the crossing. The defenders put out the flames and wounded and killed many of the attackers, many of whom drowned. It would appear that immediately following this, Fitzwalter returned to London. A second assault on the bridge brought it down.

John now shifted his focus to the town. The Anonymous says that the citizens 'made a great show of defending themselves' on the town walls. But, seeing the extent of John's siege preparations, their morale quickly collapsed and they abandoned the battlements in such haste that the garrison had to make rapidly for the refuge of the castle. John's troops poured through the gates into the town, where the King took up comfortable lodgings. The siege was pressed home intensely and unrelentingly. On 14 October John ordered all the smiths in Canterbury to work around the clock to make pickaxes which were to be delivered to him as soon as they were made. Reinforcements arrived daily. Robert of Béthune consulted with the King and both sent letters to Robert's brother, William, who hurried from Flanders to join them at the siege, as did Gautiers Bertaut with 100 knights. It would be a mistake to think of these reinforcements being deployed for the sole purpose of taking the castle: many would have been there to form an outer line of defence against an attack; and others were involved in foraging to meet the needs of the ever-growing royal army. To achieve this last purpose, the King's men ravaged Kent and plundered Rochester. The sheer weight of numbers would also hopefully intimidate the rebels and precipitate a collapse in resistance; as Wendover writes, the King's men were so numerous 'it struck fear and horror in all who beheld them.' All the while the King pounded the walls of the castle with his petraries and other siege machines, so that the garrison was constantly bombarded by a continuous barrage of stones and other weapons; underground, the pickaxes were steadily doing their work, digging their way to the walls.

Rochester was a major fortress, constructed from stone and with strong high walls twelve feet thick; internally it had a dividing wall so that the castle could be defended even if one half of it fell. The rebels knew, however, that faced with such a concentration of the King's military forces, it could stand only for a limited time. They hoped that the garrison would resist long enough for reinforcements to come to its aid from France. The Anonymous places the de Quincy diplomatic mission to Louis at this juncture; Louis was in the process of sending out the call across France for knights to fight in England and his call was being heeded. However, it was feared that Rochester could not buy enough time for this outcome, and so the barons planned their own relief force. This was probably the reason why Fitzwalter had hurried back to London after the bridge action. Wendover relates how this was also the fulfilment of a solemn pledge taken by the barons, who had sworn on the gospels to come to d'Albini's aid should Rochester be besieged. On 26 October, a large force (Barnwell exaggeratedly inflates their number to 700 knights) under the restless command of Fitzwalter headed out for Rochester. It is not clear if this was a genuine attempt at relieving the castle through a military engagement; the greater likelihood is that by sending out a force the rebels hoped that John, not known for his personal bravery and resolve on the battlefield, would turn tail and run, as he had done before. Certainly, the relief force itself displayed a remarkable lack of resolve. On reaching Dartford, they promptly turned back themselves and withdrew to the safety of London. Wendover cannot conceal his sarcasm at this abject failure to assist his patron: 'although only a mild south wind was blowing in their faces, which generally does not trouble anyone, they retreated as if beaten back by swords.' Back in the safety of the 'strongly fortified capital', they amused themselves with gambling, drinking the best wines and indulging in all manner of vices, while their comrades in Rochester faced death and endured all kinds of misery. The Barnwell annalist offers a more plausible reason: they had learned of the size of John's army positioned against them. (The royal army would have been augmented further in the time between Fitzwalter's departure from Rochester and his arrival back at Dartford.) Barnwell also suggests that they planned a further relief operation for the very end of November. This was certainly in the expectation of French troops arriving. The lengthy delay was an admission of their inability to operate effectively without Louis' help. Simultaneously, they made approaches to the King for a form of settlement, in all likelihood to gain time before a French rescue. John rebutted their approaches; he sensed victory.

D'Albini's garrison was left to fend for itself. Their resistance was nothing short of heroic. The Barnwell annalist stirringly claims that 'living memory does not recall any siege so urgently undertaken and so bravely resisted.' John went from strength to strength. With the relief force scurrying back to London, royal troops were free to roam across the countryside and forage at will. His army would be well fed while the garrison saw their meagre and hastily gathered provisions dwindle daily. Constant pressure was applied: incessant barrages from five large siege engines, crossbowmen and archers combined with repeated assaults to prevent the garrison getting any rest, day or night. While the King's large forces allowed for rotation of troops in combat, the hard-pressed garrison was always in action or on stand-by, manning and defending the curtain wall. This prolonged exposure to direct combat over six weeks was exhausting both mentally and physically. They were being ground down.

One motivation for the garrison holding out was fear of John. We have seen Philip Augustus successfully employ fear as a weapon against Rouen in 1204; it worked there because the French King could be trusted to keep his word on clemency if the city submitted. No such trust could be placed in John: Wendover says that the rebels endured their situation because they 'sought to delay their own destruction for they greatly feared the cruelty of the king'. They could only have been more determined to resist when, in an effort to stretch out their meagre supplies, they ejected their wounded and sick from the castle; according to the Barnwell chronicler, John had their hands and feet cut off.

The dogged defence inflicted serious casualties among John's troops. When mines brought down a large section of the curtain wall, John's men stormed the breach and forced the rebels to conduct a frantic, fighting retreat into the great tower. Such was the onslaught royalist troops forced their way in to this last stronghold, only to be repulsed and the tower cleared of attackers. The garrison was in such straits for lack of food it consumed horses; the knights were even driven to the extreme recourse of eating their destriers, their hugely valuable trained warhorses.

And still the onslaught continued. John issued his famous order to his justiciar to dispatch urgently 40 fat pigs to Rochester. These were not primarily to feed the troops but to assist the firing of the wooden props in the tunnel support-ing the excavated foundations of the south-western tower.[373] When the miners brought down the corner of the tower, the crisis reached its climax. D'Albini and his men continued to fight desperately from within the castle, but knew that any future resistance would be short-lived. Wendover says that they were in fact starved out and that they considered 'it would be a disgrace to die of hunger when they had not been overcome by arms'; while their provisions had failed them, the greater danger was from a storm assault in the castle that would put their lives in immediate peril. On 30 November, they surrendered.

A foremost castellologist has called the siege 'one of the greatest operations in England up to that time'.[374] Turner has argued that John's operation at Rochester shows him to be a competent military leader deserving of a positive reappraisal of his military reputation.[375] It is certainly true that John demonstrated here the determination and single-mindedness that he was occasionally capable of; but such displays were far too infrequent to mark him out as a consistently competent general. Yes, the organisation of his forces was impressive and put to excellent effect and the positive side of his military balance sheet boasts some memora-ble victories – Mirebeau, Damme, and now Rochester – but none of these had a truly lasting impact, unlike his failures on the continent. (Rochester did not remain in royalist hands for long.) Rochester was a formidably strong castle, but arraigned against it were the forces of a kingdom, whose men were well provisioned and reinforced, while the garrison was isolated and weakened by exhaustion and hunger. If John had built on this success by moving on to take London, then his military reputation would indeed merit reassessment; instead, as we shall see shortly, he embarked on another of his destructive *chevauchées* across the country. The Barnwell annalist commented that after Rochester, 'few cared to put their trust in castles', a judgement that some historians have been quick to pick up on. The truth was, in fact, that they continued to do just this; the whole war was going to continue as it had begun, centred on castles.

D'Albini's men emerged from the dust of the castle weakened but largely intact. Only one of his knights had been killed, the victim of an arrow; arrows and crossbow bolts were the most common cause of death at sieges.[376] John had a gibbet erected and ordered that the entire garrison be hanged, but he was talked out of this extreme action, hanging only some of the crossbowmen. (The Barnwell annalist believes that only one crossbowmen was hanged: someone who had served with John in his youth.) D'Albini and his knights escaped the same fate due to the intercession of John's calmer and more measured commander, Savary de Mauléon. Savary had been captured by John at Mirebeau in 1202, but served him loyally on his release, defending Niort stoutly against Philip Augustus in 1206 when other castellans defected to the French. Whereas John, enraged by the length of the siege at Rochester, its cost in blood and treasure, and, most of all, the affront of such open rebellion defiance, wished to spread terror among rebel resistance elsewhere, Savary cautioned otherwise:

> My lord king, our war is not yet over; therefore you ought carefully to consider how the fortunes of war may turn; for if you now order us to hang these men, the barons, our enemies, will perhaps by a similar event take me or the nobles of your army, and, following your example, hang us. Therefore do not let this happen, for in such a case no one will fight in your cause.[377]

Savary's self-interested pragmatism tempered John's bloodlust. Acts of terror had their place in medieval warfare, but the nature of this civil war was not so bitter as in other conflicts: divided families could understand differences of allegiances, and even royalists could not fail to appreciate the grievances against the King. Other counsels for clemency for the same reason are occasionally depicted in medieval chronicles. In 1347, having spent almost a year besieging Calais, Edward III was in a bloody mood on taking the town and wanted the defeated garrison executed; Sir Walter Mauny successfully advised him against this for the same reason given by Savary: 'My lord, you may well be mistaken, and you are setting a bad example for us. Suppose one day you send us to defend one of your fortresses; we should go less cheerfully if you have these people put to death, for they would do the same to us if they had the chance.'[378] D'Albini and his knights, who included William of Lancaster, Osbert Gyffard, William d'Einford and others named by Wendover, were imprisoned in Corfe Castle; others, such as Thomas de Melutan, Richard Gifford and Thomas of Lincoln ended up in Nottingham. John rewarded his troops by handing over to them the sergeants for ransoms. As Wendover concludes, 'By these misfortunes the cause of the barons was much weakened.'

Military activity had occurred elsewhere in the south-east, but we have only snippets of information for this. Royalist gains elsewhere include the slighting of Mountfitchet Castle in Stansted and the capitulation of a number of castles. The Anonymous of Béthune relates how his lord persuaded the Tonbridge garrison to hand over Gilbert de Clare's castle to him. Here we see a common example of castle-taking: not by force, but by negotiation. Robert warned the garrison that when John had finished at Rochester, which would be very soon, his army would make for Tonbridge and that the rebel force in London would not come to its aid. The garrison and Robert came to an agreement by which the besieged were allowed to send a messenger to London; if no help would be forthcoming from the capital, the castle would be handed over peacefully. This is what transpired, and on 28 November Robert placed his troops inside.[379] A similar agreement left William de Beauchamp's Bedford Castle in de Bréauté's hands on the same day, when Hanslope (Castlethorpe) fell to him, too. He, Bréauté and the chamberlain Geoffrey de Neville roamed freely across much of the eastern midlands.

The inability to help beleaguered rebel garrisons could only serve to under-mine the resistance of such men everywhere. John was building up a dangerous momentum in the south-east that threatened to crush the opposition there. The baronial party was more secure in the north and the east as long as John was contained in the south. Although Llywylyn's forces in Wales were holding down the forces of Ranulf of Chester and William Marshal, at the same time these earls were preventing the Welsh from making incursions into England. In the north, the teenaged Scottish king, Alexander II, failed to take the border town of Norham. But John's army was growing daily; he even had to appoint a Templar named Brother Roger whose sole purpose was to hand out funds and expenses to troops arriving from the continent. No wonder the barons appealed to Louis with the line, 'if only he would pack his clothes and come, they would give him the kingdom and make him their lord.'[380]

Negotiations between the baronial diplomatic mission and Louis entered their final phase. Saer de Quincy probably led these discussions from the English side: he was brother-in-law to Simon de Montfort, a close friend of Louis with whom he had shared the dangers of the Albigensian crusade. The barons decisively agreed not to hold any fiefs from John and made homage to Louis as their lord. The talks nearly broke down when Philip Augustus heard of the new round of negotiations between the barons and John that had begun on 9 November. If these discussions did take place, they may have been limited to Rochester Castle and the fate of its garrison. The baronial party in France did not know if this news was genuine, or whether John was up to some diplomatic skulduggery attempting to disrupt the talks. This was a perfectly reasonable suspicion: both the English and French kings had delved into the world of falsified intelligence to implicate others into their machiavellian schemes.[381] Amid accusations of treacherous behaviour, the baronial party agreed to a guarantee by sending over 24 of their sons to France as hostages. As was usual in such cases, the hostages were well cared for in comfort-able conditions. The crown was now Louis' for the taking. Practicalities of an actual coronation – there was no archbishop to perform the ceremony and hence confer spiritual authority, and there was no prospect of papal blessing when John was Innocent's vassal – were left for a later date. The first and most important step remained military success. Louis now committed himself to the baronial side and to the enterprise of England. The French had joined the war.

The first contingent of French forces had landed at the Orwell estuary by the start of December. Just as the rebel tide was at a low ebb, it now turned, carrying on it the firm hope of victory. Numbers are uncertain – perhaps 140 knights with their retinues and an unlikely total force, according to Coggeshall, of 7000 – but a sizeable division was able to make its way into London.

Louis had emulated William the Conqueror in promising followers land in England, an enticing prospect to landless younger knights. One of their leaders was the unflatteringly named William Ratsfoot.[382] Their impact was, for the time being, entirely psychological, boosting morale. A French commitment had been made, with Louis promising to arrive with his main force in the new year. The French brought with them experienced, professional soldiers to match John's; they would bring not just men, but money, supplies and vital siege equipment. But until then, the French stayed in London over winter, moaning about English beer but otherwise living comfortably and safely.

John, on the other hand, took the war to his enemies across the land with sword and fire. He wished to keep his momentum going and to make sufficient headway to render further French intervention pointless after Christmas. John travelled through Essex, Surrey and Hampshire in the first half of December, checking in on Windsor before holding a major war council in St Albans between 18 and 20 December, where the rebels were publicly proclaimed as excommunicants. Wendover (whose mother house was St Albans) writes that John 'retired with a few of his advisers into the cloister and devised plans for overcoming his enemies', adding, notably, that he also wished to address the question of 'how he might find pay for the foreigners fighting under him'.[383] The two were, of course, intimately linked. John took the opportunity to assess the strength of his resources and how they should be disposed. A document survives from this occasion which Stephen Church has identified as the earliest English muster roll.[384] This gives us some idea of the number of knights in John's service. It lists 47 household knights of the King, and 375 other knights. Very few of the latter were English; most were from the Low Countries. The conflict was never simply a matter of English against the French. In fact, Wendover suggests that one main reason for the crown being offered to Louis was because he was suzerain of so many of John's troops. Church estimates this to represent half the number of knights available to John: at a total of 800 knights, easily outmatching the knights at the barons' disposal.

A clear strategy was determined upon at St Albans and rapidly implemented.[385] John split his army into two. One, under the command of Earl William of Salisbury, supported by Falkes de Bréauté, Savary de Mauléon, William Brewer (or Gerard de Sooteghem) and the Brabantine Walter le Buck, was to conduct operations in the south while keeping the rebels pinned down in London; the other, led by the King, was to march north 'to ravage', says Wendover, 'the whole country by fire and sword'. This strategy deliberately left London to one side in the hope that by crushing resistance throughout the rest of the realm, the capital would feel its isolation and surrender. The flaw of this was that the richest city in the land stood defiant, and not just symbolically as it could absorb an influx of foreign troops to match John, provide resources and funds, and therefore continue the resistance against him. Was it wise to leave London? Even with hindsight it is not easy to judge the wisdom of John's plan. A siege of London would have been lengthy, costly and dangerous. We can not claim with any certainty to know in detail the actual relative strengths of the armies now that the French were arriving; even after John's death William Marshal and the royalists still made no move on the capital. A ravaging campaign made good sense in many ways. It was a chance to reassert the King's power over the country and thus re-establish the machinery of governance which would bring in the revenues to fund his military machine; the plundering itself would reward his mercenaries and keep them sweet; the rebels' resolve would be undermined by the catastrophic economic damage done to their estates; it carried few direct risks; and wavering barons and knights might be dissuaded from joining in with an inactive force stuck in a city in the south-east. But for all the chroniclers' mocking of the rebel forces staying holed up in the capital and not venturing forth, their strategy might be vindicated by the fact that in perhaps making London too strong for John to take, they successfully gained the time necessary for French reinforcements to appear on the scene; without these reinforcements, they had little chance of victory. This arguably should have made the capital a priority objective for John. A strong investiture may have decided the war. Warren's assessment seems a judicious one: John's decision was 'a typical example of his reluctance to commit himself to decisive military action: the rebellion would have collapsed had London been captured. The rebel head-quarters there were the nettle that he should have grasped and uprooted without flinching ... One cannot help feeling that a Richard or a Philip would have gone straight for the hardest task and sought a decisive victory.'[386] This perceptive commentary encapsulates a major weakness of John as a war leader: going for the easy success. He had missed his opportunity in 1215, before the French started to arrive. If London had fallen, it is unlikely that there would have been any rebellion left for Louis to support, and no reasonable prospect of an English crown for the French Prince.

John led his army from St Albans on the evening of 20 December to unleash devastation across his own kingdom and put fear into the hearts of his own people. Christmas 1215 ushered in an eighteen-month period of warfare that was the worst England had experienced since the anarchy of King Stephen's reign over half a century before.[387] The new year would see civil war become a national one. The French were coming.

6

THE INVASION OF ENGLAND, 1216

Fire and Sword

John and his advisers had made their war plans at St Albans just a few days before Christmas. The new year saw the plans executed with maximum force. When the King divided his army into two and set his men loose on his land, he knew that he had to achieve significant military gains, even victory, before Louis set out from France with his main force to transform the rebels' position. Although the plan was arguably flawed – the rebel stronghold of London was deliberately left until a later date in the hope that a victorious military expedition would leave it isolated and ready for surrender – the winter campaign of 1215/16 witnessed John demonstrating urgent and focused energy against his enemies, for which some historians have praised him. The campaign revealed the destructive power of the King as nothing had before.

While John made his way northward with as many as 400 knights (predominantly Flemish), his southern army made its move in the south-east. This force was under experienced leadership. William Longsword, Earl of Salisbury and John's half-brother, had been released from captivity in France following his capture at Bouvines, by means of a prisoner exchange with the high-ranking Robert de Dreux. Although he had failed to keep London out of rebel hands, he had chased the rebels away from Exeter in the south-west. With him was the notorious mercenary commander Falkes de Bréauté, a loyal (and well-paid) officer of John and heartily detested by the barons. Successful in his operations the preceding autumn, his approach to warfare was as ruthless as it was coldly professional. Accompanying them were Savary de Mauléon and the mercenary Walter Buck. Their orders were to contain the main rebel force in London, deprive them of supplies and reassert royal authority outside to the immediate north and east of the capital. They followed their orders with efficiency and, even though resistance was limited, brutality.

While the garrisons of Windsor, Hertford and Berkhamstead patrolled close to London, attempting to ensure that no troops came out and no supplies went in, Salisbury's and de Bréauté's forces ravaged and quickly subdued Essex, Hertfordshire, Middlesex, Huntingdon and Cambridgeshire by mid-January, and drove the rebels at Bury St Edmund's back to a temporary refuge on the Isle of Ely. The chronicles speak of serious destruction and brutality: everywhere the royalist forces seized booty, forced money tributes from towns and people and burned the barons' estates. The inhabitants of London could see – as the marauding soldiers meant them to – the smoke from burning land around the capital; a suburb was attacked. The retreating rebel forces were pursued to Ely and the city sacked and put to fire. Ralph of Coggeshall wrote: '[T]hey made great slaughter, as they did everywhere they went, sparing neither age, nor sex, nor condition, nor the clergy.'[388] The Earl of Salisbury managed to afford the women of the city some protection from Walter Buck's rampaging Brabançon mercenaries, but Coggeshall reports how people were horribly tortured to give up their valuables and reveal where they had been hidden. Abbot Ralph had no sympathy with the soldiers; they had just raided his Cistercian monastery and seized 22 horses from his stables. The Barnwell chronicler informs us that those who could fled to London, an indication that the royalist blockade was not secure.[389]

Meanwhile, John's larger expedition wreaked greater havoc.[390] He left St Albans with Philip d'Albini, John Marshal and continental commanders with Flemish troops and crossbowmen, 'lawless people who neither feared God nor respected man'.[391] Resting on the first night at Dunstable, he advanced through Northampton and Rockingham, reaching Nottingham by Christmas Eve: 'destroying everything in his way, he gave a miserable spectacle to all who saw it'.[392] No wonder one chronicler wrote that John spent Christmas Day at Nottingham Castle 'not in the usual fashion but as one on the warpath'.[393] On hearing of the King's approach with large forces, castellans abandoned their rebel strongholds and fled to safety, hastily leaving their provisions behind to the advantage of the advancing royalists. This was common practice of those in charge of castles when, as here, they faced clearly unfavourable odds with little or no prospect of relief from their own side if besieged.[394] However, this was often a fine judgement to make. Castellans who too readily gave up their castles might be suspected of treason or cowardice and be punished accordingly: decapitation for capitulation. This was the case at Touques in 1417 when a leading citizen was beheaded for surrendering the town too swiftly, even though help was not on its way (even the messenger was hung for being the bearer of this bad news).

John's next target was Belvoir Castle. This is where Roger of Wendover's priory stood. Its lord, William d'Albini, was languishing in the prison of Corfe castle since his capture at Rochester. From the nearby manor of Langar, John sent messengers to the castle, held by William's son Nicholas d'Albini and two of his knights, William of Studham and Hugh de Charneles. The message was simple: surrender the castle on the first time of asking or their lord would be starved to death, a 'digraceful' and 'ignominious' way to die, says Wendover. The defending knights took counsel with one another, deciding that as they could not hold out, they were better to lose their castle rather than master, as opposed to both if they resisted. Nicholas and Hugh took the keys of the castle to John at Langar. The following day John went to Belvoir and placed it under the charge of two Poitevin brothers, the mercenaries Geoffey and Oliver de Buteville, and then moved northwards to Newark. This was an important gain for John: as part of a royal castle network with Lincoln, Nottingham, Newark and Sleaford it provided him with essential military assets in a strategically vital area: the last stages of the war were to be played out here the following year. From Newark John ordered Roger of Clifford to take Geoffrey de Mandeville's castle at Hanley in Warwickshire and for Thomas of Eadington to destroy Tamworth in Staffordshire. Painter believes that 'in all probability these were the only baronial castles left to the west of the king's line of march with the possible exception of Mountsorrel.'[395] It is tempting to say that the year had ended well for John: the rebels were not daring to stand before him and his army was progressing equally well further south. But the rebels still held London in the south and there was unfinished business in the north.

By 1 January John was in Doncaster. He was taking the war against the northern barons and their chief ally in the region, the teenaged King Alexander II of Scotland. In the time honoured tradition of Scottish kings, Alexander had taken advantage of an English king's problem to add to his discomfiture. When John engaged in open war with his barons in the previous autumn, Alexander had promptly moved south into Northumbria and lain siege to Norham, close to the pivotal border town of Berwick, on 19 October.[396] Three days later the Northumbrian barons paid homage to him in return for military aid. Alexander was no doubt trying to improve the harsh conditions of the 1209 and 1212 Anglo-Scottish agreements while reasserting traditional Scottish claims to Northumberland and Westmorland. Eustace de Vescy invested Alexander with Northumberland during the siege of Norham. The garrison held out and a 40-day truce was arranged; Alexander moved on. John was now intent on once again proving his mastery over the British Isles as he done just a few years earlier. And he intended to punish the Scottish king, to 'run the sandy-eared little fox cub to his earth'.[397]

John moved northwards through Yorkshire, burning his way to Pontefract. Here the castellan, John de Lacy, Constable of Chester, submitted to the King. His lord, Earl Ranulf of Chester, spoke up on behalf of de Lacy allowing the rebel to return to John's mercy by swearing oaths of loyalty while disavowing any ties with the barons and rejecting Magna Carta; as surety, his brother was given over as a hostage. Another rebel, Roger de Montbegon, submitted to John here. Both de Montbegon and de Lacy were two of the original 25 barons. York placed itself at John's will with a votive offering of £1000, as did Beverley; Robert Oldbridge, Brian de Lisle and Geoffrey de Lacy were given extra men to hold the area. Before he moved on, John wrote to Robert de Ros demanding that he give up Carlisle to Robert de Vieuxpoint while the Earl of Chester took Richmond

Castle and probably Middleham, too. On 7 and 8 January John was at Darlington and thence quickly on to Durham, giving the charge of the latter to the powerful Philip of Oldcoates. The speed and ferocity of his march had put his enemies to flight. Alexander, who had burned Newcastle, took to his heels; on 11 January at Melrose the rebels chased out of England vowed their oaths to him again on holy relics. By the third week of January John was at Berwick, the town falling on the 15th, and sacked with great violence. A short but devastating raid across the river Tweed into Scotland was undertaken, John's forces reaching, and burning, Haddington and Dunbar; at Dunbar the castle was stormed. Roxburgh and numerous villages met with a similar onslaught; even Coldingham Priory was sacked. Keith Stringer has labelled the 'ruthless thoroughness' of John's *chevauchée* as 'shocking'.[398]

On home territory, Alexander rallied his forces from their organised retreat and harassed the English army. He may have sought an engagement with John but the latter characteristically avoided this and used intelligence from scouts to alter the direction of his march. The English raid had anyway achieved its punitive objective in the north, and a lack of supplies – exacerbated by Alexander's own retreating scorched earth policy – saw the English out of Lothian by 23 or 24 January. Matthew Paris believed that 'urgent necessity'[399] dictated this. The urgency may have been the news telling of a second wave of French reinforcements reaching London on 7 January. Berwick was torched before the English left (the Scottish chronicles claim at John's own hand); the castle and bridge across the Tweed were also reported as destroyed and the ships and their cargoes in the port profitably appropriated. Overall it appeared that John had, within a short space of time, 'delivered a mighty blow to Alexander's war effort, the more so because long-term infrastructural damage was done. Perhaps unsurprisingly, after this "extraordinary and unequalled devastation" – the Melrose chronicler's words – John appears to have thought Alexander would soon accept peace.'[400] There was no doubting that John had humiliated the Scottish king.

John now headed southwards in the last week of January, sending out his incendiaries into rebel lands once again. The castles of Morpeth, Prudhoe, Wark, Brancepeth and Mitford fell into his hands, and Alnwick was attacked.[401] The rebel Gilbert Fitzrenfrew went over to John, bringing with him his two castles and ten hostages. Robert de Ros, clearly recognising John's unstoppable momentum, granted his constable at Carlisle permission to submit to de Vieuxpont, leaving John's man in complete dominance of Cumberland and Westmoreland except for Cockermouth Castle. The castles of Lancashire were placed under Earl Ranulf's care and those of Yorkshire under Geoffrey de Neville (the barons in Yorkshire paying homage to John on 11 January). Further afield, John was issuing orders regarding the control of Manchester and Moulton. By 7 February John had taken Skelton Castle from Peter de Bruce, leaving Robert de Ros' Helmsley the only definitely rebel castle in Yorkshire, says Wendover.[402] John progressed through

Lincoln, Sleaford, Stamford and Fotheringay, arriving south in Bedford at the very end of February. The ferocious and speedy expedition witnessed victory after victory and some notable submissions. Painter is not alone among some historians in judging that 'the King's northern campaign had been highly successful.'[403]

But was it? On paper the bald recital of facts and of castles taken would appear to support this view. The reality was, yes, John had been triumphant in vanquishing all before him; but the trouble was, as ever with John, that it was all so ephemeral. John's campaign had to be fast: he did not want to be in the same position as King Harold in 1066, fighting at Stamford Bridge while an invasion force landed on the south coast. As Holt so perceptively recognises, this necessary speed 'reduced the effectiveness of John's onslaught, for the rebels could readily appreciate that he could stay in the north for a limited time'.[404] The loss of castles was a serious blow to the rebels, already outnumbered in this department, and the royal garrisons left behind had significant control of the north. But the garrisons were expensive to maintain and they could not ensure a pacified region that had as its neighbour a hostile King of Scotland and the English rebels that had retreated north of the border. The rebels had deliberately employed a strategy of non-resistance for their castles, surrendering them without a fight. Wendover says that Donnington was left vacant when John arrived there; in probability there was a skeleton garrison in place there. As Ralph Coggeshall wrote: 'The King and his army ... depopulated the lands of the barons, incessantly dedicated to plunder and burning ... The Northern barons fled before his face while a few submitted themselves to the mercy of the merciless one.'[405] This was a sensible tactical retreat that, while executed at a considerable cost, permitted them the freedom to fight later with the French on their side. Already by 20 January another contingent of French troops had arrived in London with Louis promising to come with his main force at Easter. With John back in the south, regional stability would be harder to enforce: before John had even arrived back at Bedford, the Scots had crossed over the border again to besiege Carlisle, and by spring the rebels were besieging York. John had decidedly gained the upper hand for the moment, and, in addition to peace overtures by the leading barons Robert de Ros, Eustace de Vescy and Peter de Brus, many minor figures amongst the rebels made their peace with John, reflecting the new developments. The northern rebellion was essentially over. That John was ready to come to terms with them indicates an awareness of his position: much better than it was before Rochester's fall, but still with the capital in enemy hands. If John had held London as well, Louis might have thought twice about invading.

John's successes arguably came at another cost. The sheer brutality of the campaign, with the worst excesses committed by foreign mercenaries on English soil, alienated many of his own subjects. The monastic chroniclers, never short of ammunition to fire at John, lamented the terrible sufferings of the English, but even writers on the royalist side acknowledged this, speaking of how the 'men of

Flanders, foreign knights and soldiers, who every day were set on pillage ... bent on laying waste' the land.[406] We have encountered Ralph of Coggeshall's descriptions of events at Ely and the fear created by John's army, but it is Wendover who provides us with the devastating reality of John's campaign. In a passage entitled 'On the various types of suffering endured by the Christian people', he writes of John's soldiers:

> The whole surface of the earth was covered with these limbs of the devil like locusts, who assembled ... to blot out every thing from the face of the earth, from man down to his cattle; for, running about with drawn swords and knives, they ransacked towns, houses, cemeteries, and churches, robbing everyone, and sparing neither women and children; the King's enemies wherever they were found were imprisoned in chains and compelled to pay a heavy ransom. Even the priests, whilst standing at the very altars ... were seized, tortured, robbed and ill-treated ... They inflicted similar tortures on knights and others of every condition. Some of them they hung up by the middle, some by the feet and legs, some by their hands, and some by the thumbs and arms, and then threw salt mixed with vinegar in the eyes of the wretched ... Others were placed on gridirons over live coals, and then bathing their roasted bodies in cold water they thus killed them.[407]

Such depictions may owe some literary flourish to the Anglo-Saxon Chronicle or ecclesiastical traditions (St Laurence, for example, was martyred on a gridiron), but, as I have argued in my book *By Sword and Fire: Cruelty and Atrocity in Medieval Warfare*, such medieval tales of barbarity had firm and disturbing foundations in reality. Here, the atrocities are confirmed by Ralph of Coggeshall's account of the attack on Ely. The violence was not gratuitous, or even merely punitive in nature; at its heart lay the prosaic but vital motivational force of money. Wendover makes this vividly clear:

> The wretched creatures uttered pitiable cries and dreadful groans, but there was no one to show them pity, for their torturers were satisfied with nothing but their money. Many who had worldly possessions gave them to their torturers, and were not believed when they had given their all; others, who had nothing, gave many promises, that they might at least for a short time put off the tortures they had experienced once. This persecution was general throughout England, and fathers were sold to torture by their sons, brothers by their brothers, and citizens by their fellow citizens.[408]

Wendover corroborates Coggeshall's similar but briefer account of the sacking of Ely. Here churches and even the cathedral were plundered, the latter being spared torching by handing over nine marks of silver. Stephen Ridel was dragged from the cathedral and lost all his possessions – including horses and books – and avoided torture only by handing over 100 marks.[409] Pain was the mangle that squeezed out every drop of wealth. John's winter expedition actually served a secondary purpose beyond the purely military one that was hardly less vital: he needed the campaign as a means of paying his troops and keeping them in his service. Wendover is explicit about this: 'so that … by robbery John might support the wicked agents of his iniquity. All the inhabitants of every condition and rank who did not take refuge in a churchyard were made prisoners, and, after being tortured, were forced to pay a heavy ransom.'[410] It was not just for oppressive taxes, as is often thought, that the Barnwell chronicler famously labelled John as 'a pillager of his own people'; that is exactly what he was.[411]

It has been suggested that these atrocity stories have been exaggerated by biased chroniclers. Support for this view lies in some legal records. For example, a jury statement from 1228 reveals that Ripon was spared any depredations by John's army.[412] There could be various reasons for this, such as local politics and strategy, or an understanding of some form of payment of 'goodwill' or protection money (*tenseria*). John was always on the lookout for hard cash; as Poole notes: 'wanton destruction was not John's method of revenging himself on rebels; he preferred to extort money by the threat of despoiling them.'[413] We have seen how York and Beverley handed over £1000 to John for protection; Retford and Melton Mowbray gave 100 marks; Laxton gave £100 and Thirsk paid 800 marks so as to not have their houses torched. Other evidence shows that a soldier of John's army faced the equivalent of a courts martial and had a hand amputated for the theft of a cow from a churchyard. But important as such records are, perhaps some historians make too much of them, relieved as they are to have some official documentation quantifying some aspect of history. It is worth reiterating here Colin Richmond's wise words: 'The records of government are all very well, but on issues that matter they do not tell the truth. In fact, they seek to obscure it.'[414] As I have shown elsewhere, medieval chroniclers were often very close to the fighting with first-hand reports of what happened corroborated by many different eyewitnesses. We have only to look at the war in former Yugoslavia, the Sudan and Congo to know that atrocities are always committed in time of war.[415] One of the worst charges Wendover directs at the royal soldiers is that of ransacking cemeteries. This was actually common in medieval warfare. Bodies were often buried with valuables which were worth the effort of digging up. The bodies themselves had value: they could be ransomed back at half the price of a live hostage. Recent corpses might also have nutritional value. In 1317 a Scottish invasion of Ireland coincided with the Great Famine. Foraging was very poor. A chronicle relates that the soldiers were 'so destroyed with hunger that they raised the bodies of the dead from the cemeteries'.[416] Both Ralph of Coggeshall and Roger of Wendover had first-hand knowledge of John's winter campaigning; Wendover's accounts are especially valuable for their detail of noncombatant sufferings.

The campaigns in the north and south ensured that John's men were not only paid in wages, but also received bonuses in kind. Plunder, extortion and stealing from helpless civilians was easy money; the license to do so was an attractive recruitment encouragement. This was not simply wanton destruction, but destruction with a two-fold purpose. As well as recompensing troops, ravaging destroyed the economic base of the rebels, undermining their ability to wage war. The destruction was not random but precisely targeted at John's enemies (just as they targeted royal and loyalist lands). All the chronicles tell of how the barons' lands were attacked, but Wendover, the most well-placed to comment, is the most explicit.

> Spreading his troop's abroad, [John] burned the houses and buildings of the barons, robbing them of their goods and cattle, and thus destroying everything that came in his way, he gave a miserable spectacle to those who beheld it ... burning the buildings belonging to the barons, making booty of their cattle, plundering them of their goods and destroying everything they came to with the sword.

John gave his commanders orders to 'destroy all the property of the barons, namely their castles, buildings, towns, parks, warrens, lakes and mills ... to finish the business with equal cruelty'. William Longsword was doing the same in the south, where royalist soldiers were collecting booty and indulging in pillage; they levied impositions on the towns, made prisoners of the inhabitants, burnt the buildings of their barons, destroyed the parks and warrens, cut down the trees in the orchards and, having spread fire as far as the suburbs of London, they took away an immense booty with them.[417]

Note the very specific targets, such as warrens and orchards. Wendover later gives accounts of attacks where anti-royalist forces 'observed one good rule' of only attacking the King's people and places and even individual houses within villages.[418] Armies could be very well disciplined, following ordinances for troops in the field. Even Scottish troops, feared for their seemingly unbridled savagery, proved themselves capable of such restraint, closely adhering to the command not to trouble the English clergy and only to ravage the land of King John and his supporters as they made their remarkable march to Dover later that year.

Such widespread ravaging was to be a major feature of the war that continued for the next year and a half. It was about to become a lot worse.

Louis Arrives

For all of John's success, real or superficial, he was racing violently against time. This spurred him into frantic action, the speed of which may give an illusion of efficiency. The second tranche of French troops had arrived in London on 7 January, revealing the limitations of the Earl of Salisbury's movements in the

south. Another 100 knights under the command of the marshal Gautier de
Nemours reinforced the London garrison, making a total of 240 French knights
present in England. With them came 140 crossbowmen (40 of whom were
mounted), infantry and war materiel. Forty-one ships were involved in the operation.[419] Louis had indicated that he would appear in England in person by the
end of January, but delays in his preparations required that this date be postponed.
To encourage the rebels he sent over a number of messengers and men at the end
of February, just as John was approaching Bedford. Louis sent his promises of his
own arrival on Easter Sunday and warned his English supporters to be wary of
false intelligence, hinting that this may be fabricated by John's side. It was important for Louis to give hope to the rebels: if they despaired and came to terms with
John, as many were doing, then Louis' greatest asset in England would be lost, and
with it the prospect of a successful invasion.

The psychological impact made by these French troops provided a real morale
boost to the rebels who, in addition to John's almost totally unimpeded march
north and back south again, had also to suffer at the end of February the imminent prospect of their public excommunication, along with their French allies.
The actual physical impact on the war was initially very limited. In fact, the French
first drew blood against one of their key English allies. While carrying out joint
military training exercises in the form of a tournament, a French knight called
Acroce-Meure tilted with a partially armoured Geoffrey de Mandeville, Earl of
Gloucester and Essex, and accidentally inflicted a mortal wound in his stomach.

John did not waste time and in early March, not letting up his momentum,
continued his attempts to fully reassert his authority in the kingdom with his
troops operating on the Welsh border and, crucially, in the south-east. Immediate
triumph came at Framlingham on 12 March, which simply opened its gates to
him, despite being a very strong castle. This was very satisfying to John as it was
the chief castle of Roger Bigod whom, says the Anonymous of Béthune, the
King 'greatly hated'. The Earl entered into talks with the King; John gave the
castle to Savary de Mauléon. On 14 March John was besieging Colchester with
a large army, reports Ralph of Coggeshall; this castle gave signs of resistance and
had been reinforced with French troops. After some days (John was there until
24 January) the garrison agreed to terms of surrender: the English troops were to
be held ransom while the French were to be free to return to London. Coggeshall
tells how John reneged on his promise: while the French were allowed through
his lines, the English garrison were shackled in chains and imprisoned. When the
French reached London they were met with deep suspicion: the English barons
charged them with betrayal and wondered how their fate was so different to their
English comrades. Such was the fervid atmosphere there were even threats of a
mass hanging of the French. Instead, they were imprisoned and their fate was to
be decided by Louis when he came. So far the practicality of French involvement
had been a disaster: one dead earl and a capitulation that caused massive distrust.

The Angevin Kings of England: Henry II, Richard I, John and Henry III. (The British Library Board)

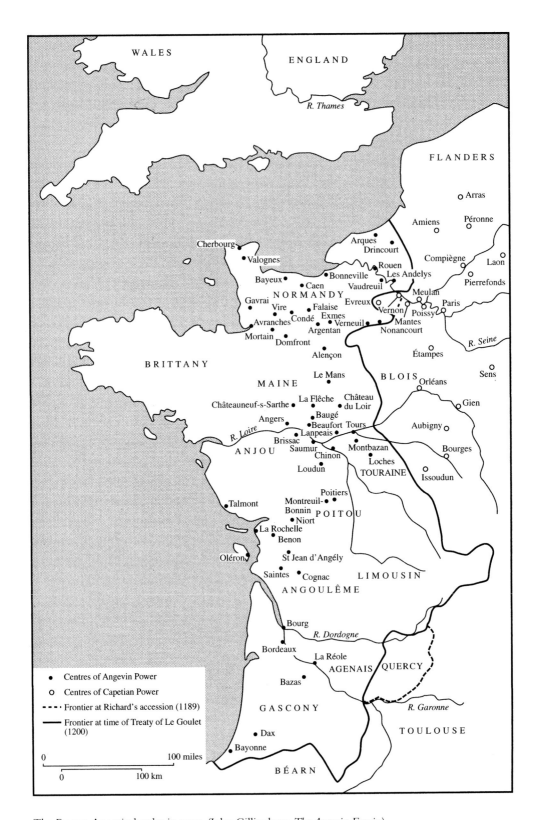

The Franco-Angevin border in 1202. (John Gillingham, *The Angevin Empire*)

The coronation of Philip II Augustus, 1179. The birth of Philip in 1165 secured the Capetian dynasty and he was therefore considered by many contemporaries in France as sent from Heaven, hence he was known as '*Dieudonné*' – 'Godgiven'. (Walters Art Gallery, Baltimore)

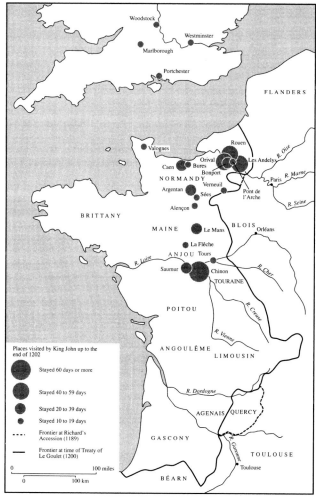

John's visits to his French domains by the end of 1202. Note the time spent at Chinon and also around Rouen, the capital of Normandy. (John Gillingham, *The Angevin Empire*)

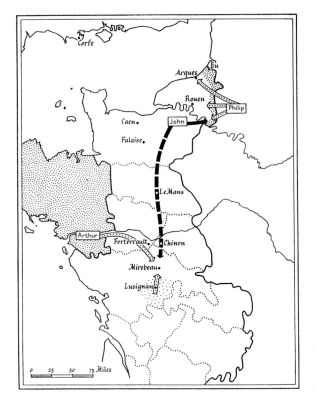

The opening stages of the
Anglo-French conflict, spring to
autumn 1202.(W.L.Warren, *King John*)

Autumn 1202 to
December 1203.The
main French-led
attack on Normandy,
with Philip leading
his forces against
Normandy and
the crucial defence
network of Château
Gaillard, which
guarded the Norman
border just north of
Paris, while his Breton
allies attack John's
Angevin territory
from the west. (W.L.
Warren, *King John*)

Château Gaillard from the Seine. Richard the Lionheart's 'Bold Castle' which he claimed he could defend even if its walls were made of butter. (Author)

View of the Seine from the ramparts of Château Gaillard. Note the isle of Andely, the scene of a fierce engagement before the castle was fully assaulted. (Author)

Château Gaillard. The thrust of Philip's main assault came from the southwest (left of picture). (Author)

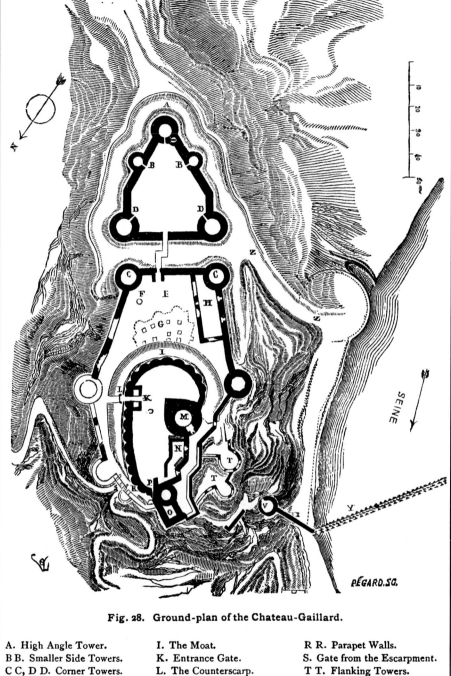

Fig. 28. Ground-plan of the Chateau-Gaillard.

A. High Angle Tower.
B B. Smaller Side Towers.
C C, D D. Corner Towers.
E. Outer Enceinte, or Lower Court.
F. The Well.
G, H. Buildings in the Lower Court.

I. The Moat.
K. Entrance Gate.
L. The Counterscarp.
M. The Keep.
N. The Escarpment.
O. Postern Tower.
P. Postern Gate.

R R. Parapet Walls.
S. Gate from the Escarpment.
T T. Flanking Towers.
V. Outer Tower.
X. Connecting Wall.
Y. The Stockade in the River.
Z Z. The Great Ditches.

Plan of Château Gaillard. (E.E. Viollet-le Duc, *Military Architecture*)

The keep of Château Gaillard. (E.E. Viollet-le Duc, *Military Architecture*)

The northeastern scarp slope of Château Gaillard. It was here that most of the hundreds of non-combatants expelled from the castle – 'the useless mouths' – died from exposure and starvation during the winter months of the siege. Neither side dared show the weakness of compassion. (Author)

The advanced design of the keep's curtain wall at Château Gaillard. Here the dramatic final moments of the siege took place. (Author)

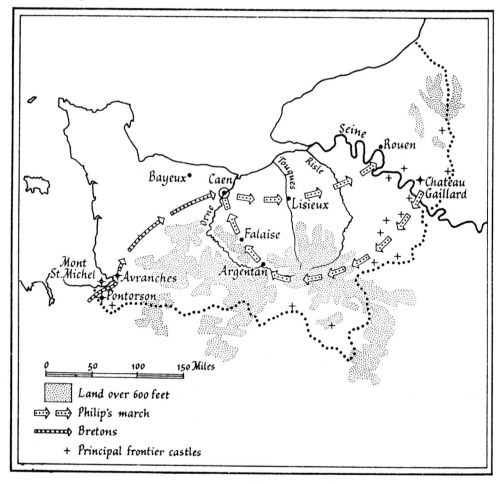

The final phase of the conquest of Normandy, showing the advances of Philip and the Bretons in the summer of 1204. (W.L. Warren, *King John*)

Falaise Castle. John spent a huge amount of resources on fortifying the castle and was outraged in 1204 at the actions of his mercenary captain Louvrecaire who commanded it for him. Arthur of Brittany was imprisoned here after the Battle of Mirebeau. (Author)

King John hunting with dogs. He came in for much criticism from some quarters for devoting too much attention to his pleasures – including his young wife – rather than to defending the Duchy of Normandy. (The British Library Board)

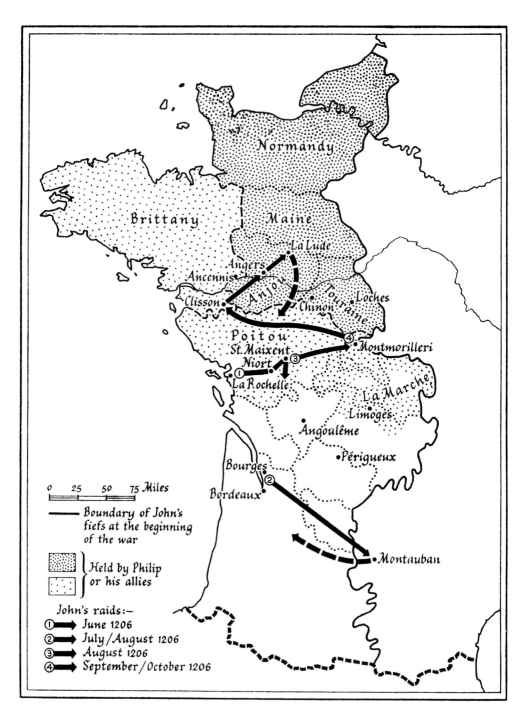

John's French campaign, 1206. His success at Montauban was deep in the south, far away from the main crucible of war to the north. (W.L. Warren, *King John*)

Left: The great seal of Philip Augustus. (Archives Nationales, Sceaux, Paris)

Below: A cavalry charge at the Battle of Bouvines, 1214, one of the most important battles of the entire Middle Ages. (Bibliothèque Nationale, Paris)

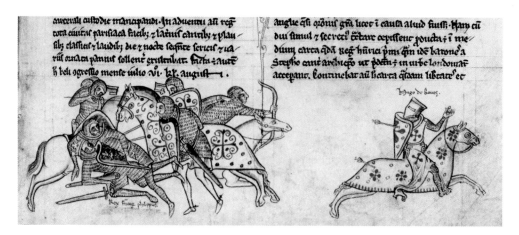

The Battle of Bouvines: King Philip lies in mortal danger while Huge de Boves makes his escape from the battlefield. (Corpus Christi College, Cambridge)

Count Ferrand of Flanders and Count Renaud de Boulogne are escorted to prison after the Battle of Bouvines. (Bibliothèque Nationale, Paris)

Philip Augustus receives the swords of his vassals in homage. (Walters Art Gallery, Baltimore)

Magna Carta. King John hoped it would buy him time to muster his forces against the rebels and prevent a French invasion. (Dean and Chapter of Lincoln Cathedral)

Seal of Robert Fitzwalter, general of the rebel army and a leading commander of Louis' forces. The other shield is that of Robert's fellow rebel, Saer de Quincy, representing their solidarity in their cause. (Trustees of the British Museum)

Left: Rochester Castle. The tower in the background was rebuilt after the original one was destroyed during the siege of 1215; it is constructed in a more advanced, rounded form. (Author)

Below: Rochester Cathedral as seen from the ramparts of Rochester Castle. John is recorded as having stabled his horses in the cathedral during the siege. (Author)

The interior cross-wall of the keep at Rochester Castle, behind which the defenders of the 1215 siege were forced to withdraw. (Author)

The fate of a defeated English garrison. Angered and frustrated by the rebels' defence of Rochester Castle, John expressed his intention at the siege of Rochester to hand out the same treatment to the garrison there. (Corpus Christi College, Cambridge)

Belvoir Castle. Roger d'Albini, who led the heroic defence at Rochester, was the master here. It was in the sights of John during his vicious campaign of 1215–16. The leading English chronicler of events for this time, Roger of Wendover, was prior at Belvoir. (Author)

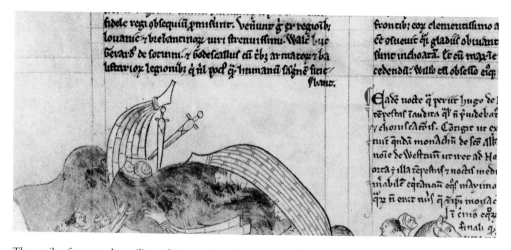

The perils of sea travel: a military ship goes down in a storm. This was the fate of many vessels in John's reinforcement fleet in the English Channel in 1215, coming to England to prepare for the French invasion. Among the victims was one of John's leading commanders. (Corpus Christi College, Cambridge)

A soldier of King John torturing prisoners. The livery of the soldier denotes him as being in the service of John's general William Marshal, considered by many contemporaries as the epitome of chivalry. (Corpus Christi College, Cambridge)

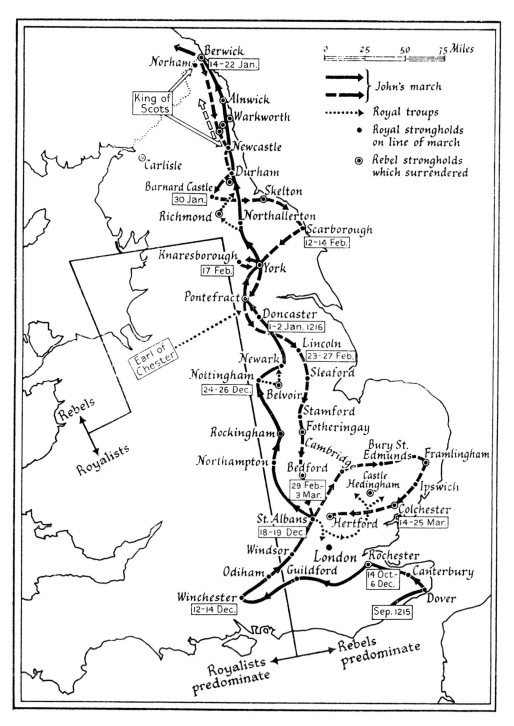

John's campaigning, September 1215 to March 1216. (W.L. Warren, *King John*)

Prince Louis with the four cardinal virtues being presented with a copy of the *Karolinus* by its author, Gilles de Paris. The work was designed to inspire Louis to emulate the deeds of the great first Holy Roman Emperor, Charlemagne. (Bibliothèque Nationale, Paris)

John's network of royal castles, a major military asset during the French invasion. (John Gillingham, *The Angevin Empire*)

Dover Castle. This massive fortress overlooking the English Channel was 'the key to England' according to Matthew Paris. It was subjected to prolonged sieges by French forces. (Author)

Siege and battle scene. Most medieval battles arose from siege situations. Note the trebuchet in action. These large machines, the heavy artillery of the day, were used to great effect against castle walls during the invasion. However, some very strong fortresses could withstand their bombardment. (Pierpont Morgan Library)

The Roman walls of Portchester looking towards the twelfth-century keep. Portchester's strong coastal position made it an important objective for Louis. (Author)

Armies on the move. The supply wagon is transporting the soldiers' armour. Logistics were key to a successful campaign and a particular problem for the French invaders. (Pierpont Morgan Library)

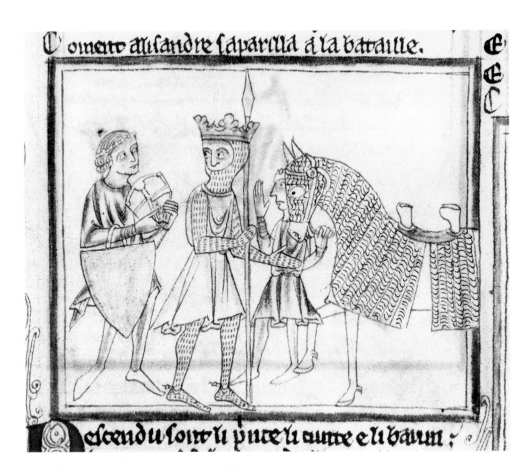

Comento alisandre saparilla a la bataille.

Descendu sont li prince li cunte e li barun :

Above: A king prepares for battle, he and his horse wearing the chainmail armour of the day. (Trinity College, Cambridge)

Left: The great seal of King Louis. (Archives Nationales, Sceaux, Paris)

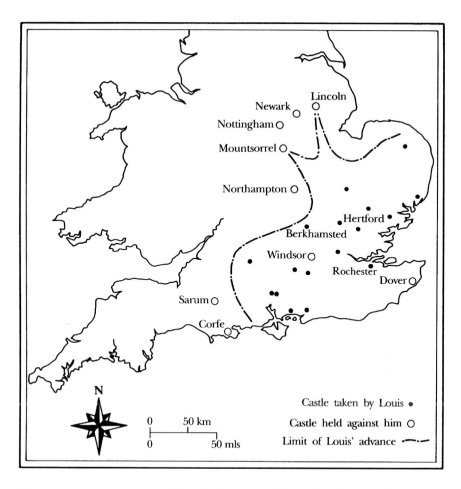

Map showing the territory consolidated by Louis during his invasion. It does not show the land of English rebels affiliated to him in the North. (N.J.G. Pounds, *The Medieval Castle in England and Wales*)

Newark Castle, the place of John's death. (Author)

Effigy of John from his tomb at Worcester Cathedral. His heart was not buried with him: it was taken from his deathbed corpse by a leading churchman. (Photograph by Mr Christopher Guy, Worcester Cathedral Archaeologist)

William Marshal's castle at Pembroke, Wales. With his other mighty royalist fortress on the Welsh border at Chepstow, the rebels and French made little permanent headway in the west. (Author)

Effigy of William Marshal from his tomb, Temple Church, London. (Author, by kind permission of The Temple Church, London)

The coronation of the boy king, Henry III. (Corpus Christi College, Cambridge)

The ruined keep of Odiham Castle, where a garrison of only thirteen men bravely held up Louis' forces for a fortnight. (Author)

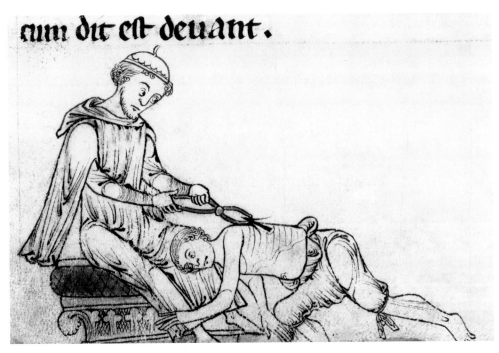

cum dit est deuant.

A surgeon removing an arrow. Bows and crossbows were the deadliest weapons at sieges, as a leading rebel commander found out to his cost, shot through the middle of his forehead with a crossbow bolt. (Trinity College, Cambridge)

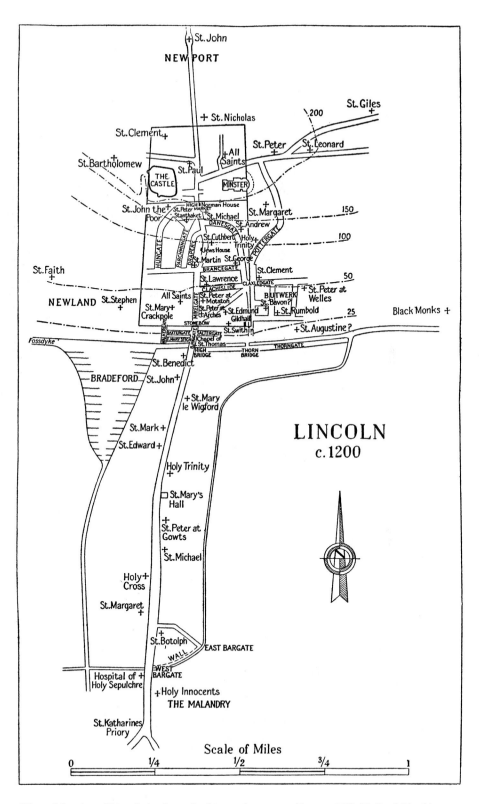

Plan of the city of Lincoln in the early thirteenth century. (Frances Hill, *Medieval Lincoln*)

Hora miracula de S. Albani

Falco de Brea[uté]

Left: The notorious royalist mercenary captain Falkes de Bréauté at St Albans. The town and abbey were pillaged by both sides during the invasion. Low-born and foreign, Falkes was a much hated military and poitical figure. (Corpus Christi College, Cambridge)

Below: Royalist troop movements at the Battle of Lincoln according to Professor David Carpenter. The Battle of Lincoln was the major land engagement of the invasion. (David Carpenter, *The Minority of Henry III*)

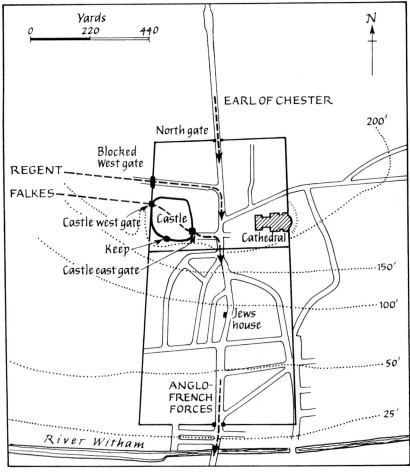

Yards
0   220   440

N

EARL OF CHESTER

North gate

Blocked
West gate

REGENT

FALKES

Castle west gate

Castle

Cathedral

Keep

Castle east gate

Jews
house

200'

150'

100'

50'

25'

ANGLO-
FRENCH
FORCES

River Witham

Left: The north gate of Lincoln Castle, scene of some fierce fighting. (Author)

Below: View along the battlements of Lincoln Castle towards the keep, from where the redoubtable Nicola de la Haye conducted a lengthy defence against French and rebel forces. (Author)

Left: Postern gate at Lincoln Castle. (Author)

Below: East gate and wall of Lincoln Castle, directly facing the cathedral. Troops poured out of this gate in retreat. (Author)

The west front of Lincoln Cathedral. Here, between the minster and the east gate of the castle, a last stand was made during the battle. (Dean and Chapter of Lincoln Cathedral)

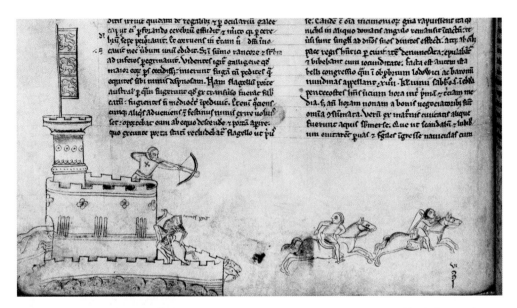

The young Count of Perche is killed by a blade which went through the eye slit of his helmet and pierced his brain. The defeated cavalry take flight. (Corpus Christi College, Cambridge)

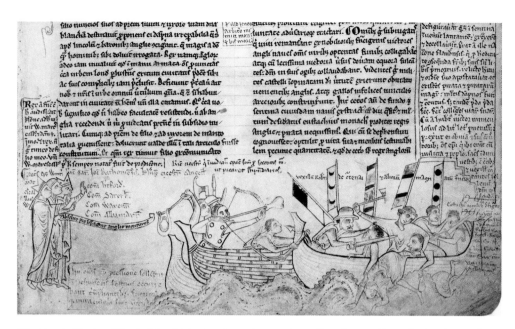

The bloody Battle of Sandwich which played a major part in ending the war. Peter des Roches, William Marshal and the papal legate Guala bless the English fleet as it engages with the French fleet bringing reinforcements for Louis' final push in England. Note the use of lime pots and grappling hooks and the grim fate of Eustace the Monk. (Corpus Christi College, Cambridge)

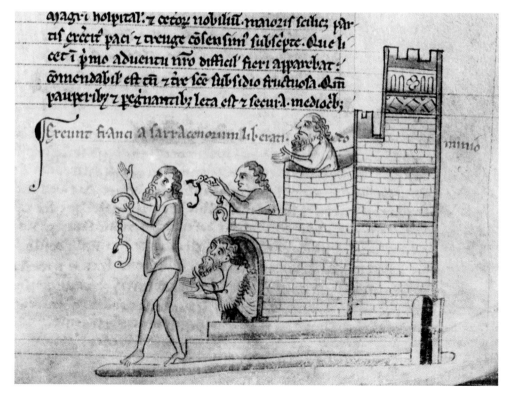

Prisoners being set free. The terms of prisoner release were central to the peace treaty. (Corpus Christi College, Cambridge)

Hedingham followed on 28 March, after John had been there three days. This was the seat of the Earl of Oxford, Robert de Vere. According to the Anonymous, after his loss the Earl swore allegiance to John, but never kept his vow and 'broke it like the traitor he was'.[420] Earl Richard of Clare asked John for safe conduct to his court about this time, indicating that more desertions to him – real or feigned – were taking place. The Earl's lands had been given to the Anonymous' patron, Robert of Béthune. John bolstered his position at Hedingham by the distribution of plunder from his winter campaign, an act which further secured the service of the thousands of mercenaries he had in his employ.

This period of campaigning ended with an interesting postscript in the form of two small engagements just outside of London which gave the rebels a fillip. John came close to London on 1 April when he spent the night at Waltham Abbey. According to Coggeshall, the citizens of the rebellious capital opened their gates and made ready for battle with their king; John, as was his habit, wished to avoid the risk of any such encounter, especially as he no doubt felt that the new year had gone satisfactorily so far. His leading captain, Savary de Mauléon, ventured closer to the city, perhaps reconnoitring its defences for possible weaknesses. He and his men were ambushed, suffering heavy casualties; Savary himself suffered a near fatal wound. Royalist forces – 'pirates', Coggeshall calls them – were also trying to blockade the Thames. The Londoners attacked them, killing, drowning or capturing 65 of them. To add to John's displeasure, and to cast a cloud over his seeming triumph in the north, the rebels had besieged York and exacted 1000 marks from its citizens in return for a truce. These were small victories, but they proved that the rebels remained an active force and one which would be of use to Louis.

The situation at the start of April was ostensibly very favourable for John:

Only the walls of London and the prospective arrival of Prince Louis stood between the baronial party and complete destruction. Except for a few isolated strongholds all the castles of England were either razed or occupied by royal garrisons. The lands of the rebels had been thoroughly ravaged by John's merce-nary troops. Moreover the mercenary captains and the Englishmen loyal to the King had been given the custody of the states of the rebellious lords and were collecting their revenues.[421]

But the shadow of the small figure of Louis loomed large from the continent: 'if it had not been for Louis of France, John could simply have sat before London until his barons made their submission.'[422] From his enemies' point of view, the situa-tion, serious as it was, clearly dictated that they await help from France.

April was marked by high political tension, intense diplomatic activity and an atmosphere of anticipation and foreboding.[423] John continued to cajole rebels over with assurances and relatively moderate sanctions. To this end, on 17 April he instructed his sheriffs to grant safe-conducts to any rebel who wished to reconcile with the King; those that remained recalcitrant were to suffer the loss of their lands by being disinherited forever. Three days previously more tangible preparations to face the French were made by his order for 21 coastal towns from Land's End to the Wash to send all their ships to the mouth of the Thames. The French had been expected at Easter, so their arrival was threatened at any time.

John directed much energy to his diplomatic efforts. Coggeshall tells of a high-ranking delegation under William Marshal and the Bishop of Winchester travelling to Philip Augustus' court to place pressure on Philip to forbid his son to make the expedition to England. The Papacy also mobilised its forces on John's behalf. At Easter papal instructions to the clergy of London finally saw the full public excommunication of the rebels and their French allies in England. (According to Wendover, this public announcement had little effect, ignored as it largely was by clergy and people alike.) The pope also sent his legate Guala Bicchieri to France to act on behalf of the church and her vassal the King of England. Guala, a lawyer steeped in civil law, met with Philip and Louis at Melun on the 24 and 25 April in an eleventh hour attempt to stop the invasion.[424] Here claim and counter-claim mixed unproductively as each side put forward their case as just.

The Capetian court presented a very weak case to the legate in an energetic but intellectually empty attempt at justification of their position. Louis' hopeful claims to the throne were reiterated and backed up with the always dubious support of negative argument to show why John was not the rightful king of England. Philip opened with the traditional expression of respect from a loyal son of the Church before moving on to attack John with the argument that England never was and never would be in Saint Peter's patrimony as John's treachery against Richard in 1194 stripped away his legal claim to the throne and thus he had no power to give up the country without the consent of the barons; and even if his crown were legal, this was forfeited by his murder of Duke Arthur of Brittany. In fact, John's succession was largely undisputed as Richard was unambiguous in naming him as his successor (if a little late in the day) and, as discussed earlier, John's killing of his nephew (which Philip reminded the legate was tried in the Capetian court) was a domestic feudal matter which had no relevance to the throne of England. The following day, a knight, acting as Louis' proctor, emphasised the Prince's claim to the throne through his wife, Blanche of Castille, a niece of Richard through his sister Eleanor. In reality, if John was not the true king, the person with the greatest claim was Arthur's sister, Eleanor of Brittany, safely incarcerated in one of John's prisons. The proctor went on to list all the wrongs John had inflicted on Louis' own lands, including the holding of prisoners without ransom.

Only the case of forfeiture based on baronial discontent following John's breaking of promises carried any real weight. Guala, as the Papacy's diplomat, understandably would hear none of this. He held to the position of John being a vassal of Rome and furthermore, having taken the vow of a crusader, John was protected from action against him for four years. Louis' man countered this last point by saying that the fact John had continued to wage war himself exempted him from this protection. Guala then played his strongest hand and threatened all those taking part in any expedition with excommunication. This had little effect on Louis, who professed to this father that he would rather undergo this from a misguided pontiff than break his word to the barons in England. The Prince reassured his vassals that he would protect them from any material damage caused by excommunication. He also reminded his father that Philip actually had no authority over him outside his French fiefs. It is unlikely that Philip needed any persuasion.

For his part the French King, anxious to avoid the same spiritual opprobrium that awaited his son, made a strong pretence of not condoning the planned invasion, and of wishing to maintain his truce with John. With cynical hypocrisy, he distanced himself from Louis and, according to William the Breton, even imposed sanctions upon him by confiscating some of his lands and those of his followers.[425] Such actions fit in with Philip's polished Machiavellianism (in both its more accurate and its more pejorative meanings). Innocent III was dubious about Philip's role, but he was dying and little came of it. Later, the Papacy acknowledged that the French King's high-profile denunciation was genuine, probably because it suited the political situation at the time to do so. There is some debate over Philip's genuine attitude to Louis' campaign after the Melun meeting, but the overwhelming likelihood was that Philip was supportive; it was just politic not to let this be widely known.[426] The well-sourced Anonymous of Béthune gives the clearest indication of this: when, at the baronial meeting at Melun, 'Louis heard their words, he sought advice from his counsellors and those of his father, who encouraged him to carry out the affair. His father, however, publicly made it appear as though he did not want to be involved because of the truce he had granted; but privately, it was believed that he had advised him.'[427] Had he wished to, Philip could easily have prevented Louis' expedition. As it was, the campaign provided the Capetians with the greatest of opportunities, holding out the possibility of enormous rewards – the final removal of the Angevin foe and England falling under Capetian rule – for little personal risk. The invasion was on.

Guala's mission had failed, as, indeed, had John's own extensive measures. It should be remembered that John's submission to the Papacy was motivated first and foremost by the threat of invasion and the need for papal condemnation of the enterprise. For all the money John had obtained from the interdict, and for all the accolades of his submission as a political masterstroke, John had failed to achieve his primary objective.

The legate's next step was to make for England and to confirm John's worst fears. To facilitate this as swiftly as possible, he asked Philip for the diplomatic courtesy of safe conduct to the Channel. The French King's response was not to his liking: 'I will gladly grant you safe conduct though my lands, but don't blame me if by chance you fall into the hands of Eustace the Monk or any of Louis' men who guard the sea and evil befalls you.'[428] Guala left the French court in a rage. Nicholas Vincent's study of the legate indicates that Guala followed a circuitous route to England, taking nearly a month to arrive at his destination, such was his anxiety to avoid Louis' forces.[429] The position of legate was no guarantee against maltreatment.

Meanwhile, in England, John was a blur of activity in the south-east. In the days immediately before the council of Melun, John had moved from Windsor, through Surrey and back to Rochester. When the council was in progress he was at Canterbury ordering his troops at Rochester to follow him immediately 'wherever he might be'; the following day he was at the key stronghold of Dover. His itinerary then shows his movements for the next three weeks 'flitting up and down along the coast of Kent', waiting in anticipation for Guala and in dread for Louis.[430] Just as he had seen to the provisioning of castles, so he had also ensured his fleet was in a state of readiness and on constant alert. The Cinque ports fulfilled their central role in his planning, their function being to provide the core of the ships and crews in the royal fighting fleet. They reinforced their support for John by oaths and the handing over of hostages. Despite the name, there were more than five coastal towns in this military confederation (there were more than 20 ports in the confederation by 1226): to the original Hastings, Dover, Hythe, Sandwich and Romney had been added with similar privileges Winchelsea, Rye and others; the chronicles report that Dunwich, Yarmouth and Lynn were just some of the other ports that sent their ships to Dover for the muster.

John was intent on the eminently sensible and traditional strategy of maritime defence. It had served him well at Damme and now he hoped to replicate that success under even more critical circumstances. In a precursor to the Royal Navy's blockading strategy in the Napoleonic Wars, John planned to sail to Calais and its neighbouring ports with all his fleet and contain Louis' huge expeditionary force there in the harbours. He placed his confidence in England's acknowledged naval superiority: the Anonymous of Béthune writes that John knew 'the little vessels of Louis could not defend themselves against his ships, which were so large; one of his was worth four of Louis's.' But John was undone by the weather: just as Louis' men were on the point of embarkation, a huge storm broke out in the Channel on 18 May. John's ships had to fly to safer havens or face destruction. The following day the battered ships were either too unseaworthy or 'they were so widely dispersed the King could not gather them altogether again'.[431] Louis seized the chance: on 20 May he ordered his troops on board their ships and made ready to sail.

A remarkably detailed breakdown of Louis' expeditionary force comes from the quill of the Anonymous of Béthune. He provides precise figures of leading knights and their contingents, not hesitating to admit that for some forces 'I do not know the number of men.' In all he estimates that Louis' army comprised 1200 knights. The scale of the army can also be gauged by the number of ships needed

to transport it across the Channel: 'a good eight hundred'. Wendover offers a figure
not too far off this one, giving a total of 680. The scale of the expedition meant
that Calais itself was insufficient to accommodate the army numbers: Boulogne,
Gravelines and Wissant were also embarkation points. The money invested in such
an enterprise was enormous, requiring the taxation of royal provinces, tellingly 'in
the name of the king' in some places. Great barons who refused to contribute were
coerced into forced loans: Duke Eudes of Burgundy had to come up with 1000
marks. When Blanche, Countess of Champagne, made excuses not to pay, soldiers
broke in as she was dining and exacted payment from her.

To these ports came many of France's great lords along with their knightly
retinues and soldiers: Robert de Dreux, Etienne de Sancerre, Gérard la Truie,
Enguerrand de Couci, Robert de Courtenay, Jean de Montmirail, Guillaume
des Roches, the Viscount of Melun, and the loyal Capetian stalwart and veteran
commander, Guillaume des Barres. These were highly experienced and respected
soldiers, representing some of France's finest fighting men. Many had performed
with distinction on the battlefield at Bouvines. The calibre of this distinguished
army was such that had Philip himself been leading the expedition, it would not
have been very different in its make up. This is an indication of two factors: one,
that Philip's position on the throne was now so secure he could afford to spare
his kingdom these men; and two, despite his protestations, his will was behind the
invasion. Amongst the army was the shady Hervé de Donzy, Count of Nevers,
'an arrogant and vicious man' according to William Marshal's biographer, with a
dazzling retinue of 100 knights. Nor were there just French knights; Flemish lords
were well represented such as Raoul de Nesle and the Count of Guines. And
more French lords were to come: in late summer the chivalrous Count of Perche
and Pierre Mauclerc, Count of Brittany, added their weight to Louis' army, the
latter laying claim to the county of Richmond. All were about to begin their
great adventure in search of new lands, rich wives and booty, echoing the aspirations of William the Conqueror's invasion force exactly 150 years earlier.[432]

The admiral in charge of the fleet and responsible for its preparation was the
infamous Eustace the Monk, one of our story's most colourful characters and one
of the most inappropriately named.[433] Eustace came from a noble family living
in the Boulonnias region of northern France. At the time of the invasion he was
probably in his mid-forties. He trained as a knight and gained experience of sea-
manship from his early travels. It is curious as to why he ever contemplated being
a monk in the first instance: his storyteller depicts him as a completely disrup-
tive character in the cloisters, causing mayhem and encouraging such unmonkish
habits as cursing. *The Romance of Eustace the Monk* portrays this ribald character as
a foul-mouthed, irredeemably dishonest trickster, fond of four-letter words and
farting (blaming the latter on his horse's saddle); but in his favour we are told that
he was not a sodomite (the *Romance* uses a far more colloquial term) and only
dressed as a woman to deceive a knight. Unsurprisingly, he renounced his holy

orders. He entered the service of Count Renaud de Boulogne, rising rapidly to become his seneschal, before falling out with him on the Count's suspicion of Eustace's likely financial irregularities. Eustace took to the woods and began his career of notoriety, this short little man becoming one of the most feared and infamous figures of the day: 'His name was enough at one time to strike terror into the hearts of Channel seamen.'[434] His feud with the Count of Boulogne soon involved Eustace in many actions, including capture and escape, after which he offered his services to King John in 1205. We are told that John hailed Eustace as 'brave and bold' and recognised in him a kindred spirit: 'You know a great deal about guile and cunning and do not need any cat's grease to help you.'[435]

Eustace deployed his naval skills to good effect by raiding the French seaboard until 1211 – something that profited him personally as well as his master – and was rewarded by John with lands in Norfolk. There appears to be some truth to the legend that he captured Sark and used it as his pirates' base. His antagonistic opportunism led him into conflict with the coastal ports of southern England, to such an extent he required safe-conducts to visit England. Eustace's reputation grew alongside daring tales in *The Romance of Eustace the Monk*, written shortly after his death, of (a temporary) recovery of the Channel Islands, raids up the Seine and of victorious encounters against Philip Augustus' leading mercenary commander, Cadoc. The *Romance* tells of how John rewarded Eustace with a large palace in London.

That two such unpleasant and self-serving figures as John and Eustace should fall out seems inevitable with hindsight. The break came between late 1212 and November 1214; the causes were familiar to those that had alienated many of the country's great barons. When Eustace failed to pay off a debt of 20 marks, John had his lands in Norfolk seized for a time; the Anonymous of Béthune also reports that his wife was taken hostage by the King. His daughter had already been handed over as a hostage. One can speculate on how they were treated by John; the *Romance* says that later John had the daughter burned, disfigured and killed, another revealing condemnation of John from a non-clerical source. There thus seems to have been growing animosity between the two over this time, exacerbated by Eustace's seemingly growing independence. It is worth considering that the ever-opportunistic Eustace may have been manoeuvring himself in light of John's defeat at Bouvines and the Capetian ascendancy, and that this was what made John uneasy about Eustace. When Eustace's old enemy the Count of Boulogne joined forces with John in 1212 it may well have motivated him to change his own allegiance. John ordered Philip d'Albini to lead a successful raid against Eustace on Sark: many of the pirate's men were captured, including family members who were incarcerated in Portchester Castle; but Eustace won these areas back during 1215–16 and in 1215 he had supplied the rebel barons with siege machines. Over the next eighteen months Eustace was to continue playing a central role in the French war effort in England right up to its bloody climactic battle.

It was on Eustace's flagship ship that Prince Louis embarked on the evening of Friday 20 May. With him were Stephen Langton's brother, Simon, the chamberlain Ours de la Chapelle and the Viscount of Melun. The winds were still high but for Louis this was an opportunity, even though some of his men waited until the seas had calmed before setting off. To deal with the winds an oblique course was charted. At 9pm the trumpets sounded their fanfare across the port of Calais to signal the departure of the invasion fleet. Louis set sail for England.[436]

One day ahead of him was the legate Guala. He had landed at Romney on the night or early morning of 20–21 May. John, anxious to exchange valuable information with him, rode out from Canterbury to meet him on the road. Guala was resplendent in his scarlet cardinal's attire riding on a white horse. With Stephen Langton suspended and in exile in Rome, Guala was the foremost ecclesiastical figure in England and now 'the uncontested guardian of the English church'.[437] He and John dismounted and embraced. The King, having received intelligence from the coast, told him that Louis' ships had been sighted; the legate immediately renewed the excommunication of John's enemies and the two went to Canterbury. Guala did not tarry here long; fearing a successful French landing, he moved quickly farther inland to avoid capture.[438]

Louis arrived in England on 21 May at Stonor on the Isle of Thanet just ahead of his main fleet, landing with just seven ships, through a combination of keenness and the compulsions and disruptions of the storm and its effects on his squadrons, many of which had turned back until the winds subsided. Louis wished to be the first ashore. He missed his footing slightly and landed in the water instead of on the earth. From a crowd that had gathered on land, a priest emerged with a crucifix. Louis kissed the crucifix and planted his lance in the ground. He had come with his army to claim the throne of England as his own.

His full force appeared off the coast the following day. John hastened to Sandwich to gauge its size for himself. For decades English armies had crossed the Channel to fight in France; now that was all turned on its head. The long-threatened French invasion of England was now a reality staring him defiantly in his face. The moment was at hand and the crisis was upon him. John had been fearing this event for years; but he had also been preparing for it. His naval force might have been rendered temporarily inoperative, but on land he had amassed his troops in readiness. At this critical juncture, John had the opportunity to seize the military initiative from the onset: he could have been in position to attempt to prevent Louis' invasion force from landing or engage with it in a pitched battle and drive it back into the sea. He did neither. Instead, he fled. The French poured onto land unopposed.

The Conquest

Was John's reaction an ignominious one of panic? William the Breton would have us believe this. According to his account, Louis sought battle even though he and his men were the worse for wear after the arduous crossing and were outnumbered three-to-one. The Anonymous, who says that Louis initially had 200 knights with him, depicts John as riding along the bank and sounding off his trumpets after the main fleet arrived but this 'little emboldened his men, and little comforted them, great was the display of French power'.[439] John is an easy target to criticise in his military role and he may indeed have lost an important chance at the onset. But as we have seen battle avoidance was a mainstay of medieval warfare and this advice was given by the old warrior William Marshal, according to the Dunstable annalist. John's decision was taken because he had an even greater fear than the French joining up with the baronial forces: he could not trust his own men. Wendover explains John's thinking: 'as he was surrounded by foreign mercenaries, he did not dare attack Louis on his landing, in case they all deserted him in battle and went over to Louis's side; he therefore chose to retreat rather than engage in battle in uncertainty.'[440] Remember that one of the attractions of Louis was that he was from the French royal family; the barons hoped that John's foreign troops, many of whom were French themselves, would not fight against the son of their overlord king. Even without this threat, the knowledge of Hastings in 1066 must have played heavily on his mind; John did not want to lose his kingdom, and perhaps his life, that day.

But, as mentioned above, John is an easy target to criticise. John had proven himself energetic and thorough in his preparations for this war, expending vast amounts of treasure and sweat in building his massive army. But at the decisive moment to what avail had it been to him? One must question the wisdom of building an army so dramatically augmented by foreign mercenaries. The idea of these was that they could be trusted above his own barons, if the pay was forthcoming. If John's position was such that he could realistically place limited faith in his own countrymen, then he had little recourse than to look across the Channel for forces. Yet if these in turn were potentially undependable then what was the massive outlay of money for? Untrustworthy himself, he placed little trust in others. The significance here is that John had not fully utilised these men when they might have had their greatest effect in the months before the invasion: had John crushed the baronial revolt and its epicentre in London, there would have been no French invasion and no potential clash of loyalties. John was in the precarious position he found himself in late May 1216 precisely because he had failed to achieve military victory against a much weaker enemy before the French arrived on the scene. He compounded this failure with the current one, leaving Louis to establish his army on land unopposed.

John seemed to realise that his reluctance to commit fully to the grim but necessary task at hand was another failure. He resorted to character and slinked speedily away from the coast and was well on the way to Dover before most of his men even knew he had gone. When captains such as Robert of Béthune and Baldwin d'Aire realised the King was no longer with them, they were angered and critical. When they followed him to Dover, they found him there greatly agitated and disheartened. John's woeful lack of leadership skills, highlighted and exposed cruelly in times of extreme pressure, did not bode well for his campaign.

While Louis took control of Sandwich on 23 May, with all its ships, wine, meat and booty, John continued his flight further inland to Guildford and thence, distressed, to Winchester by 28 May with a Flemish rearguard protecting his movements all the way. Before retreating from Dover, he left this new, powerful fortress in the capable hands of the justiciar Hubert de Burgh (a reflection of its importance); with him were a large garrison of Flemish knights (as many as 140 calculates the Anonymous) and sergeants, and plentiful supplies to withstand a long siege. Louis proceeded to subdue the whole district around eastern Kent with ease, except for Dover. Dover was to be to Louis what London had been for John: an obstinate focus of prolonged resistance. Canterbury surrendered without a struggle, Guala himself deserting the city in undignified haste ahead of the French advance, and from there Louis reached Rochester around 25 May, the scene of John's triumph the previous autumn. The barons and Louis' French troops in London were now able to leave the capital and at long last meet up with their leader at Rochester. Here Robert Fitzwalter, Hugh Bigod, Saer de Quincy, William de Mandeville, Robert de Vere, William Marshal the Younger and others paid homage to Louis.

They soon made good their earlier defeat at Rochester on 30 May, the castle holding out for less than a week. It had taken John almost two months to win it. That Rochester fell so precipitously was not merely a measure of military pressure, but its often vital concomitant: political momentum. Louis' arrival, supported by his large invasion army, transformed the situation in England. Now that he had finally made good on his word and turned up in England, there was confidence and expectation amongst many that John's reign was over and that if they were to be part of Louis' success and its consequent benefits they should declare themselves for him now. Those who had made peaceful overtures to John in the preceding months when they were completely on the defensive, now reverted to their true, pro-French colours; many waverers and even fairweather supporters of John soon followed their example, clearly sensing *fin de regime* in the spring air. These considerations outweighed any expected, wholesale national reaction to the presence of a foreign invader on English soil (this was to come later); this speaks volumes as to how far John had alienated his subjects. The momentum was with Louis, just as it was with his father in his conquest of Normandy in 1203–04.

Against this, repeated proclamations of excommunication, as again pronounced when Guala reunited with John at Winchester on 28 May, counted for little. Louis entered the capital triumphantly on 2 June to a rapturous reception. The canons of Saint Paul's, unperturbed by Guala's frantic condemnations, welcomed Louis warmly with a procession in the cathedral. No fewer than twelve of the country's twenty bishops welcomed Louis as the new defender of the English church. Perhaps Louis' satisfaction was marred a little by Westminster Abbey's refusal to grant him entry (one of only five London churches which obeyed excommunication protocol) and, more importantly, that the Tower of London remained neutral and treated him similarly, for the time being at least.[441] William Hardel, the mayor of London and a host of others paid homage to the French Prince. From the start, Louis acted in every way as the rightful King of England. He swore on the holy gospels that he would restore to his new vassals all their rightful inheritances and good laws. He wrote to Alexander of Scotland and then to all the barons who had not yet done homage to him, instructing them either to do so or 'to leave the kingdom of England with haste'.[442]

It had been a perfect start for Louis: all his forces safely across the Channel; no men lost; Sandwich, Canterbury and Rochester all secure; and now a real sense of palpable success in his claim to the throne with his experiences in London. The outcome so far had vindicated not only his careful, lengthy planning but also the stubborn, if largely passive, resistance of the barons in the capital. Louis would have hoped that the impressive impact of his arrival and the momentum that it had created would persuade his opponents that the sensible option was to abandon the despotic John and come over to him. Indeed, Wendover reports that many on the King's side abandoned him, 'quite certain that Louis would obtain the kingdom' while many of John's continental troops – but not the Poitevins – either headed home or joined with Louis.[443] But the real struggle was only just beginning.

Louis was not the type to hang around and hope for the best. He intended to capitalise on his momentum and seek out John while the Angevin was still on the back foot. He would have guessed from his own knowledge and that of the barons that John's reversal would be affecting him adversely and that he should keep the pressure on. The chronicler Robert of Auxerre reports that John had lost his nerve and was unable to act. On 6 June Louis led a large army out of London making for the King at Winchester while another force set out to assert control of the eastern counties. It was as if the forces of the long pent-up barons and early French arrivals had now combined with the massive influx of Louis' army to burst out of the capital and flood across the land. Meanwhile, Alexander of Scotland besieged Carlisle again while pro-baronial factions stirred up more trouble in Wales and Ireland. The desultory civil war was over and the driving war of conquest had begun. 'The realm was thrown into chaos,' writes Warren.[444]

The day before Louis' departure, John had actually quitted Winchester and retreated farther west to the safety of the formidable Corfe Castle. While Louis led his men, John used his as a buffer against the enemy. Louis' first objective was Reigate Castle, owned by the Earl of Warrene; he reached it on 7 June to find it abandoned. He entrusted its care to Robert de Courtenay. The following day

Louis took Guildford and on the 10th he arrived before Farnham, a castle belonging to Peter des Roches, Bishop of Winchester. Hardly had Louis set up a siege camp when the garrison surrendered the next day. By the 14th Louis was before Winchester. Here, for the first time, the French Prince met with real resistance.

Before leaving Winchester, John had reorganised his forces. He sent Falkes de Bréauté to defend the region around Oxford, centred on his royal castle there, while Savary de Mauléon was charged with preparing the defences of Oxford. We can determine here that John knew he had to draw up a defensive line before the French proceeded too far west and undermined royal support there. De Mauléon fired the suburbs to deny the oncoming enemy resources and shelter (Coggeshall claims John personally committed this incendiary act); the fire, however, spread into the city razing perhaps as much as half of it to the ground. The flames were seen by the rebel forces. Louis ordered his army to arrange itself into battle order and to approach the city quietly and carefully. He found the city deserted and entered it. However, before having left to meet up with John, Savary had left garrisons in Winchester's two castles, its main one in the west and another in the east called Wolsevey belonging to des Roches and captained by the young squire Oliver, whom the Anonymous identifies as an illegitimate son of John. Louis wished these garrisons to be checked so they could not sally forth and fire the rest of the city or make a surprise attack on his camp; he instructed Robert de Béthune and Baldwin de Belvoir to see to this task which they performed with assiduous labour. Louis' siege engines went to work on the main castle, his perriers and mangonnels bombarding its tower. The siege lasted until 24 June. On this day Savary came from the King to discuss surrender terms of the castles with Louis; the garrisons were allowed to withdraw and Louis took full possession of Winchester. Louis awarded Count Hervé of Nevers with the city and main castle. With this success emerged the first inkling of trouble in the Franco-baronial alliance. William Marshal the Younger contested Adam de Beaumont's marshalship of the army; Louis, fearing loss of English support, granted this to him. This was to be the first of many squabbles and evidence of growing friction between the rebel barons and the French over the increasing share of spoils, which did much to cause acrimony among their ranks.

More serious to John than the loss of Winchester was the flurry of high-level desertions to Louis while he was in the city and what it said about John's expected chances. These were pretty devastating to John on the political, military and personal level. Four great earls changed sides and submitted to Louis: three who were previously seemingly committed supporters of the King – Arundel, Warren and Salisbury – and Aumale. With them went 430 knights and thirteen castles. Salisbury, William Longsword, was the king's half-brother; William the Breton suggests that he was looking for vengeance for John's unwarranted advances ('incest', William claims) on the Earl's wife when he was captive in France after the defeat at Bouvines.[445] Salisbury and the consistently inconsistent Aumale soon returned to John, but it must have shaken the King at the time. Another deserter was Warin Fitzgerald, a chamberlain of the exchequer, a castellan in possession of over 100 knights' fees. Within a fortnight Hugh de Neville let John know that he was ready to hand over Marlborough, a town which owed its charter to John, and John Fitzhugh followed him. John tried to stop and even reverse this flow with increasingly desperate attempts at reconciling himself with his estranged barons, even the de Braose family, and safe-conducts were offered to any thinking of returning to his service. At the same time, rallying himself into more solid action, he checked the readiness of royal castles in Wiltshire and Dorset while instructing Bayonne to send galleys against the French.

Louis had not finished his triumphal progress yet. From Winchester he went to the south coast and the old Roman camp of Portchester, taking it and giving the castle to Nevers. At the beginning of July he moved on to Odiham, a small town belonging to des Roches. Despite its minor castle with a minimal garrison of only three knights and ten soldiers, a spirited defence was put up in the face of a barrages and assaults. The garrison commander was Engelard de Cigogné, one of the foreigners complained about in clause 50 of Magna Carta. On the third day of the siege, the garrison sortied out and caused substantial losses among the French. The garrison held out for a full week before surrendering on 9 July. As they emerged from the castles with their horses and armour – their defence ensured them honourable terms – the French were amazed at their paucity of numbers and were filled with admiration for them.

It was while at Odiham that John's chief forester Hugh de Neville offered Marlborough to Louis. The French Prince in turn handed it over to his relative Robert de Dreux. The Anonymous goes into considerable detail about the hand-over of Marlborough. De Dreux headed there with a considerable force which included Enguerrand de Coucy, Robert de Béthune and Baldwin of Belvoir. When they approached the town they feared a trap: the gates were shut, men armed the battlements and other soldiers moved around in the woods. At first they decided to return to Louis but, gathering their courage, they instead made camp for the night. As they were leaving in the morning, de Neville sent a messenger to them to arrange details of the handover. The castellan then turned up and handed over the keys to the castle. De Dreux garrisoned it with ten knights under Jean de Lisdain and returned to the host. The Anonymous judges the garrison as insufficient to protect the castle, perhaps with the benefit of hindsight, as it was soon to be retaken by the royalists.

Again, William Marshal the Younger complained about Louis' disposition of his victories, claiming the castle for himself in vain. Instead, Louis sent the young Marshal further west to capitalise on another defection, this time that of Walter de Beauchamp, Sheriff of Worcester. The younger William occupied the city, much to his father's annoyance: 'the impertinence of his heir's incursion into a region so near his own command was apparently too much for the old Earl.'[446] William

Marshal senior, who was at this time holding down the Marches for John, warned his son to quit the city. There may have been paternal care in the warning, as a royalist force under Earl Ranulf of Chester and Falkes de Bréauté retook the city on 17 July. It is likely that William Marshal saw the benefit of a division in family loyalties, as it meant a foot in both camps in very uncertain circumstances.[447]

Louis was back in London by mid-July where his cause received more fillips. Pope Innocent III died of fever at Perugia on 16 July; when the news reached London the French were delighted. The Barnwell Chronicler reports that the rebels and French were hopeful of a positive change. The new pope, Honorius III, was a less stringent character but no less supportive of John. More immediate was the knowledge that his forces under Robert Fitzwalter, William de Mandeville and William of Huntingfield were experiencing similar successes in the east of England, especially in Essex, Norfolk and Suffolk. The details of this campaign are less clear and largely absent in the chronicles. Wendover, the much and wrongly maligned chronicler, reports that the army found Norwich deserted; it was occupied and used as a base from which the freshly installed garrison could impose the new order's authority in the region, not least through taxation to assist the war effort. A more brutal way of raising war funds was achieved successfully at Lynn, a coastal town of the Wash. The town was attacked and seriously damaged and many inhabitants were taken away as prisoners for ransoming. The expedition left garrisons in strongholds before returning to London weighed down with great amounts of booty.

Gilbert de Gant came to Louis in London with more good news from further north, Gilbert presenting his lord with the sword of Lincoln. Louis rewarded him by creating him Earl of Lincoln. He gave orders to Gilbert and Robert de Ropsley to subdue the region and to hem in the royalist garrisons of Newark and Nottingham, as John's men had been making incursions from the castles to harry and destroy baronial land and property. Louis' captains took control of Lincolnshire and its principal city, imposing taxation across the region, but Lincoln Castle would not fall to them. Its castellan, the formidable lady Nichola de la Haye, negotiated a bought truce. The castle was to be besieged later for the duration of war and was to play a central role at the war's end. The two rebel commanders then went on ravage the area of Holland and impose further taxes on its people. York and Yorkshire also fell into Louis' control, due to the advance of Robert de Ros, Richard Percy and Peter de Brus. Further north again, King Alexander had, as mentioned, moved south with his host to besiege Carlisle and into Northumbria to ravage royalist lands up to Durham. 'All these provinces', says Wendover, 'were subdued and swore allegiance to Louis.'[448]

These victories were rendered all the sweeter by John's money problems; despite Guala's imposition of taxes on the clergy, the King was losing money fast. The author of *The History of William Marshal* makes the point: 'I should inform you at this point that, when the King ran out of resources, very few of the men stayed with him who were there for his money; they went their own way with their booty in hand.'[449] And then there were the desertions of as many as a sixth of John's household knights, the core of his army, including men such as Robert of Ropsley and Hugh de Neville. Stephen Church, in his valuable study of John's household knights, describes this as 'a remarkable picture of disloyalty from the rank and file ... These were the men who ... had a special relationship with the King ... Yet when John's position became seemingly untenable, or when the lands of the household knights came under threat, these men who had supped the king's wine, eaten his food, received his *benevolentia*, rejected their master and chose to look instead after their own and their families' interests.'[450] Ties of family; the need to protect their own lands; following the lead of their lords and, crucially, the expectation that John was no longer in a position to offer sufficient rewards for their service now that Louis was in the ascendant – all of these factors contributed to Louis' hugely successful initial thrust.

The Resistance

The months of June and July had produced significant and telling victories which left Louis in control of more than one-third of England, including some of its most important and prosperous regions and centres, with strong allies entrenched in areas from the south coast up to and including Scotland. This could only encourage further waverers to come over to Louis' winning side. But this picture is incomplete: Louis had not done enough to force a definitive outcome. Just as the barons had held out precariously against John, so now John was holding out against the rebels. Not everything had gone Louis' way.

On the diplomatic front, Louis' ambassadors to the papal court failed to win any concessions from the dying Innocent III. The military impact of this, like the excommunication, was slight, but it showed that the Papacy did not regard Louis' victories as being a *fait accompli* which merited a new response. Wendover thinks the diplomatic mission to be worthy of several pages in his chronicle. Louis also entered into fresh talks with Guala in mid-July, but again nothing came of them. Ironically, on the political front, the flocking of barons to Louis' banner – peaking at two-thirds of the total by the summer's end – increased the friction in the Franco-rebel camp. As exhibited by William Marshal the Younger's attitude, jealousies and suspicions increased: the more that barons offered their allegiance to Louis, the less land and spoils were available to Louis' Frenchmen.

The great swathes of territory dominated by Louis, tightly concentrated across the whole south-east and in pockets beyond, can lead to a slightly misleading impression of his position. Strong as it was, there were weaknesses in it. While victory brought men to his cause, he was actually losing some at the same time. The Count of Holland had earlier taken the cross and, unlike John, intended to fulfil his crusading vows, and so he left with his men to make his preparations for the Holy Land. Over two months of assembling at French ports and subsequent campaigning was enough for some of Louis' other troops: Hugh Havés and his men wished to return home to Artois after Winchester. From London they made to the coast along the Thames and 'reached the sea with great joy', but here had to outrun a royalist naval squadron trying to intercept them.[451]

The biggest block to Louis' momentum, however, setting limits to his expansion, was John's system of royal castles. Medieval warfare centred around sieges, none more so than this conflict. When Louis failed to take John's strongholds, the lands that he took around them remained vulnerable: hence Gilbert de Gant's operations against Newark and Nottingham. Alexander's depredations in the north failed to win the castles of Philip de Oldcoate and Hugh de Balliol who, between them, pretty much held all the castles of Northumberland; Barnard Castle and Durham Castle remained in loyal hands. Newark, Nottingham and Lincoln marked the extent of Louis' secure control into the northern midlands. While in the otherwise strongly consolidated south-east, two large thorns remained stuck in Louis' side: the powerful royal fortresses of Windsor and Dover. These defiant islands of resistance indicated, just like London did for the rebels, an enemy that remained unbroken. The chronicler's statement after the siege of Rochester in 1215 that none now placed their faith in castles was completely inaccurate. While some of his troops were occupied in small-scale warfare and raiding, John had been ensuring that the majority were securing his castles: while Louis was busy in the field, a contemporary wrote that John 'laid in good supplies of knights, provisions and arms in the castles of Wallingford, Corfe, Wareham, Bristol, Devizes and others too numerous to mention'.[452] John was playing a longer game in the hope that events would turn for him. It was not a heroic or perhaps even advisable course to take, but it suited John and it greatly discomfited the rebels in the meantime. The most significant centres of resistance were Lincoln, Windsor and Dover. Lincoln enjoyed an arranged truce until August; its fate will be discussed in the next chapter. Windsor and Dover were priorities for Louis and we shall cover his operations against these two castles shortly.

But first it is necessary to look briefly over John's other activities in leading the resistance against the invaders lest the impression be given that he had remained relatively passive. A study of government records reveal his movements from this time.[453] While Louis was at Winchester and moving through Hampshire, John was doing the rounds of his castles in Wiltshire and Dorset ensuring that they were fully readied for war. As well as his instructions to Bayonne for naval actions, granting safe-conducts and appealing to the de Broase family as mentioned above, he was issuing specific orders to his castellans across the land. One feature of these orders was castles such as Richmond and Bolsover that could not be held should be destroyed; instructions were actually sent out for the destruction of the front-line Castle of Newark before being cancelled shortly afterwards. He also granted

his men permission to submit, temporarily of course, to the French *tenserie* payments when militarily prudent to do so; in allowing this, John was recognising
that in many cases he knew help to his men might be a while in coming. The King
was probably expecting Louis to continue his advance into John's western and
south-western territory, as perhaps signalled by William Marshal the Younger's
occupation of Worcester in mid-July, and so he had concerned himself with
the border defence of this area. Just after the middle of July, John left Sherborne
and headed northwards to reach Leominster on the 31st, having passed through
Bristol, Berkeley, Gloucester, Tewkesbury and Hereford. His proximity to the
border facilitated his talks with Welsh princes as he tried to elicit their support;
on 2 August he crossed into Wales at Radnor to pursue these further. His itinerary thereafter until 19 August was Clun, Shrewsbury, Whitchurch, Bridgenorth,
Worcester, Gloucester and Berkeley. From Berkeley Castle on the 19th he wrote
a letter which explained these movements: he believed Louis intended to besiege
Hereford and Worcester.

In fact, Louis had returned to London four weeks earlier to consolidate his
position in the southeast and to oversee operations against Windsor and Dover.
One historian has therefore put John's activity in the west down to poor intelligence;[454] this may well have been the case, but throughout the war both sides
generally had a very good idea of the enemy's troop movements – indeed,
responsive strategies were commonly devised around these – and so it is worth
considering if John was consciously avoiding a decisive encounter to concentrate
on keeping his existing strongholds rather than winning back lost ones.

Although Louis had returned to London, he was still taking the fight to the
enemy. An army of barons left London to ravage Cambridgeshire and capture the
weak royal castle of the shire's principal town – a rare example of a royal castle
falling to force – and seized the twenty soldiers garrisoning it. They continued to
rampage throughout Norfolk and Suffolk, pillaging the countryside and churches
and extorting ransoms from Yarnmouth, Dunwich and Ipswich before subjecting
Colchester and its surrounding areas to the same treatment. It was a profitable
little *chevauchée* that no doubt raised morale further through full bellies, full pockets and a tangible military gain.

Dover and Windsor were harder nuts to crack. Louis had returned from his
westward advances to concentrate on these hugely important strategic fortresses.
Dover dominated the south coast and it was here that Louis arrived on 25 July to
oversee a full investiture of the castle and ensure, according to William the Breton,
'free access to England', necessary for logistical support and reinforcements.[455]
Matthew Paris offers an interesting anecdote that shows how the wise Philip
Augustus recognised Dover as 'the key to England' when he took his son to
task for not prioritising Dover from the very start of the campaign.[456] Philip,
the master castle-breaker and conqueror of Château Gaillard, was making a
very pertinent military point, which Louis appreciated. Windsor, which severely

curtailed any movements by Louis to the west and midlands, was laid under siege by Robert de Dreux and the Count of Nevers within a couple of days. The invasion forces entrenched for their first lengthy sieges of the campaign. Both were to be dramatic and violent.

Louis had been in contact with his father as the Prince requested heavier siege machinery to help with the capture of the castle. This arrived in the form of a huge stone-thrower called 'Malvoisin' ('Bad' or 'Evil Neighbour'), and joined the ranks of other machines constantly bombarding the castle; this petraria may have in fact been a trebuchet, mentioned for the first time in English sources at this siege.[457] While his ships secured the sea outside Dover, Louis' large army completed the blockade on the land side. Inside the castle were 140 knights and many soldiers, mainly Poitevin and Flemish, under Hubert de Burgh and the Flemish mercenary captain Gerard de Sotteghem. It was a strong force for a strong castle. They had been well prepared and well provisioned. Louis was billeted in a priory in the town; his leading knights also preferred the solid shelter there to life in the tented camp. They settled in for the siege.

Hubert de Burgh, 'a brave knight', says Wendover, led an active defence. The garrison made many sorties and inflicted heavy casualties on the besiegers. Louis' men kept up the pressure, eating away at the castle's defences. Louis conducted the siege operations from the field north of the castle; this gave him a clear view of the action. His first target was the north-east barbican protecting the main gates, guarded by Pierre de Créon and reinforced by strong oak timbers and a surrounding ditch. The soldiers within the garrison could be clearly seen by the besiegers as they manned the battlements to engage in crossbow exchanges with the French, one of whom, Perenaut, was obviously a crack shot because on his approach the garrison would hurry into cover. Mangonels and petrarias were repositioned to hurl their rocks at the walls and gates while from on high soldiers shot down from a tall belfry and below, under the protective mantlet of a cat, miners swung their pickaxes against the base of the ramparts. Louis then ordered his knights to make an assault; a squire by the name of Paon was the first to make his way into the barbican. Pierre de Créon stood fast at his post and was fatally struck down.

But the siege dragged on into September. The garrison's resistance increased in proportion to the level of attack. Casualties forced the French to withdraw their lines and even their tents. There were serious manpower losses, too. As the siege became ever more protracted, many of his men returned home, including leading knights such the Count de Roussi, Jean de Montmirail, Hugh de Rumegny and others. The Anonymous says that Louis' 'host dwindled marvellously'. John, meanwhile, was on the move to relieve the siege of Windsor. The siege caused Louis tremendous frustration as both his momentum and the military initiative slipped away. Wendover reports that 'he was enraged and swore that he would not leave until he had captured the castle and hanged all the garrison.' He then increased the psychological pressure: he ordered his men to construct a highly visible market in front of the castle with the clear implication that while his forces wanted for nothing, the garrison's supplies could not last forever. The intention was 'to strike terror into them' with the fear of starvation; but Wendover also implies that it was an admission of the inability of the French to take the castle by force.

A significant boost bolstered Louis, possibly around the second week of September. Alexander II of Scotland, who had taken the town of Carlisle on 8 August (the castle still held out) made a quite remarkable 400-mile march from here to Dover to greet his powerful ally.[458] Keith Stringer, who has admirably compensated for the lack of historians' attention to Alexander's role in the war, notes that the Scottish King was able to do so untroubled by John due to first-rate intelligence and the successes of the rebels: most of Yorkshire was rendered safe by the control of Robert de Ros, especially through his castle at Helmsley, and his progress was further assisted by Earl Warenne' s castles above Lincoln, where Alexander met up with the rebel besieging force. The knowledge that John was busy with his military activity in the West Country at this time was exploited fully: 'the royalists were caught completely off-guard.' His return north afterwards was more dramatic and even more successful: he made a profitable raid on John's camp. As Stringer writes: 'no one could deny that Alexander's parading through England's heartlands was a stunning feat of arms; and the unpalatable memory of his astonishing exploit remained seared on the English government's psyche for years to come.'[459] Contemporary Scottish chroniclers took note with some pride of Alexander's journey; he had, after all, led a Scottish army triumphantly from the north of England to its south-eastern most corner and back again. No wonder it shook the English government.

There had been one episode to cast a shadow on his journey southward. During a brief siege of Hugh de Balliol's castle at Barnard, he was joined by some barons, chief among whom was one of the leading northern barons, Eustace de Vescy, brother-in-law to King Alexander. As Eustace rode around the castle looking for weaknesses in the defence, he ventured in the range of a crossbowman who loosed his weapon at him. The bolt struck him through the forehead and pierced his brain. He died instantly.

Louis went to meet Alexander at Canterbury before bringing him to Dover. With Alexander was the force besieging Lincoln before the truce was arranged there. Also at Dover by now were the Counts of Perche and Brittany, recently arrived from France; Perche was to play a leading role at the climax of the war. Thus it was that a notable and sizeable congregation assembled to witness Alexander pay homage to Louis. This was a moment of great symbolic significance. It was quite something to have over two-thirds of the barons recognise the 28-year-old Louis as their lord; but here we have one king publicly acknowledging another king. In the absence of the Archbishop of Canterbury to perform the religious ceremony of coronation, Louis instead at least had the eminent satisfaction of his *de facto* role as King of England being affirmed in practical terms: as Wendover explains his action, Alexander was paying homage to Louis for the lands he held in England from 'the King of the English'.[460]

But neither the accolade nor the Scottish troops were of help to Louis at Dover. Alexander, his promise to pay homage fulfilled, had to return home and the siege of Dover continued. John, as we shall see shortly, was on the march and Louis was needed elsewhere. Efforts to take the castle were intensified. His miners had all the while been sapping away at the gatehouse towers. The tunnel, which still exists, went under one tower. The roof was propped up with timbers, which were set alight and the sappers withdrew. When the supports burned through, a tower collapsed and Louis' men charged into the breach. But they were repulsed vigorously by the defenders, who killed the French knights Guichard de Baugy and Jean de la Rivière. The gap was then refortified with large timbers, crossbeams and barricades of oak trunks. Whether this material had been brought in in readiness for the siege, or whether the defenders followed typical besieged practice and were stripping the buildings is unclear. The bodies of the knights killed were taken back to France for burial.

Louis' siege operations – and indeed his whole movement of men in the south and south-east – were severely hampered by the guerrilla activities of a royalist band of archers living in the great forests of the Weald under the inspirational leadership of a folk hero who was determined to fight against oppression. The French invasion of England in 1216 provides an historical figure as a possible inspiration for the Robin Hood stories, which may well have developed around this time. The guerrilla force's leader was William of Kensham, a royal bailiff, and his men were volunteer archers from the seven hundreds of the Weald, all loyal to the crown, who fought against the French during their occupation of southern England. Based in the great forest of the Weald in Kent and the south, this group waged highly effective ambush warfare against the French occupiers. We have only a tiny amount of information on William, but it is telling that such a little-known figure very quickly took on a popular folk name: Willikin of the Weald.[461]

Roger of Wendover writes of 'a young man named William' who, collecting a company of 1000 bowmen, took to the deep forests and 'continued to trouble the French throughout the whole war, and slew many thousands of them'.[462] The Anonymous speaks admiringly of his 'noble prowess' and how he was 'renowned in Louis's army'.[463] The author of the *History of William Marshal* confirms William's effectiveness: writing of French losses, he instructs the reader to 'witness the deeds of Willikin of the Weald'.[464] He inspired fear in French ranks as they tried to make their way from London to the southern port of Winchelsea, where at one point he even had Louis trapped. He also made an effective raid on the French siege camp at Dover. Lest he be considered too romantic and dashing a hero, he apparently had a brutal tendency to behead his prisoners. His contribution to the war effort was recognised by both John and his successor. Records suggest that William survived the war and lived to the year 1257.

Meanwhile things had not been going any better at the siege of the other great southern royal castle at Windsor.[465] The Anonymous drily comments of Robert de Dreux and the Count of Nevers and their besieging force, 'long were they there, and little did they gain.' In charge of the mighty fortress was Engelard de Cigogné with sixty knights and their retainers; despite the massive contrast to Odiham, Engelard defended his new castle with equal tenacity and his skills as 'a man well tried in war', says Wendover. As at Dover, the garrison would often burst from the castle in violent sorties that frightened the French. Twice the garrison broke the besiegers' main petraria. The Anonymous reports that during the siege a knight from Artois by the name of Gullaume de Cerisy was killed; apparently it was no great loss as his death went unlamented 'because he was hated by many'. The precarious position of Windsor and Dover spurred John into action. At the beginning of September he set out on a major campaign. It was to be his last.[466]

John's Last Campaign and the Final Defeat

We have no definitive view of John's paramount strategic objective for the last campaign: intercepting Alexander's army as it returned to Scotland; marching on Windsor to force directly its relief; or burning the lands of the barons to undermine their power bases and in the hope that the provocation would compel them to leave Windsor, Dover and Lincoln to defend their own regions. Turner and others believe that the 'furiously energetic' John only feinted at Windsor, but 'actually aimed at East Anglia, hoping to meet the Scottish King on his way north'.[467] There may appear to be a feeling of exigency about John's movements; this is not at all to say that it was directionless, but rather that John's army was flexible in its response to situations in the field. All three objectives could be part and parcel of an overall strategy; but of the three, the last – drawing away enemy forces from the great sieges – seems to dominate and it certainly fits in with the pattern of John's style of warfare: avoiding a decisive engagement and putting his energy into a defensive castle strategy and an offensive ravaging one.

There is also the question of the timing of the campaign. There clearly was an urgency to act if Dover and Windsor were to stay out of French and baronial hands. There may also have been the concern that some of the remaining loyal one-third of barons would start to go over to Louis. Whether John had fled from the initial French advances in array or beat a judicious tactical defeat can be argued; but certainly now was an opportune moment for John to counter-attack. He had held the line in the west of the country with important bases in eastern rebel territory. The desertions seemed to have reached their natural limit and now time was not on Louis' side. The Earls of Salisbury and York returned to John's side, as did William the Marshal's heir; John, calculating how much he needed the return of prodigal sons, was magnanimous in his neediness. On Louis' side, the comments from the Anonymous that Louis was losing men fast is confirmed by the annals of Dunstable: 'Day by day the followers of the French dwindled.'[468] Robert de Dreux, a leading commander of the French forces, returned to France at this juncture. Nor were the Cinque ports fulfilling their submission oath to Louis as they continued to aid John by naval actions in the Channel. The overall position was still highly favourable for Louis, but, crucially, he had lost the momentum.

John's campaign was a belated but necessary counter-attack, a testing of the strength and resolve of the enemy by a violent and intimidating incursion into their secure territory in the hope of regaining the initiative. Charting John's campaign movements is not straightforward and exact dates can be hard to confirm: Stringer notes 'the increasingly punishing and erratic nature of John's itinerary'.[469] Having secured his position in the west, on 2 September he left Cirencester with his army and Savary de Mauléon to reach Reading four days later, having travelled through Burford, Oxford (staying here for three days) and Wallingford. He was augmenting his forces by collecting men from royal garrisons along the way. After two nights at Reading he went to nearby Sonning where he stayed until the 13th. In so doing he was placing himself within striking distance of Windsor. This obviously unnerved the besiegers. Their fears increased when a contingent of John's Welsh archers approached the siege camp at night and fired into the host and a substantial skirmish broke out. The joint Franco-baronial force readied themselves in battle array for a full-scale engagement which never came.

John withdrew – the Anonymous admits he does not know who counselled this move – and on 15 September ravaged his way through baronial lands from Walton-on-Thames through Aylesbury and Bedford, reaching the recently rebel-held Castle of Cambridge the following day. The besiegers at Windsor held a quick war council and decided to follow him. 'Gaining little or no advantage at Windsor Castle', says Wendover, 'they determined to lift the siege.' They did this at night, leaving their tents behind and burning their siege machines, and made a forced march to Cambridge in an attempt to intercept John. Wendover reports the rumour that the Count of Nevers, who counselled this strategy, did do because he was in the pay of King John.[470] Had John moved away from Windsor because he felt confident matters could be left with Nevers? Or was he gambling successfully that his actions would draw off the besiegers and grant Windsor some temporary relief? The latter offers a more likely pertinent analysis. The ravaging of lands was a classic diversionary tactic of medieval commanders attempting to draw away besiegers from strongholds; it worked here and throughout the war. It was harvest time, and the damage being done was calculated and massively destructive. The barons and French may well have agreed a truce with the garrison; the latter had seen John come and then go. And again we come to John's consistent policy of battle avoidance: Coggeshall tells of how John 'fled' from the barons at Windsor.[471] It makes more sense to see the Franco-baronial force at Windsor pursuing the King to force him into a decisive engagement and protect their lands rather than a battle-shy John risking a full-scale battle to relieve Windsor.

This promotes scepticism for the suggestion that John was trying to catch Alexander on his return to Scotland. The Barnwell chronicler reports that John moved into Norfolk and 'occupied the places through which Alexander was about to return home';[472] but this does not necessarily mean that he was waiting to fight him, but might be that he was simply disrupting Alexander's movements and denying him supplies. One lesser chronicle says that John was making block-ing movements, 'destroying bridges, immobilising boats, excavating fords, and stationing troops in ambush positions'.[473] This was harassment, not engagement. And it was a failure: not only did Alexander's army march unscathed back home, it was at this time they even managed to ransack one of John's camps.

Thus it was on the night of 17 September at Cambridge that when John's scouts warned him of the approaching enemy force from Windsor he once again took to his heels, 'like a cunning traveller' says Wendover, and went further north to Stamford having first made a clever, counter-intuitive short march southwards which wrong-footed his pursuers. No battles for John, he did what he always did, resorting to the same old policy of hugely destructive *chevauchée*. John was good at this; it may have been the one military activity he was truly comfortable with. His incendiaries scorched their way through enemy territory in Norfolk and Suffolk, destroying harvests and undermining his enemy's economic capac-ity to wage war, John was at one and the same time punishing rebellious barons and trying to force them into submission, 'burning their houses and crops and inflicting great damage to his enemies', says Wendover, reporting the 'King's 'fury' against the lands of the Earl of Arundel, Roger Bigod, William de Huntingfield, Roger de Cresy and other barons: 'the cruel destruction which he wrought among the houses and crops of the barons afforded a pitiable spectacle to all who saw it.' Laying waste was a powerful diversionary weapon. As John headed rapidly out of the southern theatre of operations, the force from Windsor headed south again, to London says Wendover, gaining consolation by 'devoting' themselves in turn to the rapine and plunder of Cambridgeshire once again, while the Count of Nevers ensured Alexander's safe passage past Cambridge as the Scottish King made his way to Gilbert de Gant's small containing force at Lincoln.

On 21 September John headed west from Stamford to reach Rockingham. Before he set out for Lincoln himself to prevent a stronger baronial investiture of the castle, a tale is told of John by Matthew Paris that depicts his vengeful anger – and possible frustration – at its height. Burning his way through Oundle and the manors of the Abbey of Peterborough, John, Savary de Mauléon 'and their nefarious accomplices perpetrated unheard of wickedness'.[474] According to Paris, John ordered Savary to torch Crowland Abbey and its village while the King watched on. Savary did not carry out the order directly; instead he accepted from the fearful monks a sum of money as protection against destruction and brought this to the King. Such protection offerings, especially from monasteries, was a normal feature of the war, but John was enraged and hurled violent invective at his captain. He then picked up a torch and personally set alight the harvest fields, Paris depicting an apocalyptic figure of the King running through the flames and black smoke like a deranged demon. There may well have been method in John's madness, for Gilbert de Gant and his men had the fear of God put into them: leaving Lincoln in a hurry, they 'fled before his face, dreading his presence as if it were lightning'.[475]

John had brought relief to Windsor and now, very briefly, to Lincoln, and still he waged war with relentless energy and stamina, sometimes covering 40 miles a day. He pursued Gilbert's force to the Isle of Axholme, terrorising the land around 'by sword and fire' between 26–28 September.[476] In this brief time away, the Barnwell chronicler claims that Alexander had spent a couple of days at Lincoln during the King's absence. If John had really been after Alexander, this was a missed opportunity. John's scouts had been keeping him well informed of enemy movements, as had Alexander's for him; so who was avoiding whom? On 30 September John dispatched Savary back to Crowland Abbey to root out 'the king's enemy knights and sergeants hiding in secret places' in the surrounding area.[477] Not finding his intended prey, and probably hesitant to return to his master empty-handed, Savary forced his way into the abbey and dragged from its cloister church men and a great deal of booty, bringing these back to John, who by 9 October was in King's Lynn. The King, for his part, had kept his momentum and the fires going through early October, marching and destroying through Grimsby, Louth, Boston and Spalding. At King's Lynn, a port whose importance was exceeded only by Boston, Southampton and London, he received a very warm welcome and was laden with gifts. From here John planned to arrange for provisioning and reinforcements for his northern campaign. He had no intention of easing up. As he indulged excessively in a feast in his honour, John may have been reasonably satisfied at the gains of his persistent and energetic counter-attack. If so, his satisfaction was fleeting – perhaps only hours, if that – and crushed beyond hope in the week that followed.[478]

It is believed that John fell ill at King's Lynn with a major attack of dysentery, probably precipitated by exhaustion; according to Coggeshall, insatiable gluttony was the cause. Nevertheless, he set out for the north on the morning of 11 October, having left Savary behind in King's Lynn to fortify and defend the town. There is uncertainty over the exact date and location of what happens next, but Holt is convincing in arguing that John crossed the nearly five-mile wide estuary of the Wellstream (now the Nene) in the Wash between Long Sutton and Walpole Cross Keys on the morning of 11 October around low-tide (11.15 a.m.).[479] Not only was John attempting a well-known short-cut, but he was also avoiding the

roads in the rebel-dominated Fenlands. Stringer suggests that Alexander's movements imposed 'a sense of urgency' on John.[480] John's haste went against him.
Wendover's no doubt exaggerated account vividly relates what happened as the
King's baggage train made the crossing: 'The land opened up in the middle of the
waves and caused whirlpools which sucked in everything, men as well as horses,
so that no one escaped.' John only narrowly got away in time, but he lost 'all his
carts, wagons, baggage horses, his money, precious vessels and everything he treas-
ured'. Wendover, like John, was on uncertain ground for this episode. It may have
been the case that John did not wait until the waters had fully receded, making
navigation across the natural causeway extremely treacherous. Explorations have
revealed a thick layer of wet quicksand from medieval times at this point. There
was clearly a desperate struggle by his men to escape the catastrophe. This famous
disaster of John's lost treasure in the Wash may well be a myth, for reasons discussed in the next chapter. Coggeshall records the event as a noteworthy one but
does not resort to hyperbole: he mentions the loss of life, the royal Chapel and its
relics and some pack-horses. No victim is of sufficient rank to be named by either
chronicler, but both reveal how badly the King was affected by the loss; Wendover
attributes John's onset of illness to 'anguish of mind over his possessions swal-
lowed up by the water', causing him to be 'seized with a violent fever'.

John gathered himself at Wisbech and spent the night of 12 October at the
Cistercian Abbey of Swinesford. By this stage John is thought to have been
extremely ill, but if so this did not affect his appetite, Wendover claiming that
the notoriously gluttonous King made himself worse by stuffing himself with
peaches and by drinking new (not fully fermented?) cider. Comfort eating and
drowning his sorrows left him in a worse state than ever in the morning, and as he
made for Sleaford on 14 October he was apparently in great pain. However, the
well-placed Barnwell chronicler claims that it was at Sleaford that John began to
fall ill, which would explain his feasting and what has been seen by some as a catastrophic attack of indigestion.[481] Fearing the worst, John wrote to Honorius III
'in grave illness' and pleaded 'on bended knee' that the new pope would protect
his heir against the enemies of the King and the Holy Father.[482]

We have noted Warren's observation that John could not resist kicking a man
when he was down; now John felt what is was like to be on the receiving end.
At Sleaford he received the news from Dover that Hubert de Burgh and Gerard
de Sotteghem had arranged a truce with Louis. They had held out valiantly for
nearly three months but knew they could not resist the French siege operations
for much longer. The time was granted them to approach John for either help or
for permission to surrender. The truce came into force on 14 October. The news
'greatly angered the king' says the Anonymous, who claims that it was after this
that the King fell ill.[483] Coggeshall, a man with medical interests, says that the
blow brought on a more severe fever and the King had to be bled, but this did
nothing to improve his deteriorating condition.

Either that night or the next day John travelled to the Bishop of Lincoln's castle at Newark. Wendover says that he reached there on horseback only with great difficulty. Matthew Paris' account tells of how the King suffered so much from riding that, 'moaning and groaning' he ordered a litter to be made for him. This was roughly put together from trees along the road and seems to have piled even greater agony upon the failing King who cried out that it was killing him. At Newark Castle, the Abbot of Croxton, renowned for his medical knowledge, took charge of the fully coherent royal patient who continued to see to urgent business. Most urgent of all was his soul. He confessed his sins to the Abbot and received Holy Communion. Coggeshall writes that about midnight of 18–19 October a mighty wind arose over Newark; it was so fierce the inhabitants of the town feared their houses would be blown down. Perhaps the chronicler interpreted it as the King's spirit leaving his body, for King John died that night. His death changed everything.

7

The Battle for England, 1216–1217

A New Battlefield

There were many contingent parts to the war in England between 1215 and 1217: militarily the role of castles, foreign mercenaries and generalship were vital; politically and diplomatically, the role of patronage, finance, the handling of great lords and relations with the Papacy were central. But an overarching, dominating theme was personality; and now, with John's death, an overarching dominant personality disappeared from the cast. Even the majority of those who fought for John had little respect for the arbitrary, unstable despot; they were bound to him more by vested interest and fear than by honour and loyalty. His death was not greeted in the chronicles with a sense of respectful sympathy. The Barnwell writer offers this judicious epitaph to John: 'He was generous and liberal to foreigners but a despoiler of his own people. Since he trusted more in foreigners than in them, he was abandoned before the end by his own people, and in his own end he was little mourned'; while Matthew Paris' unsparing verdict reflected the feelings of many: 'With John's foul deeds all England is stinking / As does hell, to which he is now sinking.'[484] Speaking ill of the dead did not trouble Matthew. Over in France, William the Breton was no more sympathetic in his *Philippidos*, declaring that John's sins had caught up with him before highlighting his family values: 'condemned by the just judgement of the clergy and the people for he had been the cause of the death of his father, traitor against his brother and murderer of his nephew'; then adding, to further chasten the King's departed soul, 'O Louis, the English nation wanted to raise you on his throne.'[485]

In the days before his death, John had ordered his affairs carefully. He named his nine-year-old son Henry as his heir and made his intimate household members around him swear their allegiance to him. He had letters dispatched under his seal to all the sheriffs and castellans of England ordering them to recognise Henry as their new lord. In his testament, transcribed onto a single sheet of vellum, John leaves his affairs in the hands of the arbiters of the will, to see to 'making

satisfaction to God and holy church for damages and injuries done to them'.[486]
These arbiters, most of whom were present, were the legate Guala; Peter des
Roches, Bishop of Winchester; Richard Bishop of Chichester; Silvester Bishop
of Worcester; Brother Aimery de St Maur; Ranulf Earl of Chester; William
Earl Ferrers; Walter de Lacy; John of Monmouth; Savary de Mauléon; Falkes de
Bréauté; and William Marshal, Earl of Pembroke who, at nearly 70 years of age,
was elected regent (humbly and reluctantly, according to his biographer). This
was, in effect, John's minority council for Henry.

Stephen Church's article on John's last few days shows the King concerned for
the military situation his son would inherit. One of the John's actions on the last
day of his life was the supply of extra funds to Hubert de Burgh in order that he
could maintain the defence of Dover Castle; if Dover fell, it was likely that Louis,
not Henry, would rule England.[487] Nichola de Haye was rewarded for her defence
of Lincoln with the custody of the city, thus tying her even closer to the royalist cause. The powerful mercenary commander Falkes de Bréauté received the
Luton estates of Baldwin of Béthune, Count of Aumale who had died in 1212;
this reinforced Falkes' position as castellan of Bedford Castle and strengthened
the chain of his other crucial midlands strongholds of Hertford, Northampton,
Buckingham, Cambridge and Oxford. Eager to reach out on his deathbed to
rebel lords and the vacillating vassals who were forever changing sides as new
opportunities arose, John offered safe conducts to those who reconciled themselves to the crown through Savary de Mauléon. He also placed Savary in charge
of his 300 Welsh archers, who presumably had been with the King at the skirmish
at Windsor. Savary's role, however, was to be limited, for by December he had
returned home to Poitou.

The dominant figures of the new royalist leadership were William Marshal,
Peter des Roches, Ranulf of Chester and Guala. The first three were all experienced, supremely competent military commanders. They were supported, at
John's direction, by Falkes, Savary and William Brewer. As Church has noted, this
was a clear indication of John's determination not to compromise with the rebel
leadership: these were 'the hard men of John's regime ... Each of these men had
the taint of his master about him and no doubt there were many in the baronial camp who had suffered at their hands.' John had assembled a regency and
military council for his son of men either 'of natural authority' or 'whose "lack of
squeamishness" made them ideal royal servants'.[488] Of course, these men had been
advising the King and fighting for him all along; but John was no longer there to
overrule them or to dictate political or military strategy.

The implications of this were huge for royalists, rebels, the uncertain and the
French. The French had lost their greatest political and military asset. The baronial tide turned as anti-Johaninne rebels quickly understood the implications of
the sudden transformation and became pro-Henricians. John's death was ultimately a game changer.

The council had inherited a military situation that had certainly improved since the summer of 1216. Of the King's final campaign, Holt has judged that John's 'last convulsive actions showed a sound strategic grasp': he had strengthened royal garrisons, threatened northern baronial estates and prevented the 'danger of united action between King Alexander and Prince Louis and of the concentration of all the rebel forces against the royalist garrisons in the south'.[489] There is something to be said for this assessment, but it is too definite. John's swift decline and death distortedly preserves in aspic the successes of his last campaign. It had been energetic and with some purpose, but also frenetic, indecisive and limited in tangible gains. The French and rebels were still entrenched in a third of the country with major areas contested elsewhere.

The new council were able to build on the successes, but had John lived how much would these successes have meant in real terms? Would he have been able to keep them? Probably not. Incursions from King Alexander in Scotland and the activities of the northern rebels would in all likelihood simply have won the lands and castles back again in another round of advances and retreats. But the real issue, and the one that made John's final military successes more lasting, was the political impact of his death. The political momentum was now firmly on the loyalists' side. This is what shifted the balance.

On the morning following the King's death, a monk called John de Savigny came to the town of Newark. On entering he encountered members of John's household scurrying out of the castle laden down with all manner of goods and booty. The dead monarch was suffering the final indignity of having all his moveable valuables stolen; there was not even enough cloth left to afford his corpse a decent covering. Holt has made the intriguing suggestion that the rumours of the loss of the King's treasure at the Wash may have been started at this time, a clever diversion by those in John's household 'to cover their own acquisitive misdeeds'.[490] This is a very cynical observation and therefore a convincing one. The monk kept vigil over John's body and offered a mass for the king, who had been embalmed by the Abbot of Croxton, the Abbot having already cut out John's heart, a gift, it would seem, to his abbey. The body was transported to Worcester Cathedral in solemn procession under a mercenary guard and there, in accordance with the dead King's wishes, buried by Bishop Silvester.

On 28 October, at nearby Gloucester Cathedral, his nine-year-old son was crowned Henry III of England in an emotive ceremony led by Guala. On John's death the council members at Gloucester had sent for Henry from Devizes, William Marshal eagerly going out to meet him near Malmesbury. The first words we hear from the young King, 'the well-brought-up child', are: 'Welcome. I wish to tell you truly, that I give myself to God and yourself, so that in God's name you may take charge of me.'[491] At this, the little boy burst out crying, causing those around him to weep, too. A hasty discussion came to the rapid conclusion that Henry should be crowned as soon as possible. First Henry was knighted by William, in a scene that captures the pathos of the moment: 'they straight away dressed him in his child-sized robes of state; he was a fine little knight.'[492] From Rome, Pope Honorius III sent out reams of letters in support of Henry, and also to Philip Augustus, Louis, King Alexander and the barons to cease their hostilities and for the English to submit to the new King.

Rarely has a king of England ascended to the throne in less propitious circumstances. The royalist party were acutely aware of their precarious position. Willliam Marshal is recorded as saying: 'If all the world deserted the young boy, except me, do you know what I would do? I would carry him on my shoulders and walk with him thus, with legs astride, I would be with him and never let him down, from island to island, from land to land.'[493] Hardly had the new King changed out of his coronation robes when news came that Goodrich Castle, only eighteen miles away, was besieged that morning and already in peril of falling. Nearly three-quarters of England's 133 barons were with the rebels at the time of John's death, including nineteen of the 27 most powerful ones. Louis was secure in the south-east and most of the eastern half of the country. In the north and west, Alexander of Scotland and Prince Llewelyn harassed his enemies on the Scottish and Welsh borders. And of course there was London. Nor was there much left in the royal coffers to finance the war. On the King's death, the Earl of Salisbury advised Hubert de Burgh to give up Dover as the cause was lost and in the royalist camp a council considered that a retreat to Ireland might be necessary.[494]

The royalists looked for support from Ireland, which materialised more in the form of passive quiescence than anything else; from the still large mercenary force, if payments could be kept flowing; and, in the south-east, from Willikin of the Weald and the almost surreptitious, but still real, help of the Cinque ports. But most of all they looked to the system of royal castles. These protected the now largely subdued west while giving bases for offensives eastwards. The Anonymous offers a long list of some of these and their castellans.[495] In the north were Philip of Oldcoates at Bamburgh, Hugh de Balliol at Newcastle and Brian de Lsile at Knaresborough; stretching over the midlands were Robert de Gaugi at Newark, Philip Mark at Nottingham, Nichola de Hay at Lincoln, Falkes de Bréauté's string of castles mentioned discussed above (Bedford, Northampton, Oxford, Buckingham, Cambridge and Hertford); and in the south were Dover under Hubert de Burgh, Windsor under Engelard de Cigogné, and Peter de Maulay at Corfe (where the constable had care of Richard Fitzroy, the King's younger, illegitimate son, and the main hoard of royal treasure). The west was by now largely secure from Louis; Gloucester, Worcester and Bristol kept a check on incursions from Llewelyn; while William Marshal, as Earl of Pembroke, was a powerful force in south Wales. For all his advantages, Louis still knew that 'the royal castles were many and well fortified.'[496]

And the royalists also had Henry. The boy king's great merit was that he was not his father. Through long years of oppression, financial exactions, arbitrary justice, cruelty mistreatment of his great barons, military failures and ineptitude, John had forged the alliance against him. He united the rebels in being not just for something, but against something – against someone. There were few to defend John's odious rule for reasons other than he was King and for his followers' self interest. John's death was therefore a disaster for Louis: 'Even a child king presented a more formidable opponent than John had done.'[497] The sins of he father could not be visited on the son, especially when the son was an innocent nine-year-old. As David Carpenter has memorably expressed it: 'Henry shrugged and the weight of John's crimes fell from his shoulders.'[498]

The War Enters a New Phase

John's death came suddenly and caught all the protagonists off balance. Initially, at least, there was a stalemate, something already perhaps on the horizon indicated by the truce agreed at Dover just four days before he died.[499] The royalist council quickly tried to adapt to the new situation and set about winning back nearly half of England. The members of the council were boosted by the pope's actions and by the ecclesiastical establishment in England outside of London lining up on the new monarch's side. In November the council met in Bristol. Hubert de Burgh was there, the truce at Dover enabling him to travel. There was some friction between him and the marshal for, as justiciar, Hubert was the highest official in the kingdom after the monarch himself. William's role was clarified as *rector* of the kingdom. The council's first actions were political. Letters were sent to barons commonly offering pardons and restitutions of land for those who came back into the royalist fold. William d'Albini, captured at Rochester Castle, paid a ransom of 6000 marks and paid homage to Henry; in return he received Sleaford Castle. Then, on 12 November, in a highly significant act, Magna Carta was reissued. This 'cut the ground from beneath the feet of the rebels who had called in Louis of France' and 'removed the young King from faction and set him firmly and squarely on a legal relation with his subjects'.[500] Some changes were made to the original, for example, clause 50 was quietly dropped, as it would not do to repeat the call for removal of such alien officers such as Engelard de Cigogné while they were performing such sterling work defending royal castles at Windsor and elsewhere.

But in the medieval world the sword was mightier than the pen, and a far more significant act had already occurred at Dover. When Louis heard the news of John's death he called Hubert de Burgh to a parley, telling him that without a protector he could not hold the castle long; he promised Hubert rewards and a leading position among his advisers should he submit. Hubert took the proposition back to the garrison but they refused the offer, wishing instead to honour the rightful heir to the crown and to avoid the opprobrium of treachery and cowardice. On hearing their reply, Louis made a fateful decision: he lifted the siege. As Wendover reports, the French 'determined to subjugate the smaller castles throughout England so that, having taken these, they could attack the larger ones'.[501] Louis was making the same mistake that John had in failing to take London; he was allowing a major stronghold to exist in the heart of his territory. Louis has been much criticised for his new strategy but his actions are easily explicable: with John gone and the situation radically transformed, Louis needed to gather momentum again and to ensure that his absence did not hand that momentum to the royalists. In effect, he needed to combine itinerant kingship and military successes to reassure his own side. Nonetheless, it proved a disastrous mistake. He went quickly to London with his army to reassess the situation. As soon as they had left, the Dover garrison sortied out and burned the buildings Louis had erected before the castle. They followed this up by ravaging the countryside, pillaging and destroying it to deny the French supplies later, while stocking up the cellars in the castle to enable the garrison to survive a renewed siege for many months.

At first, it appeared that Louis' change of direction was vindicated. While the regency council was in Bristol, Louis was besieging Hertford Castle. He was here on 12 November with his engines of war arrayed around the walls, battering at them for 25 days. The garrison, under the command of Walter de Godardville, one of Falkes de Bréauté's captains, caused heavy casualties before surrendering on 6 December. Under the rules of war, the garrison were allowed to march free with their horses and arms. This arrangement appears to be part of a truce which was meant to give Berkhamstead up to Louis at the same time. But again the success was marred by squabbling over the rewards for Louis' followers. The Anonymous claims the castle was handed over to Robert Fitzwalter, to whom it had previously belonged; but Wendover says that the French complained that the castle should not be given to a baron who had betrayed his monarch – in other words, it should be given to the French. Louis procrastinated, intending to wait until after the conquest was completed.[502]

Louis moved immediately to Berkhamstead where its captain, Waleran the German, renounced the truce agreement made at Hertford. This powerful castle had recently been fortified and repaired with timbers from the local forest, so Waleran, a veteran warrior, was feeling confident. He made his intentions clear from the start. As the English barons were setting up their siege camp, knights and sergeants erupted from the castle and caused havoc, seizing supply-carts and baggage, and even snatching the standard of William de Mandeville, a major loss of face for the leading rebel commander. The garrison attempted to use the standard to confuse the besiegers in a later sortie, but the enemy had expected such a move and drove them back into the castle. The besiegers suffered many dead before Waleran was ordered to surrender the castle on 20 December under a new general Christmas truce that lasted until either 13 or 20 January.

Louis placed Raoul Plancöet in charge of the castle and made for St Albans on 21 December, extorting money from the local populace along the way. He tried to make William of Trumpington, abbot of the rich and famous abbey, pay homage to him. William refused, declaring that he would only do so if he were released from his homage to the King. At this, an enraged Louis threatened to torch the town and its abbey. Saer de Quincy, the Earl of Winchester, granted William some leeway and the fearfully intimidated abbot paid 80 silver marks to escape destruction. Such exactions were common; the Dunstable annalist reporting his home town having to pay Louis 200 marks for protection. Louis then returned to his stronghold of London.[503]

Other gains were made. The cities – but not the castles – of Ely and Lincoln were taken before the truce. Cambridge and Pleshey Castles also fell to Louis. Now, on the expiration of the first truce, a further one was under negotiation between William Marshal and Louis, the former at Oxford, the latter at Cambridge. This one, to last until 23 April, cost the royalists more castles: Hedingham, under siege, and Colchester, Norwich and Orford. Hedingham was returned to Robert de Vere while Gillon de Melun received Orford, Simon de Poissy Cambridge and William de Mandeville Pleshey.[504] The Dunstable annalist reports that all the castles of Essex and Suffolk were now in Louis' hands. Thus, by the end of January, Louis had actually strengthened his position, even though over three months had elapsed since John's death. With little effort, he now had most of the eastern half of England secured. Thus Louis had indeed regained his momentum, and the hope was that this would place greater pressure on strongholds such as Dover to appreciate the futility of further resistance.

Why was the impact of John's death so muted? Why had the royalists not reaped far greater rewards from this heaven-sent opportunity? The biographer of William Marshal was confused by the situation, believing, unpersuasively, that the 'fine, magnificent, well fortified' castles of Norwich and Orford had been handed over without the Marshal's agreement, 'and that was a wrong thing to do'.[505] (The History of William Marshal makes a reappearance as a valuable source with the onset of the new reign, disassociation with the failures of John now replaced by the accolade of the Marshal's greatest role as leader of the nation. The lengthy poem compensates for Ralph of Coggeshall's cursory treatment of just one-and-a-half pages from the coronation of Henry III to the end of the war.) One explanation for the royalists' sluggish start was simply a matter of time: many were waiting to see how the regency council responded to Louis and waiting to see if it would – or could – reverse the situation. There was the real possibility that the council would come to terms with Louis at any moment. Many barons were still sitting opportunistically on the fence. Louis' initial flurry of triumphs kept them there longer than they might otherwise have been, underlining the intent of his post-Dover strategy. The royalist camp, like the Franco-baronial one, had its own divisions, although these proved less damaging. Hubert de Burgh had some friction with the

Marshal (the latter refusing to provide more material aid to Dover), but also a real competitive hostility with Peter des Roches that later grew into a feud. Brian de Lisle, Philip Mark and the Earl of Derby were also at loggerheads over castle ownership. Perhaps the mightiest baron of all, Earl Ranulf of Chester, threatened to leave on crusade, while Savary de Mauléon was back in Poitou after Christmas and actually did embark on crusade. In fact, Ranulf did not have to go far to become a crusader: although the exact date is uncertain, probably sometime between Henry's coronation and late January, the pope decreed the royalist cause as a crusade and Guala instructed Henry's men to wear a white cross on their chests. (In the Holy Land, crusaders wore the cross on their shoulders.) More practical spiritual help followed: with John gone, the episcopacy reformed as eleven out of the twelve bishops who had abandoned John returned to the crown's service.

But there were other specific reasons, too, for caution and patience. One, proposed by David Carpenter, was simply that the Marshal was not yet in a position to counter-attack.[506] He had spent November and December in Gloucester and Bristol and waited until the new year before heading to Nottingham and offering assistance to Lincoln. It should also be noted that Louis did not make inroads into the west either, so both sides may have been using the opportunity to consolidate their positions, something that Louis achieved far more successfully. The Marshal may have feared incursions by Llewelyn and Reginald de Braose from the west, which would have left the rear of William's forces in danger; the Welsh had a tradition of attempting to exploit the moments of political uncertainty at a time of succession. The other, perennial, problem was money. The system of government had all but broken down, with revenues being collected more from local military activity, ransoming, extortions, *tenseries* and ravaging than bureaucracy. The Marshal's biographer reveals that 'the King has hardly any resources' and that 'the child has no wealth'.[507] Hard cash was in short supply and payment of royalist troops and mercenaries often had to be made in jewellery and silks. This forced the royalists to adapt the same measures as we have just seen Louis taking. Thus William Marshal threatened to torch Worcester unless it handed over £100 it had pledged to pay John. Poor old Abbot William Trumpington of St Albans was again raided on 22 January, this time by royalists. Wendover reports that Falkes de Bréauté descended on the abbey that evening with 'knights and robbers' from his garrisons and pillaged the town. Even children were taken prisoner, and someone was slain at the door of the church where he had been running to take sanctuary. These 'agents of the devil' then demanded £100 from the Abbot or else they would 'immediately burn the whole town with the monastery and other buildings'.[508] Falkes took his booty back to his stronghold at Bedford before setting out again to take some 60 clergy and noncombatants prisoner elsewhere.

This explanation may complement rather than overturn another one: that the royalist council had undertaken a deliberate strategy adopted at this time. This suggests that the royalists wanted to spread out Louis' forces and to catch them exposed beyond their bases.[509] This entailed the deliberate withdrawal of isolated and exposed garrisons in Essex, East Anglia and elsewhere, hence the swift capitulations to Louis. The men and materiel from these might be better deployed elsewhere; thus Norwich and Orford Castles, the loss of which so exercised William Marshal's biographer, had their stores transferred to Dover. The royalists may have been anxious of attack from their western flank; it is also worth considering whether a motivation for their consolidation was the fear of a co-ordinated attack from the Welsh in the west and Louis in the east. But as we have seen, Louis' focus was very much on expanding his authority through the east. In this he largely succeeded, but a visit to Lincoln failed to persuade Nichola de Haye to give up the royal castle there. Whatever the reasons behind royalist strategy – consolidation for defence, consolidation for offence, restraints of money, or a developing combination of all three – their counter-attack began in the new year.

The Battle of Rye and the Royalist Resurgence

Truces were easier to break than to maintain. Both sides accused the other of breaking the terms of the truce, and in February a bloody and bruising encounter took place at the neighbouring south-eastern ports of Rye and Winchelsea, between Hastings and Dover. The royalists moved fast to gain the initial advantage when a changing situation presented itself. The change was brought about dramatically by Louis' decision to return to France. This was a risky move necessitated by the need for men and money. We have seen how his forces were being depleted by continental troops returning home; and now with Henry on the throne, there was a well-founded fear that many barons would at best not support him and at worst desert him. The Barnwell chronicler believes Louis was summoned urgently home by his father to a council, while Wendover believes Louis was deeply anxious over the weight of religious opinion against him: an anathema with the threat of a renewed excommunication following; the English episcopate back on the royalists' side; and a crusade pronounced against him. It is possible that in addition to tangible material support, Louis might have been looking for diplomatic allies in France, too, even if his father made a pretence of not talking with him. But William the Breton, the best placed to know but least consulted on this, reports that Louis lacked money to pay his soldiers and in France found both reinforcements and funds from his friends.[510] Either way, the barons were greatly dismayed by Louis' intended departure and, uncertain about the near future, they made Louis swear to return before the truce expired. Their vulnerability was increased by a setback at Mountsorrel on 20 January. From here, the baronial garrison went on a raid to procure plunder and provisions, but the royalist garrison at Nottingham, heaving learned of this from their scouts, intercepted them; they killed three rebels and captured ten knights and 24 sergeants.[511]

From London Louis set out for the south coast to sail to France. He had heard that his castle at Rye had been lost through subterfuge. It had been taken by Philip d'Albini's flotilla. Hubert de Burgh was also operating along the coasts of Kent and Essex. Louis' grasp on the southern ports was not assured, and the Cinque ports were slipping away from even nominal obedience. From Ireland the royalists had collected a flotilla at Winchelsea, next to Rye, where they were joined by more vessels to blockade the ports. Powerful forces made for the area from both sides. The vernacular sources provide a remarkable and detailed account of what happened there.[512]

Just before reaching Winchelsea, Louis stayed in the safety of the Earl of Warenne's castle at Lewes where he fretted over supplies through the Weald. This suggests that his plan was to base himself at Winchelsea to recapture Rye before leaving for France. He may also have been making the dash to Winchelsea in the hope that he would be able to embark before royalist reinforcements made this impossible by taking this town along with Rye. His entry into the town was unresisted. The burghers burned their mills, thus hindering Louis' provisioning of his men, and took to the strong royalist ships off Rye which blockaded the ports. These were now under the command of Philip d'Albini, governor of the Channel Islands and sparring partner of Eustace the Monk. Both the Anonymous and the biographer of William Marshal confirm that these ships had strong complements of armed men and supplies. Louis' land route back to London was also blocked; Willikin of the Weald and his guerrilla force had seen to that by destroying the bridges and guarding the travel ways. The *History of William Marshal* says that Willikin was in 'no mind to play games'; many French stragglers and prisoners were beheaded. Willikin's force also had the great advantage of knowing the area intimately and they used this knowledge to great effect. As the biographer comments, the French Prince 'did not know which way to turn … Louis was harried so that he felt himself in desperate straits.' It seems to have been a classic luring to a siege to ensnare the enemy. Louis was caught in a well-made trap.

Louis' fears over supplies manifested themselves starkly, as the Anonymous tells us as he takes up the rest of the story. His men had wheat but, with the mills gone, no easy way to grind it, so they attempted to do so by hand. They were unable to catch fish and relied on large nuts found in the town for some sustenance. Truces with the enemy meant little, and the English sailors (presumably augmented by crews from Ireland and the continent) would come ashore to shoot and hurl their missiles at the weakening French. All the while Louis' losses mounted. William Marshal's biographer claims, with exaggeration, that Louis lost thousands of his troops, 'men who had been overconfident about having England in their hands'. The biographer has no sympathy for the French, whom he labels 'mercenaries'. Earlier in his poem he seems to gloat over French deaths:

> Many a barrel and cask of fine wine the French mercenaries drank, and they were
> so full of arrogance that they said England was theirs, and that the English should

vacate the land, for they had no right to it; the French, they say, would have it for
their own profit. That arrogance was of no avail whatever: subsequently I saw
a hundred of them eaten by dogs, men whom the English had killed between
Winchester and Romsey. That was the only land they managed to keep.[513]

Louis sent out men on foot to sneak through the enemy lines to seek help from
London. Some obviously broke through the enemy lines and the terrifying bands
of Willikin's decapitating guerrillas to reach the capital. Here they announced
Louis' orders 'to help them because they were in great trouble and the English
were making things wretched for them'. A relief force was dispatched as French
knights went to the assistance of their lord. This force, comprising Guillaume,
castellan de St Omer, Raoul Plancöet, Hugh Tacon, Jean de Beaumont and others
not named, was only a small one and thus feared to go the direct route through
the Weald. Instead they made for Canterbury and thence struck southwest to
Romney. We can see how Willikin's forces dominated the Weald by the relief
plan hatched: help was to come from the sea, not the land. From Romney they
sent instructions to Louis' governor in Boulogne, a Cistercian monk, to send
all the ships they could 'because their lord Louis was in very grave trouble at
Winchelsea'. The governor sent some 200, all but one sailing to Dover, the exception braving the blockade to boost the flagging morale of the French trapped
in Wincheslea with news of the relief operation. This ship may well have been
captained by Eustace, for a few lines further on the Anonymous says that he was
with Louis. French knights began embarkation at Dover but the winter weather
conditions and lack of prevailing winds prevented their departure for Winchelsea
for a fortnight. It was a long fourteen days for Louis and his men; they 'suffered
greatly because their supplies were running out'.

Louis, Eustace and his advisers held a council of war to discuss what could
be done to alleviate their predicament until reinforcements arrived. The ever
resourceful Eustace came up with a plan. He proposed adapting one of his large
galleys by building a castle-like structure upon it, presumably a large fighting platform. When completed, it was so huge it spread over the sides of the ship and
caused amazement amongst all those who saw it. Other ships the French had taken
from the English in their combats guarded it from attack. Behind this heavy ship
followed another carrying a petraria to hurl stones at the English vessels. On shore,
Louis had two other petrarias erected that caused the English flotilla great problems. But the plan came to nothing. In a pre-emptive strike, the English launched a
bold night attack that saw them capture the large galley. They taunted their enemy
with their victory by destroying it piece-by-piece 'before the eyes of the French'.
Feeling the strain of the last few weeks, Louis lashed out at the Viscount of Melun
and blamed him for the disaster, for the Viscount had been charged with the watch
that night. 'But my leader!' he responded. 'Your men are so starved I cannot find
anyone willing to perform guard duty', then adding that Louis himself would not

be able to find four knights to do so. Louis retorted that he would go on guard. A heated argument broke out. Eustace de Noeville joined in, somewhat obsequiously telling Louis that 'the viscount does not know what he is saying' and that 'forty' knights could be found. The Viscount and Eustace then went for each other, going back and forth with their contradictions of the other's statement. Eustace had he last word: he did indeed find 40 guards to man the watch.

The following day brought more intense military activity. The relief squadron from Dover appeared on the scene under the command of Raoul Plancöet, Hugh Tacon and Jean de Beaumont. The English flotilla prepared to engage with them with great bluster and display. A cog bore down on the French to attack but pulled away at the last moment; this evasive manoeuvre was so precipitous that the cog veered disastrously into one of its own ships, sinking it with the loss of its entire crew. The biographer of William Marshal believes the defeat was far greater, and that the French 'destroyed our navy'. The blockade had largely been broken. The rest of the English ships followed behind for a short while as the French squadron entered Wincheslea. Louis' army was impressively reinforced and now stood at 3000-strong. The garrison at Rye realised that they could not hold against such odds and deserted the castle; Louis found it 'full of wine and meat for which his men had great need'. Louis placed it under the command of Baldwin de Corbeil, who had just come over with the fleet from Boulogne.

The royalists put into operation either an urgent attempt to retake Rye or to relieve it. William Marshal had left Gloucester on 17 February, passed through Oxford and Reading, and met with his council at Dorking where an impressive muster of their troops was arranged, a significant statement of intent and indeed of confidence. On 28 February the council sent a letter from here to the people of Rye forbidding them from giving any hostages to Louis or entering into terms with him, promising them immediate help. And what help it was: the army comprised the Earls of Chester and Ferrers, the Count of Aumale, Richard Fitzroy, Walter de Lacy, Falkes de Bréauté, Engelard de Cigogné, and an appropriately large army of knights, sergeants, crossbowmen and Welsh archers. Even the King and legate were to follow.[514] The intent was surely for a decisive showdown with Louis. But by the time this huge host arrived at Rye, Louis had flown. He had gone to Dover and set sail for home on 27 or 28 February.

Louis had left his nephew Enguerrand de Coucy to represent him in England, ordering him to make for London and 'on no account leave it'.[515] This hints that Louis saw the royal resurgence as a real threat and that it was time to revert to the baronial plan that placed London at the heart of its strategy. However, Louis was probably hopeful that some minor trouble in Ireland around this time would escalate into a serious diversion for the Marshal.

Louis was absent for eight weeks and he was sorely missed: the Anonymous says 'the need for him in England grew acutely.'[516] Without his reassuring presence as a sign of commitment to the cause, some who had wavered crossed into the royalist camp. Within the week following Louis' departure, William Longsword, Earl of Salisbury, and William Marshal the Younger deserted the barons and Louis, a move long in the making; these close comrades had clearly been waiting for the opportune moment for further opportunism. This was a serious blow to the anti-royalist party and it played a part in a string of some 115 defections, mainly from Wiltshire, Somerset, Dorset and Berkshire.

There is no doubt that the status of crusade enhanced the royalist cause. The Barnwell annalist believes it was important as it eased the way back to the King for the Earl of Salisbury and others who were now 'fighting against pagans' as 'crusaders' in 'the army of Christ'.[517] The barons had long ceased to derive any benefit from their branding moniker as 'The Army of God', not that there was much in the first place. Historians have arguably placed too much emphasis on this positive development for the king's men: Christopher Tyerman, who has made a study of England and the crusades, judges that 'the crusade made a defi-nite, though not precisely definable, contribution' to the royalists' cause, adding that it remained very much a second-class crusade.[518] If the tangible, practical effects were real but limited, taking up the cross could only have boosted the morale, cohesion and psychological outlook of the royalist camp. But as David Carpenter has wryly and accurately noted: 'The defections in March and April were highly regional and it is difficult to believe that the men of Berkshire and Wiltshire were simply more pious than those in the north.'[519]

As I am forever telling my students, to understand the truth of the situation we have to pick up the stone and see what is underneath. There we will nearly always find self-interest scurrying or wriggling busily about in pursuit of its ends. Castles; patronage; money; office; all were strong motivating forces. When knights felt they were only receiving crumbs from Louis' French table they looked elsewhere for their dinner. Wendover captures this well: 'There was great deal of wavering amongst the barons over which King to commit to, the young Henry or the lord Louis.' He gives as the reason for their agonising the way in which many had been so 'contemptuously treated by the French'. Louis, he says, had ignored his oath and the barons' complaints to keep possession for himself the lands and castles won in the war, despite baronial help, and handed these out to his own French followers. But against this the barons did not want to face the disgrace of return-ing to allegiance to the King 'like dogs returning to their vomit'.[520] We have seen the divisions in the anti-royalist camp over the spoils of war, as when William Marshal the Younger complained and successfully contested the leadership of the army from Adam de Beaumont and resented Louis putting Marlborough Castle in the hands of Robert de Dreux instead of his. The Earl of Salisbury lacked castles for his power base, and so was on the look-out for some. He contested the ownership of Trowbridge Castle with the rebel Earl of Hereford, Henry de Bohun, who had Louis' favour (and who, in turn, was a partisan of Louis for the same, castle-seeking motives). William Marshal, however, could offer Longsword the castles of Salisbury and Sherborne, and the office of Sheriff of Wilthsire and also Somerset and Devon. The regent was keen to buy Longsword over, not least because he valued the Earl's military ability.[521] A notable character of these *reversi*, as they are called in the records, was that many of the men now changed sides for the last time and so Wendover believes that 'thus Louis' party was in large measure broken up.'[522] However, the original core of rebelling barons stayed largely constant to their cause. The desertions were serious, but not decisive.

On the military front, the royalists were now also making strong gains. The Anonymous says that the English 'chevauchéed across the land and took many castles'.[523] The sources lack detailed accounts of this military activity, leaving the historian to stitch together a rather scratchy narrative lacking in meaty details of combat and drama, in contrast to the full-bloodied descriptions they give for the end of the war. The Earl of Salisbury and William Marshal the Younger wished to prove themselves to their new lord. They quickly took Knepp Castle in Sussex, probably on 4 March, which fell immediately; it was in the hands of Roland Bloet, a brother to one of the Marshal's knights. The defecting duo then set up camp in Hyde Abbey and laid siege to the castles of Winchester on 6 March while the regent went to take Farnham during the week of 7–13 March. Its constable, Ponces de Beaumeis, was thrown into prison by des Roches and suffered there for many months, says the Anonymous; the garrison were luckier, being granted safe conduct to London. On the first day of the siege of Winchester, little was achieved, but an attack was made on the second day. The main castle was under the command of Peter Letart, one of the Count of Nevers' men. When moving about, the besiegers ensured that they maintained tight formation in case of a surprise attack. At one stage of the siege when the royalists were called away, Letart commanded some of the garrison to sortie into the town which they plundered and burned: 'They were angry, because the townsfolk had harboured their enemies and given them assistance ... The townsfolk paid a heavy price.' The sudden return of the royalist troops pushed the raiding party back into the city's two castles. The Earl of Salisbury was investing Wolvesey, the smaller of the city's two castles and the one belonging to Peter des Roches. Wolvesey was assailed for eight days, its defenders given no rest either by day or by night until it surrendered on 12 March. The Earl then went to assist his great friend William who was besieging the royal castle. The barrage of arrows and projectiles made the garrison 'greatly dismayed and afraid', says the Marshal's biographer, but the strong fortifications, recently repaired and improved by Louis, withstood it all. At this point the Marshal turned up with his great army, filling the whole area. They expected the castle's surrender, but still it held out. In mid-March, William Marshal the Younger and William Longsword were directed by the regent away from Winchester to Southampton, one of the most important ports in the country, which was comprehensively plundered: 'such was the booty taken in the town that the poor folk who wished to take advantage and had their minds on profit were all made rich by the wealth they took from their enemies.' Having installed their own governor and constable, they returned to Winchester. At the end of the second week of March they were before Portchester where a month-long siege began. The *History of William Marshal* says Rochester was taken at this point while not mentioning Portchester; this may be the result of some confusion or a reference to the operations of King John's bastard son Oliver in Kent in the third week of April or to the vaguer movements of Philip d'Albini. The siege of Portchester falls in a pattern that suggests the royalists' strategy was to advance along the coast to disrupt communications with France and deny safe ports to the French.[524] In accordance with this strategy, d'Albini took Chichester before 16 April and Portchester by the 27th; both castles had their defences destroyed. The confusing movements of troops to and from sieges continued. At the end of March, the younger Marshal went to besiege his coveted prize of Marlborough, which he took after an ardous siege of about three weeks. Winchester finally surrendered and its garrison was offered a safe conduct back to London. Odiham was also taken in the south. In the midlands, Falkes de Bréauté raided and retook Ely, where he took prisoner Adam de Nulli, a soldier greatly favoured by Louis for his steadfast service. When Louis heard the news of these setbacks in France he felt the blow of the royalist resurgence, the Anonymous announcing rather obviously that 'he was not all happy'. The Barnwell annalist paints a gloomy picture for the French Prince: 'little indeed would have remained for Louis in England had he put off his return beyond the promised time.'[525] He was back in England on 22 April. The war was about to enter its most dramatic and epic phase that would bring about its end.

The French Counter-attack

For all the defeats his army had suffered, there was nothing that could not, in theory, be won back by Louis – as he immediately set about demonstrating. William Marshal seems to have recognised this by the destruction of the castles he had retaken, excepting Farnham and Marlborough (which his son would not have countenanced anyway) when he learned of the French Prince's return. Louis still had the hardcore baronial faction that had begun the war in the first place. It is likely that the Earl of Surrey, William de Warenne, had been contemplating defecting back to the royalist cause, but Louis' return kept him in the fold. Louis had been active in France both in attending to his domestic concerns there and in building up reinforcements. He could not expect any overt help from his father. On 21 April Philip had received a letter from Honorious III thanking him for his behaviour in the whole affair; the pope would have been aware of Louis' presence back in his father's country. Louis' force comprised 'few knights' according to the Anonymous, but we are not told how much treasure he had with him to fund the war.[526] The chronicler Robert of Auxerre depicts a more substantial force with many mercenaries and infantry and the biographer of William Marshal says Louis came to England 'with his large, warlike contingent of men'.[527] Unlike Louis' first arrival in England, the Anonymous does not provide detailed numbers, rather giving an overall figure of just over 140 knights, a still sizeable force, with some powerful figures. He announces only that 'I will name the greatest men who travelled with him.' There are a number of familiar figures and some new ones: the Count of Brittany and his brother Robert de Dreux, Raoul Plonçöet, the Viscount of Melun, the Count of Perche, the Count of Guînes, the Lord of Béthune, the Seneschal of Flanders called Hellin de Waverin, the castellan of Beaumeis, Guillaume de Fiennes, Adam de Beaumont, Jean d'Osny and others 'all of whom I cannot name'. They brought with them a powerful new siege machine: the trebuchet. This was at the cutting edge of weapons technology and it provoked much discussion, 'since few had been seen in France'.[528] Louis wanted this machine to finally break the resistance of Dover. At Calais on the evening of the Friday before Easter, Louis had the horses put on board his ships; he and his men embarked the next day before sunrise. They had a good wind and a calm sea. But they raised a storm in England.

Louis arrived to a fluid situation that had put his men on the defensive. William Marshal hoped to maintain the royalist momentum by sending a force to Mountsorrel near Leicester to besiege Saer de Quincy's castle. This was an impressive force, which included the Earls of Chester, Ferrers and Aumale, Brian de Lisle, Robert de Viuexpont, William de Cantelupe and the ubiquitous Falkes de Bréauté; with them was a large force, many from the abandoned castles of the Easter truce; they were augmented along the way north by garrisons from royal castles. The regent stayed at Winchester and accepted the castle's surrender just before Louis landed; the garrison that had capitulated at Marlborough 'felt ashamed and dejected' because they had not held out longer for their lord.[529] Louis' nephew, Enguerrand de Coucy, had, in early March, sent troops from London to the siege of Lincoln. But before the opposing armies clashed in major engagements in the decisive arena of the northern midlands, Louis went on the warpath in the south.[530]

At first the omens were not good. As his fleet came into view of Dover, Louis could clearly see the buildings of the siege camp – and the smoke coming from them. King John's son Oliver and the ever reliable William of Kensham and his men had just attacked Dover, firing the camp and killing the soldiers guarding it. In so doing, they succeeded in preventing Louis from joining up with his forces there; Louis' ships diverted to Sandwich as they feared a barrage of arrows and projectiles from the cliffs at Dover. He landed at Sandwich, despite the attempts of some royal galleys to block him, and took lodging in the town before going to the priory at Dover, as before. Here, having been joined by the Count of Nevers and the few men he brought over the day after the Prince's arrival, he learned about the sieges of the Earl of Winchester's castles at Marlborough, Southampton,

Winchester and Mountsorrel. He rapidly arranged another truce with Hubert de Burgh, back in command of Dover Castle, and headed for Winchester 'with a great contingent of carters, soldiers and crossbowmen, mercenaries and riffraff', says the *History of William Marshal*.[531] But before he left, he took his revenge on Sandwich for having broken its oath to him and reverting back to the royalist cause: he burned the town. He also sent some of his troops back to France with orders to return later. On Monday 24 April he was in Canterbury; on Tuesday 25th he was at Malling, near Lewes, staying at the convent there and meeting with the Earl of Winchester, Simon Langton and some others of his English supporters. On the Wednesday he made a full day's march to Guildford, but his baggage train, presumably falling behind due to Louis' speed, only made it as far as Reigate, where it was protected by the rearguard under Gérard le Truie. At Guildford, Louis was reinforced by soldiers from the London garrison led by Enguerrand de Coucy. He was mustering his forces to strike at the royalists and retake what had been lost to him. They went into action the next day.

Louis was before Farnham by Thursday 27 April. The regent, alarmed at the advance of the French, ordered Winchester to be slighted and hurried to Marlborough with the young King on the Thursday. They feared the possibility that Louis hoped to capture the King, as Petit-Dutaillis suggests; but if this had been the case, Louis would surely have made straight for Winchester, bypassing Farnham (as, indeed, the biographer of William Marshal says he does; the Anonymous' chronology is followed here). By this time the losses of Marlborough, Southampton and Winchester had been confirmed to Louis, but his very presence had now chased the garrison out of Winchester Castle before it had time to settle in there. The Anonymous relates that Louis attacked the castle and quickly took its outer bailey, but the keep held out against him. On Friday 28 April, the baggage train and a large force of English knights turned up with Saer de Quincy. The Earl of Winchester asked Louis for a force with which to relieve the garrison at Mountsorrel in Leicestershire. Louis agreed to this. It was a fateful decision to which we will return soon.

Louis left for Winchester on the Saturday. In his rearguard with la Truie were Hugh Tacon, Florent de Hangest, the Seneschal of Flanders and Robert Lord of Béthune with three named knights. There was a real risk of harassment from the Windsor garrison who were trailing them, but the garrison was not looking for an engagement and feared even to be seen by the rearguard. Their purpose was to track the movement of the French and also possibly to capture stragglers and prevent foraging. Louis' scouts, reconnoitring ahead of the vanguard of the column and looking for lodgings for their Prince, discovered a handful of royalists still in Winchester; these fled as soon as they saw the scouts. Louis remained in Winchester from 30 April to 4 May. The fortifications were in a bad way: they had been damaged by the French assault and miners, then partially destroyed by the regent's men before they evacuated the place. Louis oversaw the initial repairs of the castle and ditch and he made such a good job of it even William Marshal's biographer was impressed: 'within a period of a very few days he had rebuilt the tower and the high walls magnificently, with stone and lime, and had restored all the fallen masonry and repaired the damage to the walls to the point they were fine and solid, just as if they were completely new.' Before he left he placed Hervé de Donzy, the powerful and faithful Count of Nevers, in charge of the city with a large force. The biographer of William Marshal calls the Count 'an arrogant and vicious man' who 'subsequently committed many a crime which was regarded as shameful on his part', disappointingly adding 'but I have no wish to go into that at this point.' Doubtless the Count conformed to the usual pattern of the conflict and oppressed the area extorting money and seizing supplies for the war effort. Louis returned to London after a remarkably successful short and sharp campaign. The south had been regained and with it greater security for communications with France. The royalist resurgence had achieved very little military advantage in terms of castles and towns; as Nicholas Vincent summarises it: 'In a matter of only a week, the royalist achievements of the spring were wiped clean away.'[532] In essence, Louis had repeated the initial success of his first arrival back in May 1216. With the exception of the defection of some barons and some more rebel places under siege, the military position was not so very different from then. But that was about to change.

Louis' stay in London was a short one of only two nights. Here news came to him that Hubert de Burgh and Gerard de Sotteghem had broken the truce at Dover in a bloody surprise assault.[533] A group of Louis' men arriving at Dover had been attacked by the garrison and many who could not escape were killed; one of the Count of Nevers' senior offices only narrowly escaped death by the personal intervention of Hubert de Burgh himself, recognising the value of a high-ranking prisoner. Louis hurried down there, not least because more of his reinforcements were due to arrive, some as instructed nearly a fortnight earlier; these would be endangered by Dover's formidable garrison. On Friday 12 May Louis set up his prized trebuchet in front of the castle and once again tried to take the key to England.

The siege camp destroyed by the garrison at the previous siege was now rebuilt and the trebuchet performed its duty well in causing considerable damage to the fabric of the castle. The following day, Louis' reinforcements appeared in the Channel in 40 ships. They attempted to dock in the harbour but high seas and a strong wind prevented all but five from doing so. The others swiftly returned to Calais to reappear two days later, on the 15th. The intervening two days gave the royalist forces the time to prepare for them. The French squadron was met by an English one over twice its size. Around 80 ships had sailed from Romney under Nicholas Haringot and the increasingly important leadership of Philip d'Albini. The ships were of all sizes, but twenty of them were 'great ships armed for battle'. The smaller French ships had been ambushed: 'they did not dare wait' for the

English so those that could turned about and made for Calais again. However, this option was not open to the 27 ships in front; these formed a tight formation and hoped that thus grouped they might chance getting through to the harbour. Fortune was with the nineteen that made it; their comrades were not so lucky. The sailors and sergeants aboard the other eight ships were seized and 'immediately killed'; the knights were thrown into the holds of the English ships in a state of terror. The squadron then sat menacingly out at sea: they 'weighed anchor before the castle and there they remained silently on guard, so that neither food nor aid could reach Louis from the sea'. Louis wrought his vengeance on Hythe and Romney just as he had done with Sandwich, by burning the towns for siding with the royalists. Willikin and his men, emboldened by the victory at sea, attacked the French on their grim mission in the towns, but were beaten off. The bloody events at Dover point to a darker turn of events; the casualties on land were high enough to be noted, but naval warfare did not accommodate safe conducts as land warfare did, as the poor French sailors and sergeants who were caught discovered. Philip d'Albini's increasingly signifiant contribution to the royalist war effort points to the substantial emphasis the royalists were placing on maritime defence. They were cutting off Louis' supply lines and they showed that they had the ships and crew to do it. This was a substantial strategic advantage which they were to exploit later. But the next engagement was to be on land in a decisive battle.

Decision by Battle

We now return to Louis' siege camp at Farnham where, it will be remembered, Saer de Quincy, the Earl of Winchester, had his request granted for a large force to relieve his Castle of Mountsorrel, besieged by the Earl of Chester who was pursuing his quarrel with Saer. This was in response to the regent's earlier dispatch at the end of April from Winchester of a powerful force to besiege the Earl's castle and raise the rebel siege of Lincoln. Earl Ranulf of Chester, Earl William of Aumale, Earl William of Ferrers (Ferrières or Derby), Robert de Vieuxpont, Brian de Lisle, William de Cantelupe, Philip Mark, Robert de Gaugi and Falkes de Bréauté led a large army collected from royalist garrisons and invested Mountsorrel with carefully positioned siege machines.[534] The Earl of Winchester's garrison comprised ten knights and some sergeants under Henry de Braybrooke. Wendover, geographically close to events, reports how they 'bravely retuned stone for stone and missile for missile against their enemy' for several days before sending to the Earl for help; they feared they had insufficient means to withstand such a concentrated force for any length of time. Louis could not refuse the Earl's request and ordered that an army, predominantly drawn from the London garrison, should follow Saer into Leicestershire to raise the siege and subdue the whole region. The Earl shared joint command of the expedition with the young Count Thomas of Perche and Robert Fitzwalter; with them were a large army and 70 French knights, including Simon de Poissy, Guillaume de Fiennes and others named by the Anonymous. Interestingly, in a sign of the exertions suffered from the intense campaign in the south, some of the French in Louis' camp refused the Prince's request to accompany Saer. Robert de Béthune and Gilbert de Copegni expressed a willingness to go, but also their inability to do so owing to the exhaustion of their men who had not had any time to recover. Hugh Tacon, a naval captain who had been a major player in the operation to save Louis at Rye, also cited exhaustion as a reason not to go. Tacon and Béthune instead joined the rearguard of Louis' army heading for Winchester, which was hardly restful as the Windsor garrison were trailing Louis. Thus Louis had, the biographer of William Marshal observes, 'divided his mighty army into two large contingents'. While the French Prince had his troubles at Dover, on Monday 30 April the main theatre of operations moved northwards.

Making for St Albans, the relief army set out in the usual manner, 'pillaging all the places they passed', records Wendover. 'These wicked mercenaries and robbers from France went through the surrounding towns, sparing neither churches nor cemeteries, and made prisoners of all ranks, and, having tortured them severely, forced ransoms from them.' It was all very reminiscent of John's northern campaign during the winter of 1215–16. And they continued as they had started. But the measured and purposeful violence of plundering, analysed earlier, is seen again here: at St Albans the army restrained itself and stole only meat and wine; seemingly Abbot William's earlier payment just before Christmas had satisfied Louis and indemnified the abbey from excessive loss. It is hard to assess the losses inflicted by such depredation. In his massive and magisterial biography of Peter des Roches, Nicholas Vincent has examined the damage done to the Bishop of Winchester's lands across the south in the early part of the war. The records reinforce general accounts of reactions to ravaging from other sources of the Middle Ages. People, livestock and grain were regularly evacuated to nearby churches and abbeys in the hope of avoiding foraging troops; buildings would be erected to accommodate these. Rents from lands were appropriated by local garrisons. Some of the Bishop's lands in Oxfordshire and Berkshire were lucky enough to have avoided any touch of war, while Hampshire was hit hard. Here the taking of livestock, grain and rents was extensive: at Merdon, the French 'made off with 14 of the manor's 20 plough horses, 4 of its 12 horses, 21 cows and a bull out of a total of 29 cattle, 225 ewes out of a flock of 253 … 26 out of 29 hogs'; seven manors in the county paid 'rents for both summer and Michaelmas terms to the Count of Nevers'.[535] This coercive requisitioning, to put it euphemistically, reinforces John Gillingham's point that 'one man's foraging is another man's pillaging';[536] the two went hand-in-hand. By this means both sides fed their troops, supplied their garrisons, and, importantly, had the horses and carts needed to move an army about. Wendover is delighted to tell the edifying tale of a robber of the church of St Amphibalus during this campaign: the man has a fit and foams at the mouth, his punishment for his crime is possession by the devil. The army spent the night at Dunstable, and were sufficiently sated by their hoard to refrain from damage there, as the local annalist reports with some relief.[537]

The army left the next morning and reached Mountsorrel a few days later, pillaging churches and cemeteries along the way. Royalist scouts informed the Earl of Chester of the approach of 'the mighty army that was making every effort to attack them'.[538] Seeking to avoid an encounter, the Earl destroyed his siege machines and withdrew his forces to Nottingham, there to wait and monitor the rebels' progress. Ranulf and his commanders believed that Louis himself was at the head of the force. Mountsorrel relieved, the barons were approached by Hugh d'Arras. Hugh had entered the barons' camp to urge them to join his forces at Lincoln so that they could win the great prize of the castle which, he believed, was now ripe for taking. A council of war was held where differences were aired; a decision was finally made to respond to the pleas and the baronial host moved east to Lincoln. It was a fateful decision that led to the major land engagement of the whole war.

The march to Lincoln saw yet another major episode of ravaging. Wendover reports the event: 'the barons therefore passed through the valley of Belvoir, where everything was seized by these robbers, because the French infantry, who were the filth and scum of their country, left nothing untouched.'[539] He portrays the footsoldiers as impoverished wretches, forced into plunder by their great need. This is where the war came closest of all to Wendover: his priory lay just below William d'Albini's Castle of Belvoir with sweeping views across the valley. When the army arrived at Lincoln its leaders lodged in the town. Gilbert de Gant and Hugh d'Arras, now greatly reinforced, renewed their assaults on the castle, which continued to defend itself bravely, as it had done since March, under the redoubtable command of Nichola de Hay.

By Friday 12 May William Marshal was appraised of the precarious situation at Lincoln. Already angered by the retreat of the royalist Mountsorrel force, he held a major war council during which he urged that now was the time for decisive action. His biographer imbues his hero with powerful oratory powers in a stirring, patriotic speech:

> Hear me, you noble, loyal knights. In God's name hear me now. Defend our name, for ourselves and for the sake of our loved ones, our wives and our children; defend our land and win for ourselves the highest honour; safeguard the peace of the Holy Church which our enemies have broken and infringed, and gain redemption and pardon for all our sins. Now that we have taken on the burden of armed combat, let us make sure there is no coward amongst us! We shall be a lily-livered lot if we do not now take revenge on those who have come from France to take for themselves the lands of our men.[540]

He told his captains that with Louis' force split, there was a great opportunity to engage with the enemy. Battles were risky and could be conclusive, and so William had advised an eagerly agreeable John against this course at Louis' landing exactly a year before – but now was the time to 'play for the highest stakes'. 'These words,' says his biographer, 'put hope in their hearts, cheered, strengthened and emboldened them.' He ordered his army to launch an attack on the large Anglo-French forces at Lincoln; his men 'did not hesitate to advance'. The time had come for battle.[541]

The regent along with Guala, Peter des Roches and other members of his council, organised a muster of royalist forces fifteen miles south-west of Lincoln at Newark on 15 May. On the command of the king, royalist castles emptied of soldiers leaving only skeleton garrisons behind as their forces converged on Newark, keen, says Wendover, to fight for their country (*pro patria*). He gives the royalist army size as 400 knights, nearly 250 crossbowmen and innumerable army auxiliaries; the *History of William Marshal* corroborates the number of knights with '405 knights' (he later says 406) but reckons there were many more crossbowmen at 'only 317', unconvincingly trying to portray the army as a small one (and hence magnifying the enemy). The muster was a major event in itself: gathered there were William Marshal, Guala and Peter des Roches, the Earl of Salisbury, John Marshal, Robert de Vieuxpont, the Earl of Derby, Brian de Lisle, Philip Mark, Robert de Gaugi, William d'Albini, Philip d'Albini and, of course, Falkes de Bréauté; representing the episcopate were the Bishops of Hertford, Bath, Exeter, Salisbury, Worcester, and Lincoln; and, the very symbol of the reinvigorated royalist cause, the young King himself. The holiness of their crusade, minor as it was, was emphasised over three days during which the clergy heard confession, administered communion and solemnly excommunicated the rebels yet again, specifically those in Lincoln. Ominously, the anathema also extended to the inhabitants of this populous city. The royalist soldiers marked themselves with their white crosses. If a soldier fell his spiritual armour thus fortified by absolution and blessings would guarantee his salvation on Judgement Day. All was not harmony, however, and, as usual, squabbles and disagreements broke out. The Earl of Chester, who had previously complained that William Marshal was too old to be in command, insisted that he had the honour of leading the front rank of the army or else he would quit the army. He was too powerful, and with too strong a contingent, to be denied. David Crouch has suggested that the habitually cautious Marshal may have been stung into a battle-seeking policy by the Earl of Chester's insults.[542] The army refreshed, armoured and prepared itself for the coming clash. On Friday 19 May, while Guala and King Henry went to Nottingham, the army set out for Lincoln and battle.

It did not take the direct route. The castle and neighbouring cathedral sit solidly atop a ridge on the original Roman site (see map in picture section). The walled city spread south from here, dropping steeply to the River Whitham,

losing 175 feet of height over 700 yards. An assault over the south wall or through
its gate would entail passing through marshy ground and crossing the river; this
would be difficult enough, but the long slog uphill – onerous enough under
normal walking conditions, never mind fighting every inch of the way encum-
bered by heavy armour and wielding weaponry – was impracticable to the point
of being impossible. Another practical consideration, somewhat overlooked, was
that the royalists would want to establish swift communications with the besieged
garrisons so as to co-ordinate movements. Therefore the royalists headed to the
north to arrive before the city on the gradual, sloping ridge that extended over
a few miles. This was the site of the First Battle of Lincoln in 1141, when King
Stephen was captured after a valiant lone stand wielding a battle-axe. The upper
city was walled internally and the castle surrounded by a deep ditch.[543] During
John's reign, 300 marks had been spent on reinforcing its defences. The besieging
forces were within the city, attacking the castle from its north and south and its
gate from the east; the west gate, opening to the plain and open countryside (and
hence to communication with royalist forces), appears not to have been secured
externally, possibly because the rebels would have felt exposed outside the walls
and more prone to a relief attack. The royalists therefore approached the city via
a detour through Torksey. The biographer of William Marshal says that the army
spent the night here; Wendover, our local guide, says they encamped at Stow,
about eight miles from the city and just off a Roman road. With an army of this
size there may well have been more than one encampment spread between the
two places. Most of the soldiers trying to settle down for the night would have
anticipated that this was the eve of battle.

That the Battle of Lincoln is an important episode in the history of the time is
clear from the space afforded it in contemporary accounts. The terse and to the
point Barnwell and Dunstable annalists devote two-and-a-half pages to it between
them. The informative factual account by Wendover takes up over eight pages; the
twenty pages of more heroic and dramatic retelling in the *History of William the
Marshal*, being in verse, amounts to about the same, although its tendency towards
grandiose and unlikely speeches by the combatants tends to reduce its utility.
These two main sources differ in some details, but overall they corroborate each
other strongly. (The Anonymous of Béthune, distant from events in the south, has
only a few short lines on Lincoln.) The battle can therefore be reconstructed in
considerable detail.

On the sunny morning of 20 May, the royalist army advanced on Lincoln in
close battle order and with their standards and shields glistening in the sun; these
'struck terror into all who saw them', says Wendover. According to the Marshal's
biographer, leading the way was Ranulf Earl of Chester, 'a brave and highly experienced knight'. Following him was the Marshal with his son, and in the third
formation was William Longsword, Earl of Salisbury. In the rear was the division
commanded by Peter des Roches. Wendover says that there were seven dense

and well-formed battalions. He convincingly reports that crossbowmen made up
the vanguard a mile to the front of the column: this was an important defensive
measure against a frontal attack or ambush. In the rear was the baggage train. It is
clear from the sources that the morale of the army was very high. Wendover says
the men 'flew to arms, mounted their horses quickly and struck camp rejoicing';
they were 'all determined to conquer or die' for their just cause. A royalist poem
written just after the battle, devoid of detail but brimful of righteous religious
hyperbole, relishes their advance on Lincoln in similar terms: 'The royal standards glitter, and the formations under oath follow, when clear faith draws out
their faces, the bright signs of the cross paint the excelling chests of the youth, a
common will strengthens their hearts; there was one sole hope of conquering.'[544]

It was in this way the royalists came within sight of the walls of Lincoln before 6
a.m. Their first action was to establish contact with the castle garrison, who must
have been tingling with anticipation at the prospect of relief. William Marshal
sent his nephew John to the castle's west gate. On his way there he met Geoffrey
de Serland, sent by Lady Nicola to meet with him. Geoffrey showed John the
castle postern gate on the western side from which sorties could be made and,
crucially, troops brought in. As John hurried back at about 6.30 a.m. to relay this
important information he was set on by some French knights. A small combat
ensued but John fought off his attackers and made his way back to his own lines.

The royalist army drew itself up in a new formation in case of a sortie from
the city. The Marshal dispatched the 317 crossbowmen under Peter des Roches'
command to his right flank and ordered them to spread out in a long line ready
to shoot down the warhorses of the enemy, should they charge. The experienced
warrior bishop does not seem to have been perturbed by an edict of the Fourth
Lateran Council in 1215 that expressly forbade clerics from commanding crossbow contingents. William Marshal then instructed 200 cavalry to be prepared to
kill their own horses with their knives 'so as to be able,' says his biographer, 'to
take shelter behind them, if necessary, in an emergency'. The subtext is that it
would also make flight from the battlefield less likely. At the Battle of Towton in
1461, Edward IV slew his horse to raise the morale of his troops and a sign of his
commitment to remain on the battlefield.[545]

A reconnoitring party under Robert Fitzwalter and the Earl of Winchester
was sent out from the city to assess the power of the enemy. It is likely that it
was this group that had the encounter with John Marshal. There followed some
confused intelligence gathering on the rebel side, which may have cost them dear.
Wendover tells of how the party reported back positively after estimating the
royalist numbers and said that the Anglo-French force should ride out to meet
them: 'The enemy come against us in good order, but we are many more than
they; therefore our counsel is that we should sortie to the top of the hill and meet
them; if we do, we shall catch them like larks.' The Marshal's biographer, who
does not record this reconnoitring mission, gives the number of French knights

as 611 and infantry as 1000, a figure that excludes the English barons with them; Wendover had given the size of the Anglo-French relief force to Mountsorrel as 600 knights in total, to which must be added those of Gilbert de Gant and the rebel forces at Lincoln. With over 400 knights recorded in the royalist army, we are talking about very large armies. Both the poet biographer and Wendover say that the French then made their own scouting party to gather intelligence. According to Wendover, Thomas, the Count of Perche, responded to the plan with the perplexing: 'You have estimated them according to your knowledge; and now we shall go out and estimate them the French way.' He and Simon de Poissy, appointed captain of the Cambridge garrison by Louis in February before Simon led his men to Lincoln, rode out beyond the city walls and on to the plain to make their own assessment of the army drawn up before them. The Marshal's biographer has them make a different judgement on the army, saying it was 'better equipped for war and more resolute to wage it' than anybody 'had ever seen in any land'. Wendover corroborates this but offers far more telling detail for the discrepancy of the two reports. The French made the mistake of counting the standards of the nobles twice, not realising that each nobleman had two standards: one with the troops – 'so that they might been known in battle' – and another in the rear with the baggage. The result was a major overestimation – doubling the size of the royalist army. On their return they held a counsel with the other leading figures – Gilbert de Gant, the Count of Hertford, William de Mowbray and the initial scouting party – and proposed a more defensive plan: while one part of their force guarded the gates to prevent a royalist irruption, the other should concentrate on taking the castle. Their siege operations had continued and even increased in urgency in the knowledge of the royalist advance: the sooner they took the castle the safer they would be. There was disagreement over this plan, probably from Robert Fitzwalter and Saer de Quincy, but a majority decision prevailed. The gates were secured and guarded and the Franco-baronial force prepared for a defence.

The Marshal's biographer says they thereby felt reasonably secure, as 'the King's men had not the power to attack them inside the city, whatever the pretence they put up.' They also believed that the rigours of the march and the prospect of a long siege (of the besiegers) would take its toll on a weary royalist army. But, as his biographer relates, the Marshal used the withdrawal to exhort his troops further: 'My lords, my friends, look how those mustered with a view to riding to attack you have already shown their true colours and retreated behind their walls; that is what God promised us. God gives us great glory!' The Marshal sent a herald to the rebels to discuss terms; he was met, a contemporary poem tells us, with insults and threats.[546]

The Bishop of Winchester, as much a wielder of weapons as of crosiers, took the initiative at this stage. At the end of his account, the biographer of the Marshal declares that 'the worthy Bishop of Winchester, Peter des Roches, who was in charge that day of advising our side, was not slow or slothful, and he knew how to make use of his arms.' This does not mean that the biographer is contradicting himself when he initially depicts William Marshal as giving battle orders. Rather, it can be read either that des Roches was, as stated, simply the chief tactician, or that while Marshal was in charge of the overall operation, des Roches was in command in the field. The biographer of the Marshal tells the story of how the Bishop rode near to the walls with his contingent of crossbowmen and there, telling them to wait, took just one soldier with him through the postern gate into the castle. He wanted to see for himself the situation within the city walls and what would be the best way to proceed with action. The castle's defences had been seriously compromised by constant bombardment from the mangonels and catapults 'which were breaking everything in sight' and which threatened the Bishop's safety. He met with Nichola de Hay before, the biographer says, leaving by another postern gate on the town side to actually enter the city. Surveying the scene, he noticed the old western gate to the upper city and close to the castle that had been blocked up with stone and cement. He gave orders for it to be knocked down so that the army outside could enter and engage the rebels within the confines of the walls. He returned to his men in high spirits and with great expectations, both militarily and politically, joking (half in jest but with earnest intent) that he should claim the Bishop's palace as his residence for 'I have arranged that entrance for the safe and valorous entry of our men.'

There are, however, problems with parts of this account. Des Roches would already have been aware of the gate on his approach from the city and from the garrison; he could have seen the gate easily from the castle battlements; it would have been problematic to say the least to tear down the wall amidst the Anglo-French troops besieging the castle; and it would have been all but impossible to wander through besieging forces around the castle at will. The last difficulty has been met with the suggestion that des Roches disguised himself as an ordinary townsperson about his everyday business – highly unlikely in the midst of a full-scale military engagement in a confined area.[547] The biographer then reports that Falkes' men attempted to storm their way through the opened gate but were repelled savagely and had to retreat to their own lines. The Bishop reported disappointedly to the Marshal: 'Upon my soul, these men of ours did badly,' claiming that they had not found the 'right gate' he had made ready for them. But as the poet admirably admits here: 'those who have given me my subject matter do not agree unanimously, and I cannot follow all of them.'

Wendover is less ambiguous, omitting the des Roches story altogether, and provides a clearer account. The biographer of William Marshal may have confused the role of Falkes' men with the more likely events described here. As the royalist army launched their main assault on the northern gate (while still applying pressure elsewhere around the walls), the rebels and French fought them off while behind them the besiegers pounded away at the castle. With this intense action taking place, Falkes and a company of his troops, including crossbowmen, were able to enter surreptitiously on foot into the castle via its western postern gate; it is possible that des Roches went with them. At a stroke, the garrison was greatly inflated in size. Falkes positioned his crossbowmen on the ramparts and roofs of the buildings. 'In the twinkling of an eye', the battlements were suddenly bristling with fresh soldiers. Suddenly, the rebel forces prosecuting the siege and defending the north gate came under a hail of heavy, concentrated missiles raining down on them. (It is possible, if unlikely, that this covering fire allowed des Roches' men to unblock the western gate.) Knights and horses were felled to the ground; as the warhorses were killed, many cavalry had to fight on as infantry. This dramatic development caused great disruption and confusion among the French and the barons. Falkes, ever the experienced opportunist, took advantage of the disarray to sortie in the city and into the enemy ranks. It is likely that either he was hoping that this moment of crisis could be developed into a tipping point for the rebels and French in which chaos would lead to flight, or that he was providing a shield for his men to unblock the western gate. However, the rebel and French troops did not break and instead turned on Falkes with vigour. A furious mêlée ensued as the two sides, no longer separated by the walls of the castle or city, battled with each other hand-to-hand. Falkes was captured but quickly rescued by the valour of some of his men. It seems probable this is the incident to which des Roches refers to in the *History of William Marshal* when he talks of Falkes' actions.

Rather than be blamed by des Roches, Falkes played an important part by his brave and aggressive tactics. He successfully diverted many of the French and rebels away from the north gate to deal with the immediate threat he posed them and also possibly protected his soldiers dismantling the blocked western gate, too. The Dunstable annalist records that the besiegers had to take men from the walls to deal with Falkes. This weakened resistance at the gates and allowed the main royalist division to force its way through them and into the city.[548] The Marshal's biographer then devotes his attention to the bravery of his patron, as all such medieval panegyrists did. He portrays the aged regent as rushing to enter the city without stopping to place his helmet on and impatient at des Roches' advice that they should first send men to ensure the way was secure. Lambasting any soldier leaving the scene of battle, the Marshal urgently exhorted his men to 'Ride on! For you will see them beaten in a short while.' With his war cry 'God is with the Marshal!' ringing out, he stormed into the city like a 'ravenous lion' and into the thick of the foe, clearing the way before him. Undoubtedly this is exaggerated, but it may have the ring of truth as the old warrior relished one final, glorious combat. With the city gates opened, the royalist army poured into the city and rushed on the enemy. The mêlée in the city became a desperate, full-scale battle.

The French and baronial forces were now assailed from the irruption through the gates, Falkes' men from the castle, and the crossbowmen from the battlements. Many were cornered. The main battleground was the crowded space between the castle and cathedral; here the day would be decided. Wendover dramatically tells of sparks and thunder from clashing metal and the sound of swords against helmets, and of how the barons suffered grievously from the shooting of the crossbow-men, 'by whose skill the barons' horses were mown down and killed like pigs'. This greatly weakened the barons and the French as the riders were then easily taken prisoner in the press of combat without anyone to ride into the enemy and rescue them. An early casualty reported by the Marshal's biographer was a catapult operator, the barons' 'most expert stonethrower'; he mistook approaching royalist knights for his own side. He therefore continued loading his catapult with a stone when they fell upon him and took his head off.

The *History of William Marshal* falls partly into the convention of portraying the battle as a series of individual combats between the great men of the day; certainly the great and the good receive his closest attention. We therefore have to be care-ful at taking his account too literally, even if it makes for exciting reading. Thus William Marshal the Younger also comes in for some special treatment, courtesy of the family's patronage. He is seen wading into the enemy, like father like son, entering the city through a breach in the wall (the unblocked western gate?). In no time at all he has inflicted great damage on his enemies. Then galloping along comes his father with the 'worthy' Earl of Salisbury. They wheeled rightwards into enemy.[549] The Earl was confronted by Robert of Ropsley who picked up a lance to joust with William Longsword; he struck the Earl so hard his lance broke into pieces. Riding on past, Ropsley was struck hard between the shoulders by the regent, a blow that nearly knocked him to the ground. It is possible that such an encounter took place, but opportunities for jousting in such a packed and confined space must have been very rare indeed. More realistic is what happened afterwards: Ropsley, fearing defeat as his comrades were being pushed downhill, slinked off to take refuge in an upper room of a nearby building.

The fate of the Count of Perche is clearer, and supported by different sources. As the Franco-baronial forces were pressed southwards into the lower city, the Count held his position on the flat ground before the imposing west front of the cathedral. This was probably intended to rally his French troops rather than as a last stand. The Count, the young, 22-year-old Thomas came from a notable family with extensive lands – and claims to land – in England. The Marshal's biographer depicts him as 'looking very arrogant and proud; he was a very tall, handsome, fine-looking man,' echoing other accounts of him. Perhaps valour got the better of discretion for this chivalrous, relatively inexperienced knight. He was quickly surrounded by the king's knights pressing all around him. They called on him to surrender to save his life but he refused point blank, disdaining to be taken by men disloyal to their true King and his: Louis. The royalists rushed on him and his men and many 'were wounded and maimed, trampled on and beaten, and many taken captive', says the biographer in a realistic depiction of the combat that took place 'in the very close of the cathedral', says the Barnwell chronicler. The royalists were in danger of being driven from the higher ground when Reginald Croc, a knight from Falkes' household, lunged forward with either his sword or dagger and thrust it through the eyehole of the Count's helmet and into his eye, inflicting a mortal wound. According to the Marshal's biographer, the young Count attacked the Marshal, his first cousin, in his death throes, taking his sword in both hands and striking the Marshal's helmet three times, and with such force that marks were left on it. He then slumped down and fell from his horse. Wendover says the wound pierced his brain and he fell to the ground without a word. The biographer reports that this caused great sadness all round and that 'it was a great pity that he had died in this manner.' By the end of the battle Croc was named as another fatality; it is likely that he was struck down after killing the Count.

The felling of their leader caused dismay among the French, who, says the Marshal's biographer in the only account of the following action, 'could no longer stand and resist'. Those that could retreated rapidly southwards down the hill to the lower city to join their comrades who already made their way there. They rallied in an open space at the top of the well-named Steep Hill; any further down and the incline would have made an upward counter-attack almost impossible, especially after the exertions of the hard-fought battle. Thus regrouped, the Anglo-French soldiers 'came riding uphill in tight battle formation'. Before they reached the top they were engaged by the royalists, who had the great advantage of fighting downhill. At this juncture, the Earl of Chester appears on the scene to the right of the rebel forces. This leads to speculation that he had been assaulting the city from the east and had broken in through the east gate. Not only did he assail them, but attack also came from the rear led by the brothers Alan and Thomas Basset. The French and rebels quickly realised that there was no hope of regaining control of the city and that the battle was lost. A rearguard was hastily formed as they undertook a fighting retreat downhill until they were pushed through the southern gate and out of the city itself.

Once outside, the *History of William Marshal* reports a stand of the French and rebels at Wigford Bridge. Although some historians have seen this as a last stand it is more likely that it was the rearguard providing protection while the rest of the army still at liberty crossed over the bridge to attempt flight and escape on the other side. Here the bar gate was a peculiar mechanism, something about which Wendover offers considerable detail. It seems to have been a swing-door design that compelled riders to dismount and pass through one at a time, closing again after each person had passed through. This was naturally a great hindrance to the escape and would have necessitated the rearguard stand to cover the slow crossing. The Marshal's biographer less convincingly blames a cow for blocking the exit. It was apparently swiftly dispatched.

Here, during the final encounter of the battle, the Marshal's biographer takes a particularly poetical turn and waxes lyrical over chivalry and the fighting that took place. 'What is armed combat? … It is much nobler work. What, then, is chivalry? Such a difficult, tough, and very costly thing to learn, that no coward ventures to take it on ... Had you been there, you would have seen great blows dealt, heard helmets clanging and resounding, seen lances fly in splinters in the air, saddles vacated by riders, knights taken prisoner.' Swords and maces delivered their blows. Horses were targets; 'their protective covering was not worth a fig' against the knives and daggers drawn against them (as at Bouvines). Amidst all this William Bloet, the banner holder of William Marshal the Younger, got carried away. He launched himself into the press of the enemy 'so heavily and head on he fell over the side of the bridge, he and his horse with him'. This bathetic episode is the last recorded action of the engagement. The battle was over.

The congestion at the bridge might have been a slaughtering ground for the French and rebels, or at least a mass corralling of prisoners. That it was neither was due to three factors. The first is that the battle had been waged over six hours; the men on both sides involved in the combat were exhausted. The second is that the nature of the war did not lend itself to massacre of fellow knights. The third was that, as Wendover puts it, 'the King's men only pretended to pursue them, and if it had not been for the effect of relationship and blood, not a single one of them would have escaped.' The Marshal's biographer, however, says that Peter des Roches energetically pursued the defeated and caught many. Only three to five fatalities are recorded for the whole battle. Wendover says these were the Count of Perche, his slayer Reginald de Croc and an unknown soldier in the baron's party. Matthew Paris later added two of the Count's knights.[550] Reginald was buried honourably at Croxton monastery. Perche, being excommunicated, was not buried in consecrated ground, but allowance was made for his position and he was laid to rest in the ground of the hospital. The unknown soldier's fate was less considerate: he was buried outside the city at a crossroads. The marked lack of recorded casualties (the figures were unlikely to cover lowly infantry deaths) earned the battle the title of 'The Tournament' or 'The Fair of Lincoln'.

Those that could fled south, Simon de Poissy and Hugh d'Arras chief among them. If the biographer of William Marshal is to be believed, so desperate was their flight that when they came to a broken bridge they killed their horses to ford the river over their bodies. Robert of Sandford, fleeing with his wife, was told by another knight: 'Leave her, you will not carry her off.' Robert turned abruptly around and, disgusted and angered, knocked the man to the floor with his lance. He and his wife reached safety. Those who made their escape 'rested neither by night or day in any house or any town'.

The magnitude of the victory is marked by the astonishing roll call of prisoners. 'No knight eager,' says the Marshal's biographer, 'to capture knights could fail to do so that day,' John Marshal bagging no less than seven barons. The baronial party had been decapitated and eviscerated as nearly all the barons who fought for Louis were taken prisoner: the Earls of Hereford, Winchester and Hertford; Gilbert de Gant, Robert Fitzwalter, William de Ros, 'and many others too tedious to mention,' says Wendover. The Barnwell chronicler records 380 knights taken prisoner, and numberless soldiers and townspeople. The Anonymous of Béthune says some barons escaped, 'but they were few'.[551] Three hundred knights were also captured and only three of the leading French captains escaped: de Poissy, Arras and Eustace de Merlinghem with about 200 knights. The ransom from the prisoners would have made many a victorious knight rich, or, in the case of the leading barons such as the Marshal family laying claim to their generous share, even richer. However, riches were also to be had elsewhere.

The greatest damage and loss of life was not at the Battle of Lincoln itself, but in the savage sacking of the city afterwards. The *History of William Marshal* does not sully the regent's great victory by offering an account of this terrible event, but Wendover, ever aware of the sufferings of noncombatants and being geographically extremely close to events, does. In a passage entitled 'Of the plunder and pillage of the city', he gives us a vivid account of what happened when the royalists had secured their victory:

After the battle was thus ended, the king's soldiers found in the city the wagons of the barons and the French, with the packhorses, loaded with baggage, silver vessels, and various kinds of furniture and utensils, all which fell into their hands without opposition. Having then plundered the whole city to the last farthing, they next pillaged the churches throughout the city, and broke open the chests and store-rooms with axes and hammers, seizing on the gold and silver in them, clothes of all colours, ornaments, gold rings, goblets and jewels. Nor did the cathedral church escape this destruction, but underwent the same punishment as the rest, for the legate had given orders to knights to treat all the clergy as excommunicated men ... This church lost eleven thousand marks of silver. When they had thus seized on every kind of property, so that nothing remained in any corner of the houses, they each returned to their lords as rich men ... Many of the women of the city were drowned in the river, for, to avoid shameful offence [rape], they took to small boats with their children, female servants and household property, and perished on their journey; but there was afterwards found in the river by the searchers, goblets of silver, and many other articles of great benefit to the finders.[552]

The Barnwell chronicler confirms the atrocities. The spoils of victory were, as ever, money and women.

Lincoln was a devastating blow to the Anglo-French party, the most decisive of the war that had started back in 1215. The poem of the battle lauds the victory as 'O famous day, to be venerated through our age!' Powicke says 'within a few hours the cause of Louis had suffered a crushing defeat'; Carpenter calls the Battle of Lincoln 'one of the most decisive in English history' with the result that 'England would be ruled by the Angevin, not the Capetian dynasty.'[553] But Louis was not finished yet.

8

The Last Campaign, 1217

The Final Push

Great as the royalist victory at Lincoln was, it did not the end the war. Although the French historian Petit-Dutaillis' judgement that the Battle of Lincoln was more important in terms of morale rather than material advantage underestimates the significance of the battle, it was not a killer blow.[554] The wheel of fortune had turned before and could turn again.

In the immediate aftermath of Lincoln, there was a flurry of activity as the protagonists responded to the dramatic events. Lincoln Castle had suffered terrible damage from the enemy's siege engines and, seeing the way the wind was now blowing and hoping to catch the breeze to its full advantage, 'the Earl of Salisbury emphasised his conversion to the king's party by advancing close on £400 towards the repair of the fortress.'[555] While Louis remained ignorant of events, the royalist high command, already gathered at Lincoln, held a council of war to decide what to do next. As to be expected, there was a difference of opinion. Some wanted to proceed to London and besiege it at last, an expression of new-found confidence after their victory at Lincoln; others thought the priority should be Dover, which Louis was still besieging. The Marshal, 'who knew most about war and had seen most of it', says his biographer, told his captains to secure their prisoners in their castles (for the profitable ransoms that would follow) and ordered a muster at Chertsey, which took place in the royal presence on 6 June. The day after the battle, news reached them that the garrison at Mountsorrel had fled, leaving the castle empty; its castellan, Henry de Braybrooke, had been at Lincoln and may have been captured there. Two days later, on 23 May, it was granted to Ranulf Earl of Chester, who had it destroyed, so that it did not create further problems for him in the region. Greater reward was in store for Ranulf: he was granted the earldom of Lincoln county. Others also received their dues: Brian de Lisle, for example, was given Knaresborough. It was for such rewards that many fought the war.

The French who escaped from Lincoln had a rough time of it as they fled to the security of London. The footsoldiers suffered especially badly, Wendover saying that most of these were killed. In comparison with the mobile cavalry, who nonetheless still incurred losses, they were less able to escape from ambushes laid for them on their journey. As the French hurried through the towns on their way to the capital, they were set upon by townspeople with swords and clubs. No doubt they were exacting revenge for the depredations of the Franco-baronial armies that had occurred during their ravaging and northward marches; with revenge came their own plundering and the opportunity to either profit or at least gain compensation for their own losses.

There was also a sense of nationalist outrage at work here at the imposition of French rule and violence in the country. Many historians, especially modernists, discount any sense of national identity at such an early date in English history, some even adhering to the extreme position of Ernest Gellner that national-ism came with industrialisation in the nineteenth century. The matter of national identity and nationalism encompasses a certain degree of obfuscating semantics on the subject. My research supports that of Patrick Wormald, John Gillingham and others influenced by Anthony Smith's more primordial approach, which rec-ognises clear signs of identification with the nation in the Middle Ages, even stretching back to the Anglo-Saxon period.[556] Thirteenth-century England meets with John Breuilly's conditions for patriotism, which he places in the early-mod-ern period. He posits nationalism as a form of politics that arises to oppose the state which is manipulated to advance the interests of the ruling elites: this is manifest in the baronial response to King John's policies and Magna Carta. The effect of war on nationalist feeling has also been well documented, but more for the early-modern period onwards.[557] Such feelings in England had been nurtured by the wars against the Celtic fringe in the twelfth century, as John Gillingham has indicated. Breuilly concurs that such military factors are crucial in the forma-tion of nationalism, and argues that the lack of ideology in English nationalism is explained by the fact that 'there has been no foreign presence which would generate nationalist opposition.'[558] But this is exactly what we have in 1216–17 with the French military occupation of England for over a year (and a reflection of just how much this important event has been overlooked or simply not known about). We have seen how at Lincoln the Marshal urged his men to fight for their country, 'pro patria' as Wendover says, and how his biographer mocked the foreign invaders. We have seen this patriotic call too in 1213. And when England was again threatened by French invasion in 1264, patriotic and anti-alien senti-ment was once more employed successfully to mobilise huge numbers of the common folk against the enemy.[559] As Alfred Smyth has shown, the Viking inva-sions fostered a real sense of national identity in Anglo-Saxon England, precisely because they posed a foreign threat.[560] Patriotism clearly existed in early thir-teenth century. It was not new, but the loss of Normandy in 1204, the oppressions of John, the break with Rome and, above all, the French invasion of England: all mark out this period as one of central importance in the development of English national identity.[561]

Some 200 French and baronial knights escaped from Lincoln and made it to London. On 25 May Louis heard the news of the disaster at Lincoln as he was pressing the siege of Dover. Unsurprisingly, the sources agree that Louis took the news badly. The *History of William Marshal* says 'Louis was full of anger and rage once he heard how his men had been defeated so badly in Lincoln, how so many had been taken prisoner there, and how the Count had been killed.' Wendover has Louis sneeringly telling those who had escaped that the fault was theirs: had they stood and fought, their companions would have been saved from capture and death. William the Breton attempts to soften the blow by blaming the defeat at Lincoln on a sneaky ambush by the English and their superior numbers, thus excusing Simon de Poissy and his knights for 'prudently' escaping to London. He says that 'vexation, sadness and lamentation burst through' the French camp.[562]

Louis' instinctive reaction on hearing the news was to return to London and secure it; besieging the capital was an option discussed at the royalist war council at Lincoln. The Marshal's biographer says Louis 'gave up the siege and went to London as quickly as possible, for he had every fear that the King's men might take it by surprise, or by force, or that they would come and launch an attack on him'.[563] However, as the reliable Anonymous of Béthune informs us from his more knowledgeable position in the south, Louis did not leave immediately. Before raising the siege and, much to his dismay, dismantling his powerful trebuchet, Louis and his advisers held a new council at which it was agreed that they should stay at Dover until Sunday.[564] This was a risky strategy: as the Marshal's biographer hints at, as well as the possibility of a quick move on London by the royalists, there was a danger that news of the defeat could dishearten the Londoners who might then go over to Henry; in 1215 the city had easily gone over to the barons and there was some danger it could just as easily switch allegiance.[565] As we shall see in a moment, this was a real threat. If London was lost, then so was Louis' whole campaign. But Louis held his nerve: he was waiting at Dover for reinforcements.

That Sunday was a clear day and the sails of the transport ships could be seen across the Channel. The next day, 29 May, the English could also see them and when they set sail, so, too, did the English; the French gave chase but to no avail. As they turned back to head into Dover, the English ships made a quick about turn and attacked the rearward vessels of the French, capturing eight of them. This seems to have been a successful naval employment of the feigned retreat of cavalry charges, most famously executed by William the Conqueror down the coast at Hastings in 1066. Despite the size of the French fleet – some 120 ships – the reinforcements they carried were few, 'all sergeants, merchants or sailors; of knights, there were only eighteen of them,' says the Anonymous.[566] When Louis went down to the shore to meet them, he was angered and dismayed at how little help had materialised. It could only have made the still fresh wound of Lincoln ache the more.

Louis held another council that evening where it was decided that he should go back to London the next day. He wrote a number of letters, which were sent to France with Guy d'Athies to his father informing the King of the changed situation, and to leading barons, seeking their help. He also sent back the ships that had just arrived, possibly in anticipation of them being used for transporting over more substantial reinforcements. The ships that were already in the harbour from earlier were burned; Louis was leaving Dover and he did not want to leave anything of use to the enemy. It is safe to assume that as soon as he left, Hubert de Burgh's garrison burst out from their incarceration within the castle to be met by local supporters, no doubt followed soon after by Willikin of the Weald. Louis spent the night in Canterbury and on Thursday 1 June was back in London.

The Anonymous says that he was received here with great ceremony; but how different and more melancholy it must have been compared to his first triumphal arrival there a year before. The atmosphere soon turned even sourer. The royalists had marched through Windsor and Staines and were now not far off mustering at Chertsey; what is more, they had opened up secret talks with the chief men of London. The sack of Lincoln would have played heavily on the Londoners' minds; the sack was, after all, not merely a plundering opportunity but a measured exercise in psychological pressure for the capital: this is what happens to those who defy us. This was the royalists' stick; their carrot was a reassuring confirmation of the city's liberties. The negotiations did not remain secret for long as Louis soon heard of them. His response was to secure all but one of the gates of the city – probably in the form of blocking them up – and to demand a renewal of the city's homage to him; he 'had little trust in the burghers of London' and thus 'dared not leave the city'.[567]

Louis stagnated in the capital for the month of June, little better off than when the rebels had taken the capital in 1215 only to find themselves on the defensive and holed up there by the autumn. The chroniclers capture this stagnation in affairs by their jump from the Battle of Lincoln in May to the last battle at the end of August; the exception is the well informed Anonymous of Béthune who thus becomes even more valuable for this period, backed up by government papers. While Louis stewed in London trying to arrange reinforcements, the Henricians went from strength to strength. The number of *reversi*, men returning to the royal camp, serves as a barometer for the changing political and military climate: from the Battle of Lincoln to early August, over 150 abandoned Louis and submitted to the king, including such major rebel figures as the Earl of Warenne (by 22 June), Reginald de Braose (by 24 June), the Earl of Arundel (by 14 July), and John de Lacy, Constable of Chester (by 9 August).[568] In the deteriorating situation the rebels found themselves, the pronouncement of a total amnesty and restoration of their lands as they held them before the war encouraged many to make the return to the English royal fold. While the majority of barons remained loyal to Louis, this was still a significant and indicative setback.

Louis was politically as well as militarily astute. He knew he had to play for time in the hope of fresh forces from France while simultaneously stalling the Henricians and hedging his bets through negotiating towards a favourable settlement. It was not a winning strategy, but the only other options were surrender or immediate departure from England. Even if he chose the latter so as to personally drum up support in France, it would have effectively ended his expedition; his leaving would have been taken as a sign of non-commitment to the cause. The political consequences would have been the collapse of the baronial party as more and more of its members availed themselves of the amnesty to lessen the retribution they feared would follow.

The opportunity for high-level negotiations overseen by leading churchmen presented itself at the start of June. A prestigious embassy of clerics had arrived in London from France under safe conduct, ostensibly to preach the Fifth Crusade (1217–19) against Egypt. The delegation was led by Archbishop Simon of Tyre from the crusader states. With him were two of Europe's foremost abbots – those of Clairvaux and Cîteaux – and the Abbot of Pontigny. Conrad, the head of the Cistercian order, was later made legate to France. It was usual for the Archbishops of Tyre to recruit help for the imperilled Holy Land: one of Simon's predecessors was in England in 1188 to seek the assistance of the aging Henry II.[569] While it was a genuine coincidence that the Archbishop's party had been in France at this time, there is more to its arrival in England than urging people to take up the cross. As the Anonymous says, Simon 'on hearing of this war crossed the sea and came to England to make peace if he could'.[570] It has been perceptively suggested that the embassy was persuaded to go to England by Philip Augustus, anxious to secure a settlement for his son;[571] indeed, it is worth speculating further and considering that the letters Louis dispatched from Dover to his father the evening before raising the siege and returning to London had specifically asked for the intervention of the Archbishop. Nicholas Vincent's detailed study of Guala's career shows how Pope Honorius III had consistently applied pressure on Philip to demand that his son made peace, commissioning the Abbots of Cîteaux and Clairvaux with this mission on 6 December 1216, threatening him with papal sanctions. On 21 April 1217 Honorius had written directly to Philip, 'mentioning the efforts at peace-making by the Archbishop of Tyre and the Abbot of Cîteaux'.[572] The Papacy's motivations behind its involvement in the peace process was determined in no small part by the fact that its desire for crusaders would be hampered by the involvement of so many English and French knights in the war in England. We have seen how Savary de Mauléon left the royalist cause at the end of 1216 to return to his native Poitou and thence to embark on crusade.

We have a detailed knowledge of the negotiations as the Archbishop recorded them and Guala sent a letter to Honorius from about 13 June also detailing the progress of the discussions.[573] There were several meetings, the last and main one being held between Brentford and Hounslow starting on Monday 12 June. Here four members each from Henry's and Louis' councils discussed terms; behind each side stood the agreed number of twenty supporting knights. A draft treaty was drawn up which, while not harsh on Louis, clearly pointed to the French Prince's defeat. He was to free the English – barons, knights and townspeople – from their oaths to him, and in the future make no further alliances with them against Henry or his heirs; likewise, the barons would swear that they would make no further alliances against the King with Louis or anyone else. Alexander II of Scotland was to restore to the English crown all lands and castles seized in the war. Similarly, Louis and the French had to return their lands, and Eustace the Monk had to return the Channel Islands he had taken on pain of confiscation of his fiefs. All rebels would have to offer security of their faith to the King. Magna Carta was reinforced. Other clauses dealt more favourably with the matter of ransoms and prisoners, reparations and absolution from excommunications.

But the talks collapsed over the matter of Louis' leading clerical supporters. To his credit, Louis insisted that Elias of Dereham, a clerk of Sephen Langton and previously of Hubert Walter, Robert de St Germain, a clerk of Louis' ally the King of Scotland, Gervase of Howbridge, dean of canons at St Paul's, and Simon Langton, Louis' chancellor in England, be included in the terms of the peace treaty. He was prepared to see them stripped of their benefices, but only if they were equally compensated with secular rents. The most important of the four was Simon, the Archbishop of Canterbury Stephen Langton's brother and previously Archbishop Elect of York. Guala, who had developed quite an antipathy to Langton, insisted that this concession was unacceptable, or at least until and if the pope acquiesced to it. He may have had the backing of some hardliners such as the Earl of Chester, who believed the treaty too lenient. Nor could Guala easily forgive them for publicly defying the decree of papal excommunication by preaching the rebels' cause. From the pulpit at St Paul's they had given sermons to the Londoners, and 'made it understood' that the excommunication could be ignored because the pope was not fully cognisant of the facts of the situation and that 'Louis and his men were good people'.[574] The Archbishop of Tyre's letter to the pope made it clear that 'Louis would in no way make peace without them.'[575] There was no movement on either side and so at the last moment the talks collapsed. War was back on the agenda.

The peace delegation returned to France in mid-June, the Archbishop of Tyre receiving a letter of consolation from Abbot Gervase of Prémontré for having so nearly achieved peace, 'which, when it was nearly accomplished, was obstructed on account of four clerks; would that they had never learned their letters'.[576] Back in England, it was the man of the cloth Guala who was agitating for an immediate military response and the seasoned warrior William Marshal who advocated caution. Guala wanted London besieged, but other commanders were against

such action. London remained a formidable fortress and it seemed better to wait
for the flow of defections to weaken Louis further. These were accelerated by the
failed peace talks: in the week that followed over 60 left Louis for Henry. There
was also a potentially serious threat from Wales to deal with: Prince Llewelyn,
enraged by the desertion of his son-in-law Reginald de Braose to Henry, invaded
his lands, seizing Swansea Castle and hence control of the Gower peninsula; the
regent looked on perturbed as Llewelyn advanced towards the Marshal's castle
at Haverford and took hostages from Pembrokeshire.[577] The regent's decision to
leave the capital alone and lead the royal court west to Gloucester for the first
week of July was probably influenced by these events; William certainly availed
himself of the opportunity to visit his castles of Goodrich and Chepstow at that
time. But the Welsh provocations were more of a distraction than anything else.
At this time Lynn submitted to the King through the hands of Falkes de Bréauté
and a sense of reclaiming political ascendancy was reinforced by the reissuing of
Magna Carta and its enforcement by the sheriffs of England. From Gloucester
on 4 July, Henry's advisers issued a summons for Oxford on 15 July to determine
what they should do next.

   While the royalists played the waiting game, which they felt secure in doing and
which may well have been employed for the want of any better strategy, it was
Louis who took the initiative. With a treaty off the table, he redoubled and redirected his energies to the familiar activity of soldiering.[578] Louis was too careful a
man to close the door on diplomacy entirely: while he again rejected the wishes
of Honorius for submission when the pope sent his confessor Brother Nicholas
to meet him, he also sent the Count of Nevers to Windsor where he held talks
with the queen mother; but although 'they spoke well together and left on good
terms', nothing was accomplished. Again, this may have simply been stalling on
Louis' part; William Marshal 'knew well' the French Prince's true intentions. And
these were not peaceful.

   Worried about the defections and also the loyalty of London, Louis moved his
residence in the capital to the Tower for greater security. Strategically, he was not
in a strong position; but nor was he a spent force. London, even if a little shaky,
was still too tough a nut to crack for the royalists at the moment, and Louis still
had a large force there, with the prospect of more men, if not on the horizon,
then just beyond it. The hardcore of baronial rebels remained and prisoners taken
at Lincoln (and elsewhere) were gradually being ransomed. And now Louis was
no longer restrained by high-level peace talks. His campaign in England set about
revitalising itself.

   The first course of action was, as ever, to go on a *chevauchée* or two. The main
purpose was a logistical one – to gather supplies for London and plunder to
pay for the troops – but on a lesser scale it also reminded the royalists that Louis
remained a force to be reckoned with and at least worthy of greater concessions in any future settlement. Making the most of the royal camp's temporary

move back to Gloucester, the first ravaging force, a large one according the Anonymous, made straight for the wealthy monastery town of Bury St Edmunds under the leadership of the Viscount of Melun, Hugh Tacon and the Flemish knight Eustace de Neville. This was not a free ride but a daring raid as the royalist garrisons surrounded London. Wendover says the French were in great want of supplies and believed themselves to be hemmed in. Bury St Edmunds rewarded their endeavour, provided rich pickings. This was followed up by a raid by the Duke of Brittany: he made 'a wonderful *chevauchée*', says the admiring Anonymous – to where he does not say – in which the lesser soldiers gained much. It was a great morale booster, and when the Duke returned to London he was warmly congratulated.[579]

The royalists had not met up at Oxford on 15 July as planned, but did so instead between about 21 and 25 July, issuing instructions on 22 July for another meeting to be held there before returning again to Gloucester; the consequent assembly held between 7 and 13 August ended with yet another summons to meet back at Oxford on 25 August. The sketchiness of the sources make it hard to judge movements and actions: were these ad hoc and unclear, reacting passively to events; or do they mask a coherent underlying plan? As the biographer of William Marshal makes no mention of the latter, and indeed depicts his hero as surprised and dismayed at the events that followed, it might be easier to assume that there was indeed no overarching plan in the royalist camp at this stage, other than to wait and see while building up their forces. However, this is not the whole picture. The war was about to enter its final and decisive stage as the theatre of operations shifted to the English Channel. Louis' future in England relied on reinforcements from France: he knew it, and William Marshal knew it. Thus the Anonymous' comments mentioned earlier that the regent 'knew well' what Louis was up to: busily recruiting more troops in France. While on land the royalists appeared to do very little, they were busily preparing and strengthening their forces at sea.

Louis' dispatches from Dover had appealed to his father and wife for help. Philip Augustus, who had reconciled himself with Honorius, was still not prepared to jeopardise his relations with the Papacy. This precluded any public support for his son, but it did not stop him from feigning ignorance of moves to help him. This task fell to his wife, Blanche of Castille. Blanche, around 32 years of age at this time, was a redoubtable female figure of the Middle Ages who went on to become regent of France between 1226 and 1234 for her celebrated son, St Louis IX. The French historian Gérard Sivéry calls her 'determined, intrepid and obstinate'.[580] She had married Louis in 1200 and proved a faithful and dedicated wife; she now threw herself into the task of finding reinforcements to send to her husband in England. If a French source from later in the thirteenth century is to be believed, she worked her charms on her father-in-law to persuade him to provide funds for her recruitment drive. 'Will you leave your son and my lord to die in a foreign country? For God's sake, sire, he ought to rule after you.' She even threatened to place the king's grandchildren and future heir as security – in effect, hostages – to secure bankers' loans.[581] This was a little over-dramatic – nobody in England had the slightest intention of stringing Louis up – but it may have worked in cajoling Philip to offer some financial assistance.

Wendover imagines the content of Louis' epistles to his father: with 'a large force marching through the cities and towns around London, which prevented he and his companions from leaving the city' (either this was written before the raids or Wendover he did not know of them), Louis tells King Philip: 'all our supplies are failing us and our followers in the city, and even if they were abundant, we do not have the money to buy them; therefore I point out to you that I have no ability to resist, or to leave England, unless you provide me with powerful military aid.' Wendover understands Philip's position and says that the King, not wishing to be rebuked by the pope again, 'lay the whole business on Louis's wife'; Blanche 'was not slow in attending to the matter that fell to her'.[582] She recruited most heavily in Louis' territory of Artois among its barons, burghers and his vassals. There was some resistance, as merchants, ship owners and sailors grumbled and protested that they had fulfilled their obligations to Louis the previous spring. She had to press them hard, with warnings that Louis was in grave danger. She may have reminded them that a ransom for their lord would prove even more costly than military assistance.

The exact size of the force that the resourceful Blanche raised is hard to determine. Wendover puts the figure at 300 'brave knights, well provisioned for war, with a large force of soldiers'; the Anonymous says there were 'barely 100 knights'. The Melrose chronicler gives exact figures of 125 French knights, 33 crossbowmen, 146 cavalry and 833 infantry. Thus Wendover may be quite accurate if we take his figure of 300 *milites* to encompass the whole cavalry element. The Dunstable annalist simply writes of 'many powerful nobles'. The Marshal's biographer is similarly vague, but emphasises the strength of the new army: it was large enough not only to 'rescue' Louis' position but also 'to conquer the realm'. Blanche 'rode through all the towns in France to seek assistance in the form of great contingents of men and coffers of money'. She went about her task with such energy that she gathered such a force they would be able to conquer 'the entire kingdom'.[583] The biographer, who says that Philip was equally active in gathering the army, was exaggerating the size of the French force for dramatic effect, but clearly it was sizeable and even if comprising 100 knights plus sergeants, would go a considerable way to replacing the prisoners taken at Lincoln (and now trickling back to Louis after the payment of their ransoms) and to prolonging his campaign well into the future.

The Battle of Sandwich

This new expeditionary force began to gather at Calais in early August. At its head was Robert de Courtnay, uncle to the French queen and a high-ranking noble in Louis' household, who had fought with the Prince in England, and the younger brother of Peter, Count of Auxerre and Nevers. His leading captains were the Parisian Ralph de la Tournelle and Michael de Harnes. The commander of the fleet was, once again, Eustace the Monk, who, Wendover reminds us, was 'a shameful man and a wicked pirate'. None of this went unnoticed by the English. After the gathering at Oxford over the second week of August, William Marshal made his way to the south coast via Reading on the 14th, Farnham on 15th–16th, Lewes on 17th, and Romney on the 19th. When the regent heard the news that he had feared and long anticipated, he was 'greatly distraught' that 'an army of such strength and might was due to arrive in England';[584] he therefore ordered his admiral Philip d'Albini and John Marshal to lead the sailors of the Cinque port and a large force of men 'to watch the seas carefully, and to reconnoitre for the French and prevent their arrival'.[585] D'Albini had been charged with coastal defence back on 20 January and we have seen his forces in conspicuous action against the French at Winchelsea and Dover.

With both sides preparing for a major encounter, it was not surprising that a number of skirmishes ensued. The English crossed the Channel to harass the French forces at Calais, shooting arrows into the harbour, hoping to keep them penned in. On one day the English sent out a large number of ships – 300 says the Anonymous – and a sizeable engagement occurred. The French, seeing the English approach, set out to meet them, capturing a staggering 140 of the lightly-manned vessels and chasing the others back to port. It seems that the English lost contact with their commander and, leaderless, panicked, abandoning their vessels at full sail and making their getaway in their skiffs. At one point the French fleet embarked and set sail, reaching Dover with the intention of sailing around to the Thames estuary and hence London, but a terrifying storm drove them back across the Channel to Boulogne and Flanders. But all knew this was just a temporary setback.

William Marshal, who spent the night of 23 August at Canterbury, had ordered a full muster of his forces at the port of Sandwich for the 24th. The leaders of the Cinque ports, sensing that the crown's need of their services and loyalty was greater than ever at this moment of approaching crisis, exploited the situation to gain advantages. The system of naval organisation had broken down during the war, leaving royalist forces to gather maritime forces in something of an ad hoc manner until the Cinque ports felt free enough from French intrusions to renew fully their allegiance to the crown. The royalist need for a coherent assembly of major naval forces was acute. The Cinque leaders complained to the Marshal of the burdens and loss of privileges suffered under John; the regent was not about to disappoint them at this critical juncture and granted them a return to their lucrative franchises as well as healthy compensation from the spoils of the coming battle, including the replacement of lost ships. Thus boosted, the Cinque representatives returned to their ships at Sandwich and prepared for combat in high spirits; the Marshal's biographer depicts the merry sailors as energetically attending to their ships, as they 'made ready their ropes, made seaworthy every one of their bowlines, guide ropes and guys, their sturdy anchors and strong cables, so that they would be able to cast anchor off the ports, should it prove necessary for them to fight and crush the arrogance of the French' and pledging to die or be taken captive before avoiding their duty, for 'if the French fleet out there were able to put to shore, then the game would have disastrous results and England would be lost'.[586]

The next day the Marshal was at Sandwich for the muster with Peter des Roches, Hubert de Burgh, who arrived from Dover in a large ship, and his other commanders. De Burgh was given command of the English fleet. The Marshal's appeals to set out with the fleet and to get stuck into the French were cried down amidst protests that he was simply too valuable to risk losing; as his biographer proudly warns, if he were 'killed there or taken prisoner, who would then defend the realm?' While obviously emphasising the central importance of his patron, this was nevertheless a real concern. Thursday 24 August was a beautiful clear day; the French fleet set sail for the mouth of the Thames with a fair and pleasant wind. The English went out to meet them. The fleets were sailing into the deciding battle of the invasion and the occupation of England. It was the day of reckoning.

The size of the English fleet is not known for certain. The biographer says that the Marshal himself had arranged for 22 ships, the best of their kind, to be fully armed and manned. The Anonymous and the Annalist of Waverley say that there were eighteen big ships present; perhaps this means that four were kept in reserve at port. It seems that these were matched by the same number of other lesser vessels. Matthew Paris, who at this stage in his writing, breaks away from merely repeating Wendover's chronicle, states that de Burgh was 'given to his command about sixteen ships well fitted out, plus small support boats numbering twenty'. Wendover corroborates this, declaring that the English had 'only a few ships, not exceeding forty in number of galleys and ships'. The biggest ship was a cog; standing high out of the water, it provided solid fighting platforms with larger 'castles' than smaller vessels for the knights and soldiers on board. No ship was thought to exceed 80 tons.[587] The cog was the Marshal's ship, crewed and garrisoned by his men. The fighting galleys in both navies were reinforced with iron prows by which they could ram enemy ships; they could take on much larger vessel, as Richard I proved in the Mediterranean on the Third Crusade, when his galleys successfully rammed a Muslim ship 'of enormous size'.[588] De Burgh's captains included some experienced men: Philip d'Albini, who directed military operations in the Channel in the war; Richard Fitzjohn, son of John and nephew to

the Earl of Warenne who had fitted out his nephew's ships with care; and two of
Hubert's trusted knights from Dover, Henry de Trubleville and Richard Suard.

We have good details of the French fleet thanks to the Anonymous of Béthune.
He and Wendover agree on a figure of about 80 ships; not, as the Marshal's biographer claims for dramatic impact, 300. The Anonymous says that these 'were
both big and small': ten large ones were ready for battle; four were full of knights
and six with sergeants; and the others were filled with supplies. The flag ship was
'the great ship of Bayone', which was so laden with treasure, horses for Louis
and a trebuchet it sat low and heavy in the water, with the waves almost washing
over it, and restricted in its manoeuvrability by its great weight. On board were
the admiral of the fleet, Eustace, Robert de Courtenay, Ralph de la Tournelle,
Neville de Canle and 36 other knights, including William des Barres the younger,
a strong knight who took his name from his father, a renowned figure of chivalry
and sword-hand of Philip Augustus. Michael de Harnes, William the castellan
of St Omer and the mayor of Boulogne commanded the other three ships with
knights. The six ships with sergeants were also battle-worthy. With the largest ships carrying some 40 knights, and four ships in all with knights on board,
the Anonymous can be seen to offering further credence to both his figure of
some 100 knights for the whole army, and the Melrose chronicler's figure of 125
knights. The English chronicles make much of being outnumbered in ships, but
the figures actually reveal a rough balance of fighting vessels, all well-equipped
and fitted for war; the extra 40 ships of the French would for the most part have
been predominantly supply ships, bringing much needed provisions, equipment,
food and wine to Louis. Heavily laden and with a fixed destination plotted, the
French lacked the flexibility and manoeuvrability of the English. However, they
had a certain strength derived from their numbers and the advantage of a strong
wind behind them. Both sides were under experienced and successful leaders;
while Eustace's reputation as an outstanding seaman was clear, Hubert de Burgh
had as a chief adviser Philip d'Albini, who, although a less colourful character
than his rival, had proven himself an equal match to the demonised pirate. On
paper, the French had the advantage of numerical superiority and hence the
upper hand, but in 1213 Wendover noted that the English 'had a superior navy
than the French king'.[589] The English had two other less tangible advantages, not
frequently remarked upon. One was their greater experience of naval warfare,
especially in the Channel; remember the French only gained the seaboard of
Normandy in 1204. Secondly, and very potently, they had the motivation that
comes from defending their homeland. In his battle speech, the Marshal warned
his men that the French now 'return to England to claim the land as theirs', echoing his battle oration at Lincoln. For the battle that was about to ensue was one
in which the enemies were divided by nation. There were no anti-Henrician
English barons commanding the French force, muddying the waters of identity
and causes. This was an English fleet against a French one.

English strategy was simple: the objective was to prevent the French from land-ing. If this sizeable force made it to London, the war could continue indefinitely. As it was, the royalists were already hesitant to besiege the capital; these significant reinforcements from France would make London unassailable and once again would have caused shifting in political movements and further realignments. This maritime strategy was an established one. During the invasion threat of 1213, John was 'determined to engage his enemies in battle at sea, to drown them before they set foot on land'. It is worth recalling Wendover's comments here on England's superior navy: in 1213 it was this in which John 'placed his chief defence'.[590] The English were doing so again. The chroniclers give the impression that William Marshal was sending out the fleet for a decisive battle; but, as with the Spanish Armada in 1588, the overriding intention was to prevent foreign troops disem-barking on English soil. The assertion by one historian that 'no medieval admiral ever sailed with the explicit intention of seeking out an enemy fleet and destroy-ing it' has to be questioned, though.[591] The most effective way to keep the enemy from landing was, as was planned in 1213, simply to destroy the French fleet and drown their army at sea.

The English went out to meet them on an oblique course from the north-east, against the wind and tide. Emboldened by the victory at Lincoln, Wendover says they dared to take on the larger force. Hubert de Burgh's ship was leading the small fleet, probably in column behind. Not far off the coast off Sandwich, he made a feint against the French, so that they thought he was approaching to engage with them head-on. The French, emboldened on their part by their recent victory over the English in the Channel, and confident in their numbers against the few vessels sent against them, hastened to meet the challenge, furling their sails and eager either to gain spoils that would pay for their expenses or to send the English to 'the bottom fishing for flounder'.[592] It is sometimes thought that naval battles were merely replications of a cavalry charge,[593] but this was not the case at Sandwich. De Burgh veered away to starboard at the last moment, as he had intended. The French then cried out 'La hart, la hart!', a call given in deer-hunting when the prey is spotted.' The term can also mean 'noose', which offers a darker, more serious interpretation of the call.[594]

William the Breton offers a unique perspective when he describes how Robert de Courtenay ordered the French flagship, Eustace's great ship of Bayonne, to make for the smaller English vessels passing by, 'thinking it would be easy to cap-ture them'.[595] However, William says that no other French ship followed him, leaving him isolated away from the main fleet. This may have been the case, but there must be some doubt over this. Yes, the flagship was the biggest in the French fleet, and the prospect of profiting from an easy catch was always tempting; but the French priority of supplying Louis was paramount, and Eustace's vessel, laden with treasure, trebuchet, horses and knights, was the most important of all. The very fact that the English's overwhelming aim was to prevent the French fleet from reaching London, meant, in turn, that reaching London was the central aim of the French. It is hard to imagine Eustace the Monk being diverted from this task. If de Courtenay, an experienced commander, had ordered the diversion it would have been an uncharacteristic display of over-confidence and of diversion from the task with which he was charged. It is only the author of *History of William Marshal* that supports William the Breton's version. While the biographer was always eager to demonstrate the arrogant presumptuousness of the French, William was no doubt trying to spare the blushes of a noble so closely related to the French royal family, demonstrating his bravery but blaming others for not supporting him and insinuating that if they had, his decision would not have been a mistake. William's account, brief as it is, also reveals his lack of detailed knowledge of the battle, as he says Robert Fitzwalter was captured during the battle; Fitzwalter was captured at Lincoln and his release was not granted until 8 October later that year. So while it is possible that de Courtenay did launch into an attack, it is far more probable that he held his course.

What is certain is that the flagship was soon fighting for its survival. The English plan involved the same tactics as the naval encounter on 29 May: to get windward of the enemy. Thus de Burgh's feint was to mislead the French and get behind them. One of the dangers in this was that if the attempt failed, the English ships could be run down.[596] But the last moment manoeuvring of de Burgh's ships worked and the English side-stepped the French. The somewhat neglected *Romance of Eustace the Monk* at this juncture confirms the tactical plan of the English: 'more than twenty ships passed in front of him [Eustace], and they attacked his fleet fiercely.' Once past, they turned about and, with a strong wind in their sails, attacked vigorously from the rear. Rather than de Courtenay making contact with the English column and engaging with Richard Fitzjohn's ship, as has been suggested by one authority, the *History of William Marshal* is probably right to say it was Fitzjohn's ship, or at least an English one, that initiated the encounter.[597] This was decapitation strategy: take the head off the enemy and its torso will collapse. We have seen how close such a strategy came to working at Bouvines, when the allies formed a cavalry unit with the sole intention of targeting Philip Augustus. In the event, infantry dragged Philip from his horse and would have killed him but for the self-sacrifice of his bodyguard.

While Fitzjohn's small ship made little impact by itself on Eustace's large vessel, the other ships at the back of the French convoy put up a strong resistance against their attackers, inflicting heavy casualties on the English. Wendover describes a battle in which Philip d'Albini takes centre stage: Philip 'with his crossbowmen and archers directing their missiles into the French soon caused many fatalities among them'. The iron-tipped English galleys rammed into the French ships, sinking many instantly. As the ships came alongside each other, a 'severe' battle ensued in which the French were mown down by arrows and javelins. The English held a greater advantage in that their ships were lighter – they were not, unlike the French, weighed down with supplies – and thus stood higher in the water; this made it easier to shoot down on the French. The English made great use of the wind to launch large pots of quicklime at the enemy. On breaking, the pots dispersed burning clouds which were carried away from the English and to the French, 'which blinded them totally', says the Anonymous. All four main sources of the battle testify to the efficacy of this tactic.

This made boarding the French ships easier. Now swords and spears were put to work. Wendover even says that the English bored holes in the bottom of the French ships to sink them. The focal point of the battle was Eustace's flagship. Fitzjohn was soon supported by three other ships, including the cog; Eustace was thus surrounded, with the cog looming high over his deck. His men returned the missile barrage and let loose their arrows at the English, putting up a fierce resistance and preventing the English from boarding them. The author of the *Romance* says they he and his men 'slaughtered a great many Englishmen and defended themselves courageously'. The enemy attacked him from all sides, using great axes and grappling hooks against the side of the ship. But when the quicklime pots hit the deck, 'the powder rose in great clouds, and it was this which caused the most damage. After that, they could no longer defend themselves, for their eyes were full of powder.'

As the English boarded, the fighting renewed into a brutal combat that would have been repeated on other ships in the battle. The *Romance* describes the 'brave and courageous' pirate leader in the thick of it as he 'knocked down a good number of them with an oar he was holding'. Elsewhere, 'some had their arms broken, some had heir heads smashed. This one was killed and that one was laid out; one was knocked down and another wounded, whilst a third had his collarbone shattered.' This no-holds-barred bludgeoning account is more realistic than that of the biographer of William Marshal, who similarly delights in providing combat detail. This can read somewhat fancifully, falling into the formulaic tradition of depicting battles as duels between leading figures. Here, there is a strong whiff of fantasy in the swashbuckling escapades. Reginald Payn of Guernsey, who 'had nothing of the coward in him, jumped from the cog onto the French flagship'. Payn's was a long leap, but his fall was broken by William des Barres; as Payn fell, he also brought down Robert de Courtenay with a well-placed blow. Hardly had he done this when Ralph de Tournelle was on him; Payn struck him with such force he spun around three times. After a tremendous fight de Tournelle was taken. And as if all this was not enough, our medieval Errol Flynn was then set upon by the rabid Theobald (possibly Count Theobald of Blois), the outcome of which the writer does not inform us about, but we can safely assume that had he done so, the remarkable Reginald would have emerged victorious.

The reality was a good deal more deadly. Sea battles were bloodier affairs than land ones; there was less scope for taking prisoners and this proved to be the case here. The flagship and other French vessels eventually succumbed to the sustained aggression and ferocity of the English onslaught; the loss of their principal ship dealt a mortal blow to the French. As an English victory became imminent, French soldiers and sailors threw themselves overboard to take their chances with the sea, rather than the certainties of capture; the Anonymous reports that 'quite a number of the smaller ships were taken, and much slaughter was carried out on those taken within them.' As the rest of the French fleet concentrated fully on fleeing rather than fighting, the English gave vigorous pursuit. The biographer of William Marshal reports that the battle became a bloody rout; when the English 'caught up with a ship, I can tell you that they lost no time at all in killing those they found on board and throwing them into the sea as food for the fish'. Only the knights were spared. He tells of how the sea was turned scarlet with blood and estimates that at least 4000 men were slain in this manner, not counting those who jumped into the sea and were drowned, who 'sunk like lead in the stormy waters' says Ralph of Coggeshall.[598]

On Eustace's flagship, the first English on board were also at French throats: they would have gladly killed 32 of their knights if the English knights had not prevented them. Such a slaughter would have cost the protectors a fortune in lost ransoms. The *Romance* says the French were treated 'very cruelly'. The high-ranking prisoners, most of whom who were on Eustace's ships, provided a rich haul indeed, including Robert de Courtenay, William des Barres, Ralph de Tournelle and Neville d'Arras. But Eustace was not among this haul. While the rest of the French fleet made their escape as best they could, Eustace abandoned the fighting on deck to hide in the hold of his ship. A long search for him was started and, at last, the perennial thorn in the royalist side Eustace the Monk was taken captive. But Eustace did not receive the same consideration as the chivalry of France. It was immediately clear that he was in mortal danger from his captors. He pleaded for his life and liberty, offering 10,000 marks to be spared and promising to serve faithfully the King of England in the future. But Eustace did not have a future: he was not to be spared on any account. Wendover has Richard Fitzjohn berating him: 'Never again in this world, wicked traitor, shall you deceive anyone with your false promises.' As he spoke these words he drew his sword and cut off Eustace's head.

However, the *History of William Marshal* offers an alternative version of Eustace's death. This has Stephen of Wincelsea playing the main part. This Stephen may well be the same as the Stephen Crave in the Anonymous' briefer account of this episode; the Anonymous says that he 'had been with him a long time', probably a reference to when Eustace had served John. He harangued Eustace with a litany of the misdeeds on land and sea that he had inflicted upon him (even though the Marshal's biographer says this was not true and so was undeserved) and then offered him a grim choice: be beheaded on the trebuchet or over the side of the ship. 'Thereupon,' says the biographer, 'they cut off his head.' Eustace's head was then stuck on a spear and later paraded through Canterbury and across the land to prove that this black legend was truly dead. The last line of the *Romance of Eustace the Monk* reads: 'No one who is always intent on evil can live for a long time.'

The sources attest to the wealth of spoils seized in the victory, which the *History of William Marshal* describes as 'a total rout': gold, silver, money, horses, provisions, plate, silk cloths, meats, wines, wheat, arms and even a trebuchet, the super weapon of the day. Hubert de Burgh had made himself even wealthier with the capture of two ships. The English fleet returned to shore to the great acclamation of crowds and religious thanksgiving for the nation being spared. The regent oversaw a fair division of the spoils so that all were well contented. 'What a fine shareout it was!' beams the Marshal's biographer: so great was the booty that the English sailors 'were able to share out the coin in bowlfuls'. With the rest of the money, he ordered the foundation of a hospital dedicated to St Bartholomew, as the day of victory was the saint's feast day. The following day the ports were awash with sailors finely attired in rich cloths and silks, boasting to each other as to who wore the most costly garments.

While the sailors paraded through the coastal towns, the valuable prisoners were secured in strong prisons. Later they were transferred to Hubert de Burgh's custody at Dover. The exact number is not known. In addition to the four Frenchmen named above, there were, at least, the other knights from the contingent of 32 on board Eustace's great ship of Bayonne. The Waverley Annalist is vague but telling in the importance of the rank of the prisoners when saying that 'ten magnates with many nobles of France were captured.'[599] There would have been more from the other ships, but there is not even an approximate number of how many of these were taken or sunk. It is clear that many escaped back to Calais as the *History of William Marshal* indicates; this was to be expected with tactics of fighting from behind the French.[600] There was also the sheer impracticality of numbers, for if the English fleet was indeed half the size of the French one, then there simply would not have been the capacity to seize all of the enemy's vessels. The Anonymous believes that it was only the flagship that was taken and that the others all escaped but this must be incorrect; it may be that he means that this was so of the ten principal ships. This does not tally with Hubert de Burgh's wins and the ships reported sunk and captured in the other sources. The Waverley Annalist reports that only fifteen ships slipped away. On 1 September William Marshal issued a writ that summoned to the Thames the Cinque ports 'with your whole navy as well as that which was recently won', indicating a good number.[601]

It was a great victory, and one which owed much to the strength of the English navy. Wendover believes the English won the battle because they 'they were skilled in naval warfare' while the French 'were not used' to it; as Philip Augustus had admitted at Damme in 1213, the French 'do not know the ways of the sea'.[602] The Battle of Sandwich has often been seen as the origins of England's great maritime reputation and formidable naval achievements,[603] but by 1217 the English navy was already an experienced and effective one.

While it is hard to quantify the scale of the victory in exact terms, it is not hard to appreciate its magnitude in military and political ones. The effects were dramatic and instantaneous. The loss to Louis in terms of men and supplies was irreparable. This was the final push of his campaign. All his resources had been invested in the fleet. Had his substantial reinforcements and supplies reached him in England, the impact on the war would have been significant; that they did not arrive was even more significant again. Financially, militarily and politically, Louis had used up all his military resources. He was ready to think about suing for peace.

Peace

Now was the time for the royalists to take the war decisively to Louis. In the months after Lincoln they had been seemingly moribund and reluctant to take resolute action against Louis in London. With the crushing victory at Sandwich, that hesitancy was now gone and they planned to capitalise on their success by a full investiture of London. Guala and the young King were already outside of London, but now William Marshal was prepared to consider joining all his forces to invest the capital fully. The writ he issued on 1 September for the southern fleet to gather on the Thames was part of his plan to blockade tightly Louis and his forces in London. He could do so now as the threat of the long-expected relief force from France had been conclusively eliminated. There was no more help coming to Louis now: with many barons in captivity after Lincoln, and no French reinforcements either, royalist forces could encircle London in security and free from outside attack. This was the endgame.[604]

News of the disaster at Sandwich reached Louis in the capital two days later on the evening of Saturday 26 August. His reaction was to be expected: 'Louis was rightly very angry,' says the Anonymous; he was 'very dejected and grieved', reports the Marshal's biographer. Wendover's estimation of the effect on him rightly gauges the scale of the defeat: 'it caused him much more pain than the misfortune at Lincoln'. The Dunstable Annalist says that Louis was 'destitute of present help and despairing of the future'. As Ralph Coggeshall comments: 'Louis, when he heard this, did not know where to turn … and so, compelled by necessity, he asked for peace.' The implications of the defeat were thus immediately apparent to him: his campaign in England was over.

On 28 August he sent his trusted cousin Robert, Count of Dreux, to the Marshal at Rochester under a safe-conduct to open peace negotiations. When Robert reached Rochester, he was exchanged with Robert de Courtenay, who thereby finally made it to London, but alone and without his army. No doubt the Henricians wanted Louis to be fully appraised of the scale of his defeat. As at Lincoln, the royalists held another council in the wake of victory, this time to discuss how to respond to Louis' overtures. Some royalists, especially those who had missed the recent battle, urged a full investiture of London; sensing that Louis' campaign was mortally wounded, they perhaps wished to gain their share of spoils that they had missed at Sandwich. They did not wish for a negotiated settlement. Others, however, counselled that now was the time for the French finally to be 'thrown out of the land', says the Marshal's biographer, and urged parleying to bring this about. The regent opted for talks, but very much kept the military option open by pressuring Louis with a full blockade of London of his combined forces complete with a huge naval presence on the Thames. Wendover says that the royalist force besieging London was a huge one; Louis was hemmed in by land and water, 'thus cutting off all supplies of provisions from the garrison'. William Marshal was making clear to Louis the overwhelming strength of the victors' bargaining position. If Louis did not come to terms, he would be starved out of London.

Louis was huddled in deep discussions with his own council. After his consultations with Robert de Courtenay and his other advisers, he decided to meet with William Marshal in face-to-face talks. These occurred just outside London on Tuesday 5 September with Louis and de Courtenay on the one side, and William Marshal and Hubert de Burgh on the other. Both sides assured the other that they would strive hard to make an honourable peace. The regent and the justiciar returned to Windsor and the Frenchmen to London. Louis waited there anxiously, expecting to hear proposals from William Marshal on how to move the peace process forward. But no word came from the regent. Louis suspected that the negotiations were being strung out to weaken his position further – and he could only grow weaker with every passing day. On Saturday 9 September he held another council privately in his chambers. Painfully aware of his deteriorating military position in the capital, and greatly troubled by the erosion of support within London, the decision they came to was a dramatic one: to make one great sortie out of the city with all their men and take on the enemy in one last great battle. This neglected episode was indeed a desperate measure, but perhaps not as desperate as it may sound. Such sorties could be remarkably effective; I would suggest that Louis had very much at the forefront of his mind the spectacular success of Simon de Montfort exactly four years earlier almost to the day. At Muret in 1213, de Montfort and his Albigensian crusaders found themselves besieged and in similarly desperate straits. Although greatly outnumbered, they sallied from the town and took on their besiegers to win a spectacular victory that left the enemy King dead and the crusaders' fortunes completely reversed. Louis' insecurity in London prompted him to act; Ralph of Coggeshall describes his predicament: he 'did not know which way to turn, for he had no safe place to rest in.'[605] If the royalists were to suffer substantial losses, with prominent leaders either killed of taken prisoner, then the whole situation would be turned radically on its head. Louis still had a substantial, if somewhat reduced, force with him in London. He had in his service many of Europe's best knights and, in London, a large population from which to draw on for auxiliary infantry. Louis and his captains steeled themselves for the great attack and made ready their men for battle.

It did not come. Later that night, at the very last moment, a letter arrived from William Marshal. He asked for a truce and for negotiations to be resumed. To these Louis acquiesced. Had this communication not arrived, the ensuing battle would have played a huge part in our story. But the preparation made for battle that day on Saturday 9 September was the last military activity of the war. The invasion had ended.

With the cessation of hostilities, our history of the war must draw to its end. The peace talks and their conclusion can be dealt with swiftly. The Marshal's letter on 9 September had asked for Hugh de Malaunay to come and talk with the regent and his council.[606] He returned with news on Monday that negotiations were set for Tuesday 12 September; the truce, guaranteed by the queen, William Marshal, the Earls of Warenne, Arundel and Salisbury and other barons, was extended to the Thursday. De Maulanay also informed Louis what was on the table in the talks from the royalists. Wendover writes that Louis was informed of the peace terms 'to which if he agreed, would swear to secure for him and his men a safe departure from England; if not, they would injure him and bring him to ruin in every way'. Louis' relief at these terms was at the French being allowed to leave England, as 'it seemed useless for them to remain there any longer.' Louis gathered about him not only his whole council but also the English barons and the leading citizens of London; they agreed to the preliminary terms. The *History of William Marshal* claims that the French excluded the English from their deliberations of this plenary council, but this is unlikely.

The next step was to formalise the peace process. On 12 September, Louis met with the regent, the king, the king's mother and the legate Guala, resplendent in his scarlet robes. The meeting place was an island in the Thames at Kingston. Louis and his party were on one bank of the river, and the royalists on the other; they were rowed out to the island. And here they made formal peace.[607] The terms were very similar to those nearly agreed upon in mid-June but for Louis' refusal to accept the exclusion of Simon Langton and the three other clerics from the peace. Louis was no longer in any position to argue their cause and so they remained excluded; Guala told them to leave the country and obtain absolution from Pope Honorius. Otherwise it was much the same. The rebel and royalist protagonists, including London and the towns, were to have their rights and lands as on the eve of war. Both sides were to release prisoners captured since Louis' arrival in May 1216; any ransoms already paid could be kept, while those that had not were not to be enforced. This helped rebels such as Robert

Fitzwalter and Gilbert de Gant, but not others such as Nicholas de Stuteville who had started payments on his ransom before the end of the war and was thus presumably released. (De Stuteville actually died between the Battle of Lincoln and September, possibly from wounds received in the battle.)[608] The terms excluded those caught as rebels, that is, those taken before Louis' arrival; the agreement applied specifically to Louis' men during his campaign. The English prisoners had to swear oaths of obedience to the king. Other terms were that: all land and property taken in the war were to be restored; King Alexander and Llewelyn could make their peace on similar terms; Louis was to write to Eustace the Monk's family and tell them to restore the Channel Islands they had taken to Henry or lose the lands they held of Louis; Louis was to absolve all those in England from their oaths to him, thus releasing them from their obligations; and the English rebels and French had to swear never again to join forces against the King and his heirs or to act against them. Louis even made a nebulous promise to exert influence on his father to return the Angevin lands to Henry taken from John. And nebulous it proved to be.

These were good terms for the defeated party, especially for the French. That the former rebels the young Marshal and the Earls of Arundel, Surrey and Salisbury formed a major part of the royalist negotiating party probably helped, as did the seeming absence in the peace talks of the more hard line Earls of Chester and Derby. Although it was to be expected that the leading rebels did not achieve the gains they had fought for (Fitzwalter, for instance, did not take ownership of Hereford Castle and the Earl of Winchester did not gain Mountsorrel), their fate was very lenient and not what would have been handed out by King John. The treatment of Louis was particularly generous. No only was he spared any reparation payments, but all debts to him were to be paid. On top of this, agreed but not written down in the final treaty, Louis was to receive an extremely generous financial settlement to encourage his departure from England: 10,000 marks (about £7000). This amounted to ten times the annual tribute John handed over to the pope and almost a quarter of the crown's annual income. William Marshal even guaranteed the money against his lands in Normandy. 4000 marks were given to Louis immediately and most of the money was stumped up within the year. A levy on knights' fees – the biographer of the Marshal records how the royalists were prepared to contribute to the peace fund[609] – helped to raise most of this sum, in effect the heftiest of insurance premiums against further French involvement in England.

The question of absolution for sins against the Church caused more of a problem. This could not be formally and ceremoniously granted to Louis and his followers on the day of the peace because the clergy present did not have their appropriate garb with them, and also because Louis contested the humiliating manner of penitence he was required to undertake: to proceed in the ceremony barefoot and shirtless, wearing only woollen undergarments as befits a true penitent. Guala, who had insisted on this, relented to the request that Louis be allowed to wear a tunic. The following day, Wednesday 13 September, the bishops and Louis duly attired, the French Prince went through the mortifying experience of public penance. By this act he and his followers were accepted back into the Church. 'There,' says Ralph Coggeshall, 'Louis in the presence of all was absolved from excommunication and renounced the kingdom of England.'[610]

Louis returned to London to prepare for his departure from England. Here he reflected on his great invasion, which a year earlier had achieved so much and which had the potential to achieve so much more. What had gone wrong to bring him to this? In reality, not a huge amount. The French campaign was a long one – fifteen months from beginning to end – and there were bound to be setbacks. Louis' great disadvantage was the royal network of castles against him, especially Dover and Lincoln. Even so, he and his followers had done extremely well in either taking or neutralising so many of these. Dover Castle was the biggest problem; Louis' inability to take this despite massive effort not only kept him bogged down in the south-east instead of expanding further into the west but also prevented him from a full consolidation of his gains in the south-east of England. He had little choice other than to try and take it as he relied on a safe highway across the Channel to bring in reinforcements and supplies from France. His failure here was a serious one but not, apart possibly from his temporary abandonment of the siege to reduce lesser castles first, a strategic error. Even the temporary abandonment had some merit: recognising how hard a nut Dover was to crack, trying to isolate it and leaving it without hope of relief might have eventually worked. It had come perilously close to falling. As Robert Bartlett has rightly noted, with over 200 castles involved in the conflict, 'the civil war was predominantly a castle war.'[611] We have only to follow troop movements, especially in the period leading up to Lincoln, to establish this. Castles were the dominant feature of all medieval warfare.

The loss of Lincoln was a very major blow, and one that should not have happened from the rebel side. There were possibly two major mistakes here from Louis' forces. One was the incomplete investiture of the castle that allowed royalists to enter it; it may have been the case that the rebel army was not strong enough to permit this and that its leaders felt that being outside of the city walls left them too vulnerable to enemy attack. The other was the lost opportunity to take advantage of their greater numbers against the royalists in the open; the Anglo-French forces were instead surprised in the city where the confines of Lincoln meant that this numerical superiority could not be deployed to the same effect. With Lincoln back in royalist hands, Louis was largely restricted once again to the south-east and was back at the position where he had started the campaign. However, his fleet from Calais in August promised to revitalise his war effort, replace the manpower lost at Lincoln and compensate with supplies the logistical shortfall that came with the subsequent loss of lands; it threatened the royalists with a prolonged and indefinite conflict in which perhaps neither side could gain the upper hand. Louis had revealed his potential to do this on his return from France in the spring, when he rapidly made good the losses in the south during his absence. The fleet's resounding defeat denied Louis both the resources he needed to continue the war and the time to rebuild them: with the Channel blocked and the royalist forces free to converge on London, Louis simply could not sit and wait for yet more reinforcements (even if they could be recruited) as he had done after Lincoln. Thus on 9 September he was considering one last sortie from the capital.

One leading authority on Angevin England believes that Louis' greatest military mistake occurred just before the Battle of Lincoln. After his successes on his return to England following Easter in 1217, Louis, when at Winchester, 'made a decision that was to cost him the war. He divided his army into two. Whilst one force was sent to relieve the Mountsorrel Castle, besieged by the Earls of Chester and Derby, Louis himself set out to complete his year-long assault on the royalist stronghold at Dover.'[612] This is the legendary military blunder of splitting one's forces and a good case can be made for it being so here. Yet was this really such a flawed strategy? It necessitated that the royalists, too, divided their own forces. More importantly, it reflected Louis' understanding of the political reality; if his English followers (in this case the powerful Earl of Winchester) did not feel supported in their battles by him, then it was but a short step for them to make their peace with the crown and change sides.

The political angle was central to all involved in the war, especially locally and in the regional interests of the barons. Everywhere barons were motivated by what they could gain from the conflict, and many were ready to lend their sword to whichever prince was more likely to fulfil their personal objectives. Thus Robert Fitzwalter had his eyes on Hereford Castle; William Mowbray wanted York; Gilbert de Gant coveted the title of Earl of Lincoln; and Alexander II wanted great swathes of the north. Louis conceded all these while trying to balance the often contesting demands of his French followers. It was a difficult path to tread and, despite the chroniclers' criticisms of Louis' preference to his fellow Frenchmen, Louis negotiated it quite successfully. The majority of barons who were with him at the beginning of the invasion were with him at the end. As David Carpenter has pointed out in his important study of the minority of Henry III in the aftermath of the war, the most bitter resentments on both sides were directed not so much towards former enemies but to former allies, those who had broken their oaths.[613]

The political situation followed the military one; success in the war generated political profits. We see this most clearly after the defeat at Lincoln when within three months 150 of Louis' followers transferred their allegiance to the crown. It could be argued strongly that John's death was a notable exception where a political event was dominant, leading to a flow back to the royalist side.

However, John's death removed not just an unloved and mistrusted ruler, but also an incompetent military leader. The biographer of William Marshal reports that King Philip of France, on hearing of John's death, believed that Louis could no longer win, as now the 'land will be well defended'.[614] Whether true or not, the sentiment is clear: the death of John was a serious blow to Louis' chances. The ebb and flow of the war is not marked by proclamations, issues of Magna Carta and excommunications, but by the bloody force of military events. Military momentum was rewarded by political momentum. Ultimately Louis lost because defeats at the engagements of Lincoln and Sandwich left him too weak to wage war. Louis failed to conquer England simply because his armies lost in battle.

The monastic chroniclers wished to believe, of course, that victory was God-given. The Barnwell annalist declared: 'It was truly a miracle that the heir of the King of France, having advanced so far into the heart of the country with a great army and having succeeded in occupying so much of it, helped by the barons, and had taken it so quickly, was forced to abandon this kingdom without hope of recovering it. It is because the hand of God was not with him.'[615] Louis felt more sorely the fact that the hand of his powerful father was not with him.

There was one other force that Louis had to contend with, and over which he had little control: national feeling. Louis could never escape from the fact that he was a foreign Prince with foreign troops laying claim to the throne of England through the force of a foreign invasion. This is a contentious point to make, not least because it is an intangible one. Most historians play down this aspect and prefer to see the royalist cause motivated more by fighting for the Church.[616] It is true, as Tyerman points out, that Louis' forces are commonly characterised as the enemies of God and the Church; this was great propaganda, but so of course was appealing to national sentiment. He still recognises that 'xenophobia and traditionalism both contributed to support for Henry' but considers it comparatively unimportant.[617] However, throughout the chronicles and poems the French are simply and constantly referred to as the French, or as *transmarine*, foreigners from across the sea. Wendover calls them 'scum' and the biographer of William Marshal never misses an opportunity to mock and humiliate the foreign enemy and its ambitions in England; both exhort defence of the homeland and fighting *pro patria*. A poem written just after Lincoln calls up 'the strength of England' and when the other sources use the term 'England' the modern reader can readily identify with it.[618] Much of the hatred for John rested, as the Barnwell chronicler noted, on the king's perverse preference for foreigners over the English.[619] The sense of the English fighting for their country against a foreign invader comes through the contemporary accounts with robustness and clarity.

Louis and his English allies had done surprisingly well. Up to May 1217 there is no telling indication that they would have to come to terms imposed upon them. But these very terms, by their very leniency, reveal what a force Louis had been. This is seen most of all in the money granted Louis. Huge as the sum was, it was still cheaper than the cost of continuing a war against a formidable foe who was the focus of the hopes of the opposition; who, even at the end, had the ability to absorb the painful and slow recovering finances of the crown in conflict at the expense of all else. William Marshal and his council also wanted Louis gone for another, overlooked, reason and were willing to pay the price to prevent this nightmare from becoming a reality. The longer that Louis was is in the country, and the longer he was in danger, the greater was the threat that his powerful and all-conquering father would intervene to help him, leading behind him the great wealth and might of France. The English, already weakened by war, did not want to provoke an even more fearful invasion.

Louis had one more main task to complete before he quit England. On Wednesday 20 September he met with his former enemies at Lambeth in a large gathering.[620] Here both sides reaffirmed the peace of Kingston which was now solemnly ratified as the treaty of Lambeth. It formally marked the end of the war and the beginning of peace. Louis and the greater part of his men left London and headed to the coast via Canterbury. He was escorted all the way by William Marshal, Guala and the leading barons of the country.[621] On 28 September he was at Dover, a painful reminder of what might have been. He set sail for France, never to return, leaving behind him a kingdom he had half won but finally lost. Louis' dream of emulating William the Conqueror's spectacular success of 150 years earlier was over. Since 1066, no one had come closer than Louis and his forgotten campaign of 1216. England was never to suffer such a powerful foreign invasion again.

King John and the Historians: Turning in Circles

When British Prime Minister David Cameron appeared on American TV's *The Late Show with David Letterman* in September 2012, the host questioned him on Magna Carta. To the question '... and the literal translation is what?', the prime minister responded with the quip 'Now you're testing me', and seemed unable to offer the correct answer: 'Great Charter' (or, when first issued, 'Big Charter'). Whether the response was contrived or not is open to debate, but with the massive attention given to the celebrations of the 800th anniversary of Magna Carta in 1215, including large-scale Parliamentary ones, no future prime minister will be able to feign ignorance of the meaning of Magna Carta.

It is no surprise that an American should question a British premier on this fundamental assertion of liberties that first appeared in England in 1215 during the reign of King John, for this foundation of the English constitution has actually had more resonance and significance across the Atlantic than in the country that gave birth to it. When one of the four surviving original copies of Magna Carta visited the States in 1983, as part of the 'Celebration of Freedom' festival, it attracted large crowds. The longest and most radical clause in the first issue exerted severe restrictions on the power of the king, appointing a twenty-five-man committee of the great and the good, acting for 'the community of the realm', to ensure that King John was no longer free to exercise arbitrary power. To Republicans fighting in the American War of Independence in the late eighteenth century, and to their proud descendants celebrating their victory, this was no minor justification of their cause; as the historian V.H. Galbraith said of the clause, this was 'the most fantastic surrender of any English king to his subjects'.

English colonists establishing a new society in seventeenth-century America deemed Magna Carta to be fundamental law, and thus it took precedence over both Crown and Parliament. The General Assembly of Maryland in 1639 declared: 'The inhabitants of this Province shall have all their rights and liberties according to the Great Charter of England.' Before and during the American War of Independence, Magna Carta provided the colonists with an intellectual and constitutional rallying cry against what many deemed to be the tyranny of kings. They followed the line from the thirteenth century to 'No taxation without representation' in the late eighteenth. The seal of the state of Massachusetts, designed by Paul Revere in 1775, depicts a militiaman with a sword in one hand and a copy of Magna Carta in the other. The 1791 Bill of Rights directly echoes clause 39 of the 1215 Charter in its proclamation that no person shall be 'deprived of life, liberty, or property, without due process of law'.

Magna Carta continued to hold sway in the modern USA. Franklin D. Roosevelt declared in his inaugural address of 1941: 'The democratic aspiration is no mere recent phase in human history ... it was written in Magna Carta.' Magna Carta was even cited in the impeachment of President Richard Nixon in 1974. It has been cited over 100 times in the Supreme Court. In a nation that has a reverenced codified constitution and is lawyered up to the gills, the respect for a medieval document that is a legally binding enshrinement of liberties is understandable. Indeed, it was left to the Americans – American lawyers, in fact – to erect the memorial at Runnymede on the Thames, marking the spot where Magna Carta was agreed. In 1957 the American Bar Association funded and oversaw the construction of the memorial with the inscription: 'To commemorate Magna Carta, symbol of freedom under law.'

So perhaps this is why some historians based in America have been more generous than others in their judgements on King John. A concerted revisionist approach started there in 1949 with the publication of Sidney Painter's *The Reign of King John* and is continued today by a pre-eminent Johannine scholar, Ralph Turner. They have not attempted to overturn entirely the Whiggish version of John as a thoroughly bad egg, but any rehabilitation is brave for a king who murdered his young nephew; lost the Duchy of Normandy and other lands in France; had the wife and son of an opponent starved to death in his prison; humiliatingly submitted his kingdom as a fief to the papacy; hanged a 7-year-old hostage; was an inveterate and blatant adulterer; fled from direct military engagement with his enemies and lost the war with France; taxed the country to the point where it was finally pushed into open rebellion; and died with London and half of his country under French rule and a majority of barons paying homage to Prince Louis of France (or, in effect, King Louis I of England).

The revisionism attempted to challenge a long-established orthodoxy. The Victorians, with some exceptions such as the constitutional episcopal historian William Stubbs, tended to like their kings masculine and chivalrous, beating up the French and giving the pagans in the Holy Land a run for their money. Unsurprisingly, they favoured the butch and vigorous Richard the Lionheart over his pusillanimous and untrustworthy younger brother who cowered in his shadow until brought tentatively out into the sunlight by the revisionists. (See, for example, the striking equestrian statue of Richard erected outside Parliament in the 1850s.) Although there were exceptions, such as J.R. Green who thought John a highly competent king, an anti-John orthodoxy held well into the twentieth century. At its beginning, the redoubtable medievalist Kate Norgate accused John of blunders in statecraft, errors in strategy, cowardice, weakness, sloth and superhuman wickedness (*John Lackland*, 1902). J.H. Ramsey condemned John as a 'selfish cruel tyrant of the worst type' (*The Angevin Empire*, 1903). John's general uselessness was firmly fixed in the popular imagination, with Stellar and Yeatman's *1066 and All That* from 1930, lampooning John as a 'bad Prince', 'an awful king' and a 'wicked' man who 'demonstrated his utter incompetence' during 'his awful reign'. By 1948, on the eve of the revisionists' emergence, even John's physiognomy came in for a battering, John Harvey imaginatively interpreting the king's effigy from his tomb at Worcester Cathedral thus: 'His face has a sly, wolfish cast, with slanting eyes faintly amused at the righteousness of better men' (*The Plantagenets*).

So what brought about the change? It is a well-known maxim that historians write history as a reflection of their times; the result is often a misleading understanding of the past. John's reputation benefitted as a result of three developments that crystallised from the late 1940s onwards. Following the horrors of the Second World War, there was a growing tiredness of and revulsion for war and military history. This was exacerbated by the Korean War, the cynicism behind the Suez Crisis and especially the era of the Vietnam conflict. In medieval studies, this meant a continued neglect of research into the warfare of the period and a concomitant persistence in misunderstanding it, while other areas began to benefit from exhaustive scholarship. Thus the central – arguably most vital – role of the king as *miles* (a warrior knight) to defend his subjects, lost currency: stocks in the bellicose Richard the Lionheart went down while those in the less gung-ho John went up. A second reason for John's partial rehabilitation was the growth of big government: Roosevelt's New Deal, the state control of war economies, and post-war welfare statism towards a new Jerusalem all helped to shift an emphasis towards bureaucratic and administrative history, an area in which John supposedly excelled. And thirdly, John's reputation was re-evaluated because historians are prone to revisionism: the need to question, challenge and reassess orthodoxies to clean and polish up, where necessary, old subjects dusty with consensus. This is, of course, a vital function of historians; but the 'where necessary' bit is often forgotten in pursuit of a new academic fad. As we shall see, with the 800th anniversaries of Magna Carta (1215) and John's death (1216) approaching, it happened again.

Painter's new John was less extreme, one who simply took centralising steps in government and administrative kingship one stage further than his predecessors; his actions were 'a question of degree not of nature'. Furthermore, among many historians a reaction set in against the seemingly hyperbolic verdicts of the excited monastic chroniclers (which we will discuss below) and, in the early 1960s, government records were preferred to the scribblings of disaffected and biased writers isolated in their scriptoriums. James Holt, one of Britain's leading historians of the period, wrote in 1963 that John's 'total achievement was enormous', helping to set a standard 'never again equalled in the medieval period' after the thirteenth century (*King John*, 1963). Revisionism became the new orthodoxy, sanctioned in the A-level history classroom by this examination board's seal of approval in its A-level supporting notes from 2001:

> Royal records showed John actively interested in the machinery of royal government and intervening frequently and intelligently in its workings. Thus emerged the picture of John as a diligent and able king ... Many historians now see John as an able king who had to face appallingly difficult circumstances and enjoyed very bad luck.

This neatly summarises the new position. But it did not stop there. Once the process of rehabilitation began, the cleansing waters flowed into other areas: John's accommodation with the papacy was not a demeaning defeat but a Machiavellian masterstroke; and his loss of Normandy was due not to military incompetence but to the greater financial resources of his French enemy. It even got to the point where John's military record – surely beyond salvaging – was reassessed. In 1973, in his biography of John, Alan Lloyd wrote of his subject:

> He was himself an ingenious administrator and a shrewd strategist. When pugnacious barons dubbed him 'Softsword', they paid unwitting tribute to his preference for negotiation rather than violence. The inference that he was a feeble soldier is a false one.

These positive interpretations are all challenged in *Blood Cries Afar*. Painter was quite open about the fact that he made 'no attempt' to look at John beyond his domestic sphere, something that allowed revisionists to play down events abroad where his most calamitous failings were exposed, and this gave time for the new interpretation of John to become established as the orthodoxy.

Time and fashion came full circle at the end of the century; 1999 marked the 800th anniversary of John's accession to the throne and prompted new research on his reign. Some leading scholars of the period, such as Prof. John Gillingham and Prof. David Carpenter, never wavered in their condemnation of John, but an essential collection of fifteen papers that year on all aspects of his reign left it in no doubt that the new scholarly consensus of John was now realigned with the original orthodoxy (*King John: New Interpretations*, edited by Stephen Church, 1999). We were now in counter-revisionist territory. On Radio Four's *In Our Time* in 2009, Prof. Nicholas Vincent happily (and accurately) spoke of John as 'an absolute rotter through and through; the worst king in English history'. In 2010, Prof. David Crouch judged John's rule as 'ham-fisted' and attacked him for his character flaws: John was 'unpredictable and unreliable', whose 'irrational capacity for abrupt, extravagant and uncontrolled resentment' put him 'outside the courtly world' ('Baronial Paranoia in King John's Reign' in *Magna Carta and the England of King John*, edited by Janet Loengard). In *Blood Cries Afar* I have detailed his disastrous military record.

That should have been that, but it has not proven to be the case. This new scholarship has not yet had time to establish itself beyond academia. A revisionist counter-attack started in 2012 with Graham Seel's *King John: An Underrated King?* It is a full-blown affirmation of the revisionist position. Seel, an experienced history teacher, targets his book primarily at A-level students and perhaps first-year undergraduates. It is a readable and sound recounting of the facts of John's reign and includes useful sources and questions. But, as the title suggests, in its interpretations it attempts to present John in a positive light once more. There is thus a danger that it will be snapped up by grateful history teachers for their courses and will therefore influence the next generation of historians. In 2012 Seel presented the findings of his research in the highly influential magazine *History Today* in an article entitled 'Good King John', which was the cover feature. (This mirrors my 'Bad King John' on a cover of *BBC History Magazine* in 2010.) It should be pointed out that *History Today* was necessarily contributing to the debate; over the last two decades it has aired the counter-revisionist position fully. At a stroke, a wide and interested readership will encounter the serial offender John not as a villain but as a victim.

Seel makes the case for 'a fiercely effective king' and he goes far beyond Turner's gentle shielding of John from total contumely. Seel has carried out some useful research and raised important, valid questions on John's reign, but he has not answered these questions convincingly. Part of the problem may be that Seel's specialism is in seventeenth-century history, and so he misses some of the nuances of the medieval past and misreads the sources, especially when focusing on the exceptions that prove the rule to formulate a new, more flattering one. His work may also display something of the exam board's settled position as laid out above.

How do the revisionists try to rescue John from the counter-revisionists? Like all good historians, Seel starts with the sources. He reiterates the case that John was certainly unlucky in not having an official royal biographer like his Capetian counterparts in Paris. But surely this is not a bad thing for historians: it is the difference between a free press and state propaganda. William the Breton's role as Philip Augustus' biographer has sometimes meant that historians are overly suspicious of his work. There is a form of chronocentric superiority among revisionists in assuming that the commentators of the time were misguided in their judgements: they were there, observed events, spoke to the protagonists – but we know better than them. The contemporary chroniclers, as a rule, did not hold back. Gerald of Wales, ever hostile to the Angevins, said the 'tyrannous' John 'feared not God, nor respected men'; Richard of Devizes depicts a raging madman with sparking eye and so consumed with rage it 'so swelled in his closed breast that it either had to burst or to vomit its venom somewhere'; William of Newburgh calls him 'nature's enemy'; even the prosaic and more equitable Barnwell writer accuses John of being 'less than successful' and 'a pillager of his own people'. Perhaps the most dramatic put-down comes, unsurprisingly, from the polemical Matthew Paris: 'Foul as it is, Hell itself is defiled by the foulness of John.' Medieval obituaries felt free to speak ill of the dead.

Seel notes that the most damning account of John is to be found in the pages of Roger of Wendover's *Flowers of History*, a writer who has stood condemned for decades, 'whom', wrote John Gillingham, 'even schoolboys are taught to mistrust' (but Gillingham does not rely just on Wendover to inform his dismissive opinion of John). Paris' own work is an exact copy of Wendover with occasional interpolations until he becomes original by the mid-1230s. Seel rightly notes that Wendover portrays John as 'cowardly, cruel, lecherous, tyrannical, duplicitous and irreligious' and that his work has been the most damaging to John's reputation. Wendover is the main chronicle source for John's reign, and by far the most detailed; from about 1201/02 he was entirely original (i.e. he did not follow previous chroniclers) until he stopped writing by the end of 1234. Practically all historians have disparaged Wendover as biased and unreliable, and further evidence of minor unreliability has been presented in recent scholarship (Colin Veach, 'King John and Royal Control in Ireland: Why William de Briouze had to be Destroyed', *English Historical Review*, cxxxix, no. 540, October 2014). With the chief chronicle source for the reign undermined and discredited, how much easier it is to rescue John from unfair criticism.

Only Wendover is really not that unreliable, and certainly not by the standards of his day. Galbraith's mid-century criticisms of Wendover as a recorder of the events of his time are often picked up on, but his mitigation is not. For on mistakes he notes: 'How could it be otherwise in so large an undertaking? And what large medieval chronicle is not?' Put to one side the religious moral fables, such as the one about the washerwoman being sucked dry by a little black pig for taking in laundry on the Sabbath (but note there is a growing scholarly debate about imaginative memory and its meaning), and Wendover is surprisingly accurate on many details, especially the all-important military ones, and, crucially, he is often corroborated by non-monastic vernacular sources. As outlined above, revisionists have tended to mitigate and excuse John's military failures but without fully engaging in the realities of medieval warfare. Turner's attempt to do so is excellent on facts, but lacks a broader and deeper understanding of this vital area ('King John's Military Reputation Reconsidered', *Journal of Medieval History*, 19, 1993).

As I hope I have shown in published research, Wendover was intimately connected to events both in terms of his first-hand sources and his geographical position; he really was extremely well informed. Nor should his anti-royal bias, clear as it is, be overplayed: he praises Fawkes de Bréauté, John's notorious mercenary commander, as a good soldier even though he ransacked Wendover's own monastery. (Paris was more partisan and could not bring himself to repeat this tribute in an otherwise predominantly faithful copy of the older monk's work.) Seel is in good company when he focuses on Wendover's factual errors and presents these as the norm rather than the exception. But rather than cut the rotten part out of an otherwise healthy apple, he, like others before him, prefers to throw the whole apple away. Wendover was supremely well placed to pass judgement on John as king; it seems strange that he has been more traduced than the monarch.

Always we hear that John did not get a fair press because the monks writing the chronicles deplored him for taxing the Church and arguing with Rome, the latter resulting in excommunication for John and interdict (a withdrawal of the church's services) for the country. All their criticisms can therefore be attributed to resentment and vested interest and so they cannot be trusted. But what is easily overlooked here is that the vernacular sources (written in Old French) also have little good to say of John. This is even the case when they are written by people whose patrons are fighting for John. The Anonymous of Béthune's *Histoire des Ducs de Normandie et des Rois d'Angleterre* is a detailed account of much of John's reign and the activities of his lord, Robert of Béthune, who served in John's army. The Anonymous labels John 'a very wicked man: he was cruel to all men ... he ashamed many of the great men of the realm for which he was much hated'. Quite simply, he says, John 'had too many bad qualities'. William Marshal was the most respected royalist baron of the realm and one of John's leading generals in the king's last days. On John's death, he became regent for his heir, the 9-year-old Henry – in effect, the ruler of royalist England. One might expect his biographer to say something positive about John. But not at all. Instead he portrays John as a suspicious and resentful ruler, heedless to reason, blinded by pride and incapable of retaining baronial affection. It was not just the monks who could not find a good word for John.

Having discounted the chronicles, the revisionists therefore turned to the increasingly plentiful records of government for a supposedly neutral and factual evaluation of John. The desire of historians to quantify their research with hard facts is understandable, but prone to problems that are arguably more acute than the chronicle sources. There is, of course, the old caveat: 'Lies, damn lies and statistics'; or as the medievalist Prof. Colin Richmond rightly warns: 'The records of government are all very well, but on issues that matter they do not tell the truth. In fact, they seek to obscure it.' But even the cold, neutral figures of the bookkeepers and clerks can reveal something of John's poor reputation among contemporaries. One entry in the chancery rolls alludes to John's serial adultery: '… the wife of Hugh de Neville gives the lord King 200 chickens that she might lie one night with her lord, Hugh de Neville.' The Anonymous of Béthune's remark that 'John ashamed many of the great men of the realm' was in no small part due to the king's lechery: the Anonymous says that John 'lusted after beautiful women', often the wives and daughters of his barons.

There is something of an obsession among some revisionists with John's supposed brilliance with administrative matters. It is clear that John had some ability in this field which should not be gainsaid, and it is this above all else that has allowed the seeds of John's rehabilitation to flourish. But his relative success here, if it can be deemed as such, is rather a marker of his abysmal failure. As Turner has rightly noted, 'modern scholars' admiration of kings such as John for attention to administration is anachronistic, applying standards of the twentieth century rather than the thirteenth'. John's improvements in government bureaucracy were driven by his need for money. These finances, in turn, were needed for his armies to win back the lands in France. It was because he had so disastrously lost these lands that he needed so much money in the first place. It did not help that the money was repeatedly wasted on military campaigns that he invariably lost. The unsurprising knock-on effect of this was that it antagonised already disgruntled groups of barons across the country. John's crass insensitivity and greed, coupled with his complete absence of people skills, pushed to the extreme a harsh and unrelenting bureaucracy that simply served to corral even more powerful barons into the rapidly growing anti-John camp. In an important recent article from 2014, Colin Veach (see article cited above) has shown this also to be true of John's 'duplicitous', 'selfish' and 'unscrupulous' methods in Ireland against the great lords there, provoking military resistance. It strikes me that their consequent and successful rebellion of 1208 must have been eagerly observed by discontents in England who would now consider what united action against the Crown could achieve.

John's failures in France turned him into to a stay-at-home king. Here he was always either under everyone's feet or stepping (and more usually stamping) on their toes. His efficient bureaucracy (on vellum, anyway) poked and prodded all and sundry to increase their payments to his exchequer in pursuit of military campaigns for which he had limited aptitude and which most barons realised had little prospect of success. John's administrative advances thereby compounded his failures by leading to open baronial revolt, Magna Carta and a major French invasion and occupation of England. But as long as the books were in order, that's okay then.

Revisionists would then say that John inherited an invidious position left to him by his father and brother: an Angevin Empire that was always prone to breaking up anyway and a bankrupt nation. The Angevin Empire (even its imperial title is disputed) stretched from the Scottish border, dissecting France down to the Pyrenees. Seel says 'it was naturally disposed to fracture'. Certainly, it lacked solid foundations in many ways but regional politics in France were available for John to exploit more effectively. Many barons there, cherishing their autonomy, preferred a weak English lord abroad to a strong French one on their doorstep. The English king was therefore a natural ally for many; but the fact that he could not be relied upon politically or militarily saw many of these barons gravitate into the French orbit. John's egregious ineptness was of greater significance. He messed up his great victory at Mirebeau in 1202, where he rescued his aged mother Eleanor of Aquitaine from a siege, when he mistreated his prisoners; many of these were related to powerful figures in Normandy, who were then more inclined to take Philip Augustus' side when the French invaded the Duchy. Warren noted that one of John's greatest failing was that 'he could not resist the temptation to kick a man when he was down'. To which I add: he couldn't even keep his balance while doing so.

To make John look better, it has been necessary to make Richard the Lionheart look worse. The financial debate is a heated one here: did Richard leave John with the bill for his excessive crusading, wars abroad and the king's ransom from captivity? It seems unlikely: when John signed the Treaty of Le Goulet with France in 1200, he agreed to hand over to the French the huge sum of 20,000 marks as a succession duty for his lands in France. Tellingly, the money had not been asked of Richard or Henry. John always found the money for his wars; and he always squandered it. Richard's wars in France were indeed expensive, but far less so than John's in 1216, when the fighting was not on French soil but English, with the king's subjects suffering the dangers and atrocities of war, the Crown's revenues collapsed and the enemy sitting comfortably in London with half the country under their rule. That, surely, is a true definition of failure.

It can be smugly chronocentric to impose modern views on the past. The view of John by contemporaries was one of a damning consensus. It remains a sound judgement 800 years later.

THE ROBIN HOOD LEGEND

When writing *Blood Cries Afar*, I, like many others who read the book, became very engaged with the guerrilla fighter William of Kensham, or, as legend calls him, Willikin of the Weald. I was struck by just how many criteria he filled for the Robin Hood legend and perplexed by how he had been completely overlooked as an inspiration for the Robin Hood story. The reason, I deduced, was because the French invasion of 1216 has been forgotten, and Willikin with it. When the book was completed, I undertook more research on him. I exhausted all that was known about William in two articles. The first, reprinted here, appeared in *History Today* in March 2013 under the title of 'The Real Robin Hood'. It was submitted with the working title of 'The First Robin Hood?'

The effect of the article was remarkable and attracted worldwide media attention, appearing in papers from Australia to Canada and triggering a blizzard of interviews and a discussion on national news in the UK. Some of the newspapers sensationalised the research with titles such as 'Robin Hood Was From Tunbridge Wells', which was amusing if somewhat misleading. My friends were overly assiduous in sending me the most disparaging comments from the internet, but my favourite comment was the Monty Python-inspired remark: 'Fwee Willikin of the Weald!'

My thanks to *History Today* for kind permission to reprint the article.

The First Robin Hood?

Lythe and listin, gentilmen,
That be of frebore blode;
I shall you tel of a gode yeoman,
His name was Robin Hode.

A Gest of Robyn Hode, fifteenth century

Robin Hood is an ever-present figure in the pantheon of English heroes, continually capturing the imaginations of historians and writers of historical fiction as much as those of the general public. Whether he was a real character or not is another matter – and one for perpetual debate. The paradox is neatly captured by an article on Robin Hood in the *Dictionary of National Biography*, an entry in which the author argues that his biographical subject was entirely mythical.

As a medievalist, I had a natural interest in the Robin Hood legends, but I never considered him as a topic to pursue. Or so it was until, while researching my recent book on a neglected French invasion of England, I learned more about a band of common men dwelling as outlaws in the forest using their bows to fight against tyranny and oppression under the charismatic leadership of a longbow-wielding folk hero. Not only has this folk hero never been identified as a possible origin of the Robin stories, this leader is no mere myth but a real flesh-and-blood man and a genuine English champion.

The latest of some sixty films and TV series dedicated to Robin was the 2010 blockbuster, *Robin Hood*. With this last major film came the inevitable flow of books in 2010 and 2011, bringing the legend up to date with a number of modern interpretations, trying to identify, if only in broad terms, Robin Hood and his Merry Men of Sherwood Forest and to place them in their real chronological and geographical context. David Baldwin puts forward the established leading contender Roger Godberd, an outlaw probably living between about 1230 and 1290. However, the timing, as we shall see, is arguably too late for the origins of the Robin Hood stories; furthermore, Godberd's reputation is a negative one of a squalid thief and killer – there is nothing of the hero here – and he lacks that most necessary accompaniment: the totemic longbow.

Nigel Cawthorne and Jim Bradbury do not commit themselves, but give more attention to the importance of popular stories of Hereward the Wake, a resistance fighter against the Normans after the 1066 conquest of England; the early thirteenth-century occasional outlaw nobleman Fulk Fitzwarren; and Eustace the Monk, a French pirate who served with and against King John. Eustace and Fulk were the heroes (or anti-heroes) of popular vernacular romances in the thirteenth century.

Bradbury, in his careful assessment, summarises the real but ultimately unknown Robin Hood as 'a criminal who pursued a criminal and violent career' who 'operated in Yorkshire, Sherwood and Nottingham' and 'became leader of an outlaw band of men skilled as archers'. None goes so far as Adam Thorpe's fictional depiction in *Hodd* (2009) of a psychotic blasphemer stoned on magic mushrooms, but research has opted for unadorned, gritty verisimilitudes to present us with an unattractive figure that falls short of the noble outlaw and popular hero as portrayed in popular ballads such as *A Gest of Robyn Hode*:

> Robyn was a prude outlaw,
> Whyles he walked on grounde;
> So courteyse an outlawe as he was one
> Was never non founde.

It is from such ballads from the mid-fifteenth century onwards that Robin becomes known to us. That is not to say earlier ballads did not exist: they almost certainly did, but they simply have not survived. In *Piers Plowman* from 1377, the priest Sloth admits he does not know his Paternoster well, but 'I kan [know] rymes of Robyn hood', indicating an existing tradition.

Where do we place Robin Hood in location and time? For the majority of historians, if Robin Hood truly existed, his activities were centred around the criminal hotspot of Barnsdale in South Yorkshire (hence Russell Crowe's heroic but ultimately doomed attempt at a northern accent). This is based on late medieval references such as 'Robin Hood in Barnsdale stood'. However, there remains some disagreement on this: Barnsdale could be confused with Bryunsdale near Nottingham; Stephen Knight, in *Robin Hood: A Mythic Biography* (2003), suggests that the reference is really to Barnsdale Forest in Rutland.

There is more disagreement on when the inspiration for the Robin Hood stories began. The two dominant schools of thought plump for the early thirteenth century and the fourteenth. Those who favour the later period often cite evidence which shows the lawlessness of the period, while a reference to King Edward in one ballad indicates one of their reigns (Edward I, II and III ruled in succession from 1272 to 1377).

Film-makers by and large choose to set the legend during the reign of King Richard (1189–99), focusing especially on the time he was held in captivity as he made his way back from the Crusades (1192–94). The Scottish chronicler John Major, writing in 1521, believed the Angevin period of Henry II, Richard I and John (1154–1216) was the time when 'flourished those most famous robbers Robert Hood an Englishman and Little John, who lay in wait in the woods, but spoiled of their goods those only that were wealthy'.

Major was perhaps not far off. There is clear evidence to suggest that the Robin Hood stories were established by the mid-thirteenth century. Criminal records from this time reveal that a suspected robber, William son of Robert le Fevere on a Memoranda Roll of 1261, had his name changed by a different scribe on the roll of the Justices in Eyre in Berkshire of 1261 to William Robehood, indicating awareness of the legend. A similar transcription occurred much earlier: in 1225 the York Assizes refer to the fugitive Robert Hod; in the margin of the 1226 Pipe Roll he is given the sobriquet of Hobbehood. The name Robert Hood is first recorded in a criminal context for the killer of Ralph of Cirencester sometime between 1213 and 1216.

For all the hints, the clues and the leads, the historian must be honest and ultimately confess his ignorance of who the real Robin is – if indeed he ever was. It is a matter of conjecture and possibility. The ever-evolving story adapted itself to different times and different places, with the name Robin Hood replacing as a matter of course the true identity of the man on whom Robin was based. The name itself is therefore possibly of minor relevance to finding the origin of the stories. Thus the trail to the true Robin Hood is always likely to lead to a dead end, as he was almost certainly a composite figure. But what seems evident is that there was some inspirational basis to the legend and this is what we should pursue if we are to understand the tradition. For all the research undertaken on Robin Hood, one real-life character who has as much, if not more, right than any other to lay claim to be the origin of the stories has gone completely overlooked: William of Kensham.

William fits the time and, crucially, the image of the heroic outlaw of legend. He is not a squalid cut-throat and thief, but a faithful servant to his king and a forest-dwelling, bow-wielding freedom fighter. What is more, such was his popular fame from his daring exploits, he became a legend in his own life-time who earned his own nickname from contemporaries: Willikin of the Weald.

William of Kensham (also known as Cassingham and variations of Collingham) appears frequently in the official records of John, Henry III and even Edward I. He was a minor servant of the crown, acting as the warden of the Seven Hundreds of the Weald in Kent, a reward for his services to John and Henry in the war against the French invaders; Kensham was a manor here. His origins are unknown. However, it is known from the records that he settled in this area with his family and that he was succeeded by his son, Ralph.

He was mentioned with high regard in contemporary writings, an unusual acknowledgement for the time as he was a lowly figure on the social scale; this is an indication of the fame that he earned. Roger of Wendover says that he was a young man in 1216, the time at which he became widely known. His name appears repeatedly in official rolls after 1217 until 1251 as he remained in the king's service, his mundane duties including temporary police work and supplying logs to friends of Henry III. His death, after forty years of service, can be calculated from the records as occurring in 1257, the year his wife was granted protection by Henry III. (Coincidentally, this is also the time of Fulk Fitzwarren's death.)

So why did he become famous? The background to his exploits is the somewhat neglected French invasion of England of 1216. The baronial revolt against King John in 1215, which led to Magna Carta in June and all-out civil war by the autumn, had left the barons in a precarious position by the end of the year. Defeated in an epic siege at Rochester castle, they were holed up in London in need of assistance. They offered the throne to Prince Louis ('the Lion'), son and heir of the powerful Capetian King Philip Augustus. Louis arrived in May 1216 with a large invasion force and established himself in England. A lightning campaign left over one-third of the country in Louis' hands, from Winchester in the south to Lincoln in the north. At one point, as many as two-thirds of the barons of England paid allegiance to the Capetian as King Louis I of England. In a remarkable progress, the young monarch of Scotland, Alexander II, travelled all the way from his home country to Dover in the far south-east to pay homage to Louis, as one king to another. The French were to remain for eighteen months. Within the French occupation zone, there were three prominent islands of opposition: the royal castles of Windsor and Dover and, in the great forest of the Weald in Kent and Sussex, there was the English resistance force of William of Kensham.

William's band comprised some 1000 archer volunteers (*sagittariis*) from the rural areas. These men knew their area intimately to take full advantage of it for hiding in the forest and laying ambushes, using their skills as bowmen to inflict serious casualties amongst the French. That William and his men were a highly effective resistance outfit is made clear from contemporary sources. Roger of Wendover writes that they took to the forests and 'continued to trouble the French throughout the whole war, and slew many thousands of them'. The Anonymous of Béthune speaks admiringly of William's 'noble prowess' and how he was feared and 'renowned in Louis' army'. The author of the *History of William the Marshal* confirms these views: 'witness the deeds of Willikin of the Weald' he exhorts his listeners, employing the already popular name for William. Recognition of his successful activities was acknowledged at the highest level: in September 1216, King John wrote to the men of the Weald to express his gratitude for their loyal service.

William continued to serve the crown loyally after John's death in October. In February 1217, Louis made for Winchelsea on the South Coast, hoping to retake the neighbouring port of Rye before returning temporarily to France for reinforcements. Even before reaching there he had been fretting over the vulnerable supply routes to these towns, as the routes went through William's operational area of the forested Weald. When he arrived at Winchelsea, Louis found himself in a well-laid trap: from the sea, royalist ships blockaded the ports; from the north, William moved in to hinder any French movements inland to the Franco-baronial stronghold of London by guarding the travel ways and destroying bridges. Fear of William grew: his men swiftly dispatched any French prisoners by beheading them. According to one source, the French leader 'did not know which way to turn … Louis was so harried that he felt himself in desperate straits'. His men began to starve before being relieved by Eustace the Monk and a French flotilla.

William is recorded being in action again in late April, when Louis returned with his reinforcements. Approaching Dover across the Channel, Louis could see smoke rising from his siege camp around the castle. A French source reports that 'Willekins de Wans and many of his men' had launched a surprise attack on the camp and killed those guarding it. This assault successfully prevented Louis from joining up with his forces there, forcing him to land at Sandwich instead. William's reputation and standing was evidently very high at this time, as he was joined in this attack by King John's illegitimate son, Oliver. In May, Louis burned the towns of Hythe and Romney, but his actions were hindered once more by William and his men.

The French occupation was finally ended in August 1217, at the epic and bloody naval battle of Sandwich, an event I would argue as a more important sea victory than those won at Traflagar and against the Spanish Armada. For his loyal services against the French oppressors, William was rewarded with favourable comments from the king, tenements in Essex and the wardenship of the Seven Hundreds of the Weald. He was also guaranteed money during his lifetime and his widow received royal protection for seven years after his death. Perhaps more valuable than this was the acclaim he received as a war hero and the honour of being awarded the affectionate and widely known nickname of Willikin of the Weald.

Thus with William we have a figure who can offer genuine inspiration for the origins of the Robin Hood story. Whereas with other contenders from this age and afterwards it is hard to find someone who is both a hero and an outlaw, in William we do have both: a heroic resistance fighter loyally protecting the crown; but also, from Louis' perspective, an egregious outlaw defying the righteous rule of his new regime. Louis had written to his new subjects demanding their support and obedience, and the men and towns of the Weald and ports in the south had indeed sworn allegiance to their new French master. And whereas other contenders at best have oblique references to bowmen (usually crossbowmen), here we have a band of archers living in the forest and laying ambushes upon their enemies and led by an enigmatic but non-noble commander who earned fame through his newly acquired sobriquet.

All this places William squarely in contention with other claimants to the origins of the Robin Hood stories; indeed, none can offer this combination of 'Robin Hood-esque' qualities. The background of the French invasion and occupation is especially important here: neglected by historians, it was understandably regarded as the major event of the era by contemporaries. Is it a coincidence that the story of Hereward the Wake became very popular by the mid-thirteenth century? In 1216, exactly 150 years after the Norman Conquest, the English must have felt history was repeating itself with another (initially successful) French invasion. The heroic resistance of an Englishman against the foreign invaders must have complemented William of Kensham's own inspirational role in the defence of the kingdom. Nor is it a coincidence that Eustace the Monk is always regarded as a major influence on the Robin Hood stories; he was a lead player in the events of the invasion, meeting his end at the Battle of Sandwich by decapitation on board his ship. His notorious reputation was such that his head was paraded on a pole around southern towns to reassure the population that this fiend was truly dead. Eustace was the subject of his own romance, which has ensured his fame – and his place in evolution of the Robin Hood story. (A genuine monk in his early career, would he not anyway serve better as a model for Friar Tuck?) Imagine if a writer had committed Willikin of the Weald's adventures to a romance story: consider then what historians would think of the part he must surely have played in the Robin Hood legend.

It can be argued that the south-east is entirely the wrong place for the legend to begin. But this argument is predicated on the uncertain assertion that Robin Hood is unquestionably connected with Barnsdale and its immediate environs and nowhere else. As we have seen, there is disagreement over which 'Barnsdale' is actually being referred to. There are also some strong associations with the south-east: in the few examples of the surname Robinhood in the second half of the thirteenth century, Holt notes that 'there is a total concentration in the south-eastern England'. He warns that this may simply reflect 'the fact that far more judicial records survive for the south-eastern England than for the North and that they happen to have been studied more intensively'; at the same time, this early concentration of the name could also reflect an area which saw the origins of the legend take hold with Willikin of the Weald. There is other incidental evidence, too, which may offer a connection to this region. I happened to stumble across some recent research by Sheila Sweetinburgh on late medieval fishing in Kent. In her discussion of names of vessels she highlighted their consistent connections with religion (e.g. saints), attributes (e.g. *The Good Fortune*) or plants and animals (e.g. *The May Flower*). Unexpected and unexplained, she noted two striking anomalies: one ship sailed under the name *Robin Hood* and another under *Little John*.

Furthermore, a link can still be made to Nottingham while preserving this south-eastern association at the time that William of Kensham was active. During the French occupation, Nottingham was the main operational headquarters for the royalist army. William's renown as a great military captain was known here as it was throughout the war zone. We have seen how King John sent his letter of thanks to the men of the Weald for their resistance to Louis. That William was very much part of central military planning can be deduced from the time when King John's son Oliver, a leading royalist commander, joined with William for the attack on the Dover siege camp in April 1217.

The royalist high command in Nottingham was acutely aware of William's resistance behind enemy lines. It would have been anxious to receive William's first-hand intelligence of Louis' troop movements in this vital sector of the war, as well as information on enemy troop numbers and morale and the local political implications. As an invaluable eyewitness with an understanding of royalist strategy, William was surely called to Nottingham to brief the war council with his invaluable first-hand knowledge of the enemy. Here he and any accompanying men would have been able to demonstrate their skills as archers and tell inspiring tales of their forest ambushes. Even in the extremely unlikely case that William, as a leading operational commander, did not visit Nottingham military HQ once during the eighteen-month French occupation, his propaganda value as a heroic, non-noble Englishman resisting the imposed tyranny of the French, was still enormous and something to be fully capitalised on at HQ in Nottingham and elsewhere. William's exploits would have been widely proclaimed to inspire people in the battle against the French. His fame was such that three contemporary chronicles felt that due attention and praise should be given to this dashing leader even though he lacked the usual prerequisite of knightly status.

Thus Nottingham may have been an area which became associated with a forest-dwelling yeoman and his band of archers fighting oppression. It is also worth noting that the city and its nearby forests of Barnsdale and Sherwood are all close to Lincoln, site of the decisive land battle of the war in May 1217. The eastern edges of Sherwood Forest were closer to Lincoln than Nottingham is; the forest may have been a base for hit-and-run sorties against the French in Lincoln, as well as harassing enemy movements and communication to and from their northern and Scottish allies. (In the legends, Robin Hood's men are famously camouflaged in 'Lincoln green'.) The success of William in the south was likely to have prompted similar tactics further north.

James Holt, in the most authoritative study of Robin Hood, argues convincingly that Robin was a legend by the 1260s. For this to have happened, he says that it would be a stretch, but 'not impossible', for there to have been 'a quick generation of the legend, perhaps even beginning in Robin's lifetime'. This is exactly what happened within ten years of William's death, to the extent that contemporary chroniclers were even aware of his folk-hero name: Willikin of the Weald.

The most probable truth behind the Robin Hood legend is that over time storytellers incorporated and conflated various characters form other tales with the alias Robin Hood becoming settled on as the instantly recognisable name of the woodsman. Inspiration would also have been taken from the dramatic exploits of known figures, which were interwoven into these stories with considerable embellishment. William of Kensham must surely be considered as one of these figures – and possibly the first – to inspire the Robin Hood phenomenon. In him not only can we reconcile the folk hero/outlaw paradox, but we are presented with a real character fighting loyally for the crown against what the propaganda of the day depicted as an unjust foe – and all the while hiding deep in the forest with his band of bowmen.

Further Reading:

J.C. Holt, *Robin Hood* (Thames and Hudson, 1989).

Jim Bradbury, *Robin Hood* (Amberley, 2010).

David Baldwin, *Robin Hood: The English Outlaw Unmasked* (Amberley, 2011).

Nigel Cawthorne, *Robin Hood: The True History Behind the Legend* (Robinson, 2010).

Appendix 3

William of Kensham: Resistance Fighter

Guerrilla warfare is always to be found in conflicts when an occupying force takes control of enemy territory or threatens borders. The medieval period was no exception. In the fifteenth century we have the Albanian–Ottoman wars, when Christian leaders worked to stretch the Ottoman Army – making divisions look for them across a broad sweep of territory, then attacking them and quickly withdrawing before reinforcements could arrive. Night attacks were another common feature of this conflict and battle avoidance was key. Guerrilla warfare was, of course, a speciality of the Welsh, as Owen Glyndower demonstrates. It was a key feature of the Swabian wars and English forces in Normandy faced numerous guerrilla or brigandage attacks towards the end of the Hundred Years War. Going further back, in the late eight century, Saxon resistance to Charlemagne's advances comprised guerrilla tactics by the Duke of Widukind, as was the case with Hereward the Wake in post-Conquest England. It was a major strategy of the Southern Resistance in Languedoc during the Albigensian Crusade (see my *Kill Them All: Cathars and Carnage in the Albigensian Crusade*, The History Press, 2015). Where the guerrilla bands were led by non-noble leaders, our knowledge of their activities is greatly reduced – in a subject that is already, by its very nature, understandably obscure. That is why William offers such a rare, invaluable insight into medieval guerrilla warfare.

The extracts here are from 'William of Kensham: Hero of the Resistance', published in vol. 3 no. 6 (2013) of *Medieval Warfare*. While there was necessarily some overlap with the *History Today* article (see Appendix 2), the focus here was on William's military activity. Here I stress that royalist war propaganda may well have promoted William as a hero (as he was clearly a legend in his own lifetime; I like to think that his exploits were celebrated in song and oral tradition). While this activity is covered in the book, the article in *Medieval Warfare* allowed me not only to bring all of William's actions together in one focused paper, but to offer some wider military context and analysis for them. The extra material here contains passages that offer additional information to that found in the *History Today* article. Between these two articles, readers will have as complete a picture as is possible of William of Kensham.

My thanks to *Medieval Warfare* for permission to reprint extracts of the article here.

William of Kensham: Hero of the Resistance

William of Kensham is one of the great unsung heroes of England. A guerrilla fighter who led a highly effective resistance against French invaders, his lack of noble status has left him bereft of the full recognition he deserves. Yet in his own lifetime he was an inspirational figure who received mention from the chroniclers of the day who recognised his role in a largely forgotten war.

Thus we know next to nothing about William before the French invasion of 1216. Unsurprisingly for the early thirteenth century, even his surname lacks absolute certainty. Matthew Paris called him William of Colingeham (or, in one variation, Collingham), but the better-placed author of the *Histoire des Ducs de Normandie et des Rois d'Angleterre* calls him Willekins of Kasingehem, identified as Cassingham in government records, which we know as Kensham near Tunbridge Wells in Kent. After the war, William was made Warden of the Seven Hundreds of the Weald, of which Rolvenden was one. Records show that the manor passed to his son Ralph and then to Ralph's son-in-law, so we can establish that William settled in the area. The *History of William Marshal* names him Wilekins de Vauz (and also Waus, in the consistently inconsistent language of Old French texts). From this we have his nickname, Willikin of the Weald, the huge forested area that enclosed extensive parts of the south-east of England. Lying between London and the South Coast, the Weald stretched from the Kent marshes to the New Forest in Hampshire, covering an area 120 miles long and 30 miles wide. Today much of the area remains heavily wooded and is designated an area of outstanding natural beauty. Willekin's name still echoes in local folklore as Willy of the Weald, even for those who know nothing of the history of the period.

In 1901, the historian Kate Norgate, suggested in her biography of King John that William was a Flemish adventurer. A brief study of William (shorter than this one) from 1941 supports this view and there is indeed much to recommend it. From 1215, King John was embroiled in the war for Magna Carta; reluctant to trust many of his own people, he imported hundreds of Flemish mercenaries to fight in his cause. So many were coming from the Low Countries to the south-eastern ports that John had to appoint a Knights Templar to oversee and register them all so as to keep an eye on payments and numbers. The familiar name of Willekins may reinforce this view, or it may simply reflect the regional identity of the author of the *Histoire des Ducs*. If he were a Flemish mercenary, I would suggest that he was already fighting for King John in 1215, possibly at the Siege of Rochester, and was not part of the huge swathes of reinforcements that came over to fight against the French invasion of 1216. This is because he settled quickly, took command of local forces from early on in the invasion and he seems to have had a thorough knowledge of the local area which was important for the success of his guerrilla warfare.

[Following Louis' invasion in May 1216] William gathered an irregular army
from men in Kent and Sussex and organised strikes against the French from
his base in the Weald. Roger of Wendover says that Louis 'conquered Sussex
with all its towns and fortresses; but here a young man named William, refusing to make his fealty to Louis, collected one thousand archers and took to the
isolated places and forests which abounded in that region' (Roger of Wendover,
Rogeri de Wendover Liber Qui Dicitur Flores Historiarum, ed. H.G. Hewlett, Rolls
Series, London, 1886–87, vol. ii, p. 182). Most of these men, being locals, had an
intimate knowledge of the area – a decided advantage over the French troops.
That they comprised a highly effective force is clear from the sources. The biographer of William Marshal exhorts his readers to 'witness the deeds of Willikin
of the Weald' when it came to killing the French (*History of William Marshal*,
eds A. Holden, D. Crouch and S. Gregory, 2002–06, vol. ii, pp. 256, 257). The
Anonymous of Béthune, author of the *Histoire des Ducs*, whose patron fought
on King John's side, wrote admiringly of William's 'noble prowess' and how
he was feared and 'renowned in Louis' army' (Histoire des *Ducs de Normandie
et des Rois d'Angleterre*, ed. F. Michel, Paris, 1840, p. 181). Interestingly, he here
identifies Willikin as 'sergeant' (*siergant*) and that 'the French called him Willekin
de Wans' (Wans being their name for the area). Roger of Wendover confirms
William's expertise at irregular warfare: 'He sought out and attacked the French
during the whole war and killed many thousands of them' (Roger of Wendover,
ii, p. 182). His actions were recognised and acknowledged by a grateful king
who wrote to the men of the Weald in September 1216 to thank them for their
loyal service to the crown. In another royal communication to William, John
paid him in money for leading military strikes against the French.

The very nature of guerrilla warfare – covert, secretive, often small-scale –
makes it difficult to track William's movements in the forests of the Weald. Even
the activities of royalty and leading knights cannot be followed completely for
this conflict, so how much the harder it is for a low-born character such as
William. William's style of irregular warfare made it difficult for regular troops
of an occupational force to deal with. His strategy was dominated by ambush,
terror and containment. William's successful containment strategy can be seen
at Rye and again at Romney and Hythe, tying down large bodies of enemy
troops and often preventing supplies from reaching them. But it was ambush
and terror that most unsettled the French and made them scared to enter the
Weald, despite their superior forces. For them, William quickly became their
bogeyman with his own nickname.

Throughout the history of warfare, the weaker side has always relied heavily on guerrilla tactics; in an area in which all but two castles were garrisoned
by the French and their allies, and with the local population compelled to pay
homage to their new lord, King Louis I, William had to resort to ambush and
terror. Without castles and fortresses, the holding and ransoming of prisoners

was a limited option: as well as the enormous problems for a guerrilla force in securing and feeding large numbers of prisoners, there would also be the issue that an exchange would force William's men into the open. The killing of prisoners, therefore, was a brutal but neat solution while serving the extra purpose of inducing terror in the enemy. That the French knew they could not expect mercy from William and his men, and that capture often meant decapitation, would have heightened the terror of operating in the dense and unfamiliar forests of the area. Many of the French, especially their commanders, had fought in the Albigensian Crusade, where in the early years from 1209 to 1211 they also faced a weaker enemy. The southerners resisting the French invasion of Languedoc were disunited and reeling from the shock of the first initial, massive onslaught of crusaders from the north; unable to field an army of note and able to resist the invaders, their only form of effective attack was, like William's strategy, ambush and terror. Just as William disrupted the lines of communication between the French stronghold in London and the coast, so the southerners ambushed crusading reinforcements and supply trains leaving the crusader headquarters of Carcassonne on the way to theatres of operation. In this way they gained some notable psychological victories. There were also many cases of crusaders being mutilated – their eyes put out and lips and other body parts cut off – as a warning to the enemy who ventured out of their strongholds. William, with only a fraction of the resources of the lords of Languedoc, had to rely on guerrilla tactics totally.

As a guerrilla force, he did have a number of factors that he could use to his advantage. The very lack of castles and strongholds meant he had a mobile force that was harder to pin down in the form of a siege. Even if he did not have as many as 1000 men as Roger of Wendover says, it is clear that it was a very substantial warrior band that constituted a small army of light, highly mobile fighters. As such, his men were probably split into smaller groups that could try to pull the enemy in different directions. Thus at Rye he forced the French to abandon land routes and take to the sea lanes instead. His knowledge of the local topography would have been invaluable, greatly aided, as in many resistance wars and insurgencies, by the support of the local population. Most of his men were from the area and so would have had connections with family and friends here. As in the Boer War and hundreds of other conflicts, the guerrillas could turn to their homes, friends and relations for supplies and information on local troop movements. Indeed, like some resistance groups, many of William's men probably operated from the comfort of their homes. This local advantage would have been one of William's greatest logistical and strategic assets.

The weapon of choice of William and his men was the bow. This suited their expertise as specialised foot soldiers hiding out in the forest where heavy armoured cavalry was largely ineffective. Their arrows could be let loose from cover and at a distance, and then the bowmen could melt away into the trees. The bow and crossbow were the deadliest weapons in medieval warfare at this time. I have made a study of this area: the overwhelming majority of deaths recorded in chronicles were the result of arrows and quarrels. In this conflict,

Eustace de Vescy, one of the leading baronial knights (and hence heavily armoured), was reconnoitring the defences of Castle Barnard when a crossbow bolt stuck him in the forehead and pierced his brain. At the Battle of Sandwich, English archers directed 'their missiles into the French and soon caused many fatalities among them … the French crews were struck down by the arrows of the English' (Roger of Wendover, ii, pp. 221–22). In Roger of Wendover's detailed chronicle, between 1214 and 1234 nearly all accounts of wounding, mortal and otherwise, are inflicted by archery. William's large force of skilled bowmen thus had the opportunity to cause maximum damage without having to expose itself to the battlefield where the French superiority in numbers and armour would have been telling. When William engaged more openly with the enemy in the surprise attack on the French camp at Dover, is it notable that he did so with the support of regular troops under Oliver Fitzroy.

The fact that we have any mention of William at all in the sources is, on the one hand, surprising as these sources tended to focus on figures of nobility and chivalry, but on the other hand, it is a testament to the very real impact William made on the war and hence on contemporaries. All the sources mentioned were written within a relatively short time of the conflict – possibly all within the first decade of its end. The Old French texts were written by those who patrons fought in the war, while Roger of Wendover's had excellent access to first-hand sources. Thus William, a completely obscure person before the invasion, was made famous by the war.

The letters and payment from the kings, and the joint operation at Dover with Oliver Fitzroy, prove that William was known at the very highest levels of the royalist command during the war and that he was thought highly enough of for the king's son to join with him in combat. It is likely that William was promoted to fame by the royalist leadership, for here was a superb propaganda opportunity to encourage and inspire the English people with a low-born warrior fighting bravely behind enemy lines against the evil invader: the common man resisting the French occupier. This would enhance his renown in his own lifetime and the nicknames afforded him. The late twelfth and early thirteenth centuries were an age when national identity was growing. (It is a sociological and historically chronocentric error to believe that such sentiment is the preserve of the modern era.) One of the most influential defining factors in any nation's development of national sentiment is the role of war, especially when faced by a foreign invader; very quickly, a sense of 'us an them' is created to meet with the threat. And so it was with the eighteen-month French invasion and occupation of England. Thus we hear from the contemporary sources of the English fighting for their country (*pro patria*). At the Battle of Lincoln in May 1217, William Marshal rallies his troops and exhorts them 'to defend our land' (*History of William Marshal*, ii, p. 309). It is highly possible that it was royal policy to make William more famous, and hence this offers another reason why he features in our three most important sources of the invasion.

With the war over, further royal recognition was made of William's substantial contribution to the victory. Henry III wrote highly of him and rewarded him with lands and office: tenements in Essex and wardenship of the Seven Hundreds of the Weald. It can be estimated that he had 120 acres of land at his disposal and that he rose to the rank of squire. He was granted an annual income and his wife received a widow's pension for seven years. His position as an officer of the crown ensures that his name appears in government records but no further mention is made of his career in the chronicles. The war was followed by a relatively peaceful few decades and William seems to have settled down into a quiet way of life in the king's service with none of the excitement of the war years. The only knowledge we have of his activities in this time are some policing duties and the menial task of supplying a friend of the king with some logs. It was quite the anticlimax to his career as a war hero.

Further Reading:

Sean McGlynn, 'The Real Robin Hood', *History Today,* 63 (3), 2013
G.R. Stephens, 'A Note on William of Cassingham', *Speculum,* 16 (2), 1941

THE LEGACY OF MAGNA CARTA

As part of the rebuilding process after the French were driven from England, the Charter of Liberties was reissued for a second time in November 1217 (the first reissue being in Bristol in November 1216 following John's death). Once again it was modified with deletions and additions, the forty-two clauses of the 1216 reissue now being increased to forty-seven. One of the major changes was the dropping of the three forest clauses. These were now incorporated into a new Charter of Forest Liberties. Thus from 1218, to differentiate between the two charters, the larger Charter of Liberties became known as the Great Charter: Magna Carta.

From here it went from strength to strength in the thirteenth century. In 1225 it was reissued; as with the original of 1215, it was the result of a bargain being struck between the monarch and his subjects. Henry III needed money: in return for the third reissue he received the proceeds of a general taxation.

The 1225 Magna Carta is the definitive and enduring version that finally became enshrined in law. Pared down to thirty-seven clauses (some were dropped, others were merged into one), it begins by stating that these liberties were granted by the king 'of our own spontaneous freewill' and concludes with the promise that the Crown will do nothing 'whereby the liberties contained in this Charter shall be infringed or weakened'. Adherence to Magna Carta was thus established as the keystone of stable relations between monarch and subjects.

Henry declared his commitment to Magna Carta nearly a dozen times during his reign, which lasted until 1272. By the 1250s the Charter was being copied out not only in Latin and French, but also in English, ensuring it became further embedded in the consciousness of the people. Each time Magna Carta was distributed among the shires and cathedrals of the land it was sent out with the king's seal attached.

In times of unrest, crisis or financial need, appeals were made for the full implementation of the Great Charter. The 1225 Charter was reissued in 1265, again as the result of a second baronial rebellion: Simon de Montfort, wishing to see Magna Carta fully implemented, had led the barons against the financial pressures imposed by Henry III to fund the king's failed foreign policy. In 1297, Edward I, needing, as ever, taxation to fund his wars, also reissued it. Under pressure from his subjects once more, in 1300 Edward announced what turned out to be the final reissue of the Magna Carta. It had become a permanent feature of the constitutional landscape in medieval England.

By the time of the last reissue of Magna Carta in 1300, it was nearly a century old and in some ways feeling its age, many of its clauses seeming antiquated in light of a changing society. But in its fundamental affirmation of freedoms it remained deeply important.

The growth of Parliament, which was in no small part spurred on by Magna Carta, ensured its continuing relevance. For a long period in the Middle Ages, Parliament opened with a public reading of the Charter and made over forty renewals of its confirmation by the early 1400s. During the crises of weak kingship in the reigns of Edward II (1307–27) and Richard II (1377–99), both reflecting King John's own reign, the idea of baronial committees again came to the fore to play a major role in politics and the restriction of the monarch's power.

The reign of the powerful and effective King Edward III (1327–77) saw the further entrenchment of the Charter. In 1354 he extended its provisions beyond just freemen of the realm to encompass 'every man, of whatever estate or condition that he be'. Furthermore, he added that no one should suffer punishment without 'due process of the law'. In 1369, Parliament passed a statue that declared that 'if any Statute be made to the contrary' of Magna Carta, it was to be ignored.

However, as the Middle Ages drew to a close, Magna Carta receded into the background. The upheaval of the Wars of the Roses (1455–85) was more concerned with the rivalry between competing kings than between monarchs and subjects. With the arrival of the Tudor dynasty (1485–1603) and the imposition of strong, royal government, especially under Henry VIII, and the further development of Parliament, there seemed little opportunity to extol the virtues of the Charter. Some Catholics tried to invoke its first clause protecting the independence of their Church against its absorption into the state at a time of Reformation, but to little avail. Many were wary of anything that might seem to promote rebellion against the monarch. Therefore, surprising as it may still be, Shakespeare's *The Life and Death of King John* (c. 1595) makes no mention of Magna Carta whatsoever.

It was the great Crown versus Parliament crisis of the seventeenth century that saw Magna Carta propelled back to the very forefront of English constitutional politics. At this juncture it was the lawyers who called upon the Charter to defend the rights of individuals against what they saw as the growing despotism of King Charles I (1625–49). Once again, the Crown's need for money and the subsequent treatment of its subjects led to the dust being blown off the Charter. Charles attempted to bypass Parliament and impose a forced loan on the country in 1626; by the following summer he had imprisoned 150 men in London who refused to pay. When Charles re-established a number of feudal taxes that had long been forgotten and violated the Forest Charter, Magna Carta was once again on many lips.

Those who invoked the Charter presented it as part of Britain's ancient constitution and the birthright of her subjects and thus inviolable. As the lawyer Edward Coke declared: 'Magna Carta is such a fellow, that he will have no sovereign.' He reminded Charles that 'the king ought to be under no man, but under God and the law'. During the Civil War period of the 1640s the Charter was repeatedly raised as justification for resistance to an unjust and overbearing king.

Although the medieval meaning of Magna Carta was often misunderstood in this period, it was the symbolism of what it represented that mattered most. Thus when the English rebelled against King James II in 1688, Magna Carta was instrumental in shaping the consequent 1689 Bill of Rights. This 'Act Declaring the Rights and

Liberties of the Subject and Settling the Succession of the Crown' forms the basis of Britain's modern constitution.

As monarchy in Europe veered towards absolutism, Britons could feel that Magna Carta and the Bill of Rights afforded them some protection against such a direction. In 1762, when Arthur Beardmore was arrested for seditious libel, he had arranged things so that he was teaching his son Magna Carta at the time the officers of the law called to his house; this scene became a popular print that was circulated widely. When the French Revolution and subsequent Napoleonic Wars erupted (1789–1815), many in Britain then held up the Magna Carta as a constitutional defence against political terror and dictatorship.

However, in the great reforming period of the Victorian age there was a comprehensive overhaul of legislation that repealed many old and outdated laws, including seventeen clauses of Magna Carta in 1863. By 1892 another five were gone. Further revisions in the twentieth century, such as the 1965 Law Commission's call for the removal of laws that were 'obsolete and superseded', meant that by 1970 only four clauses from 1215 (numbers 1, 13, 39 and 40) remained active in English law.

Yet Magna Carta still looms large in the public consciousness when it comes to ideals of political freedom and rights. One reason for this is due to the phenomenon that while the Charter declined in practical use in Britain, its importance had been growing across the Atlantic in the development of the United States of America.

English colonists establishing a new society in seventeenth-century America deemed Magna Carta to be fundamental law, and thus took precedence over both Crown and Parliament. The General Assembly of Maryland in 1639 declared: 'The inhabitants of this Province shall have all their rights and liberties according to the Great Charter of England.' Before and during the American War of Independence, Magna Carta provided the colonists with an intellectual and constitutional rallying cry against what many deemed to be the tyranny of kings. The seal of the state of Massachusetts, designed by Paul Revere in 1775, depicts a militiaman with a sword in one hand and a copy of Magna Carta in the other. The 1791 Bill of Rights directly echoes clause 39 of the 1215 Charter in its proclamation that no person shall be 'deprived of life, liberty, or property, without due process of law'.

Magna Carta holds great sway in the modern USA. Franklin D. Roosevelt declared in his inaugural address of 1941, 'The democratic aspiration is no mere recent phase in human history … it was written in Magna Carta.' It has been cited over 100 times in the Supreme Court. To mark the legal and constitutional importance of Magna Carta, in 1957 the American Bar Association erected the memorial that now stands at Runnymede. The inscription carved into it reminds us why this ancient medieval parchment remains so relevant today: 'To commemorate Magna Carta, symbol of freedom under law.'

Appendix 5

Magna Carta Translation

JOHN, by the grace of God King of England, Lord of Ireland, Duke of Normandy and Aquitaine, and Count of Anjou, to his archbishops, bishops, abbots, earls, barons, justices, foresters, sheriffs, stewards, servants, and to all his officials and loyal subjects, Greetings.

KNOW THAT BEFORE GOD, for the health of our soul and those of our ancestors and heirs, to the honour of God, the exaltation of the holy Church, and the better ordering of our kingdom, at the advice of our reverend fathers Stephen, archbishop of Canterbury, primate of all England, and cardinal of the holy Roman Church, Henry archbishop of Dublin, William bishop of London, Peter bishop of Winchester, Jocelin bishop of Bath and Glastonbury, Hugh bishop of Lincoln, Walter bishop of Worcester, William bishop of Coventry, Benedict bishop of Rochester, Master Pandulf subdeacon and member of the papal household, Brother Aymeric master of the knighthood of the Temple in England, William Marshal earl of Pembroke, William earl of Salisbury, William earl of Warren, William earl of Arundel, Alan de Galloway constable of Scotland, Warin Fitz Gerald, Peter Fitz Herbert, Hubert de Burgh seneschal of Poitou, Hugh de Neville, Matthew Fitz Herbert, Thomas Basset, Alan Basset, Philip Daubeny, Robert de Roppeley, John Marshal, John Fitz Hugh, and other loyal subjects:

1   FIRST, THAT WE HAVE GRANTED TO GOD, and by this present charter have confirmed for us and our heirs in perpetuity, that the English Church shall be free, and shall have its rights undiminished, and its liberties unimpaired. That we wish this so to be observed, appears from the fact that of our own free will, before the outbreak of the present dispute between us and our barons, we granted and confirmed by charter the freedom of the Church's elections – a right reckoned to be of the greatest necessity and importance to it – and caused this to be confirmed by Pope Innocent III. This freedom we shall observe ourselves, and desire to be observed in good faith by our heirs in perpetuity.

TO ALL FREE MEN OF OUR KINGDOM we have also granted, for us and our heirs for ever, all the liberties written out below, to have and to keep for them and their heirs of us and our heirs:

2   If any earl, baron, or other person that holds lands directly of the Crown, for military service, shall die, and at his death his heir shall be of full age and

owe a 'relief', the heir shall have his inheritance on payment of the ancient scale of 'relief'. That is to say, the heir or heirs of an earl shall pay – 100 for the entire earl's barony, the heir or heirs of a knight 100s, at most for the entire knight's 'fee', and any man that owes less shall pay less, in accordance with the ancient usage of 'fees'.

3   But if the heir of such a person is under age and a ward, when he comes of age he shall have his inheritance without 'relief' or fine.

4   The guardian of the land of an heir who is under age shall take from it only reasonable revenues, customary dues, and feudal services. He shall do this without destruction or damage to men or property. If we have given the guardianship of the land to a sheriff, or to any person answerable to us for the revenues, and he commits destruction or damage, we will exact compensation from him, and the land shall be entrusted to two worthy and prudent men of the same 'fee', who shall be answerable to us for the revenues, or to the person to whom we have assigned them. If we have given or sold to anyone the guardianship of such land, and he causes destruction or damage, he shall lose the guardianship of it, and it shall be handed over to two worthy and prudent men of the same 'fee', who shall be similarly answerable to us.

5   For so long as a guardian has guardianship of such land, he shall maintain the houses, parks, fish preserves, ponds, mills, and everything else pertaining to it, from the revenues of the land itself. When the heir comes of age, he shall restore the whole land to him, stocked with plough teams and such implements of husbandry as the season demands and the revenues from the land can reasonably bear.

6   Heirs may be given in marriage, but not to someone of lower social standing. Before a marriage takes place, it shall be made known to the heir's next-of-kin.

7   At her husband's death, a widow may have her marriage portion and inheritance at once and without trouble. She shall pay nothing for her dower, marriage portion, or any inheritance that she and her husband held jointly on the day of his death. She may remain in her husband's house for forty days after his death, and within this period her dower shall be assigned to her.

8   No widow shall be compelled to marry, so long as she wishes to remain without a husband. But she must give security that she will not marry without royal consent, if she holds her lands of the Crown, or without the consent of whatever other lord she may hold them of.

9   Neither we nor our officials will seize any land or rent in payment of a debt, so long as the debtor has movable goods sufficient to discharge the debt. A debtor's sureties shall not be distrained upon so long as the debtor himself can discharge his debt. If, for lack of means, the debtor is unable to discharge his debt, his sureties shall be answerable for it. If they so desire, they may have the debtor's lands and rents until they have received satisfaction for the debt that they paid for him, unless the debtor can show that he has settled his obligations to them.

10 If anyone who has borrowed a sum of money from Jews dies before the debt has been repaid, his heir shall pay no interest on the debt for so long as he remains under age, irrespective of whom he holds his lands. If such a debt falls into the hands of the Crown, it will take nothing except the principal sum specified in the bond.

11 If a man dies owing money to Jews, his wife may have her dower and pay nothing towards the debt from it. If he leaves children that are under age, their needs may also be provided for on a scale appropriate to the size of his holding of lands. The debt is to be paid out of the residue, reserving the service due to his feudal lords. Debts owed to persons other than Jews are to be dealt with similarly.

12 No 'scutage' or 'aid' may be levied in our kingdom without its general consent, unless it is for the ransom of our person, to make our eldest son a knight, and (once) to marry our eldest daughter. For these purposes only a reasonable 'aid' may be levied. 'Aids' from the city of London are to be treated similarly.

13 The city of London shall enjoy all its ancient liberties and free customs, both by land and by water. We also will and grant that all other cities, boroughs, towns, and ports shall enjoy all their liberties and free customs.

14 To obtain the general consent of the realm for the assessment of an 'aid' – except in the three cases specified above – or a 'scutage', we will cause the archbishops, bishops, abbots, earls, and greater barons to be summoned individually by letter. To those who hold lands directly of us we will cause a general summons to be issued, through the sheriffs and other officials, to come together on a fixed day (of which at least forty days notice shall be given) and at a fixed place. In all letters of summons, the cause of the summons will be stated. When a summons has been issued, the business appointed for the day shall go forward in accordance with the resolution of those present, even if not all those who were summoned have appeared.

15 In future we will allow no one to levy an 'aid' from his free men, except to ransom his person, to make his eldest son a knight, and (once) to marry his eldest daughter. For these purposes only a reasonable 'aid' may be levied.

16 No man shall be forced to perform more service for a knight's 'fee', or other free holding of land, than is due from it.

17 Ordinary lawsuits shall not follow the royal court around, but shall be held in a fixed place.

18 Inquests of novel disseisin, mort d'ancestor, and darrein presentment shall be taken only in their proper county court. We ourselves, or in our absence abroad our chief justice, will send two justices to each county four times a year, and these justices, with four knights of the county elected by the county itself, shall hold the assizes in the county court, on the day and in the place where the court meets.

19 If any assizes cannot be taken on the day of the county court, as many knights and freeholders shall afterwards remain behind, of those who have attended the court, as will suffice for the administration of justice, having regard to the volume of business to be done.

20 For a trivial offence, a free man shall be fined only in proportion to the degree of his offence, and for a serious offence correspondingly, but not so heavily as to deprive him of his livelihood. In the same way, a merchant shall be spared his merchandise, and a husbandman the implements of his husbandry, if they fall upon the mercy of a royal court. None of these fines shall be imposed except by the assessment on oath of reputable men of the neighbourhood.

21 Earls and barons shall be fined only by their equals, and in proportion to the gravity of their offence.

22 A fine imposed upon the lay property of a clerk in holy orders shall be assessed upon the same principles, without reference to the value of his ecclesiastical benefice.

23 No town or person shall be forced to build bridges over rivers except those with an ancient obligation to do so.

24 No sheriff, constable, coroners, or other royal officials are to hold lawsuits that should be held by the royal justices.

25 Every county, hundred, wapentake, and tithing shall remain at its ancient rent, without increase, except the royal demesne manors.

26 If at the death of a man who holds a lay 'fee' of the Crown, a sheriff or royal official produces royal letters patent of summons for a debt due to the Crown, it shall be lawful for them to seize and list movable goods found in the lay 'fee' of the dead man to the value of the debt, as assessed by worthy men. Nothing shall be removed until the whole debt is paid, when the residue shall be given over to the executors to carry out the dead man's will. If no debt is due to the Crown, all the movable goods shall be regarded as the property of the dead man, except the reasonable shares of his wife and children.

27 If a free man dies intestate, his movable goods are to be distributed by his next-of-kin and friends, under the supervision of the Church. The rights of his debtors are to be preserved.

28 No constable or other royal official shall take corn or other movable goods from any man without immediate payment, unless the seller voluntarily offers postponement of this.

29 No constable may compel a knight to pay money for castle-guard if the knight is willing to undertake the guard in person, or with reasonable excuse to supply some other fit man to do it. A knight taken or sent on military service shall be excused from castle-guard for the period of this service.

30 No sheriff, royal official, or other person shall take horses or carts for transport from any free man, without his consent.

31 Neither we nor any royal official will take wood for our castle, or for any other purpose, without the consent of the owner.

32 We will not keep the lands of people convicted of felony in our hand for longer than a year and a day, after which they shall be returned to the lords of the 'fees' concerned.

33 All fish-weirs shall be removed from the Thames, the Medway, and throughout the whole of England, except on the sea coast.

34 The writ called precipe shall not in future be issued to anyone in respect of any holding of land, if a free man could thereby be deprived of the right of trial in his own lord's court.

35 There shall be standard measures of wine, ale, and corn (the London quarter), throughout the kingdom. There shall also be a standard width of dyed cloth, russett, and haberject, namely two ells within the selvedges. Weights are to be standardised similarly.

36 In future nothing shall be paid or accepted for the issue of a writ of inquisition of life or limbs. It shall be given gratis, and not refused.

37 If a man holds land of the Crown by 'fee-farm', 'socage', or 'burgage', and also holds land of someone else for knight's service, we will not have guardianship of his heir, nor of the land that belongs to the other person's 'fee', by virtue of the 'fee-farm', 'socage', or 'burgage', unless the 'fee-farm' owes knight's service. We will not have the guardianship of a man's heir, or of land that he holds of someone else, by reason of any small property that he may hold of the Crown for a service of knives, arrows, or the like.

38 In future no official shall place a man on trial upon his own unsupported statement, without producing credible witnesses to the truth of it.

39 No free man shall be seized or imprisoned, or stripped of his rights or possessions, or outlawed or exiled, or deprived of his standing in any other way, nor will we proceed with force against him, or send others to do so, except by the lawful judgement of his equals or by the law of the land.

40 To no one will we sell, to no one deny or delay right or justice.

41 All merchants may enter or leave England unharmed and without fear, and may stay or travel within it, by land or water, for purposes of trade, free from all illegal exactions, in accordance with ancient and lawful customs. This, however, does not apply in time of war to merchants from a country that is at war with us. Any such merchants found in our country at the outbreak of war shall be detained without injury to their persons or property, until we or our chief justice have discovered how our own merchants are being treated in the country at war with us. If our own merchants are safe they shall be safe too.

42 In future it shall be lawful for any man to leave and return to our kingdom unharmed and without fear, by land or water, preserving his allegiance to us, except in time of war, for some short period, for the common benefit of the realm. People that have been imprisoned or outlawed in accordance with the law of the land, people from a country that is at war with us, and merchants – who shall be dealt with as stated above – are excepted from this provision.

43 If a man holds lands of any 'escheat' such as the 'honour' of Wallingford, Nottingham, Boulogne, Lancaster, or of other 'escheats' in our hand that are baronies, at his death his heir shall give us only the 'relief' and service that he would have made to the baron, had the barony been in the baron's hand. We will hold the 'escheat' in the same manner as the baron held it.

44   People who live outside the forest need not in future appear before the royal justices of the forest in answer to general summonses, unless they are actually involved in proceedings or are sureties for someone who has been seized for a forest offence.

45   We will appoint as justices, constables, sheriffs, or other officials, only men that know the law of the realm and are minded to keep it well.

46   All barons who have founded abbeys, and have charters of English kings or ancient tenure as evidence of this, may have guardianship of them when there is no abbot, as is their due.

47   All forests that have been created in our reign shall at once be disafforested. River-banks that have been enclosed in our reign shall be treated similarly.

48   All evil customs relating to forests and warrens, foresters, warreners, sheriffs and their servants, or river-banks and their wardens, are at once to be investigated in every county by twelve sworn knights of the county, and within forty days of their enquiry the evil customs are to be abolished completely and irrevocably. But we, or our chief justice if we are not in England, are first to be informed.

49   We will at once return all hostages and charters delivered up to us by Englishmen as security for peace or for loyal service.

50   We will remove completely from their offices the kinsmen of Gerard de Athée, and in future they shall hold no offices in England. The people in question are Engelard de Cigogné, Peter, Guy, and Andrew de Chanceaux, Guy de Cigogné, Geoffrey de Martigny and his brothers, Philip Marc and his brothers, with Geoffrey his nephew, and all their followers.

51   As soon as peace is restored, we will remove from the kingdom all the foreign knights, bowmen, their attendants, and the mercenaries that have come to it, to its harm, with horses and arms.

52   To any man whom we have deprived or dispossessed of lands, castles, liberties, or rights, without the lawful judgement of his equals, we will at once restore these. In cases of dispute the matter shall be resolved by the judgement of the twenty-five barons referred to below in the clause for securing the peace (61). In cases, however, where a man was deprived or dispossessed of something without the lawful judgement of his equals by our father King Henry or our brother King Richard, and it remains in our hands or is held by others under our warranty, we shall have respite for the period commonly allowed to Crusaders, unless a lawsuit had been begun, or an enquiry had been made at our order, before we took the Cross as a Crusader. On our return from the Crusade, or if we abandon it, we will at once render justice in full.

53   We shall have similar respite in rendering justice in connexion with forests that are to be disafforested, or to remain forests, when these were first afforested by our father Henry or our brother Richard; with the guardianship of lands in another person's 'fee', when we have hitherto had this by virtue of a 'fee' held of us for knight's service by a third party; and with abbeys founded in another person's 'fee', in which the lord of the 'fee' claims to

own a right. On our return from the Crusade, or if we abandon it, we will at once do full justice to complaints about these matters.

54 No one shall be arrested or imprisoned on the appeal of a woman for the death of any person except her husband.

55 All fines that have been given to us unjustly and against the law of the land, and all fines that we have exacted unjustly, shall be entirely remitted or the matter decided by a majority judgement of the twenty-five barons referred to below in the clause for securing the peace (61) together with Stephen, archbishop of Canterbury, if he can be present, and such others as he wishes to bring with him. If the archbishop cannot be present, proceedings shall continue without him, provided that if any of the twenty-five barons has been involved in a similar suit himself, his judgement shall be set aside, and someone else chosen and sworn in his place, as a substitute for the single occasion, by the rest of the twenty-five.

56 If we have deprived or dispossessed any Welshmen of lands, liberties, or anything else in England or in Wales, without the lawful judgement of their equals, these are at once to be returned to them. A dispute on this point shall be determined in the Marches by the judgement of equals. English law shall apply to holdings of land in England, Welsh law to those in Wales, and the law of the Marches to those in the Marches. The Welsh shall treat us and ours in the same way.

57 In cases where a Welshman was deprived or dispossessed of anything, without the lawful judgement of his equals, by our father King Henry or our brother King Richard, and it remains in our hands or is held by others under our warranty, we shall have respite for the period commonly allowed to Crusaders, unless a lawsuit had been begun, or an enquiry had been made at our order, before we took the Cross as a Crusader. But on our return from the Crusade, or if we abandon it, we will at once do full justice according to the laws of Wales and the said regions.

58 We will at once return the son of Llywelyn, all Welsh hostages, and the charters delivered to us as security for the peace.

59 With regard to the return of the sisters and hostages of Alexander, king of Scotland, his liberties and his rights, we will treat him in the same way as our other barons of England, unless it appears from the charters that we hold from his father William, formerly king of Scotland, that he should be treated otherwise. This matter shall be resolved by the judgement of his equals in our court.

60 All these customs and liberties that we have granted shall be observed in our kingdom in so far as concerns our own relations with our subjects. Let all men of our kingdom, whether clergy or laymen, observe them similarly in their relations with their own men.

61 SINCE WE HAVE GRANTED ALL THESE THINGS for God, for the better ordering of our kingdom, and to allay the discord that has arisen between us and our barons, and since we desire that they shall be enjoyed in their entirety, with lasting strength, for ever, we give and grant to the barons the following security:

The barons shall elect twenty-five of their number to keep, and cause to be observed with all their might, the peace and liberties granted and confirmed to them by this charter.

If we, our chief justice, our officials, or any of our servants offend in any respect against any man, or transgress any of the articles of the peace or of this security, and the offence is made known to four of the said twenty-five barons, they shall come to us – or in our absence from the kingdom to the chief justice – to declare it and claim immediate redress. If we, or in our absence abroad the chief justice, make no redress within forty days, reckoning from the day on which the offence was declared to us or to him, the four barons shall refer the matter to the rest of the twenty-five barons, who may distrain upon and assail us in every way possible, with the support of the whole community of the land, by seizing our castles, lands, possessions, or anything else saving only our own person and those of the queen and our children, until they have secured such redress as they have determined upon. Having secured the redress, they may then resume their normal obedience to us.

Any man who so desires may take an oath to obey the commands of the twenty-five barons for the achievement of these ends, and to join with them in assailing us to the utmost of his power. We give public and free permission to take this oath to any man who so desires, and at no time will we prohibit any man from taking it. Indeed, we will compel any of our subjects who are unwilling to take it to wear it at our command.

If one of the twenty-five barons dies or leaves the country, or is prevented in any other way from discharging his duties, the rest of them shall choose another baron in his place, at their discretion, who shall be duly sworn in as they were.

In the event of disagreement among the twenty-five barons on any matter referred to them for decision, the verdict of the majority present shall have the same validity as a unanimous verdict of the whole twenty-five, whether these were all present or some of those summoned were unwilling or unable to appear.

The twenty-five barons shall swear to obey all the above articles faithfully, and shall cause them to be obeyed by others to the best of their power.

We will not seek to procure from anyone, either by our own efforts or those of a third party, anything by which any part of these concessions or liberties might be revoked or diminished. Should such a thing be procured, it shall be null and void and we will at no time make use of it, either ourselves or through a third party.

62   We have remitted and pardoned fully to all men any ill-will, hurt, or grudges that have arisen between us and our subjects, whether clergy or laymen, since the beginning of the dispute. We have in addition remitted fully, and for our own part have also pardoned, to all clergy and laymen any offences committed as a result of the said dispute between Easter in the sixteenth year of our reign [i.e. 1215] and the restoration of peace.

In addition we have caused letters patent to be made for the barons, bearing witness to this security and to the concessions set out above, over the seals of Stephen archbishop of Canterbury, Henry archbishop of Dublin, the other bishops named above, and Master Pandulf.

63 IT IS ACCORDINGLY OUR WISH AND COMMAND that the English Church shall be free, and that men in our kingdom shall have and keep all these liberties, rights, and concessions, well and peaceably in their fullness and entirety for them and their heirs, of us and our heirs, in all things and all places for ever.

Both we and the barons have sworn that all this shall be observed in good faith and without deceit. Witness the abovementioned people and many others.

Given by our hand in the meadow that is called Runnymede, between Windsor and Staines, on the fifteenth day of June in the seventeenth year of our reign [i.e. 1215: the new regnal year began on 28 May].

Notes

Introduction Warfare and Medieval History

1 C. von Clausewitz, *On War*, Harmondsworth, 1968 [original German edition 1832], 101, 402, 119. John Keegan, following J. J. Graham's 1908 translation (used here in the Penguin Classics edition), discusses the interpretation of this famous quote on politics and war in J. Keegan, *A History of Warfare*, London, 1993, 3.

2 A detailed analysis of this is presented in C. Allmand, *Henry V*, London, 1992, chs. 19 and 20, summarised, 435–8.

3 Counter-factual history based on military events is hypothesised in R. Cowley (ed), *What If?*, London, 2000. See also idem (ed), *More What If?*, London, 2004; A. Roberts, *What Might Have Been*, 2004; N. Ferguson, *Virtual History: Alternatives and Counterfactuals*, London, 1997.

4 The millennium saw a proliferation of studies on the battles of 1066: J. Bradbury, *The Battle of Hastings*, Gloucester, 1999; S. Morillo (ed), *The Battle of Hastings*, Woodbridge, 1996; F. McLynn, *1066: The Year of Three Battles*, London, 1999; K. de Vries, *The Norwegian Invasion of England in 1066*, Woodbridge, 2000; M. Lawson, *The Battle of Hastings 1066*, Gloucester, 2002. See also F. W. Brooks, *The Battle of Stamford Bridge*, York, 1963; I. Walker, *Harold: The Last Anglo-Saxon King*, Gloucester, 1997, 142–82.

5 We shall see later how the Papacy, acting as a temporal and diplomatic institution, influenced events and bestowed crusading status upon the conflict; but this 'crusade' was always patently political, and not of the same nature as those perpetrated against the Muslims or even against heretics (the Albigensian crusade directed against the Cathars in southern France was launched in 1208).

6 Kingship roles are discussed in R. Kaeuper, *War, Justice and Public Order: England and France in the Later Middle Ages*, Oxford, 1988, 1, 95–7, 342; R. Kaeuper, *Chivalry and Violence in Medieval Europe*, Oxford, 1999, 93–5 and passim; P. Maddern, *Violence and Social Order: East Anglia, 1422–1442*, Oxford, 1992, 12–14; W. Ullman, *Medieval Political Thought*, Harmondsworth, 1979 (originally 1965); idem., *Principles of Government and Politics in the Middle Ages*, London, 1961; J. E. A. Joliffe, *Angevin Kingship*, 2nd edn., 1963, ch. 1; S. B Chrimes, *An Introduction to the Administrative History of Medieval England*, 2nd edn., Oxford, 1959, 1–27; W. L. Warren, *The Governance of Anglo-Norman and Angevin England, 1086–1272*, London, 1987, 15–19, 177–82; E. Kantorowicz, *The King's Two Bodies: A Study in Medieval Political Theology*, Princeton, 1957; A. Duggan, *Kings and Kingship in Medieval Europe*, London, 1993; M. Clauss, 'Kings as Military Leaders', *OEMW*, Oxford, 2010, ii, 466; S. McGlynn, *By Sword and Fire: Cruelty and Atrocity in Medieval Warfare*, London, 2008, 36–61.

7 P. Contamine, *War in the Middle Ages*, trans. M. Jones, Oxford, 1984, xii.

8 An example of this line of thought is encapsulated in the title of a scholarly work: C. Kidd, *British Identities Before Nationalism: Ethnicity and Nationhood in the Atlantic World, 1600–1800*, Cambridge, 1999. I shall later endeavour to loosen the over-prescriptive semantic terminology and taxonomical divisions of nationalism, ethnicity and nationhood.

9   For a fuller analysis of Wendover's utuility in matters of warfare, see S. McGlynn, 'Roger of Wendover and the Wars of Henry III, 1216–34', in B. Weiler and I. Rowlands (eds), *Britain and Europe During the Reign of Henry III*, Aldershot, 2002.

10 Wendover puts John's army in 1213 at '60,000' strong (RW, ii, 67). He also employs this figure for the Muslim enemy at Seville in 1189 (this figure is arrived at from '47,000' casualties and '13,000' survivors) (RW, i, 157). Jordan Fantosme, an otherwise excellent contemporary source for medieval warfare, uses the same figure of 60,000 in an even more implausible context at the town of Dol in 1173: 'The knights in their battle array have come forth from the town: some sixty thousand of them…' (R. C. Johnston, ed. and trans., *Jordan Fantosme's Chronicle*, Oxford, 1981, 15).

11 Simeon of Durham, *Opera Omnia*, ed. T. Arnold, 2 vols., RS, London, 1882–85, ii, 191–2. Simeon (fl. 1100–1150) was not an eyewitness to these events, but was well informed. For the context of this episode, see J. Gillingham, 'Conquering the Barbarians: War and Chivalry in Britain and Ireland', *The English in the Twelfth Century: Imperialism, National Identity and Political Values*, Woodbridge, 2000, and McGlynn, *By Sword and Fire*, 202, 208–16.

12 Clausewitz, *On War*, p. 163. Tolstoy captures this well in *War and Peace*, Harmondsworth, 1978 edn., 766.

13 Dust was a problem at the summer Battle of Bouvines. Sleet hampered visibility at the Battle of Towton in March 1461: A. W. Boardman, *The Battle of Towton*, Gloucester, 1994, 107 ff.; P. A. Haigh, *The Military Campaigns of the Wars of the Roses*, Gloucester, 1995, 60–3.

14 J. Gillingham, 'Richard I and the Science of War in the Middle Ages', *Richard Coeur de Lion*, 1994, 212. Verbruggen also makes the case for vernacular sources over Latin ones: J. F. Verbruggen, *The Art of Warfare in the Western Europe During the Middle Ages From the Eighth Century to 1340*, trans. S. Willard and R. W. Southern, 2nd edn., Woodbridge, 1997, 10–14. For studies of contemporary sources and their uses for medieval warfare, see: K. De Vries, 'The Use of Chronicles in Recreating Medieval Military History', *JMMH*, ii; C. Hanley, *War and Combat: The Evidence of Old French Literature, 1150–1270*, Woodbridge, 2003; C. Saunders, F. Le Sau and N. Thomas (eds), *Writing War: Medieval Literary Responses to Warfare*, Woodbridge, 2004.

15 J. Beeler, *Warfare in Feudal Europe, 730–1200*, Ithaca, 1971, xii.

16 For the priest at Le Puiset: Suger, *Vita Ludovici Grossi Regis*, ed. H. Waquet, Paris, 1964 edn., 138. For laws affecting the clergy: M. Keen, *The Laws of War in the Late Middle Ages*, London, 1965, 195; T. Meron, *Henry's Wars and Shakespeare's Laws: Perspectives on the Law of War in the Later Middle Ages*, Oxford, 1993, 96–101. Christopher Tyerman has observed 'the clergy's love of war in general': C. Tyerman, *England and the Crusades, 1095–1588*, Chicago, 1988, 262. For aspects of the clergy and war in general: T. Reuter, 'Episcopi cum sua militia: the Prelate as Warrior in the Early Staufer Era', in T. Reuter (ed), *Warriors and Churchmen in the High Middle Ages*, London, 1992; the section on 'Violence and the medieval clergy' in D. J. Kagay and L. J Andrew Villalon (eds), *The Final Argument: The Imprint of Violence on Society in Medieval and Early Modern Europe*, Woodbridge, 1998, pp. 3–52; B. Arnold, 'German Bishops and their Military Retinues in Medieval Europe', *German History*, 7 (2), 1989, 161–83; M. Prestwich, *Armies and Warfare in the Middle Ages: The English Experience*, New Haven, 1996, 168–70; Kaeuper, *Chivalry and Violence*, 41–84; McGlynn, *By Sword and Fire*, 61–71; A. Murray, 'Roles in Warfare of Clergy', *OEMW*, i, 404–6. For a fuller discussion of what follows, see McGlynn, 'Roger of Wendover'.

17 For Guérin's career, see J. Baldwin, *The Government of Philip Augustus*, Berkeley, 1986, 115–22.

18 Quoted in Contamine, *War*, 211.

19 Barbara English, 'Towns, Mottes and Ring-works of the Conquest', in A. Ayton and J. L. Price (eds), *The Medieval Military Revolution: State, Society and Military Change in Medieval and Early Modern Europe*, London, 1995, 45.

20 F. Paxton, 'Power and the Power to Heal: The Cult of St Sigismund of Burgundy', *Early Medieval Europe*, 2 (2), 1993, 101.

21 H. Cowdrey, 'Pope Gregory VII', *Medieval History*, 1 (1), 1991, 28.

22 Quoted by Timothy Reuter in Reuter, 'Episcopi cum sua militia', 93.

23 St Bernard, himself a son of a knight, was originally destined for the knighthood. There is a large literature on the military orders: M. Barber, *The New Knighthood: A*

History of the Order of the Temple, Cambridge, 1994; A. Forey, *The Military Orders: From the Twelfth to the Early Fourteenth Centuries*, London, 1992; D. Selwood, *Knights of the Cloister: Templars and Hospitallers in Central-Southern Occitania, 1100–1300*, Woodbridge, 1999; J. M. Upton-Ward, ed. and trans., *The Rule of the Templars*, Woodbridge, 1992; H. Nicholson, *Templars, Hospitallers and Teutonic Knights: Images of the Military Orders, 1128–1291*, Leicester, 1995; idem., *The Knights Templar: A New History*, Gloucester, 2001; J. Upton-Ward, *The Military Orders: Volume IV*, Ashgate, 2008; L. Marvin, 'Monastic Military Orders', *RGMH*, 383–4; J. Porter, S. Cerrini and C. Jensen, 'Military Orders', *OEMW*, iii, 76–85. Brother Guérin was a Knight Templar (see n. 17 above).

24   C. Oman, *The Art of War in the Middle Ages*, Oxford, 1885; idem., revised and expanded 3rd edn., 2 vols., London, 1924.

25   H. Delbrück, *Medieval Warfare*, trans. W. J. Renfroe, Lincoln, 1982 (original German edn. 1924). For a very interesting but ultimately unconvincing reassessment of Delbrück and army sizes, see B. Bachrach, 'Early Medieval Military Demography: Some Observations on the Methods of Hans Delbrück', in D. J. Kagay and L. J. Andrew Villalon (eds), *The Circle of War in the Middle Ages*, Woodbridge, 1999.

26   R. C. Smail, *Crusading Warfare, 1097–1193*, Cambridge, 1956.

27   Note the reminisces of M. Keen, *Nobles, Knights and Men-at-Arms in the Middle Ages*, London, 1996, ix.

28   J. F. Verbruggen, *The Art of Warfare in Western Europe During the Middle Ages From the Eighth Century to 1340*.

29   Ibid., 16.

30   See ns. 7 and 14.

31   Critical evaluations of this expansive literature are to be found in: S. McGlynn, 'Land Warfare, 1000–1500', in C. Messenger (ed), *Reader's Guide to Military History*, London, 2002; J. France, 'Recent Writing on Medieval Warfare: From the Fall of Rome to c. 1300', *Journal of Military History*, 65 (2), 2001 (my thanks to Prof France for forwarding an early copy of this comprehensive article). The literature on medieval warfare is also discussed in: M. Strickland, 'Introduction', in M. Strickland (ed), *Anglo-Norman Warfare: Studies in Late Anglo-Saxon an Anglo-Norman Military Organization and Warfare*, Woodbridge, 1992 (itself an invaluable collection of revisionist papers chiefly from the 1980s); A. Curry, 'Medieval Warfare: England and Her Continental Neighbours, Eleventh to the Fourteenth Centuries', *JMH*, 21 (3), 1997; S. McGlynn, 'The Myths of Medieval Warfare', *History Today*, 44 (1), 1994; idem., 'Battle Honours', *Medieval World*, no.7, 1992; idem., 'Medieval Warfare', *European Review of History-Revue Européene d'Histoire*, 4 (2), 1997.

32   See n.25.

33   John France, *Western Warfare in the Age of the Crusades, 1000–1300*, 1999.

34   William Blake, *The Complete Poems*, Harmondsworth, 1977, pp. 59–60.

1 Enemies: The Angevin-Capetian Struggle

35   *Gesta Stephani*, eds. K.R. Potter and R.H.C. Davis, Oxford, 1976, 224.

36   J.C Holt considers this treaty as neither a treaty nor a charter, but rather a 'formal promulgation of terms previously agreed.' ('The Treaty of Winchester', in Edmund King (ed), *The Anarchy of King Stephen Reign*, Oxford, 1994, 293–5). Holt's essay is one of a number of valuable pieces in this important collection. Stephen's reign has seen a proliferation of significant recent studies, notably: Keith Stringer, *The Reign of Stephen*, London., 1993; R.H.C Davis, *King Stephen*, 3rd edn, Harlow, 1990; Jim Bradbury, *Stephen and Matilda: The Civil War of 1139–53*, Gloucester, 1996; David Crouch, *The Reign of King Stephen, 1135–1154*, Harlow, 2000; Donald Matthew, *King Stephen*, London, 2002; Paul Dalton and Graeme White (eds), *King Stephen's Reign, 1135–1154*, Woodbridge, 2008.

37   The Capetian house ruled France from 987 to 1328. Louis has come in for much criticism for divorcing Eleanor and hence losing such a great amount of territory, but it should be noted that he did go on to produce a son and thus ensured uncomplicated further successions to the crown; France therefore avoided the strife caused by disputed successions in England. For Capetian France, see: Elizabeth Hallam, *Capetian France, 987–1328*, Harlow, 1980 (2nd edition with Judith Everard, 2001); Jean Dunbabin, *France in the Making, 843–1180*, Oxford, 1985; Robert Fawtier, *The Capetian Kings of France:*

Monarchy and Nation, 987–1328, Basingstoke, 1960; Georges Duby, *France in the Middle Ages, 987–1460,* Oxford, 1991; Ivan Gobry, *Les Capétiens,* Paris, 2001; Jim Bradbury, *The Capetians,* 2007.

38 Ralph of Diss remarked on Henry's itinerant kingship: 'now in Ireland, now in England, now in Normandy, he must fly rather than travel by horse or ship' (*Radulphi de Diceto Opera Historica,* ed. W. Stubbs, RS, 1876, i, 351

39 For Eleanor: Bonnie Wheeler and John C. Parsons, *Eleanor of Aquitaine: Lord and Lady,* Basingstoke, 2002; D.D.R. Owen, *Eleanor of Aquitaine: Queen and Legend,* Oxford, 1993. Her life is also comprehensively covered, if a little romantically, by Amy Kelly, *Eleanor of Aquitaine and the Four Kings,* London, 1950; and more recently by Alison Weir, *Eleanor of Aquitaine: A Life,* London, 2000. Two useful articles are: Jane Martindale, 'Eleanor of Aquitaine: The last Years', in Church, *King John;* and Ralph V. Turner, 'Eleanor of Aquitaine and her Children', *JMH,* 14 (3), 1998.

40 A.L. Poole covers these events and discusses the importance of the gains in *From Domesday Book to Magna Carta, 1087–1216,* 2nd edn, Oxford, 1955, 323–6. For these and other territories see *Richard Couer de Lion,* 25–33.

41 For Henry's reign, the best account is the magisterial work by W.L. Warren, *Henry II,* London, 1973. For his early years, Emilie Amt's *The Accesion of Henry II in England, Royal Government restored, 1149–1159,* Woodbridge, 1993, is very insightful. See also Richard Barber, *Henry Plantagenet,* Woodbridge, new edn, 2001. An excellent collection of papers has recently been published: Christopher Harper-Bill and Nicholas Vincent (eds), *Henry II: New Interpretations,* Woodbridge, 2007. Also of interest is Ruth Kennedy and Simon Meecham-Jones (eds), *Writers of the Reign of Henry II,* Basingstoke, 2006. Of relevance is John Gillingham, 'Conquering Kings: Some Twelfth-Century Reflections on Henry II and Richard I, in *Richard Couer de Lion.* For a detailed account of events in 1173–4, see M. Thomas, *War of the Generations: The Revolt of 1173–4,* Michigan, 1980. Military aspects of this war are authoritatively dealt with in two papers by Matthew Strickland: 'Securing the North: Invasion and the Strategy of Defence in Twelfth-Century Anglo–Scottish Warfare', in *ANW;* 'Arms and the Men: Loyalty and Lordship in Jordan Fantasome's Chronicle', in Christopher Harper-Bill, *Medieval Knightood, 4,* Woodbridge, 1992. Also important here is John D. Hosler, *Henry II: A Medieval Soldier at War, 1147–1189,* Woodbridge, 2007. The danger of 1183 was further exacerbated by Lord Rhys of Wales, who had taken the opportunity of Henry's distraction by these troubles to lead a Welsh Rebellion, as Gillingham explores in 'Henry II, Richard I and the Lord Rhys', *Peritia,* 10, 1996 (I am grateful to Prof Gillingham for allowing me to read an advanced copy of this paper).

42 W. Stubbs (ed), *Itinerarium Regis Ricardi* in *Chronicles and Memorials of The Reign of Richard I,* 2 vols, RS, 1864, i, xvii. The standard account of Richard's reign, is John Gillingham's *Richard I,* London, 1999. This is augmented by his *Richard Couer de Lion,* London, 1994. This can be usefully supplemented by Kate Norgate, *Richard the Lionheart,* London, 1924; Jean Flori, *Richard the Lionheart: Knight and King,* trans. Jean Birrell, Westport, 2006 and Janet Nelson (ed), *Richard Coeur de Lion in History and Myth,* London 1992. An important collection of articles on Richard is to be found in Louis Le Roc'h Morgère (ed), *Richard Couer de Lion, Roi d'Angleterre, Duc de Normandie,* Caen, 1999. Less favourable views of Richard are to be found in: Ralph V. Turner and Richard R. Heiser, *The Reign of Richard Lionheart: Ruler of the Angevin Empire, 1189–1199,* Harlow, 2000, which offers a measured alternative perspective; John Appleby, *England Without Richard, 1189–1199,* London, 1965; and especially James Brundage, *Richard Lionheart,* New York, 1973. The debate on Richard is continued in M. Markowski. 'Richard Lionheart: Bad King. Bad Crusader?, *Journal of Medieval History,* 23, 1997. Ralph V. Turner's 'Good or Bad Kinsghip? The Case of Richard the Lionheart', *Haskin's Society Journal,* 8, Woodbridge, 1999, is a sustained critique of Gillingham's defence of Richard; although extremely helpful in summarising the debate, the article, in common with all Ricardian studies, fails to consider the grand strategy addressed in this chapter and is thus too sympathetic to John's predicament in 1203–04.

43 See Richard Benjamin, 'A Forty Years War: Toulouse and the Plantagenets,' *Historical Research,* 61 and P.N. Lewis, 'The Wars of Richard I in the West,' unpublished MPhil dissertation, University of London, 1977, for the military ramifications of this.

44   J.C. Holt, *Magna Carta and Medieval Government*, London, 1985, 82. Richard Heiser has demonstrated that Richard's judicious appointments to shrievalties indicate care and foresight: 'Richard I and His Appointments to English Shrievalties', *EHR*, 112 (445), 1997. He also makes the valid point that Richard's constant shuffling and exploitation of the sherrif's office was common medieval practice and therefore not proof of Richard's personal cupidity; Philip Augustus treated the office of *bailli* in a similar fashion and is praised for doing so (p.10).

45   J. Cookson, 'What if Napoleon had Landed?', *History Today*, 53 (9), 2003, 17.

46   Robert J. McMahon, *The Cold War*, Oxford, 2003, 12.

47   Anthony Tuck, *Crown and Nobility*, 1985, 186. See pp. 177–86 for a discussion of strategy during this period. Charles VI called off the invasion in November, probably due to financial reasons.

48   WB, i, 204.

49   Holt, *Magna Carta and Medieval Government*, 39.

50   His classic study, *The Angevin Empire*, reprinted in *Richard Couer de Lion*, discusses the economic issues, especially on 46–8. The Angevin Empire is also explored in Ralph V. Turner, 'The Problem of Survival for the Angevin "Empire": Henry's II's and his Sons' Vision versus Late Twelfth-Century Realities, *American Historical Review*, 100 (1), 1995; John Le Patourel, 'Angevin Succesions and the Angevin Empire', in his *Feudal Empires: Norman and Plantagent*, London, 1984; Richard Benjamin, 'The Angevin Empire', in Nigel Saul (ed), *England in Europe, 1066–1453*, London, 1994; Robert Bartlett, *England under the Norman and Angevin Kings, 1075–1225*, Oxford 2000, 21–8; Warren, *Henry II*, 207–37; Donald Matthew, *Britain and the Continent, 1000–1300*, London, 2005, 88–128.
     Adam Smith, writing in 1776, noted the prerequisite importance of river systems to growing economies: 'So it is upon the sea coast, and along the banks of navigable rivers, that industry of every kind naturally begins to divide and improve itself … A broad wheel wagon attended by two men and drawn by eight horses in about six weeks' time carries and brings back between London and Edinburgh near four tons of goods. In about the same time a ship navigated by six or eight men and sailing between the ports of London and Leith frequently carries and brings back 200 ton weight of goods' (Adam Smith *The Wealth of Nations*, Harmondsworth 1982, [originally published in 1776],122. Thus the continental Angevin Empire, despite its disparate regions, distance from England and its separation from it by sea, was geographically and economically well-placed to be a thriving commercial entity. For geographical determinants of economic growth, see also Jeffery Sachs, 'The Limits of Convergance: Nature, Nurture and Growth', *The Economist*, 14 June, 1997. For the economy in Richard and John's reign, additional to Gillingham above, see the essays by Jim Bolton and Paul Latimer in Church, *King John*. The most up-to-date survey is James Masschaele, 'The English Economy in the Age of Magna Carta', in Janet Loengard (ed.), *Magna Carta and the England of King John*, Woodbridge, 2010.

51   *RHF*, 24, 758.

52   For example: Michael Clanchy, *England and its Rulers, 1066–1272*, London, 1983, 112; Gillingham, *Richard Couer de Lion*, 8.

53   *The Song of Dermot and the Earl*, ed. and trans. G.H. Opren, Oxford, 1892, 22.

54   Bartlett, *England Under the Norman and Angevin Kings*, 23.

55   Turner, 'Survival of the Angevin "Empire"', 88–9.

56   Good general surveys of this struggle are provided in the appropriate chapters of Poole, *Domesday Book;* Clancy, *England and Its Rulers;* Frank Barlow, *The Feudal Kingdom of England, 1042–1216*, 4th edn, Harlow 1998; Gillingham, *Richard Couer de Lion*; Kate Norgate, *England Under the Angevin Kings*, 2 vols, ii, London 1887; Hallam, *Capetian France;* Achille Luchaire *Philippe Auguste et son Temp*, Paris 1980 (originally published in 1902); Malcolm Vale, *The Ancient Enemy: England, France and Europe from the Angevins to the Tudors*, 2007.

57   There are a number of important accounts of John's reign, analysing both his domestic and foreign policies in substantial details. W.L Warren offers the standard survey, on which I have relied heavily, *King John*, 3rd edn, London, 1998. To this may be added three differing but excellent surveys: R.V. Turner, *King John*, London, 1994; Kate

Norgate, *John Lackland,* London, 1902; Sidney Painter, *The Reign of King John,* Baltimore, 1949. Also enjoyable, if less rigourous, is Alan Lloyd, *King John,* Trowbridge, 1973. A useful brief survey, with documents, can be found in J.A.P. Jones, *King John and Magna Carta,* Harlow, 1971. An important collection of conference papers has already been referenced for John's reign, counter-revisionist in tone: Church, *King John.* Also of great value is the collection from Janet S. Loengard (ed) *Magna Carta and the England of King John,* Woodbridge, 2010. John's rule is afforded much detailed discussions in Gillingham, *Richard Couer de Lion* and in the essential writings of J. C. Holt: *Magna Carta and Medieval Government; Magna Carta,* 2nd edn, Cambridge, 1992; idem, *The Northerners,* 2nd edn, Oxford 1992.

58   W.C. Sellar and R.J. Yeatman, *1066 and All That,* Gloucester, 1993 [1930], 26–8.

59   Norgate, *John,* 286.

60   Lloyd, *John,* 392. This conclusion is based on Gervase of Canterbury's contemporary opinion, expressed in *The Historical Works of Gervase of Canterbury,* ed. W. Stubbs, RS, 1880, ii, 92–3. Ralph Turner also argues that John deserves a favourable assessment of his generalship: Turner, 'King John's Military Reputation Reconsidered', *JMH,* 19, 1993.

61   For an example of the extremes taken in nineteenth-century Britain by admirers of chivalry, see Ian Anstruther, *The Knight and the Umbrella,* London, 1963. For a brief discussion of this phenomenon, see my review article in *History Today,* 47 (2), 1997. A broad survey is given in Mark Girouard, *The Return to Camelot,* Yale, 1981.

62   Holt writes that John's 'total achievement was enormous, fit to stand alongside that of Henry II or Edward I. Together, these two and John represent a standard which was never again equalled in the medieval period' (*Magna Carta and Medieval Government,* 96).

63   Colin Richmond, 'Identity and Morality: Power and Politics During the Wars of the Roses', in *Power and Identity in the Middle Ages: Essays in Memory of Rees Davies,* Oxford, 2007, 234.

64   Turner, *King John,* 3–4.

65   The collection is Church, *King John.* David Carpenter and Nicholas Vincent have engaged in a robust debate over 1199 and the origins of chancery rolls in Nicholas Vincent (ed), *Records, Administration and Aristocratic Society in the Anglo-Norman Realm,* Woodbridge, 2010, xvi–xviii, 1–28. See also Mark Hagger's article in the same volume, 'Theory and Practice in the Making of Twelfth-Century Pipe Rolls', which raises questions over the reliability of even Pipe Rolls. The quotation is from David Crouch, 'Baronial Paranoia in King John's Reign', in Leongard, *Magna Carta* 51, 62.

66   Gerald of Wales in *Giraldi Cambrensis Opera,* (8 vols), eds. J.S. Brewer, J.F. Dimcock and G.F Warner, RS. 1861–91, viii, 214; Richard of Devizes in *Chronicon,* ed. and trans. J.T. Appleby, London, 1963, 32; the Barnwell chronicler (BC) in *Memoriale Walteri de Coventria,* ed. W. Stubbs, 2 vols, RS, 1879–80, ii, 232, Anonymous of Béthune in *Histoire des Ducs de Normandie et des Rois d'Angleterre,* ed. F. Michelet, Paris, 1840; the anonymous biographer of William Marshal (HWM) in *History of William Marshal,* 3 vols., ed. A. Holden, D. Crouch and S. Gregory, Anglo-Norman Text Society, 2002–2006, 124–7 (I will use page rather than line numbers); I am indebted to the kindness of Prof Holden, Dr Gregory and especially Prof Crouch for their kindness in allowing me to see draft versions of this invaluable edition.

67   Charles Petit-Dutaillis, *The Feudal Monarchy in France and England,* London, 1936, 215.

68   Vivian Green, *The Madness of Kings: Personal Trauma and the Fate of Nations,* Gloucester, 1993, 43–7.

69   Warren, 71. This comment beautifully encapsulates more about John than any amount of psychoanalysis.

70   Gillingham, *Richard I,* 166–71; McGlynn, *By Sword and Fire,* 100–12. Bradbury sums up the differing perceptions of the two kings thus: 'Richard may have been rash and aggressive, but he was widely respected; his brother came to be respected by none': Jim Bradbury, *Philip Augustus: King of France, 1180–1223,* Harlow, 1998, 116.

71   See Gervase, n. 20. The term becomes more perjorative as John's reign progresses. For discussions of John's image see, in particular: Warren, ch. 1; Turner, ch. 1; and Turner's same argument in 'King John in his Context: a Comparison with his Contemporaries', in *The Haskins Society Journal,* 3, 1991; C. Warren Hollister, 'King John and the Historians', *Journal of British Studies,* 1, 1961. For a modern comparison with difficulties

in the perceptions of political leadership, see also Sean McGlynn, 'British Nationalism and Europe: a Medieval Comparison', *Politics*, 16(3), 1996.

72 Winston Churchill, *A History of the English Speaking Peoples*, I, London, 1956, 190.

73 Jean Flori, *Philippe Auguste*, Paris, 2007, 9. My translation.

74 Good broad accounts of the salient features of Philip's reign can be found in: Hallam, *Capetian France*; Robert Fawtier, *Capetian Kings*; Duby, *France in the Middle Ages*. Alexander Cartellieri's *Philipp II. August*, 4 vols, Leipzig, 1899–1922, is a massive, if severely dated, achievement. For Philip's historical reputation, see Georges Duby, *The Legend of Bouvines*, Cambridge, 1990. French biographies, though useful, can be over-flattering. See Georges Bordonove, *Philippe Auguste*, Paris, 1986; Gérard Sivéry, *Philippe Auguste*, Paris, 1993; Flori, *Philippe Auguste* and Luchaire's *Philippe Auguste*. Much of the same information is to be found in the English sources cited above, especially in Warren and Norgate. Two biographies in English on Philip are: William Hutton, *Philip Augustus*, London, 1896; and the more comprehensive Bradbury, *Philip Augustus*. But best of all on Philip's reign are two magnificent works: John Baldwin, *The Government of Philip Augustus*, Berkeley, 1986; and R-H. Bautier (ed), *La France de Philippe Auguste: Le Temps des Mutations*, Paris, 1982, a collection of invaluable essays.

75 Turner, 'King John in his context', 188; Steven Runciman, 'Richard Couer-de-Lion', in *History Today*, 41(6), 1991 (originally 1955), 51; Fawtier, *Capetian Kings*, 24; Charles Petit-Dutaillis, *La Monarchie Féodale en France et en Angleterre*, Paris, 1933, 290; Flori, *Philippe Auguste*, 10.

76 John Gillingham, 'Richard I and the Science of War', *ANW*, 195. (This essay is also in his *Richard Couer de Lion* collection.)

77 For these events, see Gilbert of Mons, *Chronicle of Hainaut*, trans. Laura Napran, Woodbridge, 2005, 90–1.

78 Fawtier, *Capetian Kings*, 25.

79 R-H. Bautier, 'La Personalité de Philippe Auguste', in Bautier, *La France de Philippe Auguste*, 56. This essay offers a detailed character analysis of the French king. The personalities of John and Philip are contrasted in Jim Bradbury, 'Philip Augustus and Jim Bradbury: Personality and History', in Church, *King John*.

80 See Sean McGlynn, 'Philip Augustus: Too Soft a King?, *Medieval Life*, 1 (4), 1996.

81 Gillingham, 'Richard I', *ANW*, 197; Poole, *Domesday Book*, 342; Lloyd, *John*, 30.

82 W. Paden, T. Sankovitch and P. Stalein (eds), *The Poems of Bertran de Born*, Los Angeles, 1986, 393, 380. Surprisingly, I have not come across any writer who uses this quotation to support the notion of Philip as a poor soldier.

83 For Anglo-Imperial relations see Poole, *Domesday Book*, 366–7 and 452–55. For John's reign, Theo Holzapfel covers the English-Guelph alliance in *Papst Innozenz III, Philip II August, König von Frankreich und die englisch-welfische Verbindung, 1198–1216*, Frankfurt, 1991. He also covers the treaty 45–51. (I am grateful to John Gillingham for bringing this book to my attention.) Also of value is Natalie Fryde, 'King John and the Empire', in Church, *King John*.

84 The treaty is discussed in Warren, 54–6; F.M. Powicke, *The Loss of Normandy*, 2nd edn, Manchester, 1961, 134–8; Turner, 53–4; Baldwin, 96–7; Bradbury, *Philip Augustus*, 133–5. Contemporaries' views on Le Goulet are discussed by John Gillingham: 'Historians Without Hindsight: Coggeshall, Diceto and Howden on the Early Years of John's Reign', in Church, *King John*.

85 Turner, *King John*, 54.

86 Baldwin, 97. Bradbury agrees, evaluating the treaty as 'recognition of Philip's strength' (Bradbury, *Philip Augustus*, 133). In concordance with this view are Hallam, *Capetian France*, 183 and Jacques Boussard, 'Philippe Auguste et les Plantgenêts', in R.H. Bautier, *La France de Philippe Auguste* ('un grand success pour Philippe Auguste', 279).

87 Warren, 55.

88 Turner, 14.

89 See above, n. 26. But see also Gillingham, 'Historians Without Hindsight', 22–3 and Holt, 'King John', in *Magna Carta and Medieval Government*, 102–3.

90 See, for example, Warren, *King John*, 57.

91 Richard's religious life is discussed by Gillingham, *Richard I*, 257–60.

92 Examined by Ralph V. Turner, 'Richard Lionheart and English Episcopal Elections', *Albion*, 29 (1), 1997.

93 Ralph V. Turner, 'Richard Lionheart and the Episcopate in His French Domains', *French Historical Studies*, 21 (4), 1998, 520. This paragraph relies heavily on Turner's article.

94 See Baldwin, *The Government of Philip Augustus*, 307, 328 and his 'Philip Augustus and the Norman Church', *French Historical Studies*, 6 (1), 1969.

95 Turner, 'Richard Lionheart and the Episcopate', 528; Quentin Griffiths, 'The Capetian kings and St. Martin of Tours', *Studies in Medieval and Renaissance History*, 9, 1987.

96 Turner, 'Richard Lionheart and the Episcopate', 535. Turner believes the implications of this to be stark: 'The Angevin monarchs' failure to forge close links with the bishops of their southern domains contributed to their inability to construct a lasting political structure for their would-be empire' (537). See also his 'The Problems of Survival for the Angevin "Empire"', 92–6.

97 Fuller details of this incident are to be found in Gillingham, *Richard I*, 301–4.

98 For events leading to Andely's burning, see Robert de Tourigny, *Chronica*, in *Chronicles of the Reigns of Stephen, Henry II and Richard I*, ed. Richard Howlett, 4 vols., Rolls Series, London, 1884–9, 4, 229–32 (Robert calls Andely an 'excellent town'); Yves Sassier, *Louis VII*, Paris, 1991, 387; Warren, *Henry II*, 106.

99 'Rex Francie petiit ad opus sum Andeli' Roger of Howden, *Chronica*, ed. W. Stubbs, 4 vols., Rolls Series, London 1868–71, 4, 3–4. Andely changed hands more than once during the confused wars of the 1190s. For the peace of Louviers, see Gillingham, *Richard I*, 297–8 and F.M. Powicke, 'King Philip Augustus and the Archbishop of Rouen (1196)', *EHR*, 27 (1), 1912.

100 HGM, 3, 159. The Archbishop was not alone in expressing his anxieties this way, Geoffrey de Vinsauf lamenting: 'O Normandy, once safe beneath king Richard's shield, but undefended now…' (*Poetria Nova of Geoffrey of Vinsauf*, trans. M.F. Nims, Toronto, 1967, 28). In some versions, 'England' replaces 'Normandy': see Gillingham, *Richard I*, 321 and n. 3. Bartlett's translation is used here (Bartlett, *England Under the Norman and Angevin Kings*, 25).

2 The Conquest of Normandy, 1200–1204

101 For John's tour see Warren, *King John*, 64; Norgate, *John*, 74 (the source of the quotation); Norgate, *Angevin Kings*, ii, 397–8; Howden, iv, 125.

102 Warren's *King John* (69) makes this point. For Isabella, see Nicholas Vincent, 'Isabella of Angoulême: John's Jezebel', in Church, *King John*.

103 Daniel Power, *The Norman Frontier in the Twelfth and Early Thirteenth Centuries*, Cambridge, 2004, 424. Kate Norgate suggests that John may have deliberately intended to goad the Lusignans into rebellion, thereby providing him with the pretext to recover La Marche (Norgate, *John*, 77). If this had been the case the plan had backfired disastrously for John.

104 Howden, iv, 163. This episode is not quite as blatant as Henry IV's scam in 1407, when he persuaded parliament to stump up finances for a proposed campaign in Wales. Henry cancelled the campaign and absorbed many of the funds into his household: Edmund Wright, 'The Recovery of Royal Finance in 1407', in Rowena Archer and Simon Walker (eds), *Rulers and Ruled in Late Medieval England*, London, 1995, 77–81.

105 Bautier, *La France de Philippe Auguste*, 251–2; Luchaire, *Philippe Auguste*, 142; Theodore Evergates, *Feudal Society in the Bailliage of Troyes under the Counts of Champagne, 1152–1284*, Baltimore, 1975, 47.

106 Gervase of Canterbury, ii, 93.

107 WB, i, 207. William the Breton is the only source to mention that Tillières was similarly treated (ii, 159–60) and that the siege took three weeks. For events in Normandy, the best detailed accounts are in Power, *The Norman Frontier*, 413–45, and F.M. Powicke, *The Loss of Normandy, 1189–1204*, 2nd edn, Manchester, 1960, 148–69.

108 According to Roger of Wendover, Philip also besieged Radpont for eight days at the beginning of July, but hastily retreated from there when John suddenly appeared on the scene (RW, i, 313–14).

109 For Gournay, see Powicke, 149–50; Bradbury, 141–2; WB, ii, 160–2; Robert of Auxerre, *Roberti Canonici Sancti Mariani Autissiodorensis Chronicon*, Monumenta Germania Historica Scriptores xvii, 265. Above all, for Gournay and the campaign in eastern Normandy, see the important appendix in Power, *The Norman Frontier*, 532–38. Gournay Castle is briefly commented on in André Châtelain, *Châteaux Forts en Île de France*,

Paris, 1983, 185. For John's intentions at Arques see Powicke, 150 and *Rot. Pat.* 15. For the Cinque Ports, see N.A.M. Rodgers, 'The Naval Service of the Cinque Ports', *EHR*, 111 (442), 1996. These ports were, as Stephen Church has observed, 'the most important ports in the land': S. D. Church, *The Household Knights of King John*, Cambridge, 1999, 47.

110 For Mirebeau see Coggeshall, 137–8; WB, ii, 166–9; RW, i, 314–15; AB, 93–5; and Bradbury, *Philip Augustus*, 143–4, for the politics.

111 At Courcelles in 1189 in a trap laid by Richard I (WB, ii, 139) See John Gillingham, *Richard the Lionheart*, 2nd edn, 1989, 272–3. For intelligence gathering in the Middle Ages see J.O. Prestwich, 'Military Intelligence under the Norman and Angevin Kings' in G. Garnett and J. Hudson (eds), *Law and Government in Medieval England and Normandy*, Cambridge, 1994. Wendover writes that John's march was 'faster than is to be believed': RW, i, 314.

112 These examples are from William the Breton: WB, ii, 73, 75, 102, 125–6. Cf. Richard's remarks with Hugh de Boves: 'delays are always dangerous when things are ready' (RW, ii, 107). For Aumâle see WB, ii, 132 and Gillingham, *Lionheart*, 267–8.

113 Warren, 79. Cf. Poole's remark in Poole, *From Domesday Book to Magna Carta*, 382.

114 RW, i, 315. Poole suggests that 'shortage of provisions may have expedited the retirement' (Poole, *From Domesday Book to Magna Carta*, 382). See above for John's intention that the Cinque Ports should cut off the supplies to Philip by sea. Bradbury writes that 'Philip's retreat was the one occasion when militarily John out-trumped' (Bradbury, 143).

115 AM, i, 26; *Rot. Pat.*, 1, 33b, 37b, 44b, 55b; H.J Chaytor, *Savaryc de Mauléon*, Cambridge, 1939, 14. The sources concur that John was a harsh captor. However, such was a medieval *realpolitik*, this did not prevent some of the prisoners from later forging alliances with John: see Lyons, 'The Capetian Conquest of Anjou', 35.

116 RC, 139–41; Matthew Paris, *Historia Anglorum*, ed. F. Maddern, RS, 1866, ii, 95; AM, i, 27; WB, ii, 173–4. Arthur's historical role is explored most fully in K. Carter, 'Arthur I, Duke of Brittany, in History and Literature', unpublished PhD, The Florida State University, 1996, and J. A. Everard, *Brittany and the Angevins*, Cambridge, 2000, 159–75. Judith Everard's bbok is to be much recommended for events in Brittany which we do not have space to go into here. See also Powicke, *The Loss of Normandy*, 309–28; Michael Jones, 'The Capetian and Brittany', *Historical Research*, 63 (1), 1990, 9–12; M. D. Legge, 'William the Marshal and Arthur of Brittany, *Historical Research*, 55 (1), 1982. Legge draws attention to William de Braose as a common source for both William the Breton and the annalist of Margam (19).

117 Powicke, 153–4. For the political and territorial shake-up that followed des Roches' move to Philip, see Lyons, 'The Capetian Conquest of Anjou', 39–64. John ensured that des Roches was unable to carry all his military power with him.

118 RW, i, 317. For Count Robert's defection see Power, *The Norman Frontier*, 438–40, and for this and John's alienation of the Norman aristocracy, see Daniel Power, 'King John and the Norman Aristocracy', in Church, *King John*.

119 Poole, *From Domesday Book to Magna Carta*, 383–4. Daniel Power's massive and brilliant *The Norman Frontier* is comprehensive for this period. For an excellent survey of ties between England and Normandy see David Bates and Anne Curry (eds), *England and Normandy in the Middle Ages*, London, 1994. Also, Bartlett, *England Under the Norman and Angevin Kings*, 11–28; Power, 'King John'; V. D. Moss, 'The Norman Exhequer Rolls of King John', in Church; Powicke, *The Loss of Normandy*, chs. 3 and 5. Historians who make a convincing case for cracks in the Anglo-Norman relationship include: Ralph Turner, 'Good or Bad Kingship: The Case of Richard Lionheart', *Haskins Society Journal*, 8, 1999, 72–73; idem, 'Richard Lionheart and the Episcopate'; idem, 'The Problems of Survival'; Lucien Musset, 'Quelques problèmes poses par l'annexion de la Normandie au domain royale français', in Bautier, *La France de Philipp Auguste*; and J.C Holt, 'the End of the Anglo-Norman Realm', in his *Magna Cart and Medieval Government*, where he writes of the 'signs that Normandy and England were beginning to go their separate ways' (47). All the while, ties with France had been growing stronger: Judith Green, 'Lords of the Norman Vexin', in J. C Holt and John Gillingham (eds), *War and Government in the Middle Ages'*, Woolbridge, 1984; idem, 'Unity and Disunity in the

Anglo-Norman State', *Historical Research*, 62 (1), 1989. Warren believes that by the early thirteenth century Normans considered their union with England to be 'a curious anachronism': W. L. Warren, *Henry II*, London, 1973, 627. David Crouch writes that by the beginning of the thirteenth century one can 'conclude that it was only the fraction of the magnates with Anglo-Norman interests which supported the King of England's desire to keep Normandy': Crouch, 'Normans and Anglo-Normans: A Divided Aristocracy?', in Bates and Curry, *England and Normandy in the Middle Ages*, 67.

120 For commentaries on the siege of Château Gaillard see: E. E. Viollet le Duc, *Military Architecture*, London, 1990, 80–94 (originally published in 1860); Raymond Quenedy, 'Le Siège de Château Gaillard en 1203–1204', *Bulletin de la Société des Amis des Monuments Rouennais*, 1913, 51–89. These works contain good physical descriptions of the castle, as does J. F. Fino, *Fortresses de la France Mediévale*, Paris, 1967, 115–83. See also: Paul Boutellier, 'Le Siège et la Prie du Château Gaillard', *Revue Historique de l'Armée*, 1946, 15–26; Philip Warner, *Sieges of the Middle Ages*, London, 1968, 124–34; Cartellieri, *Philipp II*, iv, 166–70, 173–179; Powicke, 253–6 (which sees the siege as one important event amongst many); Warren, 93–5. The most complete previous account in English is Norgate, *Angevin Kings*, ii, 411–23; also of note is her *John Lackland*, 94–100. I have, to my knowledge, provided here the fullest account of the siege in English. See n. 27 for contemporary sources. Bradbury (*Philip Augustus*, 145–151) and Wade ('Warfare and Armies in Capetian France', 140–56) provide good recent accounts. For its strategic importance, see Dominique Pitte, 'Château-Gaillard dans la Défense de la Normandie orientale (1196–1204)', *ANS*, 24 (2002).

121 Of contemporary sources, William the Breton provides two invaluable accounts: WB, i, 212–19 and ii, 176–209. Rigord covers the siege in Rigord (WB), i, 159; Roger of Wendover offers a slightly different perspective in RW, ii, 8–9. Brief mentions appear in AM, ii, 255–6; and AB, 102–3; and also the Anonymous of Béthune's narrative in *RHF*, xxiv, 762.

122 See Norgate, *John*, n. 20.

123 RW, i, 317.

124 Baldwin, 168. See also ch. 3.

125 The accounts in the *Philippidos* and *Gesta* differ here: the former attributes this commando-style mission solely to Galbert; the latter conflates the earlier breaking of the stockade with the later attack on the isle into one episode.

126 Powicke (*The Loss of Normandy*, 254–6) casts doubt on the existence of these trenches, judiciously reminding us of Charles VII's siege operations at Château Gaillard in 1449; but he is wrong to say that William the Breton does not mention these trenches, as he clearly does so: WB, i, 216 and ii, 193; so also does the extremely rarely mentioned account of the siege by the Anonymous of Béthune in *RHF*, xxiv, 762.

127 For what follows, see William the Breton's prose account in WB, i, 216–218; his lengthier verse account is in WB ii, 195–200. Historians who cover this event tend to do so only within a few lines at most: see Lloyd, *King John*, 139–40; Philip Warner, *Sieges of the Middle Ages*, London, 1968, 133–134; Powicke, *Normandy*, 256; Luchaire, *Philippe Auguste ou la France Rassemblée*, Paris, 1979, 157–158. Kate Norgate's *Angevin Kings*, ii, 417–418 gives the most detail, and is the only one to add an original insight into the subject. But see also Sean McGlynn, 'The Useless Mouths', *History Today*, 48 (6), 1998, idem, *By Sword and Fire*, 161–70, and Wade, 'Warfare and Armies in Capetian France', 149–50. The expulsion of 'useless mouths' was commonplace: the French garrison besieged at Calais turned out non-combatants in 1346, as that of Rouen did in 1418 (see n. 30). As a siege measure, we can see it in operation as late as 1870 at the siege of Paris: Alistair Horne, *The Fall of Paris: The Siege and Commune, 1870–71*, London, 1965, ch. 11; Susan Watkins, 'War on God', (review article), *London Review of Books*, 21 (10), 20, who uses the phrase 'les bouches inutiles' in a modern context.

128 There is a large painting by Tattegrain, considered by many to be a masterpiece, with this title ('Les bouches inutiles'), which is exhibited in the mayorial offices at Les Adelys. The lower of the figures cited is more likely. The numbers are calculated from William the Breton's figures.

129 William refers to this tragic ending only in his chronicle (WB, i, 218); he probably did not wish for such an unhappy ending to mar the compassion of the French king in

his panegyric *Philippidos*. For the Parzival episode, see Paul Strohm's review of Herman
Pleij, *Dreaming of Cockaigne: Medieval Fantasies of the Perfect Life* (Columbia, 2001) in *The
London Review of Books*, 21 June, 2001, 17.
William's account of the siege is given extra authenticity by this description of the fatal
consumption of food by the surviving starving refugees. In 1945 British soldiers who
had liberated Belsen concentration camp gave food to the skeletal inmates; several of
the internees died from the induced gastrointestinal bleeding, the result of too much
food acting on acutely empty stomachs (see Thomas Stuttaford, MD, writing in *The
Times*, 22 May 1995 and also *The European Journal of Gastroenterology and Hepatology*, May
1995). The veracity of this episode is further underlined by the case of the shipwrecked
survivors of the whaleship *Essex* in 1820: when rescued from being adrift in their
lifeboat, two remaining sailors were reluctant to surrender the bones on which they had
been gnawing and relying for sustenance (the drama is related in Nathaniel Philbrick,
In the Heart of the Sea: The Tragedy of the Whaleship 'Essex', London, 2000; Owen Chase,
Shipwreck of the Whaleship Essex, London, 2000). That these bones were human (from
victims of the disaster) makes the William the Breton's claims of cannibalism at
Château Gaillard more believable. Modern authorities are too ready to dismiss William's
reference as sheer sensationalism (eg, Wade, 'Armies and Warfare', 150, n. 93) or as a
literary topos. Desperate sieges could prompt desperate responses. During the Battle of
Leningrad in the Second World War, between early December 1941 and 15 February
1942 Soviet authorities investigated no less than 886 cases of cannibalism in just three
months (John Erickson, 'The Ultimate Wound', *The Times Literary Supplement*, 28 August
1998, 11).

130   For the events at Calais see: Jim Bradbury, *The Medieval Siege*, Woodbridge, 1992,
      157–158; Jonathon Sumption, *The Hundred Years War*, London, 1990, 577; Warner,
      Sieges, 172. For Rouen see: Desmond Seward *Henry V as Warlord*, London, 1987, 117; J.
      Bradbury, *The Medieval Siege*, Woodbridge, 1992, 169–170; and John Page's eyewitness
      account A.R. Myers (ed), *English Historical Documents*, iv, 1969, 219–222. William the
      Breton was not only an experienced observer of warfare, he was also something
      of a classic scholar, and he himself used his knowledge of ancient wars to draw
      comparisons with his own time. This is partly revealed in the way that the sufferings
      of the non-combatants at Château Gaillard are paralleled with the harshness of war
      in early history, thereby displaying his awareness of the widespread misery that war
      always creates. Taking his lead in from Caesar's *De Bello Civili*, William relates how
      Roman soldiers were compelled by circumstances to drink the urine of their horses.
      This incident is more familiar to modern readers from Shakespeare's *Anthony and
      Cleapatra*, when Caeser reminisces on the hardships that Anthony had to endure for
      success in war:

      At thy heal
      Did famine follow, whom thou fought'st against –
      Though daintily brought up – with patience more
      Than savages could suffer. Thou didst drink
      The stake of horses, and the gilded puddle
      Which beasts would cough at. Thy palate then did deign
      The roughest berry on the rudest hedge.
      Yea, like the stag when snow the pasture sheets,
      The barks of trees thou browsed. On the Alps
      It is reported thou didst eat strange flesh.
      Which some did die to look on ...
      (I, iv, ll. 58–68)

131   Rigord in WB, ii,159; RC,144; Wendover, RW, ii, 8.
132   AB, 103.
133   Norgate (*Angevin Kings*, ii, 417) lays this blame on de Lacy. The quote is from Susan
      Reynolds, *Fiefs and Vassals*, Oxford, 1994, 37.
134   The letter is briefly discussed in Norgate, *John Lackland*, 99 and in Powicke, *Normandy*,
      255–6. The letter fell into Philip's hands and is preserved in his earliest register, now

lodged in the Vatican, under the title 'Littere quas misit Rex Anglie onsessis in Gaillard.' ('Letter sent by the King of England to the besieged in Gaillard'), Register A.f. 38v. Powicke suggests (note 25, 256) that the letter was sent with John's 'intimate clerk' in January: ie, after de Lacy had expelled the noncombatabants.

135 *The Paston Letters*, ed. J. Gairdner, London, 1872, i, 260–261, no. 191. For some examples of the fate of garrison captains who capitulated too precipitously, see Maurice Keen, *The Laws of War in the Later Middle Ages*, London, 1965, 124–126, and McGlynn, *By Sword and Fire*, 150.

136 Cf. Odo de Dueil's *De Profectione de Ludovici VII I Orientum*, New York, 1948, ed. Virginia Berry, 40, when, during the Second Crusade, the Greeks kept the French out of their cities for fear of food riots.

137 Norgate makes this suggestion (*Angevin Kings*, 418). The only other reference that I have found alluding to this possibility is in Lloyd, *John*, 140); but he is clearly following Norgate. The French sources are quiet on this idea. Wade suggests that Philip acted out of fears of papal condemnation; unlikely given the imperatives of war ('Armies and Warfare', 150, n. 94).

138 Wendover, ii, 311–313.

139 RW, ii, 319.

140 Ambroise, *The Crusade of Richard Lionheart by Ambroise*, ed. and trans. M. J. Hubert and J.L. La Monte, New York, 1976 (reprint), ll. 3625–60.

141 Robert of Auxerre, 253.

142 Norgate believes that the lower-level was, in fact, a storehouse (*Angevin Kings*, ii, 421; Warner believes the outlet of the latrine (*forica*) was used (*Sieges*, 132). During the Battle of Verdun in 1916, a small Germany party, led by Sergreant Künst (playing the Bogis part), slipped through a small aperture in the renowned and formidable Fort Douamont to take it with ease. 'Its reconquest cost the lives of 100,000 French troops': Alistair Horne, 'Letter From Verdun', *Prospect*, August/September 1999, 45.

143 AB, 102–3.

144 RW, ii, 8. Norgate dismisses Wendover's account as 'not worthy of consideration' (*Angevin Kings*, ii, 423, n. 1). Wade raises the relevant issue that 'Wendover assumes that there were still horses left, after a blockade of several months' ('Armies and Warfare', 155, n. 102).

145 Painter, *John*, 40.

146 Powicke, *Normandy*, 254.

147 For what follows see Coggeshell, 144–6; RW, ii, 8; AB, 97–9; WB, i, 220–1, Rigord (WB), i, 160–1 and WB ii, 210–17.

148 RW, i, 319; ii, 8. See also Sean McGlynn, 'Philip Augustus', *Medieval Life*, 1 (4), 23–5.

149 Nicholas Vincent, 'Introduction: The Record of 1204', in Vincent (ed), *Records, Administration and Aristocratic Society*, xiii; David Carpenter, *The Struggle for Mastery*, 270. The following offer analysis of the implications of the duchy's loss: Clanchy, *England and its Rulers*, 181–2; Robert Stacey, *Politics, Policy and Finance under Henry III, 1216–45*, Oxford, 1987, 160–3; J.C Holt, 'The Loss of Normandy and Royal Finance', in J. Gillingham and J. C. Holt *War and Government in the Middle Ages*, Woodbridge, 1984; Gillingham, *Richard Couer de Lion*, 71; Poole, 431–2; Robin Frame, *The Political Development of the British Isles, 1100–1400*, Oxford, 1990, 44–5; Hugh M. Thomas, *The English and the Normans: Ethnic Hostility, Assimilation, and Identity, 1066–.c.1220*, Oxford, 2003, 332–5.

3 War, Politics and the First Invasion Attempt, 1205–1213

150 Despite Winston Churchill's opinion that the loss benefitted England. See ch. 1, n.38.

151 For the Treaty of Paris, see: Le Patourel, *Feudal Empires*, IV,453; Gillingham, *Angevin Empire*, 115; F.M. Powicke, *King Henry III and the Lord Edward*, 2 vols., Oxford, 1947, i, 253–71; idem, *The Thirteenth Century*, Oxford, 2nd edn, 1962, 84, 122–8; Jacques le Goff, *Saint Louis*, Paris, 1996, 257–64; Hallam, *Capetian France*, 219–20, 266–7; Bjorn Weiler, *Henry III of England and the Staufen Empire, 1216–1272*, Woodbridge, 2006, 166–7; Michael Prestwich, *Plantagenet England 1225–1360*, Oxford, 2005, 296–8. Powicke and Gillingham argue that the terms were generous for Henry.

152 This age-old antagonism is entertainingly surveyed in Robert Gibson, *Best of Enemies: Anglo-French Relations Since the Norman Conquest*, 1995. See also Vale, *The Ancient Enemy*.

153 Frank Barlow, *The Feudal Kingdom of England, 1042–1216*, 4th edn, Harlow, 1988, 195. For Anglo-Imperial relations see: idem, 359–60, 411–14; A.L. Poole, 'Richard the First's Alliances with the German Princes in 1194', in R.W. Hunt, W.A. Pantin and R.W. Southern (eds), *Studies in Medieval History Presented to F.M. Powicke*, Oxford, 1948; idem, *Domesday Book to Magna Carta*, 326–8, 376–7, 449–52; Benjamin Arnold, 'Germany and England, 1066–1453', in Nigel Saul (ed), *England in Europe, 1066–1453*, 1994; idem, 'England and Germany', in Michael Jones and Malcolm Vale (eds), *England and Her Neighbours, 1066–1453*, 1989; Bartlett, *England Under the Norman and Angevin Kings*, 103–6; Weiler, *Henry III of England*; Holzapfel, *Papst Innocent III* (which takes little account of the following book); Jens Ahlers, *Die Welfen und Die Englische Könige 1165–1235*, Hildesheim, 1987 (my thanks to John Gillingham for bringing this book to my attention); Nichola Fryde, 'King John and the Empire', in Church, *King John*; Cuttino, *English Medieval Diplomacy*, 38–53; J. Huffman, *The Social Politics of Medieval Diplomacy: Anglo-German Relations, 1066–1307*, Michigan, 2000. For Frederick II, see: *Frederick II: A Medieval Emperor*, Harmondsworth, 1988; W. Stürner, *Friedrich II: Die Königsherrscahft im Sizilien und Deutschland, 1194–1210*, Band I, Darmstadt, 1992.

154 Arnold, 'England and Germany, 1066–1453', 80, where Arnold also notes 'Not all Englishmen approved of the German emperor's pretensions to this type of world dominion'. Further adverse reaction is noted in Bartlett, *England Under the Norman and Angevin Kings*, 105 and, in similar vein to John of Salisbury, in Bjorn Weiler, *Kingship, Rebellion and Political Culture: England and Germany, c.1215–c.1250*, Basingstoke, 2007, 174.

155 Poole, *Domesday Book to Magna Carta,* 326. For Henry the Lion: K. Jordan, *Henry the Lion,* trans. P.S. Falla, Oxford, 1986.

156 Poole, 'Richard the First's Alliances', 91.

157 See Gillingham, *Richard I*, 312.

158 Poole, *Domesday Book to Magna Carta*, 453.

159 At this stage Henry's son and heir Frederick was still an infant living in Sicily.

160 For a recent summary of Otto's career in English, see Sean McGlynn, 'Otto IV', in Clifford J. Rogers, *Oxford Encyclopedia of Medieval Warfare and Military Technology*, Oxford, 2010.

161 Poole, *Domesday Book to Magna Carta*, 451; *Foedora*, i, 103.

162 Fryde, 'King John and the Empire', 343.

163 *Foedora*, i, 104.

164 Suger, *Vie de Louis le Gros*, ed. and trans. by H. Waquet, Paris, 1964 [1929], 218–226. The Capetians, unlike English kings, were fortunate in having a succession of authorised royal biographies. For what follows, I have relied heavily on Fryde, 'King John and the Empire'. Also for Franco-Imperial relations, see n. 4 above and: Hallam, *Capetian France*, 131–2; Luchaire, *Philippe Auguste*, 165–79; Baldwin, *Government of Philip Augustus*, ch. 9; Slyvian Gougenheim, 'Les Grands Traits de la Vie Politique', in Michel Parisse (ed), *L'Allemagne au XIIIe Siècle*, Paris, 1994, 19–24.

165 Gillingham, *Richard I*, p. 236. Gillingham covers the consequences of Richard's imperial imprisonment in detail, 230–53.

166 Gervase of Canterbury, *The Historical Works of Gervase of Canterbury*, ed. W. Stubbs, 2 vols., RS, 1879–80, i, 514.

167 But see Baldwin, *Government of Philip Augustus*, 81–2. Baldwin believes the marriage may have been to bluff England into greater insecurity. For Philip and Denmark, see Thomas Riis, 'Autour de Marriage de 1193: l'Epouse, son Pays et les Relations Franco-Danoises', in Bautier, *La France de Philippe Auguste*. Of related interest is Kathleen S. Schowhalter, 'The Ingeborg Psalter: Queenship, Legitimacy, and the Appropriation of Byzantine Art in the West', in Kathleen Nolan (ed) *Capetian Women*, Basingstoke, 2003.

168 Howden, iii, 217.

169 Howden provides the quotes: Howden, iii, 196–7, 204–5.

170 Howden, iii, 216–17.

171 Horst Fuhrman, *Germany in the High Middle Ages*, trans. Timothy Reuter, Cambridge, 1986, p. 186; Alfred Haverkampf, *Medieval Germany, 1056–1273*, trans. H. Braun and R. Mortimer, Oxford, 1988, 242–4.

172 Luchaire, *Philippe Auguste*, 167–8.

173 There is no room to discuss the crusade here. It was, for the French, primarily an offensive war; it was a sideshow that never threatened the Capetian dynasty in the

way the Anglo-Imperial menace did. Two recent accounts of the crusade are: Laurence Marvin, *The Occitan War*, Cambridge, 2008, and Mark Gregory Pegg, *A Most Holy War: The Albigensian Crusade and the Battle for Christendom*, Oxford, 2008. Of interest here is Nicholas Vincent, 'England and the Albigensian Crusade', in Weiler and Rowlands, *England and Europe in the Reign of Henry III*.

174 For Innocent, see: Jane Sayers, *Innocent III: Leader of Europe, 1198–1216*, London, 1994; James M. Powell (ed), *Innocent III: Vicar of Christ or Lord of the World?*, Boston, 1963; Colin Morris, *The Papal Monarchy: The Western Church from 1950 to 1250*, Oxford, 1989, 417–51.

175 For these events, see Baldwin, Government of Philip Augustus, 80–87, 178–9; Bradbury, *Philip Augustus*, 173–85. For Philip's relations with the Papacy in general, see: Bradbury, ibid, 166–94; Sivéry, *Philippe Auguste*, 232–6; Luchaire, *Philippe Auguste*, ch. 3; R. Foreville, *Le Pape Innocent III et la France*, Stutthart, 1992; Brenda Bolton, 'Philip Augustus and John: Two Sons in Innocent III's Vineyard?', in her *Innocent III: Studies on Papal Authority and Pastoral Care*, Aldershot, 1995, especially at 121–2; M. Maccarrone, 'La Papauté et Philippe Auguste: la Décrétale *Novit Ille*', in Bautier, *La France de Philippe Auguste*. The text of *Novit Ille* can be read in C.R. Cheney and W. H. Semple (eds), *Selected Letters of Pope Innocent III Concerning England, 1198–1216*, 63–8.

176 Poole, *Domesday Book to Magna Carta*, 443.

177 For what follows, I have relied heavily on Christopher Harper-Bill's excellent 'King John and the Church', in Church, *King John*. See also: Warren, *King John*, ch. 5; Painter, *Reign of King John*, ch. 5; F.M. Powicke, *Stephen Langton*, Oxford, 1928. A new biography on Stephen Langton from Nicholas Vincent is anticipated. For a broader context, see: C. H. Lawrence, 'The Thirteenth Century', in C.H. Lawrence (ed), *The English Church and the Papacy in the Middle Ages*, 1965; R. Brentano, *Two Churches: England and Italy in the Thirteenth Century*, Berkely, 1968; C.R. Cheney, *The Papacy and England: Twelfth to Fourteenth Centuries*, 1982; ibid, *From Becket to Langton: English Church Government, 1170–1213*, Manchester, 1956; ibid, *Innocent III and England*, Stuttgart, 1979. Innocent's letters to John can be found in Cheney and Semple, *Selected Letters*.

178 Gillingham, *Richard I*, 275; Holt, *Magna Carta and Medieval Government*, p. 82.

179 Painter, *Reign of King John*, 161, 163–4.

180 RW, ii, 37.

181 Turner, *King John*, p. 159. For a more favourable picture: Warren, *King John*, 169; Barlow, *Feudal Kingdom*, 399–400.

182 Turner, *King John*, 158. See also Christopher Harper-Bill, 'John and the Church of Rome', 301. For his time in Paris, see also Powicke, *Stephen Langton*, 23–74.

183 Robert Fawtier, 'Un Fragment du Compte de l'Hôtel de Prince Louis', in Fawtier, *Autour de la France Capétienne: Personnages et Institutions*, 1987 [1933], IX, 228, 238. The payment details are recorded in item 101, 244. This is a much overlooked source. The quote is from Powicke, *Stephen Langton*, 135.

184 For the Interdict, see Harper-Bill, 'John and the Church of Rome', 304–7; Warren, *King John*, 163–73; Turner, *King John*, 160–3, 165, 170–2, 175; Painter, *Reign of King John*, 173–97. For context, see Peter D. Clarke, *The Interdict in the Thirteenth Century*, Oxford, 2007.

185 Turner, *King John*, 162. Poole takes a different view: *Domesday Book to Magna Carta*, 446.

186 Annals of Margam, in *Annales Monastici* [AM], ed. H.R. Luard, Rolls Series, 1864–6), iii, 28; Turner, *King John*, 163.

187 Warren, *King John*, 169.

188 Harper-Bill, 'John and the Church of Rome', 306–7.

189 BC, ii, p.210. For Wendover's accurate comment, see RW, ii, p. 64. The patriotically minded Matthew Paris lambasted the agreement, labelling it 'detestable': *Matthei Parisiensis Historia Anglorum*, ed. F. Maddern, 3 vols., Rolls Series, 1886–9, ii, 146–8.

190 Cheney and Semple, *Selected Letters of Pope Innocent III*, 157, 163.

191 Ibid, 141.

192 Some of the more effusive accolades from scholars are summarised in Turner, *King John*, 169. A portion of the financial restitution was redirected to John's financing of his continental campaign in 1214 (Vincent, *Peter des Roches*, 92). Christopher Harper-Bill draws attention to the important ecclesiastical consequences of the haggling over compensation: Harper-Bill, 'John and the Church of Rome', 308–9.

193 For military organisation in England, see: Prestwich, *Armies and Warfare*, chs. 3 and 4;
     Bartlett, *England Under the Normand and Angevin Kings*, 261–9; Powicke, *The Loss of
     Normandy*, 209–32; John Beeler, *Warfare in England, 1066–1189*, Ithaca, 1966, chs. 10–11;
     Michael Powicke, *Military Obligation in Medieval England*, Oxford, 1962, especially chs.
     3–5; Strickland, *Anglo-Norman Warfare*, 28–127; C. W. Hollister, *The Military Organization
     of Norman England*, Oxford, 1965. Indispensable for knights in John's reign is S.D.
     Church, *The Household Knights of King John*, Cambridge, 1999 and his articles listed
     therein. Important articles which shed light on John's forces both directly or indirectly,
     include Nicholas Vincent, 'A Roll of Knights Summoned to Campaign in 1213',
     Historical Research, 66 (1), 1993 and J. Critchley, 'Summonses to military service early in
     the reign of Henry III', *EHR*, 86 (1), 1971.

194 As records become more abundant and complete in the later Middle Ages, so (but
     still with reservations), a fuller picture can emerge from the records. See, for example,
     the fine study by Andrew Ayton, *Knights and Warhorses: Military Service and the English
     Aristocracy Under Edward III*, Woodbridge, 1994.

195 Smail, *Crusading Warfare*, 97.

196 For Henry VII and Bosworth, see: Michael Jones, *Bosworth 1485*, Stroud, 2002; Michael
     Bennett, *The Battle of Bosworth*, Stroud, 1985. For Henry IV and Richard II, see Nigel Saul,
     Richard II, 1997; Ian Mortimer, *The Fears of Henry IV*, 2007. Anthony Tuck estimates that
     Henry's retinue as 'probably numbering no more than forty or fifty'; 'Richard had little to
     fear from Henry and his small band of exiles' (Tuck, *Crown and Nobility*, 215–16). In the
     Annales Ricardi Secundi, Thomas Walsingham, a monk of St Albans continuing the literary,
     anti-royalist tradition of Roger of Wendover and Matthew Paris, wrote: 'the number of
     fighting men accompanying him did not amount … to more than fifteen … With such
     a small force, it is a wonder that he dared to invade the kingdom of England, but even
     more astonishing is the fact that within such a short time … he was able to pacify the
     whole realm' (in C. Given-Wilson, ed. and trans., *Chronicles of the Revolution, 1397–40: The
     Reign of Richard II*, Manchester, 1993, 116–17). Nigel Saul doubts that at this stage Henry
     had designs on the crown but was merely seeking to regain his inheritance (Saul, *Richard
     II*, 406). Either way, the episode shows just how events take on a momentum of their own.
     Many military actions were begun as exploratory moves to test the waters.

197 See Matthew Bennett, 'Wace and Warfare', in *ANW*, 241. Wace was writing in the
     twelfth century. The whole question of the introduction of knight service into England
     is persuasively challenged by John Gillingham, *The English in the Twelfth Century*,
     Woodbridge, 2000, 187–208, which includes a succinct summary of scholarship on this
     debate. Stephen Church has made the important observation that despite the move to
     money, land was still central to retaining (or failing to retain) the loyalty of his knights
     (Church, *The Household Knights of King John*, ch. 4).

198 Robert de Torigny, *Chronica*, in *Chronicles of the Reigns of Stephen, Henry II and Richard I*,
     ed. R. Howlett, 4 vols., Rolls Series, 1884–9, iv, 193. The campaign lasted four months.

199 Prestwich, *Armies and Warfare*, 67. See also Poole, *Domesday Book to Magna Carta*, 370–1.
     For recent summaries and discussion of feudal service, see Frederick C. Suppe, 'Military
     Obligation' and Sean McGlynn, 'Servicium Debitum', both in *OEMW*.

200 Bartlett, *England Under the Norman and Angevin Kings*, 263.

201 Ibid, 203–5, 263–4. For a cogent discussion of quota reductions and knighthood in
     general, see: Peter Coss, *The Knight in Medieval England, 1000–1400*, Stroud, 1993, ch.3;
     Prestwich, *Armies and Warfare*, pp. 68–71. Knighthood in England is debated in articles
     by John Gillingham, Peter Coss, David Crouch and Michael Prestwich, in *Transactions of
     the Royal Historical Society*, Sixth Series, v, 1995, 129–220.

202 The Assize of Arms can be found in D.C. Douglas and G. Greenaway (eds), *English
     Historical Documents, II: 1042–1189*, 449–51, and Howden, ii, 261–3, who also covers
     France at 270. The Count of Flanders also followed these reforms. For a discussion, see
     Powicke, *Military Obligation*, 58–60; John D. Hosler, *Henry II: A Medieval Soldier*, 96–100.

203 Powicke, *Military Obligations*, 58–60, offers a good discussion of these mobilisations.

204 Church, *Household Knights of King John*, 153.

205 Bartlett, *England Under the Norman and Angevin Kings*, 265.

206 See R. Allen Brown, *English Castles*, 3rd edn, 1976, 185. Castle garrisons are studied
     in John Moore, 'Anglo-Norman Garrisons', *ANS* 22, 2000; Michael Prestwich, 'The

Garrisoning of English Medieval Castles' in Richard Abels and Bernard S. Bachrach, *The Normans and Their Adversaries at War*, Woodbridge, 2001. Castles needed supplies as well as men, and this too could reflect the political climate. For supplying, see Michael Prestwich, 'The Victualling of Castles' in Peter Coss and Christopher Tyerman (eds), *Soldiers, Nobles and Gentlemen: Essays in Honour of Maurice Keen*, Woodbridge, 2009.

207 Powicke, *The Loss of Normandy*, 225.

208 For Philip's war finances and organisation see: Baldwin, *Government of Philip Augustus*, 166–75, and E. Audouin, *Essai sur l'Armée Royale au Temps de Philippe Auguste*, Paris, 1913.

209 Bradbury, *Philip Augustus*, 246.

210 For what follows the starting point is Baldwin's *Government of Philip Augustus*, chs. 7, 11 and 15. Good summaries with useful commentaries are to be found in Bradbury, *Philip Augustus*, pp. 238–44; Philippe Contamine, 'L'Armée de Philippe Auguste', in Bautier, *La France de Philippe Auguste*; Laurence Marvin, 'Warfare and the Composition of Armies in France, 1100–1218: An Emphasis on the Common Soldier', unpublished PhD thesis, University of Illinois, 1996, 133–40. For detail, see E. Audouin, *Essai sur l'Armée de Philippe Auguste*, Paris, 1913. Brief accounts are available in Hallam, *Capetian France*, 161–3; Powicke, *Loss of Normandy*, 220–1; Luchaire, *Philippe Auguste*, 260–66.

211 Baldwin, *Government of Philip Augustus*, 283.

212 Bradbury, *Philip Augustus*, 280.

213 A. Erlande-Brandenburg, 'L'Architecture Militaire au Temps de Philippe Auguste: une Nouvelle Conception de la Défense', in Bautier, *La France de Philippe Auguste*; idem, 'Organisation du Conseil d'Architecture et des Corps des Spécialistes sous Philippe Auguste', in X.B. Altet (ed), *Artistes, Artisans et Productions Artistique au Moyen Age*, Paris, 1987; P. Curnow, 'Some Devlopments in Military Architecture c. 1200: Le Courdray-Salbart', *ANS* 2, 1979; Peter Purton, *A History of the Early Medieval Siege, Volume I: c.450–1200*, Woodbridge, 2010, 328–30.

214 Charles Coulson, 'Fortress Policy in Capetian Tradition and Angevin Practice', in *ANS*, 6, 1983, 15. See also his important article '"National" Requisitioning for "Public" Use of "Private" Castles in Pre-Nation State France', in Alfred Smyth (ed), *Medieval Europeans: Studies in Ethnic Identity and National Perspectives in Medieval Europe*, 1998.

215 For naval matters, see: Warren, *King John*, 120–5; F.W. Brooks, *The English Naval Forces, 1199–1272*, 1933; N.A.M. Rodger, *The Safeguard of the Sea: A Naval History of Britain, Volume I: 660–1649*, 1997, ch. 4; W.L. Clowes, *The Royal Navy, Volume I* 1897, ch. 9. Bradbury, *Philip Augustus*, pp. 242–3; Michel Mollat du Jourdin, 'Philippe Auguste et la Mer', in Bautier, *La France de Philippe Auguste*. For medieval shipping, in addition to Rogers above, see Ian Friel, *The Good Ships: Ships, Shipbuilding and Technology in England, 1200–1520*, 1995, and Susan Rose, 'Ships and Shipping', *OEMW*. For the Cinque Ports, F.W. Brooks, 'The Cinque Ports', *Mariner's Mirror*, xv, 1929.

216 Warren, *King John*, 121–2.

217 Ibid, 123.

218 Turner, *King John*, 128.

219 John Gillingham, 'Richard I, Galley Warfare and Portsmouth: The Beginnings of a Royal Navy', *TCE*, 6, 1997.

220 Helen Nicholson (ed and trans), *Chronicle of the Third Crusade: A Translation of the Itinerarium Peregrinorum et Gesta Regis Ricardi*, Aldershot, 1997, 157.

221 Bradbury, *Philip Augustus*, 242; Mollat du Jourdin, 'Philippe Auguste et la Mer', in Bautier, *La France de Philippe Auguste*, 622. The importance of Flanders to the nascent French navy can be seen in S. Curveiller, 'Le Bois et la Flandre Maritime au Moyen Âge', *Le Moyen Âge*, 106 (2), 2000.

222 P.D.A. Harvey, 'The English Inflation of 1180–1220, *Past and Present*, 61, 1973; J.L. Bolton, 'Inflation, Economics and Politics in Thirteenth-Century England', *TCE*, 4, 1992; idem, 'The English Economy in the Early Thirteenth Century', in Church, *King John*; Paul Latimer, 'Early Thirteenth-Century Prices', in ibid; M. Allen, 'The Volume of the English Currency, 1158–1470', *Economic History Review*, 54 (4), 2001; D.H. Fischer, *The Great Wave: Price Revolutions and the Rhythm of History*, Oxford, 1996, ch.1.

223 Respectively: Harvey, 'English Inflation', 7; D. Stenton, *English Society in the Early Middle Ages*, Harmondsworth, 1952, 44. Warren also sympathises (*King John*, 145). A different view is expressed in Bolton, 'The English Economy'.

224 Georges Duby, *The Early Growth of the European Economy: Warriors and Peasants from the Seventh to the Twelfth Centuries*, Ithaca, 1974, 263; Fischer, *The Great Wave*, 17. Although Fischer does not cite Bolton, both are in broad agreement on this issue.

225 James Masschaele, 'The English Economy in the Age of Magna Carta', in Loengard, *Magna Carta*, 167.

226 R.I. Moore, *The Formation of a Persecuting Society*, Oxford, 1987, 102.

227 J.C. Holt, 'The Loss of Normandy and Royal Finance', in John Gillingham and J.C. Holt (eds), *War and Government in the Middle Ages*, Woodbridge, 1984; John Gillingham, *The Angevin Empire*, 2nd edn., 2001, 95–102; Nicholas Barratt, 'The Revenues of king John and Philip Augustus Revisited', in Church, *King John*; idem, 'The Revenue of King John', *EHR*, 111 (443), 1996; Turner, *King John*, 91–4; Baldwin, *Government of Philip Augustus*, 44–58, 117–19, 144–75, 239–48, 277–79.

228 Bolton, 'English Inflation', 4. Holt's influential essay (see n. above) also puts forward this view.

229 Gillingham, *Angevin Empire*, 98.

230 Barratt, 'Revenues of John and Philip Augustus', 84.

231 See Turner, *King John*, 12.

232 Holt, *The Northerners*, 144.

233 For the events of 1205–06, see: Warren, *King John*, 100–120; Turner, *King John*, 127–30; Norgate, *John Lackland*, 103–18; Baldwin, *Government of Philip Augustus*, 194–6; A. Lyons, 'The Capetian Conquest of Anjou', unpublished PhD thesis, John Hopkins University, 1976; Guy Gauthier, *Philippe Auguste*, Paris, 2002, 242–56. The events are dispersed through the chronicles; see the references in the following footnotes.

234 WB, i. 161–2.

235 RC, 146.

236 Ibid, 152–4; Gervase of Canterbury, ii, 98.

237 Turner, *King John*, 129; Warren, *King John*, 115.

238 RW, ii, 13–14.

239 Cited in Jones, *King John*, 122. See Gilbert of Mons, 101, for an example of how readily allegiances could be shifted.

240 Rigord says that he 'totally destroyed the city' (WB, i,163); the local chronicle of St Aubin restricts the damage to a bridge (see Norgate, *John Lackland*, 115, n. 5).

241 Peter Coss (ed), *Thomas Wright's Political Songs of England: From the Reign of John to that of Edward III*, Cambridge, 1996 [1839], 2–3.

242 Turner, *King John*, 130.

243 The Channel Islands had previously fallen with Normandy: J.A. Everard and J.C. Holt, *Jersey 1204*, 2004, 85–6. For the truce, see Norgate, *John Lackland*, 117 and Rigord, WB, i, 174.

244 Warren, *King John*, 119.

245 Baldwin says that military operations began after the expiry in 1208 (Baldwin, *Government of Philip Augustus*, 199). French writers go with the date of 1207.

246 I am currently working on a military history of this conflict (see chapter seven and bibiliography.) A recent account can be found in Marvin, *The Occitan War*.

247 Baldwin, *Government of Philip Augustus*, 196–207.

248 See ns. 213 and 214 above.

249 Painter, *Reign of King John*, 253–6. For Anglo-Scottish relations, see: A.A.M. Duncan, 'John King of England and the King of Scots', in Church, *King John*; Owen, *William the Lion*, ch. 5 passim.

250 RW, ii, 50–1.

251 HWM, ii, 214–15. For Anglo-Irish relations around this time, see: Sean Duffy, 'John and Ireland: the Origins of England's Irish Problem', in Church, *King John*; F.X. Martin, 'John, Lord of Ireland', in Art Cosgrove (ed), *A New History of Ireland, Vol II: Medieval Ireland, 1169–1534*, Oxford, 1993.

252 Duffy, 'John and Ireland', 242.

253 *Brut y Tywysogion*, 1210, cited in Norgate *John Lackland*, 157–8, n. For Anglo-Welsh relations around this time, see Ifor W. Rolands, 'King John and Wales', in Church, *King John*.

254 BC, ii, 203.

255 Warren, *King John*, 199–200, offers a brief summary of the 1212 revolt.

256 RW, ii, 61. The Welsh and Irish regularly decapitated their enemies. This led to English reciprocation in the Anglo-Welsh conflict: in 1231, the heads of Welsh raiders were

delivered to Henry III; in 1245, Matthew Paris tells of an English division of troops returning the camp with over 100 Welsh heads. See McGlynn, *By Sword and Fire*, 242; Frederick C. Suppe, *Military Institutions on the Welsh Marches: Shropshire, 1066–1300*, Woodbridge, 1994, 22; idem, 'The Cultural Significance of Decapitation in High Medieval Wales and the Marches', *Bulletin of the Board of Celtic Studies*, 36, 1989. Gerald of Wales offers a grisly account from Ireland in 1069 when about 200 heads are laid before the victorious King Dermot. The king inspected each in turn, jumping with joy. On recognising the head of one man that he particularly loathed, he lifted it by its ears and hair and gnawed at its nose and cheeks. See Gerald of Wales, *Expugnatio Hibernica*, ed. and trans. by A.B. Scott and F.X. Martin, Dublin, 1978, 37; McGlynn, *By Sword and Fire*, 218.

257 Rowlands, 'King John and Wales', 282–3.

258 RW, ii, 63.

259 WB, ii, 248. See also RW, ii, 63–4. Baldwin supports the idea of a crusade (*Government of Philip Augustus*, 208).

260 For the events that follow, see: Warren, *King John*, 202–5; Baldwin, *Government of Philip Augustus*, 210–12; Norgate, *John Lackland*, 185–6; Sivéry, *Phillipe Auguste*, 261–70; Nicholas, *Medieval Flanders*, 152–3; F.W. Brooks, 'The Battle of Damme, 1213', *Mariner's Mirror*, 19, 1933; RW, ii, 67–80; WB, i, 249–53, and ii, 252–75; AB, 129–31; BC (Walter of Coventry), ii, 211; HWM, ii, 230–33.

261 Poole, *Domesday Book to Magna Carta*, 453; Baldwin, *Government of Philip Augustus*, 207. For Renaud, see Glynn Burgess, *Two Medieval Outlaws: Eustace the Monk and Fouke Fitz Waryn*, Woodbridge, 1997, 24–7.

262 RW, ii, 67. Royalist forces repeatedly appealed to patriotism throughout the conflict, especially after the French arrived.

263 RW, ii, 67–8.

264 BC, 216. See Cheney, *Innocent III and England*, 335 and Innocent's letters to John in Cheney and Semple, *Selected Letters of Innocent III*, 161–3, 168–71.

265 Warren, *King John*, 203.

266 There is some uncertainty among historians as to whether Philip intended to follow through with his invasion after the papal threat delivered by Pandulf. Norgate says that Philip 'dared not go on in the teeth of the papal prohibition' (*John Lackland*, 185); Bradbury writes his plans had been 'frustrated', reasonably telling of how the Capetian unleashed his readied forces into Flanders instead (*Philip Augustus*, 286). Baldwin seems to assume that the invasion was to go ahead, as do I (*Government of Philip Augustus*, 211). As he showed in his Normandy campaign, Philip turned a deaf ear to ecclesiastical entreaties for peace when it suited him; much of his great success is owed to his great tenacity and perseverance in the field. William the Breton dutifully claims that Philip abandoned the invasion, but this may well be because a papal order to do so was more palatable to admit as a reason than the drumming taken by the French at Damme (WB, i, 259).

267 RW, ii, 78. William the Breton confirms the extensive ravaging: WB, i, 251. David Nicholas says that Flanders was 'devastated' (Nicholas, *Medieval Flanders*, 153). See n. 111 for primary source quotations.

268 RC, 167.

269 See Vincent, 'A Roll of Knights', 90.

270 Harper-Bill, 'John and the Church', 310.

271 Poole, *Domesday Book to Magna Carta*, 464.

272 RC, 168; Turner, *King John*, 132.

273 Turner, *King John*, 132.

4 The Battle of Bouvines, 1214

274 For this campaign, its political background and culminating battle, see: WB, i, 260–96; WB, ii,. 281–347; RW, ii, 105–110; HWM, 235–43; RC, 168–9; MGH, 390–1; AB, 142–4; Anonymous of Béthune, *Recueil des Historiens des Gaules et de la France*, xxiv, 768–70; Warren, *King John*, 217–24; Turner, *King John*, 132–5; Norgate, *John Lackland*, 196–203; John Gillingham, *Richard Couer de Lion*, 78–9; Baldwin, *The Government of Philip Augustus*, 220–6; Bradbury, *Philip Augustus*, 279–316; Cartellieri, *Philip II*, iv, 402–80. French historians understandably devote much space to this seminal battle in their nation's formation: Georges Duby, *France in the Middle Ages, 987–1460*, Oxford, 1991,

220–6; Luchaire, *Philippe Auguste*, 193–212; Bordonove, *Philippe Auguste*, 213–53; Sivéry, *Philippe Auguste*, 271–311; Antoine Hadenague, *Philippe Auguste et Bouvines*, Paris, 1978 [1935]; Georges Duby, *La Dimanche de Bouvines*, Paris, 1973; Guy Gauthier, *Philippe Auguste*, Paris, 2002, 300–9; and, most recently, Jean Flori, *Philippe Auguste*, Paris, 2007, 84–9. The international and diplomatic scene is closely followed in Holzapfel, *Papst Innozenz III*, 223–80. The military angle is analysed Duby's *La Dimanche de Bouvines* and also in Verbruggen, *The Art of Warfare*, 220–37; Wade, *Armies and Warfare*, 156–74; John France, *Western Warfare in the Age of the Crusades*, 235–41 (see n. 10, 294, for France's differences with Verbruggen's account). Prof France offers a brief but up-to-date account in France, 'Battle of Bouvines', *OEMW*,163–5.

275 *Rot. Lit. Pat.*, 115a; Poole, *Domesday Book to Magna Carta*, 466.
276 RW, ii, 99–100.
277 AB, 143; RW, ii, 104; WB, i, 254. In the *Philippidos*, William claims that Robert was caught in an underhand ambush (WB, ii, 283 ff.). For the Dreux family, see Sidney Painter, *The Scourge of the Clergy: Peter of Dreux, Duke of Brittany*, New York, 1969 [1937]. For Brittany, see Everard, *Brittany and the Angevins* and Michael Jones, 'The Capetians and Brittany', *Historical Research*, 63, 1990.
278 WB, i, 260–4; WB, ii, 287–94; RW, ii, 104–5; *Chroniques d'Anjou*, 252–4. The most detailed secondary accounts before this one are, not surprisingly, French: Petit-Dutaillis, *Louis VIII*, 48–50; Sivéry, *Louis VIII*, 121–3. The exception, as ever, is the quantity provided by Cartellieri, *Philipp II*, 419–30. See also Bradbury, *Philip Augustus*, 293–5.
279 WB, ii,287–9, with the quote at 289. Here *parma* is almost certainly a mantlet of the type frequently seen in later medieval manuscript depictions of besieging forces.
280 For Louis, see: Sivéry, *Louis VIII*; Hallam, *Capetian France*, 132–6; and most useful despite its age, Petit-Dutaillis, *Louis VIII*. For a snapshot of Louis' personal and financial life a year earlier in 1213, including details of military expenditure and pre-invasion contacts with disaffected forces in England, see Fawtier, 'Un Fragment du Compte de l'Hôtel du Prince Louis de France pour le Terme de la Purification, 1213'.
281 WB, ii, 290. William was almost certainly not an eye-witness to events here as he would have been accompanying Philip Augustus to Flanders at this time. His account is therefore most likely to have been constructed from the leading French protagonists involved in the engagement.
282 RW, ii,105. Bradbury calls John's retreat 'a panic move': Bradbury, *Philip Augustus*, 293–5.
283 *Rot. Pat.*, i, 118.
284 Poole, *Domesday Book to Magna Carta*, 467; Sivéry, Louis VIII, 134.
285 Turner, *King John*, 132.
286 Power, 'King John and the Norman Aristocracy' and 'The End of Angevin Normandy'.
287 Mathhew Paris, *Historia Minor*, ii, 150. William the Breton portrays La Roche as a great victory only in his *Philippidos*, and not in his earlier *Gesta*; this may reflect William's sensitive awareness as to who was on the throne at the time of writing.
288 Anonymous of Béthune, *Chroniques des Rois*, 198.
289 For the German alliance: A.L. Poole, 'Richard the First Alliances with the German Princes in 1194'; Bartlett, *England Under the Norman and Angevin Kings*, 103–6; Gillingham, *Richard I*, 311–12; Fryde, 'King John and the Empire' and the references in ch. 3.
290 See Sean McGlynn, 'Philip Augustus', *Medieval Life*, 24
291 What follows is taken from the contemporary sources cited in note 274.
292 RW, ii 107. For Henry's and Richard's similar comments see WB, ii, 75 (Richard in particular remarks that 'To those who are well prepared, delay has always been and always will be dangerous'). Hugh's remark is noted in *HWM*, 241. See also chapter 4, n. 12.
293 RW, ii, 105.
294 See Powicke, *The Thirteenth Century*, 187.
295 For 1124, see Suger, *Vie de Louis VI le Gros*, ed. H. Waquet, Paris 1964, 226: 'ustar castellorum in corona locarentur'. For the Battle of Alençon see *Chroniques des Comtes d'Anjou*, 146; the battle is discussed in depth by Jim Bradbury in his *Medieval Archer*, Woodbridge, 1985, 44–5 and in *ANW*, 188–9. For 1197 the episode is also briefly discussed in Gillingham, *Richard Couer de Lion*, 233.

296 The numbers are analysed by Verbruggen, *The Art of Warfare* 223–9. See also Baldwin, *Philip Augustus*, 450.

297 John France offers a viable different perspective for the dispositions (see France, *Western Warfare in the Age of the Crusades*, pp. xiv-xv and appendix 1, 235–41). As explained in the text, I believe that that a lull in the fighting allowed for Ferrand and Guérin to align themselves practically, if not regimentally, into the overall order of battle.

298 All quotes in what follows are from William the Breton unless otherwised cited.

299 WB, ii, 235–326. I have not attempted to versify William's poetic form from the *Philippidos*. Matthew Strickland suggests that infantry casualties were 'probably high': *War and Chivalry*, 165. This was almost certainly the case, given the last stand of Boulogne's pikemen at the end of the battle. See also n. 32 below.

300 In Wendover's version, it is, less plausibly but more dramatically for literary effect, Count Renaud of Boulogne who knocks Philip from his horse with a lance and who is on the point of finishing him off with his sword when a bodyguard intercedes and receives the fatal blow (RW, ii, 108).

301 At this time the new style great helms were replacing the older Norman conical ones; perhaps this new dagger was designed for infantry to overcome this greater degree of protection. Alberic of Trois-Fontaines confusingly calls this new knife a *falsarium*, probably confusing it with a falchion, a curved, cleaver-like sword (akin to a scimitar) which was also appearing at this time (the cover shows an early version of this deadly weapon) (*MGSS*, xxiii, 901).

302 Even if caught, des Barres was not easily held: at Gisors in 1188 he was seized but freed by his men (*HGM*, 91). Roger of Howden (*Gesta*, ii, 46) accuses des Barres of escaping by breaking his parole, a distinctly unchivalrous act by France's greatest knight.

303 These tactics were witnessed over twenty years before Bouvines and are described by contemporaries: see Ambroise, *La Guerre Sainte*, ll. 11396–592; *Chronicle of the Third Crusade: A Translation of the Itinerarium Peregrinorum et Gesta Regis Ricardi*, ed. H. Nicholson, Aldershot, 1987, 362; and Ralph of Coggeshall (*Chronicon*, RC, 47) who based his account on information supplied by Hugh of Neville, who was present at this engagement. For the Battle of Jaffa in general, see Gillingham, *Richard I*, 214–15.

304 Anonymous of Béthune, *Chroniques des Rois*, 770.

305 Casualty figures for any battle, especially medieval ones, are notoriously difficult to determine. Verbruggen estimates that 169 knights were killed: this may be too high (William the Breton only gives two knights as killed) but is more plausible if it includes sergeants, light cavalry and, possibly, mounted mercenaries (Verbruggen, *The Art of Warfare*, 236).

306 This catalogue, known as 'Register C', is discussed by Baldwin, *Philip Augustus*, 413–18. For the list of prisoners, also see Baldwin 219, 343, 380; Sivéry discusses the captured enemy in *Philippe Auguste*, 297–300.

307 RW, ii, 109–110.

308 Baldwin, *Philip Augustus*, 219.

309 For example, Luchaire, *Philippe Auguste*, 214 (clearly following William the Breton, WB, i, 298).

310 Baldwin, *Philip Augustus*, 219.

311 Gillingham, *Richard Couer de Lion*, 79

312 Ibid, pp. 78–9. Gillingham offers a convincing argument here. See also R. Hasdju, 'Castles, Castellans, and the Structure of Politics in Poitou, 1152–1271', *Journal of Medieval History*, iv, 1978, in support of this thesis.

313 RC, 170. Jones writes that Coggeshall confuses this payment with the one of 60,000 marks made by John to Philip in 1216 (Jones, *John*, 18).

314 Painter, *John*, 228.

315 Carpenter, *The Struggle for Mastery*, 286.

316 Vincent, *Peter des Roches*, 103–4. Vincent shrewdly suggests that the merchants, ships and goods seized 'might also serve as a bargaining counters in negotiations for the release of prisoners taken at Bouvines, including the Earl of Salisbury whose ransom the justiciar was instructed to obtain … The merchants were eventually released, having promised not to put into any hostile ports or to carry cargoes to the detriment of King John' (104). Commerce with Flanders increased following the free trade clause in Magna

Carta (41) but Flemish merchants remained distinctly uneasy at political vicissitudes and the possibility of sequestration of goods by the English (see David Nicholson, *Medieval Flanders*, Harlow, 1992, 154). The nature of Welsh incursions into England is explored by F. Suppe, *Military Institutions on the Welsh Marches*, Woodbridge, 1994.

317 Flanders had the Treaty of Paris imposed upon it on 24 October 1214. By this many fortresses were not permitted repairs and the key ones – Ypres, Cassel and Oudenarde – were completely destroyed; these three strongholds comprised the Flemish line of defence against French incursions. For the consequences of Bouvines on Flanders, see Nicholson, *Medieval Flanders*, 153–6.

318 Anonymous of Béthune, *RHF*, xxiv, 770. Elizabeth Hallam has written of the Capetian's ascendancy: 'From kings too powerless and obscure even to find biographers, there had sprung a hero-king, whose grandson was to become a saint' (*Capetian France*, 179). For the most detailed discussions of the seminal historic importance of Bouvines and its legendary status in France, see: Baldwin, *Philip Augustus*, 380–9; Duby, *France in the Middle Ages*, 222–7; Duby, *The Legend of Bouvines*, 141–79; Hallam, *Capetian France*, 178–9; Luchaire, *Philippe Auguste*, 211–17; Hadenauge, *Philippe Auguste*, 233–51; Bradbury, 326–8; and the section on 'L'image du roi et du règne' in Bautier (ed), *Philippe Auguste*, 115–213 *passim*. Of especial note, which includes unlikely moves to have Philip canonised, see John Baldwin, 'Le Sens du Bouvines', *Cahiers de Civilisation Médiévale*, 30, 1987. One less expected result came in the form of parody: see John Haines, 'A Parody of Songs in Praise of War', *Speculum*, 82 (2), 2007, which focuses on later interpretations of Bouvines.

319 Matthew Bennet has suggested to me that Philip, shaken by his near fatal experience at Bouvines, may have shunned any further military role for fear of the personal dangers involved. This fits in with Philip's cautious and unheroic character.

320 Unedited chronicle, in MS 553, Bibliothèque Mazarine, folio 373; and Luchaire, *Philippe Auguste*, 198.

5 Magna Carta, Civil War and the Countdown to Invasion, 1215

321 Michael Clanchy, *England and Its Rulers, 1066–1272*, 2nd edn., London, 1998, 129. For Peter des Roches see Nicholas Vincent's magisterial study, *Peter des Roches*.

322 There is a wealth of material and analysis for these events and Magna Carta. In addition to the general histories already cited, see: J.C. Holt, *The Northerners: A Study in King John*, 2nd edn. Oxford, 1992; J.C Holt, *Magna Carta*, Cambridge, especially 183–266, 347–77; J.C.Holt, *Magna Cart and Medieval Government*; Turner, *King John*, 201–54; Warren, *King John*, 217–51; Norgate, *John Lackland*, p 210–256; Painter, *King John*, 226–366; Ralph Turner, *Magna Carta*, London, 2003, 40–79; Hugh Thomas, *Vassals, Heiresses, Crusaders and Thugs*, Pennsylvania, 1993, 168–92. The recent (2010) collection edited by Loengard, *Magna Cart and the England of King John* is a valuable collection of papers for this aspect of John's reign.

323 Carpenter, *The Struggle for Mastery*, 286.

324 For financial matters, see references in ch. 3 notes and, specifically for discontent, see: Warren, *King John*, 182–4; Turner, *King John*, 215–24, 231–2; for a discussion of scutage, see Painter, *King John*, 125–8. The principle of taxation and consent for the period 1189–1227 has recently been addressed by J.R.Maddicott, *The Origins of the English Parliament, 924–1327*, Oxford, 2010, 119–26.

325 *Pipe Roll 12 John*; Warren, *King John*, 182.

326 Turner, *King John*, 220.

327 Holt, *The Northerners*, 34. See Brian Golding, 'Simon of Kyme: the Making of a Rebel', *Nottingham Medieval Studies*, 27, 1983, for a case study of one of the rebels.

328 Carpenter, *The Struggle for Mastery*, 279. For a detailed analysis of the de Braose case, see Painter, *King John*, 238–50, and, most recently (2010), Crouch, 'Baronial Paranoia' and 'The Complaint of King john against William de Braose', in Loengard (ed), *Magna Carta and the England of King John*. For an overall context see the innovative study by J.S. Bothwell, *Falling From Grace: Reversal of Fortune and the English Nobility, 1075–1455*, Manchester, 2008.

329 Annals of Margam, *Annales Monastici*, i, 27; Warren, *King John*, 82–3. The Annals were probably written after de Braose's fall.

330 RW, ii, 48–9.

331 Warren, *King John*, 184, 187.

332 Crouch, 'Baronial Paranoia', 51; Painter, *King John*, 249–50.

333 AB, 105.

334 Cited in Painter, *King John*, 231. Painter suggested that she was probably John's mistress and was buying her way out of the king's bed (231).

335 The quotes are from Nicholas Vincent, 'Introduction', in Vincent, *Records, Administration and Aristocratic Society in the Anglo-Norman Realm*, xiv. See also Marie Lovatt, 'Archbishop Geoffrey of York: A Problem in Anglo-French Maternity' from the same volume and Vincent, 'Isabella of Angôuleme'.

336 BC, 207.

337 Crouch, 'Baronial Paranoia', 60.

338 RC, 167.

339 Holt, *The Northerners*, 34.

340 Crouch 'Baronial Paranoia', 62.

341 The quote is from Turner, *King John*, 222. For the composition of the baronial party, see Painter, *King John*, 284–99. Painter emphasises the youth of the baronial faction. The question of knights is addressed by Holt, *The Northeners*, 35–60; Kathryn Faulkner, 'The Knights in the Magna Carta Civil War', in *TCE*, 8, 2001; J.R. Maddicott, 'Magna Carta and the Local Community, 1215–19', *Past and Present*, 101, 1984. On the question of loyalty, see also S.D. Church, *The Household Knights of King John*, Cambridge, 1999, 100–16.

342 Paul Latimer, 'Rebellion in South-western England and the Welsh Marches, 1215–1217', *Historical Research*, 80 (208), 2007.

343 Poole, *Domesday Book to Magna Carta*, 470; Warren, *King John*, 230.

344 AB, p 116–18. Fitzwalter's retinue was only about 50, so the figures here are clearly inflated, but the point is made. It is unlikely that John would have hung an earl for this.

345 Turner, *King John*, 223.

346 See n. 2 for events leading to Magna Carta.

347 Holt, *The Northerners*, p 103–4 for figures.

348 Keith Stringer, 'The War of 1215–17 in its Context', in Richard Oram (ed), *The Reign of Alexander II, 1214–49*, Leiden, 2005. My thanks to Prof Stringer for sending me an early draft of this important and detailed study.

349 BC, 218. This was not actually mentioned in the charter.

350 RW, ii, 114; RC, p 171–2.

351 Painter, *King John*, 303.

352 BC, 220. Generational splits were a feature of rebellions.

353 RW, ii, p 137. For London and its relationship with the rebels, see Tony Moore, '"Other Cities Have Citizens, London's are Called Barons." Connections between London and Essex During the Magna Carta Civil War (1215–17')', forthcoming. Many thanks to Dr Moore for sending me a draft of his important essay. Also for London, see his 'Government and Locality in Essex in the Reign of Henry III', unpublished doctoral thesis, University of Cambridge, 2006, 62–76. Again, I am indebted to Dr Moore for his kindness in forwarding me a copy of his important thesis. Also: Natalie Fryde, *Why Magna Carta? Angevin England Revisited*, Munster, 2001, 73–81; C.N.L. Brooke and Gillian Keir, *London, 800–1216: the Shaping of a City*, London, 1975, 49–56.

354 RW, ii, 117–18.

355 RC, 171–2.

356 Baldwin says that Philip Augustus was at best reluctant and at worst hostile to intervention in England after Bouvines (Baldwin, *Philip Augustus*, 332). This is areal possibility, but he may have indulged the ambitions of his son Louis. Philip would also have been keenly aware from his father Louis VII of the efficacy of sowing internal dissent in England.

357 See AB, 148–9 for events.

358 Painter, *King John*, 308.

359 Ibid, 309.

360 For the full text of Magna Carta, see Holt, *Magna Carta*, 441–73; Warren, *King John*, 265–77; Turner, *Magna Carta*, 226–36.

361 Warren, *King John*, 239.
362 Matthew Paris, ii, 611.
363 Holt, *Magna Carta*, 228.
364 BC, 222.
365 Warren, *King John*, 108. For John's relations with Salisbury, see Brock Holden, 'The Balance of Patronage: King John and the Earl of Salisbury', *Haskins Society Journal*, 8, 1996.
366 For Falkes, see Daniel Power, 'Bréauté, Sir Falkes de', *Dictionary of National Biography*, Oxford, accessed online at www.oxforddnb.com.
367 Turner, *King John*, 251. Turner summarises the positions well (251–3) and I have borrowed from him heavily for the following passage.
368 See Richard Eales, 'Castles and Politics in England, 1215–1214', *TCE2*, 1988.
369 Painter, *King John*, 352–3.
370 Ibid, 353.
371 Turner, *King John*, 252.
372 Half a century later, another rebel, Simon de Montfort, and another king, Henry III, viewed Rochester in similar terms: see J.R. Maddicott, *Simon de Montfort*, Cambridge, 1994, 268. For Rochester, see RW, 145–51; AB, 158–60, 163; BC, 226. I have, as far as I am aware, provided here the most detailed account of the siege.
373 The result of this action is clearly seen at Rochester today; the south-western tower was rebuilt immediately after the siege in the more modern and effective circular form, standing incongruously next to its older partners.
374 R. Allen Brown, *Rochester Castle*, 2nd edn., English Heritage, 1986, 10–11. I was fortunate to have taken postgraduate studies with Prof Allen Brown at King's College, London.
375 Ralph Turner, 'King John's Military Reputation Reconsidered', *Journal of Medieval History*, 19, 1993.
376 For example, a detailed study of Wendover's chronicle reveals that most woundings and fatalities in this period were from crossbows and bows. See McGlynn, 'Roger of Wendover and the Wars of Henry III', 188. Much has been written on these weapons, for example: Kelly de Vries, *Medieval Military Technology*, Peterborough, 1992, 33–44; David Nicolle, *Arms and Armour of the Crusading Era, 1050–1350: Western Europe and the Crusader States*, London, 1999, passim; Vernon Foley, George Palmer and Werner Soedel, 'The Crossbow', *Scientific American*, 1985. Matthew Strickland and Robert Hardy, *The Great Warbow*, Stroud, 2005; Jim Bradbury, *The Medieval Archer*, Woodbridge, 1985. Readers will discover here elements of the longbow debate, ie: the longbow was a radical new weapon which revolutionised English tactics in the Hundred Years War leading to such great victories as Crécy and Agincourt. For my mind, I think it highly improbable that it was a new weapon: in age of technological wonders such as castles and cathedrals, it seems impossible that medieval man would not have realised a longer bow would have greater power. As armour developed, so the bow would have too to attempt to counter it. Gerald of Wales gives a vivid depiction of the penetrative power of bows in the late twelfth century: Gerald of Wales, *The Journey Through Wales / The Description of Wales*, London, 1978, 113.
377 RW, ii, 150, confirmed by AB, 163.
378 Froissart, Chronicles, 106. For a discussion of threats, see McGlynn, *By Sword and Fire*, 189–94.
379 AB, 161–2.
380 Ibid, 160.
381 See Petit-Dutaillis, *Louis VIII*, 71. Ralph of Coggeshall says that John had passed on forged letters: RC, 176–7.
382 See AB, 160–1 for a list of French knights and Petit-Dutaillis, *Louis VIII*, 70–96, for Louis' preparations.
383 RW, ii, 161.
384 S. D. Church, 'The Earliest English Muster Roll, 18/19 December, 1215', *Historical Research*, 67 (162), 1994. Also see S.D.Church, 'The Knights of the Household of King John: a Question of Numbers', *TCE*, 4, 1992. His monograph is extremely insightful: Church, *The Household Knights of King John*.
385 RW, 162.

386 Warren, *King John*, 248–9.
387 There has been a tendency in recent years to play down the extent of the Anarchy, but Hugh Thomas has reassuringly countered this misperception in an important article: Hugh Thomas, 'Violent Disorder in King Stephen's England: A Maximum Argument', in Paul Dalton and Graeme White (eds), *King Stephen's Reign, 1135–1154*, Woodbridge, 2008.

6 The Invasion of England, 1216

388 RC, 178.
389 BC, 229.
390 For John's campaign, see: RW, ii, 162–6; AB, 163–4; McGlynn, *By Sword and Fire*, 222–33; Turner, *King* John, 254; Warren, *King John*, 248–9; Painter, *King* John, 368–70; Norgate, *John Lackland*, 255–7 Holt, *The Northerners*, 133.
391 RW, ii, 162.
392 RW, ii, 162.
393 BC, 228.
394 See Strickland, 'Securing the North' for castle strategy.
395 Painter, *King John*, 368.
396 For events in Scotland in the years 1215–17, see Keith Stringer, 'Kingship, Conflict and State-Making in the Reign of Alexander II: The War of 1215–17 and its Context', in Richard Oram (ed), *The Reign of Alexander II, 1214–49*, Lieden, 2005. This is the only article that deals at length with the events discussed here; it is an invaluable study on which I have drawn heavily.
397 Stringer, 'Kingship, Conflict and State-Making', 123, n. 88; AB, 163–4.
398 Stringer, 'Kingship, Conflict and State-Making', 144.
399 MP, ii, 642.
400 Stringer, 'Kingship, Conflcit and State-Making', 145.
401 See: Painter, *King John*, 370; Holt, *The Northeners*, 133–5.
402 There is uncertainty over Alnwick and Warwick-on-Tweed: Holt says they remained untaken by John (*The Northeners*, 134); Painter says otherwise (*King John*, 370). According to Wendover, Mountsorrel was the only castle remaining to the rebels in the north (RW, ii, 167).
403 Painter, *King John*, 370.
404 Holt, *The Northerners*, 137.
405 RC, 178–9.
406 HWM, ii, 225. William Marshal was in Ireland at this time.
407 RW, ii, 165–6. See McGlynn, *By Sword and Fire*, 227–31, for a detailed analysis of what follows.
408 RW, ii, 166.
409 RW, ii, 171–2.
410 RW, ii, 162.
411 BC, 232.
412 Holt makes the case for no payment in *The Northerners*, 134, n.1.
413 Poole, *Domesday Book to Magna Carta*, 481.
414 Richmond, 'Identity and Morality', 234.
415 McGlynn, *By Sword and Fire*, explains the rationale behind atrocities in medieval warfare.
416 David Green, *Edward the Black Prince*, Harlow, 2007, 35.
417 RW, ii, 162–7. See also McGlynn, 'Roger of Wendover', 194–7.
418 McGlynn, 'Roger of Wendover', 195.
419 The Anonymous gives the names of some of the knights: AB, 160–1; *Chronique des Rois de France*, 770–1. For events leading up to Louis' arrival, see: RW, ii, 165–80; AB, 162–8; WB, i, 305–8; RC, 178–81; Petite-Dutaillis, *Louis VIII*, 90–100; Painter, *King John*, 370–4; Turner, *King John*, 254–5; Warren, *King John*, 251–1.
420 AB, 164–5.
421 Painter, *King John*, 372.
422 Painter, *King John*, 372.
423 For the events of April, see: RW, ii, 176–80; WB, ii, 359; WB, I 306–7; Baldwin, *The Government of Philip Augustus*, 332; Bradbury, *Philip Augustus*, 318–19; and note 32.

424 For Guala, see: Nicholas Vincent (ed), *The Letters and Charters of Cardinal Guala Bicchieri*, Woodbridge, 1996; Fred A. Cazel, 'The Legates Guala and Pandulf', in *TCE* II.

425 These sanctions can not be verified.

426 Bradbury, *Philip Augustus*, 319–20; Baldwin, *Government of Philip Augustus*, 335.

427 See AB, 187 and again in his *Chroniques des Rois de France*, 770.

428 RW, ii, 180. Cf. WB, i, 306–7 where William says a safe passage was granted.

429 Vincent, *Letters and Charters*, xl–xli.

430 Norgate, *John Lackland*, 267.

431 AB, 168; RC, 181.

432 AB, 166–7; WB, i, 307.

433 For Eustace, see: Glyn Burgess (ed and trans), *Two Medieval Outlaws: Eustace the Monk and Fouke Fitz Waryn*, Woodbridge, 1997; Maurice Keen, *The Outlaws of Medieval Legend*, 1977.

434 Maurice Keen, *The Outlaws of Medieval Legend*, 54.

435 Burgess, *Two Medieval Outlaws*, 77.

436 RC, 181; Petit-Dutaillis, *Louis VIII*, 100.

437 Vincent, *Letters and Charters*, xli.

438 AM, ii, 46.

439 AB, 169. In his *Chroniques des Rois de France*, the Anonymous says that did not wait there (*Recueil*, xiv, 771).

440 RW, ii, 180.

441 It opened its gates to Louis on 6 November.

442 RW, ii, 181.

443 RW, ii, 181–2.

444 Warren, *King John*, 252. For the events of June and July, see: RW, ii, 190–2; AB, 171–4; BC, ii, 230–1; AM, ii, 46–7; Petite-Dutaillis, *Louis VIII*, 106–8; Norgate, *John Lackland*, 271–4; Painter, *King John*, 374–5. Wendover and Anonymous remain the chief sources here.

445 WB, i, 311.

446 Sidney Painter, *William Marshal: Knight-Errant, Baron, and Regent of England*, Toronto, 1982 [1933], 188. Walter de Beauchamp was soon back in John's camp.

447 Painter, *King John*, 375.

448 RW, ii 191.

449 WM, 257.

450 Church, *Household Knights of King John*, 111. For the comings and goings of these vacillating vassals see chapter 5 of this excellent study.

451 AB, 176–7.

452 RW, ii, 183.

453 Norgate, *John Lackland*, 274–5, on whom I have drawn heavily for this paragraph.

454 Norgate, *John Lackland*, 275. For intelligence, see: Michael Prestwich, 'Military Intelligence under the Norman and Angevin kings', in George Garnett and John Hudson (eds), *Law and Government in Medieval England and Normandy*, Oxford, 1994; McGlynn, 'Roger of Wendover', 191–2.

455 WB, i, 311–12, where he calls Dover 'impregnable'. For a recent study of Dover Castle, see John Gillingham, 'The King and the Castle', *BBC History*, 10 (8), 2009. For an analysis of the castle's military architecture during the siege, see John Goodall, 'Dover Castle and the Great Siege of 1216', *Château Gaillard XIX*, 2000.

456 MP, ii, 664.

457 AM, ii, 49. For the initial phase of the siege of the Dover, see: AB, 177–80; RW, ii, 191–2.

458 The exact date is uncertain; Wendover suggests that the meeting took place in August (RW, ii, 194). See Stringer, 'Kingship, Conflict and State-Making', 128 and 131 for a discussion of Alexander's march.

459 Stringer, 'Kingship, Conflict and State-Making', 128, 129.

460 RW, ii, 194.

461 For Willikin, see: G. R. Stephen, 'A Note on William of Cassingham', *Speculum*, 16, 1941; Sean McGlynn, 'King John and the French Invasion of England', *BBC History*, 11 (6), 2010, 28.

462 RW, ii, 182.

463 AB, 181.

464 WM, 257.

465 For the siege of Windsor and events surrounding it, see: RW, ii, 192–3; AB, 177, 179.

466 For events up to mid-October, see: RW, ii,193–7; 180; RC, 182–4; Turner, *King John*, 256–7; Warren, *King John*, 253–6; Painter, *King John*, 376–7; Norgate, *John Lackland*, 277–81; Petit-Dutaillis, 109–110.

467 Turner, *King John*, 256.

468 AM, ii, 149.

469 Stringer, 'Kingship, Conflict and State-Making', 129.

470 RW, ii, 193; see also AM, ii 47.

471 RC, 182.

472 BC, 231.

473 See Stringer, 'Kingship, Conflict and State-Making', 128.

474 MP, ii 667. See also his *Historia Anglorum*, ii, 189–90.

475 RW, ii, 193.

476 BC, 231.

477 BC, 232.

478 For events see Holt, *Magna Carta and Medieval Government*, 111–22 and the references in n.466.

479 Holt, *Magna Carta and Medieval Government*, 117–18; see also Warren, *King John*, 278–85 (Appendix C).

480 Stringer, 'Kingship, Conflict and State-Making', 129 n.113.

481 Baldwin, *Government of Philip Augustus*, 333.

482 Jane E. Sayers, *Papal Government and England During the Pontificate of Honorius III, 1216–1227*, Cambridge, 1984, 166–7.

483 AB, 182.

7 The Battle for England, 1216–1217

484 BC, 232; MP, ii, 669.

485 WB, ii, 259.

486 S.D. Church, 'King's John Testament and the Last Days of his Reign', *EHR*, 125, 2010, 517.

487 The following paragraph draws heavily on Church's detailed study, especially at 521–2.

488 Church, 'King John's Testament', 528.

489 Holt, *The Northeners*, 139.

490 Holt, *Magna Carta and Medieval Government*, 122; RC, 184.

491 HWM, 265.

492 HWM, 269.

493 HWM, 287.

494 MP, iii, 3–4; HWM, 285.

495 AB, 180–1.

496 BC, 232.

497 Gillingham, *Angevin Empire*, 108.

498 Carpenter, *The Minority of Henry III*, 1990, 22.

499 For a narrative of the events of Henry's first year, see: Carpenter, *Minority*, ch. 2; K. Norgate, *The Minority of Henry III*, 1912, ch.1; F.M. Powicke, *King Henry III and the Lord Edward: The Community of the Realm in the Thirteenth Century: Volume One*, Oxford, 1947, 1–18; F.M. Powicke, *The Thirteenth Century, 1216–1307*, 2nd edn, Oxford, 1–14; Petit-Dutaillis, *Louis VIII*, chs. 8 and 9; Sivéry, *Louis VIII*, ch.7. For Henry's reign and aspects of it, see also David Carpenter, *The Reign of Henry III*, 1996; Robert Stacey, *Politics, Policy and Finance under Henry III, 1216–1245*, Oxford, 1987; Weiler and Rowlands, *England and Europe un the Reign of Henry III*; Vincent, *Peter des Roches* (ch.4 deals with the civil war and its immediate aftermath); and the important series, *TCE*.

500 Powicke, *Thirteenth Century*, 4. For the reissue of Magna Carta, see Holt, *Magna Carta*, 378–82; Turner, *Magna Carta*, 80–4; Norgate, *Minority*, 10–15; Stacey, *Politics, Policy and Finance*, 3–4. The Barnwell chronicler stresses the religious activity at this time: BC, 233–4.

501 RW, ii, 199. See also AB, 182, who says a further truce was arranged.

502 For Hertford and Berkhamstead: RW, ii, 200–1; AB, 182; HWM, 289. Hertford may have surrendered sooner: AM, ii 287.

503   AM, iii, 47 and RW, ii, 201 for St Albans. St Albans was Wendover's mother house.

504   AB, 182.

505   HWM, 289.

506   See Carpenter, *Minority*, 26, for what follows.

507   HWM, 275, 285.

508   RW, ii, 205. See also MP, ii, 12–13 for Falkes' later attempt at a very insincere reconciliation with the abbey.

509   Norgate, *Minority*, 19; BC, 235.

510   BC, 235; RW, ii, 206; WB, i, 312–13.

511   RW, ii, 205; BC, 235 for the oath.

512   For the combat at Rye, see AB 183–7; Anonymous of Béthune, *Recueil des Historiens de France*, xiv, 774 (which closely follows the *Histoire des Ducs*); HWM, 291–5.

513   HWM, 257.

514   Painter, *William Marshal*, 210–11.

515   AB, 187.

516   AB, 187.

517   BC, 235–6.

518   Christopher Tyerman, *England and the Crusades*, 133–44. The quote is at 139.

519   Carpenter, *Minority*, 29. And note how the Barnwell chronicler draws attention to Guala's unpopularity: BC, 236.

520   RW, ii, 205.

521   Carpenter, *Minority*, 30–1, has fuller details.

522   RW, ii, 205.

523   AB, 187–8. Our main source for this period is HWM, 297–303. Petit-Dutaillis offers a brief paragraph (*Louis VIII*, 145). For what follows, see David Crouch's valuable notes, HWM, iii, 169–70.

524   David Crouch makes the point about the south coast movements: Crouch, *William Marshal*, 121.

525   BC, 236.

526   AB, 188.

527   Robert of Auxerre, 36; HWM, 303.

528   AB, 188–9.

529   HWM, 305.

530   For military activity in the south, see: AB, 189–93; HWM, 305–7; BC, 236–7. *The History of William Marshal* confirms the chronology at Winchester; see also David Crouch's notes: HWM, iii, 171.

531   HWM, 305. The biographer of William Marshal mistakingly notes that Louis' army of heavily equipped knights 'wisely rode straight past Farnham' (305).

532   Vincent, *Peter des Roches*, 136.

533   AB, 192–3, is the only contemporary account of what follows.

534   For Mountsorrel, see: RW, ii, 208–9, 211; HWM, 307; BC, 236–7; AM, iii, 49.

535   Vincent, *Peter des Roches*, 127–31 (at 128–9). For the impact of ravaging, see: E.B. Fryde. *Peasants and Landlords in Later Medieval England*, Stroud, 1996, 220–26; J.J.N. Palmer, 'The Conqueror's Footprints in Domesday Book', in Ayton and Price, *The Medieval Military Revolution*; J.J.N. Palmer, 'War and Domesday Waste', in Strickland, *Armies, Chivalry and Warfare*; McGlynn, *By Sword and Fire*, ch. 5; Sean McGlynn, 'Sheer Terror' and the Black Prince's *Grand Chevauchée* of 1355', in *The Hundred Years War: Volume 3*, eds Donald Kagay and Andrew Villalon, Leiden, 2011.

536   Gillingham, 'William the Bastard at War', *ANW*, 151.

537   AM, iii, 49.

538   HWM, 307.

539   RW, ii, 207.

540   HWM, 309–13. I have omitted sections of the speech and adapted it here.

541   For Lincoln, see: RW, ii, 211–19; HWM, 309–55; BC, 237; AM, iii, 49–50; 194–5; WB, ii, 313–14; Coss, *Political* Songs, 19–27; F.W. Brooks and F. Oakley, 'The Campaign and Battle of Lincoln, 1217', *Associated Architectural Societies' Reports and Papers*, vol. 26., part 2, 1922; J.W.F. Hill, *Medieval Lincoln*, Cambridge, 1948, 201–5; T.F. Tout, 'The Fair of Lincoln and the "Histoire de Guillaume le Maréchal"', *EHR*, 18. For Nichola de

Hay, see Charles Petit-Dutaillis, 'Une femme de Guerre au XIIIe siècle: Nicole de la Haie, Gardienne du Château de Lincoln', in *Mélanges Julien Havet. Recueil de TRavaux d'Erudition Dedies à la Memoire de Julien Havet (1853–93)*, Paris, 1895. I am very grateful to Louise Wilkinson for drawing my attention to this article and for sending me a copy of her paper on Nichola which she presented to the Late Medieval Seminar at the Institute of Historical Research in March 1998, and to David Carpenter for suggesting to her that this paper might be of use to me (as indeed it was).

542 David Crouch makes this interesting suggestion: HWM, iii, 173.

543 Detailed descriptions of medieval Lincoln are to be found in Hill, *Medieval Lincoln*, and Brooks and Oakley, 'The campaign and Battle of Lincoln, 1217',

544 Coss, *Political Songs*, 24.

545 The most recent literature on Towton is: Gorge Goodwin, *Fatal Colours: Towton, 1461 – England's Most Brutal Battle*, 2011; John Sadler, *Towton: The Battle of Palm Sunday Field*, Barnsley, 201; Sean McGlynn, 'The Wars of the Roses', in Clifford Rogers (ed), *The Oxford Encyclopedia of Medieval Warfare and Technology*, vol. 3, Oxford 2010; McGlynn, *By Sword and Fire*, 129–31.

546 Coss, *Political Songs*, 25.

547 The suggestion is made in an appendix in Norgate, *Minority*, 273–4. Cf. the comments by Brooks and Oakley, 'The Campaign and Battle of Lincoln, 1217', 303–4.

548 There is a slight possibility that it was in fact the western blocked/unblocked gate that was forced. Carpenter suggests that the gate may have been unblocked at this juncture (*Minority*, 39). See also Brooks and Oakley, 'The Campaign and Battle of Lincoln, 1217', 306.

549 This rightward wheel prompts David Carpenter to believe that the regent had entered through the unblocked west gate (*Minority*, 39).

550 *Historia Anglia*, ii, 213.

551 See Norgate, *Minority*, 44, n.6 for a detailed list of prisoners; also AB, 195. For the Count of Perche, see K. Thompson, *Power and Border Lordship in Medieval France: the County of Perche, 1000–1226*, Woodridge, 2002, 151–63.

552 RW, ii, 218–19. See also the Dunstable annalist who confirms that 'many drowned' (AM, iii, 50) and also BC, 238. For sacking of cities, see McGlynn, *By Sword and Fire*, ch.4, with Lincoln at 187–8.

553 Coss, *Political Songs*, 27; Powicke, *King Henry III*, 12; Carpenter, *Minority*, 40. But see also the dissenting views of Brooks and Oakley, 'The Campaign and Battle of Lincoln, 1217', 312.

8 The Last Campaign, 1217

554 Petit-Dutaillis, *Louis VIII*, 153. Nor had Lincoln completely 'destroyed the barons' as the Merton Chronicle believes (Petit-Dutaillis, 514). However, the barons suffered more than their French comrades as they did not have a reservoir of manpower to draw upon from across the Channel.

555 Powicke, *King Henry* III, 13. For events immediately following Lincoln, see: AB, 195–200; HWM, 355–9; BC, 238; RW, ii, 219–20; AM, iii, 50; and the secondary sources in note 16, chapter seven.

556 See: Sean McGlynn, 'British Nationalism and Europe: A Medieval Comparison', *Politics*, 16 (3), 1996; A.D. Smith, *National Identity*, 1991; Patrick Wormald, 'Engla Lond: The Making of an Allegiance', *Journal of Historical Sociology*, 7 (1), 1994; Patrick Wormald, 'The Making of England', *History Today* 45 (2), 1995; John Gillingham, 'Henry of Huntingdon and the Twelfth-Century Revival of the English Nation', *The English in the Twelfth Century* (and pages 93–162 for other relevant essays); Jospeh Llobera, 'State and Nation in Medieval France', *Journal of Historical Sociology*, 7 (3), 1994; Len Scales and Oliver Zimmer (eds), *Power and Nation in European History*, Cambridge, 2005 (Part Two for the Middle Ages); Len Scales, 'Identifying "France" and "Germany": Medieval Nation-Making in Some Recent Publications', *Bulletin of International Medieval Research*, 6, 2000; Len Scales, 'Bread, Cheese and Genocide: Imagining the Destruction of Peoples in Medieval Western Europe', *History*, 92 (3), 2007; Simon Forde, Lesley Johnson and Alan Murray, *Concepts of National Identity in the Middle Ages*, Leeds, 1995; Michael Clanchy, *England and its* Rulers, 173–89; A.D. Smith, 'Gastronomy or Geology? The Role of Nationalism in the Reconstruction of

Nations', *Nations and Nationalism* 1 (1), 1995; Ernest Gellner, *Nations and Nationalism*, Oxford, 1983.

557 See, for example, Bertrand Taithe and Tim Thornton (eds), *War: Identities in Conflict, 1300–2000*, Stroud, 1998. War and identity are main themes in Smith, *National Identity*; John Breuilly, *Nationalism and the State*, 2nd edn., Manchester, 1993; E. Shils, 'Nations, Nationalism and Civil Society', *Nations and Nationalism*, 1 (1), 1995. See Gillingham, *The English in the Twelfth Century*, 123–62, for the role or war within the British Isles on the formation of identity.

558 Breuilly, *Nationalism and the State*, 87.

559 David Carpenter, 'English Peasants in Politics, 1258–1267' *Past and Present*, 136, 1992.

560 Alfred Smyth, 'The Emergence of English Identity, 700–1000', in Alfred Smyth (ed), *Medieval Europeans: Studies in Ethnic Identity and National Perspectives in Medieval Europe*, Basingstoke, 1998.

561 McGlynn, 'British Nationalism and Europe: A Medieval Comparison' extends this argument.

562 HWM, 355–7; RW, ii, 219–20; WB, i, 313–14.

563 HWM, 357.

564 AB, 195.

565 See again Tony Moore, 'Other Cities have Citizens, London's are called Barons' for London.

566 AB, 195–6.

567 AB, 196–7. For the unsettled atmosphere in London, see AB, 196–7 and AM, ii, 287.

568 Powicke, *King Henry III*, 13; Petit-Dutaillis, *Louis VIII*, 157.

569 Tyerman, *England and the Crusades*, 59.

570 AB, 197–8.

571 Powicke, *King Henry III*, 13.

572 Vincent, *Letters and Charters*, 109.

573 Vincent, *Letters and Charters*, 106–110 for the letter and commentary. See also Petit-Dutaillis, *Louis VIII*, 157–8, n.9, and Powicke, *King Henry III*, 14, n.1.

574 AB, 197.

575 *Recueil des Historiens des Gaules et de la France*, 1734–1904, xix, 636, in Carpenter, *Minority*, 42.

576 Cited in Vincent, *Letters and Charters*, 110.

577 Carpenter, *Minority*, 42–3, covers this episode.

578 AB, 199–200 for what follows in London.

579 AB, 199–200.

580 Sivéry, *Louis VIII*, 186. For Blanche of Castille, see: Gerard Sivéry, *Blanche de Castille*, Paris, 1990; Régine Pernoud, *Blance of Castile*, London, 1975; Jacques le Goff, *Saint Louis*, Paris, 1996.

581 The Minstrel of Reims, in Petit-Dutaillis, *Louis VIII*, 163.

582 RW, ii, 220–1.

583 RW, ii, 221; AB, 198; AM, iii, 50; HWM, 357–9; Melrose, 127–8.

584 HWM, 359.

585 RW, ii, 221. For what follows and the Battle of Sandwich, see: RW, ii, 221–3; HWM, 357–77; AB, 201–2; BC, 238–9; RC, 185; WB, i, 314; *The Romance of Eustace the Monk* in Burgess, *Two Medieval Outlaws*, 77–8. Matthew Paris also covers the battle, but less reliably so when he moves away from Wendover's account: MP, iii, 26–9; *Historia Anglia* 216–21. A detailed secondary account of the battle is to be found in H.L. Cannon, 'The Battle of Sandwich and Eustace the Monk', *EHR*, 27, 1912. More briefly, see Norgate, *Minority*, 50–4; I follow a different chronology to Norgate who places the initial English defeat on the day of battle, instead of in the previous weeks.

586 HWM, 363–5. The return to full allegiance of the Cinque ports was essential in preparing the English fleet. For medieval naval matters, see: N.A.M. Rodger, *The Safeguard of the Sea: A Naval History of Britain. Volume One: 660–1649*, 1997; F.W. Brooks, *The English Naval Forces, 1199–1272*, n.d.; Archibald Lewis and Timothy Runyan, *European Naval and Maritime History, 300–1500*, Bloomington, 1985; Ian Friel, *The Good Ship: Ships, Shipbuilding and Technology in England, 1200–1520*, 1995; John Gillingham, 'Richard I, Galley-Warfare and Portsmouth: the Beginnings of a

Royal Navy', *TCE* 6, 1997; Susan Rose, *Medieval Naval Warfare, 1000–1500*, 2002; John Hattendorf and Richard Unger (eds), *War at Sea in the Middle Ages and Renaissance*, Woodbridge, 2003.

587 For cogs, see Rodgers, *Safeguard of the Sea*, 62–3; Friel, *The Good Ship*, 35–8.

588 For this episode, see Helen Nicholson (ed and trans), *Chronicle of the Third Crusade: A Translation of the* Itinerarium Peregrinorum et Gesta Ricardi, Aldershot, 1997, 197–9.

589 RW, ii, 67–8.

590 RW, ii, 68.

591 David Loades, 'The King's Ships: the Keeping of the Seas, 1413–1480', *Medieval History*, 1 (1), 1991, 94.

592 HWM, 369.

593 Loades, 'The King's Ships', 94.

594 The hunting analogy is usually the one accepted. However, in *The History of William Marshal*, from which this phrase comes (370–1), 'hart' is translated as 'noose'. Here it is feminine. In English, 'hart' usually refers to a male deer, especially a stag, 'Noose' in Old French is a masculine noun. The inconsistencies of Old French apply to gender as much as to any aspect of its variable language.

595 WB, i, 314.

596 As is pointed out by Carpenter, *Minority*, 43.

597 Cannon believes the French broke order to attack: 'The Battle of Sandwich', 663.

598 RC, 185–6.

599 AM, ii, 287–8. Prisoner numbers are discussed in Cannon, 'The Battle of Sandwich', 666–7.

600 As Carpenter has noted (*Minority*, 43).

601 *Patent Rolls*, 1216–25, 89 in Cannon, 'The Battle of Sandwich', 666, where the number of ships taken is discussed.

602 RW, ii, 272; WB, ii, 271.

603 See, for example, W.L. Clowes, *The Royal Navy: A History from the Earliest Times to 1900*, 1996 [1897], i, 190.

604 For the immediate aftermath and impact of the battle, see RC, 186; RW, ii, 223; AB, 203–5.

605 RC, 186. Note the worry Louis had over London's loyalty in *Recueil*, xviii, 240 and Vincent, *Letters and Charters*, xliii. The most detailed account of the Battle of Muret will be found in Sean McGlynn, '*Kill Them All!' Crusaders, Cathars and Carnage: Warfare in the Albigensian Crusade*, forthcoming.

606 For the peace talks and settlement, see: AB, 202–5; RW, ii, 223–6; HWM, 385–9; RC, 186; AM, iii, 50–1; BC, 239.

607 For the treaty, see: J. Beverley Smith, 'The Treaty of Lambeth, 1217', *EHR*, 94, 1979'; Norgate, *Minority*, 57–8; Carpenter, *Minority*, 44–9, which simultaneously examines some of the implications of the settlement in the early years of Henry's minority; Powicke, *Thirteenth Century England*, 13–15; Painter, *William Marshal*, 223–4; Crouch, *William Marshal*, 125; Powicke, *King Henry III*, 17–19.

608 Carpenter, *Minority*, 46.

609 HWM, 385–7. Note William the Breton's figure for the total amount of the payment to Louis: WB, i, 314–5.

610 RC, 186.

611 Bartlett, *England Under the Norman and Angevin Kings*, 275. See also Eales, 'Castles and Politics in England'.

612 Vincent, *Peter des Roches*, 136.

613 See Carpenter, *Minority*, 31–4, for locality and allegiance.

614 HWM, 357.

615 BC, 239.

616 For example: Powicke, *King Henry III*, 16.

617 Tyerman, *England and the Crusades*, 139–40.

618 Coss, *Political Songs*, 22.

619 BC, 232.

620 For this meeting and a discussion of dates, see Smith, 'The Treaty of Lambeth', 562–5.

621 AB, 205; RW, ii, 225.

BIBLIOGRAPHY

Please note that the excellent and authoritative three-volume reference work *Oxford Encyclopedia of Medieval Warfare and Military Technology* edited by Clifford J. Rogers (Oxford, 2010) is too comprehensive to list separately all the articles relevant to this book, excepting the indulgence of my own germane entries. As a general rule in the bibliography, unlike in the endnotes, articles are not cited separately when they appear in volumes of collected papers of the authors' works.

Place of publication is London unless otherwise stated.

Abulafia, D., *Frederick II: A Medieval Emperor*, Harmondsworth, 1988

Ahlers, J., *Die Welfen und Die Englische Könige, 1165–1235*, Hildesheim, 1987

Ailes, M. and Barber, M. (eds and trans), *The History of the Holy War*, Woodbridge, 2003

Allen, M., 'The Volume of the English Currency, 1158–1470', *Economic History Review*, 54 (4), 2001

Allmand, C. (ed), *Society at War: The Experience of England and France during the Hundred Years War*, Woodbridge, 1998

Allmand, C., 'The Reporting of War in the Middle Ages', in Diana Dunn (ed), *War and Society in Medieval and Early Modern Britain*, Liverpool, 2000

Allmand, C., 'War and Non-Combatants in the Middle Ages', in Keen, *Medieval Warfare*

Allmand, C., *Henry V*, 1992

Allmand, C., *The Hundred Years War: England and France at War, c.1300–c.1450*, Cambridge, 1988

Ambroise, *The Crusade of Richard Lionheart by Ambroise*, ed. and trans. M. J. Hubert and J.L. La Monte, New York, 1976 (reprint)

Amt, E., *The Accession of Henry II in England: Royal Government Restored, 1149–1159*, Woodbridge, 1993

Annales Monastici, [AM], ed. H.R. Luard, Rolls Series, 1864–69

Anonymous of Béthune, [AB], *Histoire des Ducs de Normandie et des Rois d'Angleterre*, ed. F. Michelet, Paris, 1840

Anonymous of Béthune, *Chroniques des Rois de France*, in *Recueil des Historiens de Gaules et de la France*, xxiv, ed. L. Delisle

Anstruther, I., *The Knight and the Umbrella*, 1963

Appleby, J. (ed and trans), *The Chronicle of Richard of Devizes*, 1963

Appleby, J., *England Without Richard, 1189–1199*, 1965

Arndt, W. (ed), *Gisleberti Chronicon Hanoniense*, Hanover, 1869

Arnold, B., 'England and Germany', in Michael Jones and Malcolm Vale (eds), *England and Her Neighbours, 1066–1453*, 1989

Arnold, B., 'German Bishops and their Military Retinues in Medieval Europe', *German History*, 7 (2), 1989

Arnold, B., 'Germany and England, 1066–1453', in Nigel Saul (ed), *England in Europe, 1066–1453*, 1994

Arnold, B., *Princes and Territories in Medieval Germany*, Cambridge, 1991

Audouin, E., *Essai sur l'Armée Royale au Temps de Philippe Auguste*, Paris, 1913

Ayton, A., *Knights and Warhorses: Military Service and the English Aristocracy under Edward III*, Woodbridge, 1994

Bachrach, B., 'Early Medieval Military Demography: Some Observations on the Methods of Hans Delbrück', in D. J. Kagay and L. J. Andrew Villalon (eds), *The Circle of War in the Middle Ages*, Woodbridge, 1999

Bachrach, B., Rogers, C. J., DeVries, K. (eds), *Journal of Medieval Military History*, Woodbridge, 2002-

Baldwin, J., 'Le Sens du Bouvines', *Cahiers de Civilisation Médiévale*, 30, 1987

Baldwin, J., 'Philip Augustus and the Norman Church', *French Historical Studies*, 6 (1), 1969

Baldwin, J., *The Government of Philip Augustus*, Berkeley, 1986

Baraz, D., *Medieval Cruelty*, Ithaca, 2003

Barber, M., *The New Knighthood: A History of the Order of the Temple*, Cambridge, 1994

Barber, R. (ed), *Life and Campaigns of the Black Prince*, 1979

Barber, R., *Edward: Prince of Wales and Aquitaine*, Woodbridge, 1978

Barber, R., *Henry Plantagenet*, Woodbridge, new edn, 2001

Barber, R., *The Knight and Chivalry*, Woodbridge, 1995

Barlow, F., *The Feudal Kingdom of England, 1042–1216,* 4th edn, Harlow 1998

Barnie, J., *War in Medieval English Society: Social Values in the Hundred Years War, 1377–99*, New York, 1974

Barnwell Chronicler [BC], *Memoriale Walteri de Coventria*, ed. W. Stubbs, 2 vols, RS, 1879–80

Barrat, N.,'The Revenues of King John', *EHR*, 111 (443), 1996

Barratt, N., 'The Revenues of King John and Philip Augustus Revisited', in Church, *King John*

Barrow, G.W.S., 'The Scots and the North of England', in Edmund King (ed), *The Anarchy of King Stephen's Reign*, Oxford, 1994

Bartlett, R., *England Under the Norman and Angevin Kings, 1075–1225*, Oxford, 2000

Bartlett, R., *The Making of Europe: Conquest, Colonization and Cultural Challenge, 950–1350*, Harmondsworth, 1993

Bates, D. and Curry, A. (eds), *England and Normandy in the Middle Ages*, London, 1994

Bautier, R-H. (ed), *La France de Philippe Auguste: Le Temps des Mutations*, Paris, 1982

Beeler, J., *Warfare in Feudal Europe*, Ithaca, 1971

Benjamin, R., 'The Angevin Empire', in Nigel Saul (ed), *England in Europe, 1066–1453*, London, 1994;

Bennett, M., 'Military Masculinity in England and Northern France, *c.*1050–*c.*1215', in D.M. Hadley (ed), *Masculinity in Medieval Europe*, 1999

Bennett, M., 'Wace and Warfare', in *ANW*

Bennett, M., *Agincourt 1415: Triumph Against the Odds*, 1991

Bennett, M., *The Battle of Bosworth*, Stroud, 1985

Bloch, M., *Feudal Society*, Chicago, 1961

Boardman, A., *The Battle of Towton*, Stroud, 1996

Bolton, B., 'Philip Augustus and John: Two Sons in Innocent III's Vineyard?', *Innocent III: Studies on Papal Authority and Pastoral Care*, Aldershot, 1995

Bolton, J., 'Inflation, Economics and Politics in Thirteenth-Century England', *TCE*, 4, 1992

Bolton, J., 'The English Economy in the Early Thirteenth Century', in Church, *King John*

Bordonove, G., *Philippe Auguste*, Paris, 1986

Bothwell, J.S., *Falling From Grace: Reversal of Fortune and the English Nobility, 1075–1455*, Manchester, 2008

Bouet, P. and Gazeau, V. (eds) *La Normandie et l'Angleterre au Moyen Âge*, Caen, 2003

Boussard, J., 'Philippe Auguste et les Plantgenêts', in R.H. Bautier, *La France de Philippe Auguste*

Boutellier, P., 'Le Siège et la Prie du Château Gaillard', *Revue Historique de l'Armée*, 1946

Bradbury, J, *The Medieval Siege*, Woodbridge, 1992

Bradbury, J., 'Philip Augustus and Jim Bradbury: Personality and History', in Church, *King John*

Bradbury, J., *Philip Augustus: King of France, 1180–1223*, Harlow, 1998

Bradbury, J., *Stephen and Matilda: The Civil War of 1139–53*, Gloucester, 1996

Bradbury, J., *The Battle of Hastings*, Gloucester, 1999

Bradbury, J., *The Capetians*, 2007

Bradbury, J., *The Medieval Archer*, Woodbridge, 1985

Bradbury, J., *The Medieval Siege*, Woodbridge, 1992

Brentano, R., *Two Churches: England and Italy in the Thirteenth Century*, Berkely, 1968

Breuilly, J., *Nationalism and the State*, 2nd edn., Manchester, 1993

Brooke, C. and Gillian Keir, G., *London, 800–1216: the Shaping of a City*, 1975

Brooks, F.W., 'The Battle of Damme, 1213', *Mariner's Mirror*, 19, 1933

Brooks, F.W., 'The Cinque Ports', *Mariner's Mirror*, 25, 1929

Brooks, F.W. and Oakley, F., 'The Campaign and Battle of Lincoln, 1217', *Associated Architectural Societies' Reports and Papers*, vol. 26., part 2, 1922

Brooks, F.W., *The Battle of Stamford Bridge*, York, 1963

Brooks, F.W., *The English Naval Forces, 1199–1272*, 1933

Brown R. A. (ed), *The Norman Conquest: Documents of Medieval History*, 1984

Brown, A. L., *The Governance of Late Medieval England*, 1989

Brown, R. A., *English Castles*, 3rd edn., 1976

Brown, R. A., *The Normans and the Norman Conquest*, Woodbridge, 1985

Brown, R.A., *Rochester Castle*, 2nd edn., English Heritage, 1986

Brundage, J., *Richard Lionheart*, New York, 1973

Burgess, G., *Two Medieval Outlaws: Eustace the Monk and Fouke Fitz Waryn*, Woodbridge, 1997

Cannon, H., 'The Battle of Sandwich and Eustace the Monk', *EHR*, 27, 1912

Carpenter, D., 'English Peasants in Politics, 1258–1267' *Past and Present*, 136, 1992

Carpenter, D., *The Minority of Henry III*, 1990

Carpenter, D., *The Struggle for Mastery: Britain, 1066–1284*, 2003

Carpenter, *The Reign of Henry III*, 1996

Cartellieri, A., *Philip II. August, König von Frankreich*, Leipzig, 1899–1922

Carter, K., 'Arthur I, Duke of Brittany, in History and Literature', unpublished PhD thesis, The Florida State University, 1996

Cazel, F., 'The Legates Guala and Pandulf', in *TCE* 2.

Charles Petit-Dutaillis, C., *The Feudal Monarchy in France and England*, 1936

Châtelain, A., *Châteaux Forts en Île de France*, Paris, 1983

Chaytor, H., *Savaryc de Mauléon*, Cambridge, 1939

Cheney, C.R. and Semple, W. (eds), *Selected Letters of Pope Innocent III Concerning England, 1198–1216*, 1953

Cheney, C.R., *From Becket to Langton: English Church Government, 1170–1213*, Manchester, 1956

Cheney, C.R., *Innocent III and England*, Stuttgart, 1979

Cheney, C.R., *The Papacy and England: Twelfth to Fourteenth Centuries*, 1982

Choffel, J., *Louis le Lion: Roi de France Méconnu, Roi d'Angleterre Ignoré*, Paris, 1983

Chrimes, S.B., *An Introduction to the Administrative History of Medieval England*, 2nd edn., Oxford, 1959

Chroniques des Comtes d'Anjou et des Seignuers d'Amboise, ed. L. Halphen and R. Poupardin, Paris, 1913

Church, S.D., 'The Earliest English Muster Roll, 18/19 December, 1215', *Historical Research*, 67 (162), 1994

Church, S.D., 'The Knights of the Household of King John: a Question of Numbers', *TCE*, 4, 1992

Church, S.D. (ed), *King John: New Interpretations*, Woodbridge, 1999

Church, S.D., *The Household Knights of King John*, Cambridge, 1999

Church, S.D., 'King John's Testament and the Last Days of His Reign', *EHR*, 125, 2010

Churchill, W., *A History of the English Speaking Peoples*, 1956

Clanchy, M., *England and its Rulers, 1066–1272*, 1983

Clarke, P., *The Interdict in the Thirteenth Century*, Oxford, 2007.

Clausewitz, C.von, *On War*, Harmondsworth, 1968 [1832]

Clowes, W., *The Royal Navy, Volume I*, 1897

Connelly, J, 'Rampaging', *London Review of Books*, 22 June 2006

Contamine, P. and Guyotjeannin, D. (eds), *La Guerre, la Violence, et Les Gens au Moyen Âge* (2 vols), Paris, 1996

Contamine, P., 'L'Armée de Philippe Auguste', in Bautier, *La France de Philippe Auguste*

Contamine, P., 'Rançons et Butins dans la Normandie Anglaise, 1424–1444', in Actes du 101e Congrès National des Sociétés Savantes (Lille, 1976), *La Guerre et la Paix: Frontières et Violences au Moyen Age*, Paris, 1978

Contamine, P., Giry-Deloison, C. and Keen, M. (eds), *Guerre et Société en France, en Angleterre et en Bourgogne, XIVe-XVe Siècle*, Lille, 1991

Contamine, P., *War in the Middle Ages*, Oxford, 1984

Cookson, J., 'What if Napoleon had Landed?', *History Today*, 53 (9), 2003, 17

Coss, P. and Lloyd, S. (eds), *Thirteenth Century England*, Woodbridge, 1985–

Coss, P. (ed), *Thomas Wright's Political Songs of England: From the Reign of John to that of Edward III*, Cambridge, 1996 [1839], 2–3

Coss, P., and Tyerman, C. (eds), *Soldiers, Nobles and Gentlemen: Essays in Honour of Maurice Keen*, Woodbridge, 2010

Coss, P., *The Knight in Medieval England, 1000–1400*, Stroud, 1993

Coulson, C., '"National" Requisitioning for "Public" Use of "Private" Castles in Pre-Nation State France', in Alfred Smyth (ed), *Medieval Europeans: Studies in Ethnic Identity and National Perspectives in Medieval Europe*, 1998

Coulson, C., 'Fortress Policy in Capetian Tradition and Angevin Practice', in *ANS*, 6, 1983, 15

Coulson, C., *Castles in Medieval Society: Fortresses in England, France, and Ireland in the Central Middle Ages*, Oxford, 2003

Cowdrey, H. E. J., *Popes, Monks and Crusaders*, 1984

Cowley R. (ed), *What If? Military Historians Imagine What Might Have Been*, 2000

Cowley, R. (ed), *More What If? Eminent Historians Imagine What Might Have Been*, 2004

Critchley, J., 'Summonses to Military Service early in the Reign of Henry III', *EHR*, 86 (1), 1971.

Crouch, D., *The Reign of King Stephen, 1135–54*, Harlow, 2000

Crouch, D., *William Marshal: Court, Career and Chivalry in the Angevin Empire, 1147–1219*, 1990

Crouch, D., 'Baronial Paranoia' and 'The Complaint of King John against William de Braose', in Loengard (ed), *Magna Carta and the England of King John*

Crouch, D., 'The Complaint of King John against William de Braose', in Loengard (ed), *Magna Carta and the England of King John*

Crouch, D., 'Normans and Anglo-Normans: A Divided Aristocracy?', in Bates and Curry, *England and Normandy in the Middle Ages*

Crouch, D., *The Reign of King Stephen, 1135–1154*, Harlow, 2000

Curnow, P., 'Some Devlopments in Military Architecture c. 1200: Le Courdray-Salbart', *ANS* 2, 1979

Curry, A., *Agincourt: A New History*, Stroud, 2005

Curry, A., 'Medieval Warfare: England and Her Continental Neighbours, Eleventh to the Fourteenth Centuries', *JMH*, 21 (3), 1997

Curveiller, S., 'Le Bois et la Flandre Maritime au Moyen Âge', *Le Moyen Âge*, 106 (2), 2000.

Cuttino, G.P., *English Medieval Diplomacy*, Bloomington, 1985

Dalton, P. and White. G. (eds), *King Stephen's Reign, 1135–1154*, Woodbridge, 2008

Davies, R.R., *The First English Empire: Power and Identities in the British Isles, 1093–1343*, Oxford, 2000

Davis, R.H.C., *King Stephen*, 3rd edn, 1990

Delbrück, H., *Medieval Warfare*, trans. W. J. Renfroe, Lincoln, 1982 [1924]

Dockray, K., *Henry V*, Stroud, 2004

Douglas, D.C. and Greenaway, G. (eds), *English Historical Documents, II: 1042–1189*, 2nd edn., Oxford, 1981

Douglas, D.C., *William the Conqueror*, 1964

Duby, G., *France in the Middle Ages, 987–1460*, Oxford, 1991

Duby, G., *The Early Growth of the European Economy: Warriors and Peasants from the Seventh to the Twelfth Centuries*, Ithaca, 1974,

Duby, G., *The Legend of Bouvines*, Cambridge, 1990

Duffy, S., 'John and Ireland: the Origins of England's Irish Problem', in Church, *King John*

Duggan, A. (ed), *Kings and Kingship in Medieval Europe*, 1993

Dunabin, J. *France in the Making, 843–1180*, Oxford, 1985

Dunbabin, J., *Captivity and Imprisonment in Medieval Europe, 1000–1300*, Basingstoke, 2002

Duncan, A., 'John King of England and the King of Scots', in Church, *King John*

Edbury, P.W. (ed and trans), *The Conquest of Jerusalem and the Third Crusade: Sources in Translation*, Aldershot, 1996

English, B., 'Towns, Mottes and Ring-works of the Conquest', in A. Ayton and J. L. Price (eds), *The Medieval Military Revolution: State, Society and Military Change in Medieval and Early Modern Europe*, London, 1995

Erickson, J., 'The Ultimate Wound', *The Times Literary Supplement*, 28 August 1998

Erlande-Brandenburg, A., 'L'Architecture Militaire au Temps de Philippe Auguste: une Nouvelle Conception de la Défense', in Bautier, *La France de Philippe Auguste*

Erlande-Brandenburg, A., 'Organisation du Conseil d'Architecture et des Corps des Spécialistes sous Philippe Auguste', in X.B. Altet (ed), *Artistes, Artisans et Productions Artistique au Moyen Age*, Paris, 1987

Everard, J. and Holt, J.C., *Jersey 1204*, 2004

Everard, J., *Brittany and the Angevins*, Cambridge, 2000

Evergates, T., *Feudal Society in the Bailliage of Troyes under the Counts of Champagne, 1152–1284*, Baltimore, 1975

Faulkner, K., 'The Knights in the Magna Carta Civil War', in *TCE*, 8, 2001

Fawtier, R., 'Un Fragment du Compte de l'Hôtel de Prince Louis', in Fawtier, *Autour de la France Capétienne: Personnages et Institutions*, 1987 [1933]

Fawtier, R., *The Capetian Kings of France: Monarchy and Nation, 987–1328*, Basingstoke, 1960

Feodora, conventiones, litterae, ed. T. Rymer, 1703

Ferguson, N., *Virtual History: Alternatives and Counterfactuals*, 1997

Fino, J., *Fortresses de la France Mediévale*, Paris, 1967

Fiorato, V., Boystlon, A., and Knüsel, C., *Blood Red Roses: The Archaeology of a Mass Grave from the Battle of Towton AD 1461*, Oxford, 2000

Fischer, D., *The Great Wave: Price Revolutions and the Rhythm of History*, Oxford, 1996

Flori, J., *Philippe Auguste*, Paris, 2007

Flori, J., *Richard the Lionheart: Knight and King*, trans. Jean Birrell, Westport, 2006

Foley, V., Palmer, G. and Soedel, W., 'The Crossbow', *Scientific American*, 1985

Forde, S., Johnson, L. and Murray, A., *Concepts of National Identity in the Middle Ages*, Leeds, 1995

Foreville, R., *Le Pape Innocent III et la France*, Stutthart, 1992

Forey, A., *The Military Orders: From the Twelfth to the Early Fourteenth Centuries*, 1992

Frame, R., *The Political Development of the British Isles, 1100–1400*, Oxford, 1990

France, J., 'Recent Writing on Medieval Warfare: From the Fall of Rome to c.1300', *Journal of Military History*, 65 (2), 2001

France, J., *Western Warfare in the Age of the Crusades, 1000–1300*, 1999

Friel, I., 'Oars, Sails and Guns: The English and War at Sea, c.1200–c.1500', in Hattendorf and Unger, *War at Sea*

Friel, I., *The Good Ships: Ships, Shipbuilding and Technology in England, 1200–1520*, 1995

Froissart, *Chronicles*, ed. and trans. Geoffrey Brereton, Harmondsworth, 1978

Fryde, E., *Peasants and Landlords in Later Medieval England*, Stroud, 1996

Fryde, N., 'King John and the Empire', in Church, *King John*

Fryde, N., *Why Magna Carta? Angevin England Revisited*, Munster, 2001

Fuhrman, H., *Germany in the High Middle Ages*, trans. Timothy Reuter, Cambridge, 1986

Gauthier, G., *Philippe Auguste*, Paris, 2002

Gauvard, C., 'Justification and Theory of the Death Penalty at the *Parlement* of Paris in the Late Middle Ages', in Christopher Allmand (ed), *War, Government and Power in Late Medieval France*, Liverpool, 2000

Gellner, E., *Nations and Nationalism*, Oxford, 1983

Gerald of Wales, *Expugnatio Hibernica*, ed. and trans. by A.B. Scott and F.X. Martin, Dublin, 1978

Gerald of Wales, *Giraldi Cambrensis Opera*, (8 vols), eds. J.S. Brewer, J.F. Dimcock and G.F Warner, RS, 1861–91

Gerald of Wales, *The Journey Through Wales / The Description of Wales*, 1978

Gervase of Canterbury, *The Historical Works of Gervase of Canterbury*, ed. W. Stubbs, RS, 1880

Gesta Stephani, eds. K.R. Potter and R.H.C. Davis, Oxford, 1976, 224

Gilbert of Mons, *Chronicle of Hainaut*, ed. and trans. Laura Napran, Woodbridge, 2005

Gillingham, J., 'The Anonymous of Béthune, King John and Magna Carta', in Loengard, *Magna Carta and the England of King John*

Gillingham, J., 'Historians Without Hindsight: Coggeshall, Diceto and Howden on the Early Years of John's Reign', in Church, *King John*

Gillingham, J., 'Richard I and the Science of War', in *ANW*

Gillingham, J., 'Richard I, Galley Warfare and Portsmouth: The Beginnings of a Royal Navy', *TCE*, 6, 1997.

Gillingham, J., 'The King and the Castle', *BBC History*, 10 (8), 2009

Gillingham, J., 'War and Chivalry in the *History of William the Marshal*' in *ANW* and *Richard Couer de Lion*

Gillingham, J., *Richard Couer de Lion*, 1994

Gillingham, J., *Richard I*, 1999.

Gillingham, J., *Richard the Lionheart*, 2nd edn, 1989

Gillingham, J., *The Angevin Empire*, 2nd edn., 2001

Gillingham, J., *The English in the Twelfth Century: Imperialism, National Identity and Politics*, Woodbridge, 2000

Gillingham, J., *The Wars of the Roses: Peace and Conflict in Fifteenth-Century England*, 1981

Girouard, M., *The Return to Camelot*, Yale, 1981.

Given-Wilson, C. (ed. and trans), *Chronicles of the Revolution, 1397–40: The Reign of Richard II*, Manchester, 1993

Gobry, I., *Les Capétiens*, Paris, 2001

Goff, J. Le, *Saint Louis*, Paris, 1996

Golding, B., 'Simon of Kyme: the Making of a Rebel', *Nottingham Medieval Studies*, 27, 198

Gonthier, N., *Le Châtiment du Crime au Moyen Âge*, Rennes, 1998

Goodall, J., 'Dover Castle and the Great Siege of 1216', *Château Gaillard XIX*, 2000

Goodwin, G., *Fatal Colours: Towton, 1461 – England's Most Brutal Battle*, 2011

Gorby, I., *Louis VIII, 123–1226: Fils de Philippe II*, Paris, 2009

Gougenheim, S., 'Les Grands Traits de la Vie Politique', in Michel Parisse (ed), *L'Allemagne au XIIIe Siècle*, Paris, 1994, 19–24

Green, D., *Edward the Black Prince*, Harlow, 2007

Green, D., *The Battle of Poitiers, 1356*, 2002

Green, J., 'Lords of the Norman Vexin', in J. C Holt and John Gillingham (eds), *War and Government in the Middle Ages*, Woolbridge, 1984

Green, J., 'Unity and Disunity in the Anglo-Norman State', *Historical Research*, 62 (1), 1989

Green, V., *The Madness of Kings: Personal Trauma and the Fate of Nations*, Gloucester, 1993

Griffiths, Q., 'The Capetian kings and St. Martin of Tours', *Studies in Medieval and Renaissance History*, 9, 1987

Grimsley, M. and Rogers, C.J. (eds), *Civilians in the Path of War*, 2002

Hadenague, A., *Philippe Auguste et Bouvines*, Paris, 1978 [1935]

Hagger, M., 'Theory and Practice in the Making of Twelfth-Century Pipe Rolls', in Leongard, *Magna Carta and the England of King John*

Haines, J., 'A Parody of Songs in Praise of War', *Speculum*, 82 (2), 2007

Hajdu, R., 'Castles, Castellans and the Structure of Politics in Poitou, 1152–1271, *JMH*, 4, 1978

Hallam, E., *Capetian France, 987–1328*, Harlow, 1980 (2nd edition with Judith Everard, 2001)

Hanley, C., *War and Combat, 1150–1270: The Evidence of Old French Literature*, Woodbridge, 2003

Harper-Bill, C. and Vincent, N. (eds), *Henry II: New Interpretations*, Woodbridge, 2007

Harper-Bill, C., 'John and the Church of Rome', in Church, *King John*

Harriss, G.L., *Henry V: The Practice of Kingship*, Oxford, 1985

Harvey, P., 'The English Inflation of 1180–1220, *Past and Present*, 61, 1973

Hattendorf, J. and Unger, R. (eds), *War at Sea in the Middle Ages and Renaissance*, Woodbridge, 2003

Haverkampf, A., *Medieval Germany, 1056–1273*, trans. H. Braun and R. Mortimer, Oxford, 1988, 242–4.

Heiser, R., 'Richard I and His Appointments to English Shrievalties', *EHR*, 112 (445), 1997

Hericher, A.M.F. and Gazeau, V., *1204: la Normandie entre Planatagenêts et Capétiens*, Caen, 2007

Hill, J.W.F., *Medieval Lincoln*, Cambridge, 1948

History of William Marshal, [HWM], ed. A. Holden, D. Crouch and S. Gregory, Anglo-Norman Text Society, 2002–2006

Holden, B., 'King John, the Braoses and the Celtic Fringe, 1207–1216', *Albion*, 33 (1), 2001

Holden, B., 'The Balance of Patronage: King John and the Earl of Salisbury', *Haskins Society Journal*, 8, 1996

Hollister, C.W., 'King John and the Historians', *Journal of British Studies*, 1, 1961

Hollister, C.W., *The Military Organization of Norman England*, Oxford, 1965.

Holt, J.C., 'The Loss of Normandy and Royal Finance', in J. Gillingham and J. C. Holt (eds), *War and Government in the Middle Ages*, Woodbridge, 1984

Holt, J.C., 'The Treaty of Winchester', in Edmund King (ed), *The Anarchy of King Stephen Reign*, Oxford, 1994

Holt, J.C., *Magna Carta and Medieval Government*, London, 1985

Holt, J.C., *Magna Carta*, 2nd edn, Cambridge, 1992

Holt, J.C., *The Northeners*, Oxford, 1992

Holzapfel, T., *Papst Innozenz III, Philip II August, Koënig von Frankreich und die englisch-welfische Verbindung, 1198–1216*, Frankfurt, 1991

Horne, A., 'Letter From Verdun', *Prospect*, August/September 1999

Hosler, J., *Henry II: A Medieval Soldier at War, 1147–1189*, Woodbridge, 2007

Howlett, R. (ed), *Chronicles of the Reigns of Stephen, Henry II and Richard I*, 1884, 4 vols, Rolls Series

Hudson, J., *The Formation of the English Common Law: Law and Society in England from the Norman Conquest to Magna Carta*, 1996

Huffman, J., *The Social Politics of Medieval Diplomacy: Anglo-German Relations, 1066–1307*, Michigan, 2000

Hutton, W., *Philip Augustus*, 1896

Jane Martindale, 'Eleanor of Aquitaine: The last Years', in Church, *King John*

Johnston, R.C. (ed and trans), *Jordan Fantosme's Chronicle*, Oxford, 1981

Joinville and Villehardouin, *Chronicles of the Crusades*, ed and trans M R B Shaw Harmondsworth, 1963

Joliffe, J.E.A., *Angevin Kingship*, 1963

Jones, J., *King John and Magna Carta*, Harlow, 1971

Jones, M., 'War and Fourteenth-Century France', in Anne Curry and Michael Hughes (eds), *Arms, Armies and Fortifications in the Hundred Years War*, Woodbridge, 1994

Jones, M., 'The Capetians and Brittany', *Historical Research*, 63 (1), 1990

Jones, M., *Bosworth 1485*, Stroud, 2002

Kaeuper, R.W. and Kennedy, E. (eds and trans), *The Book of Chivalry of Geoffroi de Charny*, Pennsylvania, 1996

Kaeuper, R.W., *Chivalry and Violence in Medieval Europe*, Oxford, 1999

Kaeuper, R.W., *War, Justice and Public Order: England and France in the Later Middle Ages*, Oxford, 1988

Kagay, D.J. and Villalon, L.J.A. (eds), *The Circle of War in the Middle Ages*, Woodbridge, 1999

Kagay, D.J. and Villalon, L.J.A. (eds), *The Final Argument: The Imprint of Violence on Society in Medieval and Early Modern Europe*, Woodbridge, 1998

Kantorowicz, E., *The King's Two Bodies: A Study in Medieval Political Theology*, Princeton, 1957

Kapelle, W.E., *The Norman Conquest of the North, 1000–1135*, 1979

Keegan, J., *A History of Warfare*, 1993

Keen, M. (ed), *Medieval Warfare: A History*, Oxford, 1999

Keen, M., 'Chivalry, Nobility and the Man-at-Arms', in Christopher Allmand (ed), *War, Literature and Politics in the Late Middle Ages*, Liverpool, 1976

Keen, M., *Chivalry*, 1984

Keen, M., *Nobles, Knights and Men-at-Arms*, 1996

Keen, M., *The Laws of War in the Later Middle Ages*, 1965

Kelly, A., *Eleanor of Aquitaine and the Four Kings*, 1950

Kennedy, R. and Meecham-Jones, S. (eds), *Writers of the Reign of Henry II*, Basingstoke, 2006

Kidd, C., *British Identities Before Nationalism: Ethnicity and Nationhood in the Atlantic World, 1600–1800*, Cambridge, 1999

Latimer P., 'Early Thirteenth-Century Prices', in Church, *King John*

Latimer, P., 'Rebellion in South-western England and the Welsh Marches, 1215–1217', *Historical Research*, 80 (208), 2007

Lawrence, C., 'The Thirteenth Century', in C.H. Lawrence (ed), *The English Church and the Papacy in the Middle Ages*, 1965

Legge, M.D., 'William the Marshal and Arthur of Brittany, *Historical Research*, 55 (1), 1982

Lewis, A. and Runyan, T., *European Naval and Maritime History, 300–1500*, Bloomington, 1985

Lewis, P., 'The Wars of Richard I in the West,' unpublished MPhil dissertation, University of London, 1977

Llobera, J., 'State and Nation in Medieval France', *Journal of Historical Sociology*, 7 (3), 1994

Lloyd, A., *King John*, 1973

Loades, D., 'The King's Ships: the Keeping of the Seas, 1413–1480', *Medieval History*, 1 (1), 1991

Loengard, J. (ed) *Magna Carta and the England of King John*, Woodbridge, 2010

Luchaire, A., *Philippe Auguste et son Temps*, Paris 1980 [1902]

Luchaire, A., *Social France at the Time of Philip Augustus*, 1912

Lyons, 'The Capetian Conquest of Anjou', unpublished PhD thesis, John Hopkins University, 1976

Maccarrone, M., 'La Papauté et Philippe Auguste: la Décrétale *Novit Ille*', in Bautier, *La France de Philippe Auguste*

Maddern, P., *Violence and Social Order: East Anglia, 1422–1442*, Oxford, 1992

Maddicott, J.R., 'Magna Carta and the Local Community, 1215–19', *Past and Present*, 101, 1984

Maddicott, J.R., 'Responses to the Threat of Invasion, 1085', *EHR*, 122 (498), 2007

Maddicott, J.R., *Simon de Montfort*, Cambridge, 1994

Maddicott, J.R., *The Origins of the English Parliament, 924–1327*, Oxford, 2010

Markowski, M., 'Richard Lionheart: Bad King, Bad Crusader?, *Journal of Medieval History*, 23, 1997

Martin, F.X., 'John, Lord of Ireland', in Art Cosgrove (ed), *A New History of Ireland, Vol II: Medieval Ireland, 1169–1534*, Oxford, 1993.

Martindale, J. and Nelson, J. (eds), *Studies in Medieval History Presented to R Allen Brown*, Woodbridge, 1989

Marvin, L, 'Monastic Military Orders', in Martel, *Reader's Guide to Military History*, 383

Marvin, L., 'Warfare and the Composition of Armies in France, 1100–1218: An Emphasis on the Common Soldier', unpublished PhD thesis, University of Illinois, 1996

Marvin, L., *The Occitan War*, Cambridge, 2008

Masschaele, J., 'The English Economy in the Age of Magna Carta', in Loengard, *Magna Carta*

Matthew Paris, [MP], *Matthei Parisiensis, Monachi Sanctii Albani, Chronica Majora*, ed. H.R. Luard, RS, 1884–9

Matthew Paris, *Matthei Parisiensis Historia Anglorum*, ed. F. Maddern, RS, 1866–9

Matthew, D., *Britain and the Continent, 1000–1300*, London, 2005

Matthew, D., *King Stephen*, 2002

Mayer, H.E., *The Crusades*, Oxford, 1988

McGlynn, S., 'Britain and Europe: A Medieval Comparison', in *Politics*, 16 (3), 1996

McGlynn, S., '*Kill Them All!' Crusaders, Cathars and Carnage: Warfare in the Albigensian Crusade*, forthcoming

McGlynn, S., 'King John and the French Invasion of England', *BBC History*, 11 (6), 2010

McGlynn, S., 'Land Warfare, 1000–1500', 'Siege Warfare', 'Richard I (The Lionheart)'in C. Messenger (ed), *Reader's Guide to Military History*, London, 2001

McGlynn, S., 'Medieval Warfare', *European Review of History-Revue Européene d'Histoire*, 4 (2), 1997

McGlynn, S., 'Philip Augustus: Too Soft a King?', *Medieval Life*, 7, 1997

McGlynn, S., 'Politics and Violence in the Late Middle Ages', *Canadian Journal of History*, 26 (3), 2001

McGlynn, S., 'Recent Research on Medieval Warfare', *European Review of History-Revue Européene d'Histoire*, forthcoming, 2012

McGlynn, S., 'Roger of Wendover and the Wars of Henry III, 1216–1234', in B. Weiler and I.W. Rowlands (eds), *England and Europe in the Reign of Henry III, 1216–1272*, Aldershot, 2002

McGlynn, S., '*Servicium Debitum*', 'Otto IV', 'William Marshal', 'Philip II of France', 'John, King of England', 'Louis VII of France', 'Louis VIII of France', 'Marshal, William', 'Richard I of England and Anjou', 'Sandwich, Battle of', 'Siege Warfare: Tactics and Technology' in *OEMW*

McGlynn, S., 'Sheer Terror' and the Black Prince's *Grand Chevauchée* of 1355', in *The Hundred Years War: Volume 3*, eds Donald Kagay and Andrew Villalon, Leiden, 2011

McGlynn, S., 'The Myths of Medieval Warfare', *History Today*, 44 (1), 1994

McGlynn, S., 'Violence and the Law: Popular Attitudes to Judicial Violence in Medieval England', *History Today*, 57 (4), 2008

McGlynn, S., 'War Crimes', in G. Martel (ed), *Blackwell Encyclopedia of War*, Oxford, 2011

McGlynn, S., *By Sword and Fire: Cruelty and Atrocity in Medieval Warfare*, 2008

McGlynn, S., *Medieval Generals*, forthcoming, 2012

McMahon, R., *The Cold War*, Oxford, 2003

Meron, T., *Henry's Wars and Shakespeare's Laws: Perspectives on the Law of War in the Middle Ages*, Oxford, 1993

Messenger, C. (ed), *Reader's Guide to Military History*, London, 2001

Meyerson, D., Thiery, D. and Falk, O., *'A Great Effusion of Blood?': Interpreting Medieval Violence*, Toronto, 2004

Michel, F. (ed), *Histoire des Ducs de Normandie et des Rois d'Angleterre*, Paris, 1840

Milner, N.P. (ed and trans), *Vegetius: Epitome of Military Science*, Liverpool, 1993

Mollat du Jourdin, M., 'Philippe Auguste et la Mer', in Bautier, *La France de Philippe Auguste*.

Moore, A., 'Government and Locality in Essex in the Reign of Henry III', unpublished doctoral thesis, University of Cambridge, 2006

Moore, A.,'"Other Cities Have Citizens, London's are Called Barons". Connections between London and Essex During the Magna Carta Civil War (1215–17)', forthcoming

Moore, J., 'Anglo-Norman Garrisons', *ANS* 22, 2000

Morillo, S. (ed), *The Battle of Hastings*, Woodbridge, 1996

Morillo, S., *Warfare Under the Anglo-Norman Kings*, Woodbridge, 1994

Morris, C., *The Papal Monarchy: The Western Church from 1950 to 1250*, Oxford, 1989

Mortimer, I., *The Fears of Henry IV*, 2007.

Moss, V., 'The Norman Exhequer Rolls of King John', in Church, *King John*

Musset, L., 'Quelques problèmes poses par l'annexion de la Normandie au domain royale français', in Bautier, *La France de Philipp Auguste*

Nelson, J. (ed), *Richard Coeur de Lion in History and Myth*, 1992

Nicholas, D., *Medieval Flanders*, 1992

Nicholson, H. (ed and trans), *Chronicle of the Third Crusade: A Translation of the Itinerarium Peregrinorum et Gesta Regis Ricardi*, Aldershot, 1997

Nicholson, H., *Medieval Warfare*, Basingstoke, 2004

Nicholson, H., *Templars, Hospitallers and Teutonic Knights: Images of the Military Orders, 1128–1291*, Leicester, 1995

Nicholson, H., *The Knights Templar: A New History*, Gloucester, 2001

Nicolle, D., *Arms and Armour of the Crusading Era, 1050–1350: Western Europe and the Crusader States*, 1999

Norgate, K., *England Under the Angevin Kings*, 2 vols, 1887

Norgate, K., *John Lackland*, 1902

Norgate, K., *Richard the Lionheart*, 1924.

Odo de Dueil, *De Profectione de Ludovici VII I Orientum*, New York, 1948, ed. Virginia Berry

Oman, C., *The Art of War in the Middle Ages*, Oxford, 3rd edn., 1924

Otto of Freising, *The Deeds of Frederick Barbarossa*, trans. by Charles Mierow, Toronto, 1994

Owen, D.D.R., *Eleanor of Aquitaine: Queen and Legend*, Oxford, 1993

Owen, D.D.R., *William the Lion: Kingship and Culture, 1143–1214*, East Linton, 1997

Paden, W., Sankovitch, T., and Stalein, P. (eds), *The Poems of Bertran de Born*, Los Angeles, 1986

Painter, S., *The Reign of King John*, Baltimore, 1949

Painter, S., *The Scourge of the Clergy: Peter of Dreux, Duke of Brittany*, New York, 1969 [1937]

Painter, S., *William Marshal: Knight-Errant, Baron, and Regent of England*, Toronto, 1982 [1933]

Palmer, J., 'The Conqueror's Footprints in Domesday Book', in Andrew Ayton and J L Price (eds), *The Medieval Military Revolution: State, Society and Military Change in Medieval and Early Modern Europe*, 1995

Palmer, J., 'War and Domesday Waste', in Matthew Strickland (ed), *Armies, Chivalry and Warfare in Medieval Britain and France*, Stamford, 1998

Patourel, J. Le,'Angevin Succesions and the Angevin Empire', in his *Feudal Empires: Norman and Plantagent*, London, 1984

Pegg, M., *A Most Holy War: The Albigensian Crusade and the Battle for Christendom*, Oxford, 2008

Pernoud, R., *Blanche of Castile*, 1975

Petit-Dutaillis, C., 'Une femme de Guerre au XIIIe siècle: Nicole de la Haie, Gardienne du Château de Lincoln', in *Mélanges Julien Havet. Recueil de TRavaux d'Erudition Dedies à la Memoire de Julien Havet (1853–93)*, Paris, 1895

Petit-Dutaillis, C., 'Une Nouvelle Chronique de Règne de Philippe Auguste, l'Anonyme de Béthune', *Revue Historique*, 50, 1892

Petit-Dutaillis, C., *Etude sur la Vie et le Règne de Louis VIII 1187–1226*, Paris, 1894

Pitte, D., 'Château-Gaillard dans la Défense de la Normandie orientale (1196–1204)', *ANS*, 24, 2002

Pleij, H., *Dreaming of Cockaigne: Medieval Fantasies of the Perfect Life* (Columbia, 2001) in *The London Review of Books*, 21 (12), 2001

Poole, A. L., *From Domesday Book to Magna Carta*, Oxford, 1955

Poole, A.L., 'Richard the First's Alliances with the German Princes in 1194', in R. W. Hunt, R., Pantin, W., and Southern, R. (eds), *Studies in Medieval History Presented to F.M. Powicke*, Oxford, 1948

Porter, J., Cerrini, S., and Jensen, C., 'Military Orders', *OEMW*

Potter, K.R. (ed), *Gesta Stephani*, Oxford, 1955

Powell, J. (ed), *Innocent III: Vicar of Christ or Lord of the World?*, Boston, 1963

Power, D., *The Norman Frontier in the Twelfth and Early Thirteenth Centuries*, Cambridge, 2004

Power, D., 'Bréauté, Sir Falkes de', *Dictionary of National Biography*, Oxford, www.oxforddnb.com.

Power, D., 'King John and the Norman Aristocracy', in Church, *King John*.

Power, D., 'The End of Angevin Normandy: the Revolt at Alençon (1203)', *Historical Research*, 74, 2001

Powicke, F.M., 'King Philip Augustus and the Archbishop of Rouen (1196)', *EHR*, 27 (1), 1912

Powicke, F.M., *King Henry III and the Lord Edward*, 2 vols., Oxford, 1947

Powicke, F.M., *Stephen Langton*, Oxford, 1928

Powicke, F.M., *The Loss of Normandy*, 2nd edn., Manchester, 1961

Powicke, F.M., *The Thirteenth Century*, Oxford, 2nd edn, 1962

Powicke, M., *Military Obligation in Medieval England*, Oxford, 1962

Prestwich, J.O., 'Military Intelligence under the Norman and Angevin Kings' in G. Garnett and J. Hudson (eds), *Law and Government in Medieval England and Normandy*, Cambridge, 1994

Prestwich, M., 'The Garrisoning of English Medieval Castles' in Richard Abels and Bernard S. Bachrach, *The Normans and Their Adversaries at War*, Woodbridge, 2001

Prestwich, M., 'The Victualling of Castles' in Peter Coss and Christopher Tyerman (eds), *Soldiers, Nobles and Gentlemen: Essays in Honour of Maurice Keen*, Woodbridge, 2009

Prestwich, M., *Armies and Warfare in the Middle Ages: The English Experience*, 1996

Prestwich, M., *Plantagenet England 1225–1360*, Oxford, 2005

Purton, P., *A History of the Early Medieval Siege, Volume I: c.450–1200*, Woodbridge, 2010

Quenedy, R., 'Le Siège de Château Gaillard en 1203–1204', *Bulletin de la Société des Amis des Monuments Rouennais*, 1913

Ralph of Coggeshall, [RC], *Radulphi de Coggeshall Chronicon Anglicanum*, ed. J. Stevenson, RS, 1875

Ralph of Diss, *Radulphi de Diceto Opera Historic,* ed. W.Stubbs, RS, 1876

Reuter, T., '*Episcopi cum sua militia*: The Prelate as Warrior in the Early Staufer Era', in Timothy Reuter (ed), *Warriors and Churchmen in the Middle Ages*, 1992

Reynolds, S., *Fiefs and Vassals,* Oxford, 1994, 37.

Richard of Devizes, *Chronicon*, ed. and trans. J.T. Appleby, London, 1963

Richards, D.S. (ed and trans), *The Rare and Excellent History of Saladin*, Aldershot, 1992

Richmond, C., 'Identity and Morality: Power and Politics During the Wars of the Roses', in *Power and Identity in the Middle Ages: Essays in Memory of Rees Davies*, Oxford, 2007

Riis, T., 'Autour de Marriage de 1193: l'Epouse, son Pays et les Relations Franco-Danoises', in Bautier, *La France de Philippe Auguste*.

Robert de Tourigny, *Chronica*, in *Chronicles of the Reigns of Stephen, Henry II and Richard I*, ed. Richard Howlett, 4 vols., Rolls Series, London, 1884–9, iv

Robert of Auxerre, *Roberti Canonici Sancti Mariani Autissiodorensis Chronicon*, Monumenta Germania Historica Scriptores, xvii

Roberts, A., *What Might Have Been*, 2004

Roc'h Morgère, L. le (ed), *Richard Couer de Lion, Roi d'Angleterre, Duc de Normandie*, Caen, 1999

Rodger, N., 'The Naval Service of the Cinque Ports', *EHR*, 111 (442), 1996

Rodger, N., *The Safeguard of the Sea: A Naval History of Britain, Volume I: 660–1649*, 1997

Roger of Howden, *Chronica*, ed. W. Stubbs, 4 vols., Rolls Series, London 1868–71, 4, 3–4

Rogers, C.J. (ed), *Oxford Encyclopedia of Medieval Warfare and Military Technology*, [*OEMW*], Oxford, 2010

Rogers, C.J. (ed), *The Wars of Edward III: Sources and Interpretations*, Woodbridge, 1999

Rogers, C.J., 'By Fire and Sword: *Bellum Hostile* and "Civilians" in the Hundred Years' War', in Grimsley and Rogers, *Civilians in the Path of War*

Rogers, C.J., 'The Age of the Hundred Years War', in Keen, *Medieval Warfare*

Rogers, C.J., *War Cruel and Sharp: English Strategy under Edward III, 1327–1360*, Woodbridge, 2000

Rolands, I., 'King John and Wales', in Church, *King John*.

Rosenwein, B., (ed), *Anger's Past: The Social Uses of an Emotion in the Middle Ages*, Ithaca, 1998

Runciman, S., 'Richard Couer-de-Lion', in *History Today*, 41(6), 1991 (originally 1955)

Russell, F., *The Just War in the Middle Ages*, Cambridge, 1976

Sachs, J., 'The Limits of Convergance: Nature, Nurture and Growth', *The Economist*, 14 June, 1997

Sadler, J., *Towton: The Battle of Palm Sunday Field*, Barnsley, 2011

Sassier, Y., *Louis VII*, Paris, 1991

Saul, N., *Richard II*, 1997

Saunders, C., Le Saux, F. and Thomas, N., *Writing War: Medieval Literary Responses to War*, Woodbridge, 2004

Sayers, J., *Innocent III: Leader of Europe, 1198–1216*, London, 1994

Sayers, J., *Papal Government and England During the Pontificate of Honorius III, 1216–1227*, Cambridge, 1984

Scales, L. and Zimmer, O. (eds), *Power and Nation in European History*, Cambridge, 2005

Scales, L., 'Bread, Cheese and Genocide: Imagining the Destruction of Peoples in Medieval Western Europe', in *History*, 92 (3), 2007, 300

Scales, L., 'Bread, Cheese and Genocide: Imagining the Destruction of Peoples in Medieval Western Europe', *History*, 92 (3), 2007

Scales, L., 'Identifying "France" and "Germany": Medieval Nation-Making in Some Recent Publications', *Bulletin of International Medieval Research*, 6, 2000

Scohwalter, K., 'The Ingeborg Psalter: Queenship, Legitimacy, and the Appropriation of Byzantine Art in the West', in Kathleen Nolan (ed) *Capetian Women*, Basingstoke, 2003.

Sellar, W. and Yeatman, R., *1066 and All That*, Gloucester, 1993 [1930]

Seward, D., *Henry V as Warlord*, 1987

Shils, E., 'Nations, Nationalism and Civil Society', *Nations and Nationalism*, 1 (1), 1995

Simeon of Durham, *Opera Omnia*, ed. T. Arnold, 2 vols., RS 1882–85

Sivéry, G., *Blanche de Castille*, Paris, 1990

Sivéry, G., *Philippe Auguste*, Paris, 1993

Smail, R.C., *Crusading Warfare, 1097–1193*, Cambridge, 1956

Smith, A., 'Gastronomy or Geology? The Role of Nationalism in the Reconstruction of Nations', *Nations and Nationalism* 1 (1), 1995

Smith, A., *National Identity*, 1991

Smith, A., *The Wealth of Nations*, Harmondsworth 1982, [1776]

Smith, J.B., 'The Treaty of Lambeth, 1217', *EHR*, 94, 1979

Smyth, A. (ed), *Medieval Europeans: Studies in Ethnic Identity and National Perspectives in Medieval Europe*, Basingstoke, 1998

Smyth, A. 'The Emergence of English Identity, 700–1000', in Alfred Smyth (ed), *Medieval Europeans*

Speed, P. (ed), *Those Who Fought: An Anthology of Medieval Sources*, New York, 1996

Spiegel, G., *Romancing the Past: The Rise of Vernacular Prose Historiography in Thirteenth-Century France*, Berekeley, 1993

Stacey, R., 'The Age of Chivalry', in Michael Howard, George Andreopoulis and Mark Shulman (eds), *The Laws of War: Constraints on Warfare in the Western World*, New Haven, 1994

Stacey, R., *Politics, Policy and Finance under Henry III, 1216–45*, Oxford, 1987

Stenton, D., *English Society in the Early Middle Ages*, Harmondsworth, 1952,

Stephen, G., 'A Note on William of Cassingham', *Speculum*, 16, 1941

Stephenson, J. (ed) [RC], *Radulphi de Coggeshall Chronicon Anglicanum*, Rolls Series, 1875

Stones, E.L.G. (ed and trans), *Anglo-Scottish Relations, 1174–1328*, Oxford, 1965

Strickland, M., 'Against the Lord's Anointed: Aspects of Warfare and Baronial Rebellion in England and Normandy, 1075–1265', in George Garnett and John Hudson (eds), *Law and Government in Medieval England and Normandy*, Cambridge, 1994

Strickland, M. (ed), *Anglo-Norman Warfare: Studies in Late Anglo-Saxon an Anglo-Norman Military Organization and Warfare*, Woodbridge, 1992

Strickland, M., 'A Law of Arms or a Law of Treason? Conduct in War in Edward I's Campaigns in Scotland, 1296–1307', in Richard W. Kaeuper (ed), *Violence in Medieval Society*, Woodbridge, 2000

Strickland, M., 'Arms and the Men: Loyalty and Lordship in Jordan Fantasome's Chronicle', in Christopher Harper-Bill and Ruth Harvey (eds), *Medieval Knightood*, 4, Woodbridge, 1992

Strickland, M., 'Killing or Clemency? Ransom, Chivalry and Changing Attitudes to Defeated Opponents in Britain and Northern France, 7–12th Centuries', in Hans-Henning Kortum (ed), *Krieg im Mittelalter*, 2001 (from www.deremilitari.org/strickland)

Strickland, M., and Hardy, R., *The Great Warbow*, Stroud, 2005

Strickland, M., *War and Chivalry: The Conduct and Perception of War in England and Normandy, 1066–1217*, Cambridge, 1996

Stringer, K.J., 'Nobility and Identity in Medieval Britain and Ireland: the de Vescy Family, c.1120–1314', in B. Smith (ed), *Britain and Ireland, 900–1300: Insular Responses to Medieval European Change*, Cambridge, 1999

Stringer, K.J., 'The War of 1215–17 in its Context', in Richard Oram (ed), *The Reign of Alexander II, 1214–49*, Leiden, 2005

Stringer, K.J., *The Reign of Stephen*, 1993

Stubbs, W. (ed), *Itinerarium Regis Ricardi* in *Chronicles and Memorials of The Reign of Richard I*, 2 vols, RS, 1864

Stürner, W., *Friedrich II: Die Königsherrscahft im Sizilien und Deutschland, 1194–1210*, Darmstadt, 1992

Suger, *Vita Ludovici Grossi Regis*, ed. H. Waquet, Paris, 1964 edn

Suppe, F., 'The Cultural Significance of Decapitation in High Medieval Wales and the Marches', *Bulletin of the Board of Celtic Studies*, 36, 1989

Suppe, F., *Military Institutions on the Welsh Marches: Shropshire, 1066–1300*, Woodbridge, 1994

Taithe, B. and Thornton, T. (eds), *War: Identities in Conflict, 1300–2000*

Thomas, H., 'Violent Disorder in King Stephen's England: A Maximum Argument', in Paul Dalton and Graeme White (eds), *King Stephen's Reign, 1135–1154*, Woodbridge, 2008

Thomas, H., *The English and the Normans: Ethnic Hostility, Assimilation, and Identity, 1066–.c.1220*, Oxford, 2003

Thomas, M., *War of the Generations: The Revolt of 1173–4*, Michigan, 1980

Thompson, K., *Power and Border Lordship in Medieval France: the County of Perche, 1000–1226*, Woodridge, 2002

Tout, T.F., 'The Fair of Lincoln and the "Histoire de Guillaume le Maréchal"', *EHR*, 18, 1903

Tuck, A., *Crown and Nobility (1272–1461)*, 1985

Turner, R.V. and Heiser, R., *The Reign of Richard Lionheart: Ruler of the Angevin Empire, 1189–1199*, Harlow, 2000

Turner, R.V., 'Good or Bad Kingship: The Case of Richard Lionheart', *Haskins Society Journal*, 8, 1999

Turner, R.V., 'King John in his Context: a Comparison with his Contemporaries', in *The Haskins Society Journal*, 3, 1991

Turner R.V., 'Eleanor of Aquitaine and her Children', *JMH*, 14 (3), 1998

Turner, R.V., 'Good or Bad Kingship? The Case of Richard the Lionheart', *Haskin's Society Journal*, 8, Woodbridge, 1999

Turner, R.V., 'King John's Military Reputation Reconsidered', *JMH*, 19, 1993

Turner, R.V., 'Richard Lionheart and English Episcopal Elections', *Albion*, 29 (1), 1997

Turner, R.V., 'Richard Lionheart and the Episcopate in His French Domains', *French Historical Studies*, 21 (4), 1998

Turner, R.V., 'The Problem of Survival for the Angevin "Empire": Henry II's and his Sons' Vision versus Late Twelfth-Century Realities, *American Historical Review*, 100 (1), 1995

Turner, R.V., *King John*, Harlow, 1994

Tyerman, C., *England and the Crusades, 1095–1588*, Chicago, 1988

Ullman, W., *Medieval Political Thought*, 1975

Ullman, W., *Principles of Government and Politics in the Middle Ages*, 1961

Upton-Ward, J.M. (ed and trans), *The Rule of the Templars*, Woodbridge, 1992

Upton-Ward, J.M. (ed), *The Military Orders: Volume IV*, Ashgate, 2008

Vale, M., *The Ancient Enemy: England, France and Europe from the Angevins to the Tudors*, 2007

Vale, M., *War and Chivalry: Warfare and Aristocratic Culture in England, France and Burgundy at the End of the Middle Ages*, Athens, Georgia, 1981

Verbruggen, J.F., *The Art of Warfare in the Western Europe During the Middle Ages From the Eighth Century to 1340*, trans. S. Willard and R.W. Southern, 2nd edn., Woodbridge, 1997

Vincent, N. (ed), *Records, Administration and Aristocratic Society in the Anglo-Norman Realm*, Woodbridge, 2010

Vincent, N. (ed), *The Letters and Charters of Cardinal Guala Bicchieri*, Woodbridge, 1996

Vincent, N., 'A Roll of Knights Summoned to Campaign in 1213', *Historical Research*, 66 (1), 1993

Vincent, N., 'Introduction: The Record of 1204', in Vincent (ed), *Records, Administration and Aristocratic Society*

Vincent, N., *Peter des Roches*, Cambridge, 1996

Viollet le Duc, E., *Military Architecture*, London, 1990, 80–94 [1860]

Vries, K. de, *Medieval Military Technology*, Peterborough, 1992

Vries, K. de, *The Norwegian Invasion of England in 1066*, 2000

Vries, K. de, 'The Use of Chronicles in Recreating Medieval Military History', *JMMH*, 2, 2004

Walker, I., *Harold: The Last Anglo-Saxon King*, Gloucester, 1997

Warner, P., *Sieges of the Middle Ages*, London, 1968

Warren, W.L., *King John*, 1978

Warren, W.L., *Henry II*, 1973

Warren, W.L., *The Governance of Anglo-Norman and Angevin England, 1086–1272*, 1987

Watkins, S., 'War on God', *London Review of Books*, 21 (10), 2001

Weiler, B., *Henry III of England and the Staufen Empire, 1216–1272*, Woodbridge, 2006

Weiler, B., *Kingship, Rebellion and Political Culture: England and Germany, c.1215–c.1250*, Basingstoke, 2007

Weir, A., *Eleanor of Aquitaine: A Life*, 2000

Wendover, R., [RW], *Rogeri de Wendover Liber Qui Dicitur Flores Historiarum [The Flowers of History]*, ed. H.G. Hewlett, RS, 1886–7

Wheeler, B. and C. Parsons, J.C., *Eleanor of Aquitaine: Lord and Lady*, Basingstoke, 2002

Wilkinson, L., 'Women as Sheriffs', in A. Jobson (ed), *English Government in the Thirteenth Century*, Woodbridge, 2004

William the Breton, [WB], *Oeuvres de Rigord et de Guillaume le Breton*, ed. H.F. Delaborde, Paris, 1882

Wormald, P., 'Engla Lond: The Making of an Allegiance', *Journal of Historical Sociology*, 7 (1), 1994

Wormald, P., 'The Making of England', *History Today* 45 (2), 1995

Wright, E., 'The Recovery of Royal Finance in 1407', in Rowena Archer and Simon Walker (eds), *Rulers and Ruled in Late Medieval England*, London, 1995

Wright, N., *Knights and Peasants: The Hundred Years War in the French Countryside*, Woodbridge, 1998

Zajac, W., 'Captured Property on the First Crusade', in Jonathan Phillips (ed), *The First Crusade: Origins and Impact*, Manchester, 1997

INDEX